Roadside History of
OKLAHOMA

Francis L. and Roberta B. Fugate

Mountain Press Publishing Company
Missoula, Montana — 1991

Unless otherwise noted, all photos by the authors.
Cartography by Carla Majernik

Library of Congress Cataloging-in-Publication Data

Fugate, Francis L., 1915-1992.
  Roadside history of Oklahoma / Francis L. Fugate and Roberta
B. Fugate.
        p.   cm. — (Roadside History series)
  Includes bibliographical references and index.
  ISBN 0-87842-279-X : $24.95—ISBN 0-87842-272-2 (pbk.)
$20.00
      1. Oklahoma—History, Local. 2. Automobile travel—Oklahoma—
Guide-books. 3. Oklahoma—Description and travel—1981—Guide-
books. 4. Historic sites—Oklahoma—Guide-books. I. Fugate,
Roberta B.   II. Title. III. Series
F694.F84   1991   91-17509
976.6—dc20   CIP

Mountain Press Publishing Company
P. O. Box 2399 • Missoula, MT 59806
406-728-1900

To
C. L. "Doc" Sonnichsen
a treasured friend

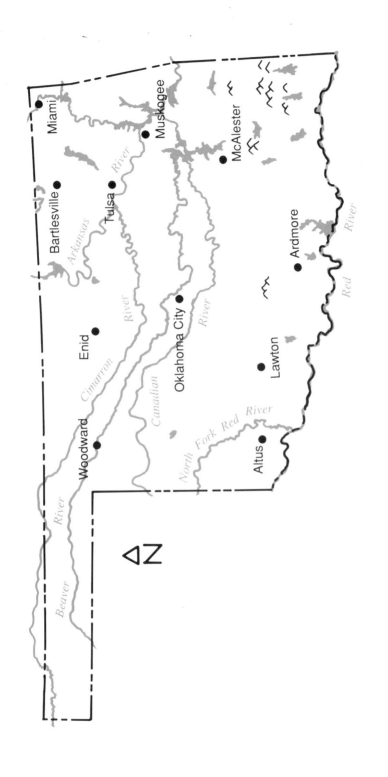

Table of Contents

The authors visit their namesake towns, Francis and Roberta, Oklahoma.

About the Authors

Francis Fugate was a freelance writer on Western topics for more than half a century. In addition to hundreds of articles and short stories, his works included *The Spanish Heritage of the Southwest* and *Viewpoint: Key to Fiction Writing.* For twenty-five years he conducted classes in professional writing at the University of Texas at El Paso, and he served as president of Western Writers of America from 1986 to 1988.

Roberta Fugate graduated from the University of Missouri in 1938 and taught in public schools in Missouri, Oklahoma, Florida, and Texas. She and Francis married in 1939, and they arrived in Oklahoma in 1946. There Francis worked on the *Cushing Daily Citizen,* and he immediately became an avid student of Oklahoma history. For three years the Fugates traveled the state from border to border, scouring libraries and archives while Francis authored "Oklahoma Vignette," a syndicated historical newspaper feature.

In 1977 Francis left the university to devote more time to writing. Roberta retired from teaching to join him as a collaborator. Together the Fugates wrote several books, including *Roadside History of New Mexico.*

Roberta died in October 1991 and Francis died in December 1992.

Foreword

To appreciate Oklahoma's beauty to the fullest, leave the freeways and turnpikes for leisurely driving through the towns and countryside. Your reward will be a kaleidoscopic panorama of farms and ranches, oil and gas fields, prairies and forests, and tiny hamlets and bustling cities. Man-made lakes cover more than a million acres with water. A wealth of state parks provide a variety of outdoor recreation.

The ambience of Oklahoma's rich past can be experienced only by visiting the historic communities which formed the leading edge of America's frontier scarcely more than a century ago. There you can rub elbows with the past through an abundance of historic sites and museums.

Oklahoma has experienced a history like that of no other state in the Union. When the area was acquired from France as part of the Louisiana Purchase it was conceived as a reservation for Indian tribes who were in the way of agricultural and industrial expansion in the East. Treaties guaranteed the land to the Indians "as long as grass grows and the rivers run."

Within three-quarters of a century, railroads invaded the territory. Avaricious railroad officials spread glowing reports of unoccupied stretches of verdant prairies, hoping to secure a share of the Indian lands if the country was opened to white settlement. Railroads and other entrepreneurial interests hired "Boomers" to mobilize clamoring homesteaders on the borders of the incipient state, and the United States found excuses to violate the solemn treaties by which the Indians had been promised homes in perpetuity.

Beginning in 1889, Oklahoma attracted white emigrants by a series of land "runs"—races during which prospective settlers vied with each other to stake claims in "unassigned lands." Industrious homesteaders flooded across the borders to drive their stakes in quarter-sections and townsite lots. They settled in tents, sod houses, and frame shanties; they broke the virgin sod and tilled the land. And eventually they sapped its strength. Nature retaliated with a drought which produced the catastrophe called the Dust Bowl. Some have maintained it was the Indians' Great Spirit meting out punishment for sins against His children and Mother Earth.

The settlers fought back. They built dams and conserved water to counteract future drought. They planted belts of trees to forestall soil erosion. Prosperity returned as geologists and engineers pierced the earth and sucked out its oil. Entrepreneurs reacted to the consequent boom by overdevelopment and—again—economic retribution was dealt out. Once more the fiber of Oklahomans was put to test by economic woes.

Notwithstanding Rand McNally's omission of the state from its 1989 atlas, Oklahoma is a very real and very large parcel of Western Americana, stretching 69,919 square miles from border to border. The forty-sixth state to enter the Union ranks eighteenth in size. It has prairies, forests, deserts, mountain ranges, and more than 200 lakes.

Oklahoma has the second largest Indian population of any state in the Union. Descendants from the 67 tribes inhabiting Indian Territory in 1889 still live in Oklahoma, and 35 tribes are headquartered in the state. Today, Oklahoma's Indian citizens straddle two cultures with one hand grasping their ancestral heritage and the other clutching the daily realities of modern life.

As we traveled the state, we found all of the customary apparatus of the West compressed and encapsulated within the memory of living man or inscribed in books, newspapers, and county histories by those with vivid remembrance of stories told by their parents and grandparents. Spanish conquistadors, Indians, trappers, traders, freighters, buffalo hunters, ranchers, outlaws, gold-seekers, lawmen, homesteaders, entrepreneurs, farmers, oil drillers, and Dust-Bowl fugitives have woven the colorful fabric of Oklahoma's past.

We have probed the history of these people in libraries and museums; we have traveled the highways and byways to trace their footsteps and to visit the scenes of their deeds. We have found many evidences of their passing, stories of heroism and of villainy.

We have met Okies who returned after fleeing to the Promised Land in California during the Dust Bowl days; we have met businessmen who lost fortunes during the deflation following the oil boom. And we have met fresh young opportunists to whom such disasters are vague buzz words from the hazy pasts of their parents and grandparents. We have met Indians who shared fascinating stories of the folkways of their ancestors, ancient customs which make them a unique part of the state's fiber.

Most of the people we meet are imbued with a boisterous exuberance seldom found outside the State of Oklahoma. Their voices are an echo of the state song adopted from Rodgers and Hammerstein's *Oklahoma!*

We know we belong to the land
And the land we belong to is grand!
And when we say—Yeeow! A-yip-i-o-ee ay!
We're only sayin' You're doin' fine. Oklahoma! Oklahoma—O.K.

Francis L. & Roberta B. Fugate

Acknowledgments

It would be impossible for us to name all of those in a more than forty-year succession of friends, colleagues, acquaintances, and fellow travelers who have contributed to our knowledge of Oklahoma. However, we would be remiss not to recognize some of the special people who have helped us during the past two years of collection and consolidation.

H. Dick Clarke, of Norman, ranks high on the list. An inveterate traveler and dedicated Oklahomaphile, Dick read our manuscript and opened his collection to enable us to fill holes and seal cracks. Robert and Evelyn Conley, of Tahlequah, were of invaluable assistance during our pursuit of Cherokee lore.

Without the help of David Lopez, Systems Supervisor, and Gary B. Taylor, Mapping Supervisor, in the Planning Division of the Oklahoma Department of Transportation, we would surely have gotten lost. David reached into the past to track down the Ozark Trails and Gary provided maps to keep our project on the right road. Fred W. Marvel, Oklahoma Tourism and Recreation Department, was most helpful.

We are indebted to Robert L. Klemme, of Enid, for leading us along the Chisholm Trail and guiding our pursuit of John Wilkes Booth's mummy. Jay D. Smith, of El Paso, shared his store of knowledge concerning George Armstrong Custer and the Plains Indians. By the time Smith Luton, Jr., finished showing us Hugo our enthusiasm for the community was on a par with his.

Curator Donald Dewitt and the entire staff of the superb Western History Collections, University of Oklahoma, were extremely helpful. John R. Lovett, Photo Archivist, went far beyond the call of duty in ferreting out historic photographs to provide illustrations.

Towana D. Spivey, Director of the Fort Sill Museum, and Linda Roper, Photo Archivist, enhanced our knowledge of the part played by Fort Sill in Oklahoma's past and provided photographs. Joe Caldwell, of the Southwest Natural and Cultural Association at the Wichita Mountains

Wildlife Refuge, helped us during our investigation of the buffalo herd. Joe Carter, Executive Director of the Will Rogers Memorial at Claremore, guided us in our pursuit of the Cherokee Kid.

Naming chamber of commerce and city representatives who helped us would take more space than we can afford, but some deserve particular mention: Janet Pierce, Gage; Joanne Wood, Pawhuska; Joan T. Walton, Boise City; Brett C. Smith, Freedom State Bank, Freedom; Robert P. McSpadden, Vinita; John M. Wylie II, Oologah; Mary Lou Sherrod, of Blue, for information about the Blue Warriors; and Eleanor Brown, the Municipal Clerk of Mule Barn, for introducing us to her town with its population of three.

Our visits to libraries were highlighted by associations with several very special people: Mary B. Ruhl, Reference Librarian, Ardmore; Renita Edigen, Beaver; Joan Singleton, Public Service Supervisor, Bartlesville Public Library; JoAnn Hunt, Pawhuska Public Library; and Michael Sinkovitz, Audio Visual Librarian, El Paso Public Library.

We must recognize David Shindo, of Darst-Ireland Photography of El Paso, Texas, for exercising his magic to bring faded photographs back to life. William H. Healy provided the name for our mobile office, "The Writer's Cramp"; and we would be negligent not to mention Gerry Carpenter's labors to save our strawberries and provide consolation to Simon and Pierre during our long absences.

Were it not for David Flaccus, the publisher who sent us on this trek, the book would not exist. We feel particularly blessed to have the artistry of cowboy-artist Joe Beeler to provide a setting for this volume.

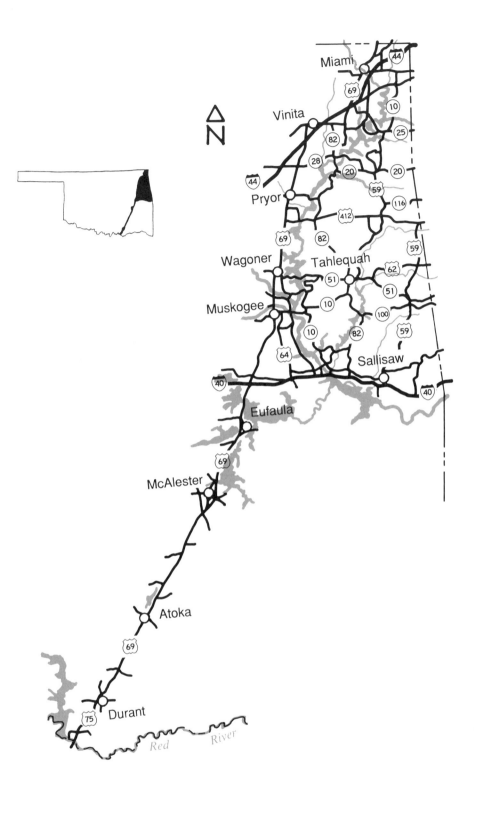

I. The Texas Road

The Texas Road slanted from the northeast corner of present-day Oklahoma southwest across the eastern part of the state to the Red River, roughly along the same route of US Highway 69. The warlike Osage Indians used the trail long before President Thomas Jefferson began casting covetous eyes toward the prairie land west of the Mississippi. Indians packed furs from Oklahoma across Missouri to the French frontier town of St. Louis, where the Chouteaus and other traders gave them ammunition, woolen cloth, knives, beads, vermillion, and other trade goods in exchange for their year's catch. In Missouri the trail became known as the Osage Trace.

The route was never surveyed; it grew as a natural result of travel into Indian Territory. It entered through the Cherokee country, passing through the site of present-day Vinita and Big Cabin, crossed the Creek Nation, and continued to Three Forks, where the Verdigris and Grand rivers empty into the Arkansas.

In 1824 the U.S. Army established Fort Gibson near Three Forks, hoping to put a stop to Osage depredations against the Civilized Tribes and establish peace along the frontier. The Texas Road continued southwest through the Choctaw Nation and crossed the Red River into Texas at Colbert's Ferry. Traffic became heavy with hunters, trappers, explorers, traders, emigrants to Texas, cattlemen, freighters, and military detachments.

During the Mexican War there was a steady stream of white-topped wagons and caravans. In March 1845, a thousand wagons crossed the Red River into Texas in six weeks. Exposure to the country along the road helped create an insatiable thirst for land that had been solemnly granted to the Indians by a long succession of treaties:

> The United States hereby agree that the district of country embraced within the following limits, . . . shall be and is hereby set apart for the absolute and undisturbed use and occupation of the tribes who are parties to this treaty.

1

On October 21, 1832, Count Albert-Alexandre de Pourtalès, a young Prussian nobleman who came to the area with Washington Irving, made an entry in his journal pointing to an ominous future for the Indians:

> If ever I settle in America, it will be in this area, the only place in the United States which offers a romantic way of life plus absolute independence. I would surround myself with a double rampart of Osages to protect me against the Americans, those commercial Thebans of the New World.

An east-west California Road through the Indians' land intersected the Texas Road at present-day McAlester. A flood of emigrants from the southern states and the eastern seaboard came during the California gold rush. Later, the discovery of gold in Colorado precipitated another wave. The Texas Road and the California Road brought white traders and entrepreneurs, some licensed by the commissioner of Indian Affairs and some clandestine, particularly those who came to sell whiskey to the Indians.

In 1861 the Civil War brought conflict. The Battle of Honey Springs, the turning point of the Civil War in Indian Territory, took place along the Texas Road. The Indian tribes of Oklahoma were divided in their loyalties, some siding with the Union and some with the Confederacy. Following the war, regardless of their loyalties, all Oklahoma Indians were treated much the same: The United States was on a course of westward expansion, and the Indians were in the way. The Civil War provided an excuse, albeit flimsy, to undo treaties and make way for white settlement.

After the war, Texan soldiers returned home to find their ranges teeming with cattle, which had multiplied during the four years of conflict. There was little or no market for cattle in Texas. If a buyer could be found, beeves might bring from three to four dollars a head, but prices in the North and East were skyrocketing.

Getting cattle to market was the problem. Earlier, cattle driven through Missouri had brought an epidemic of Texas fever to local stock, and southwest Missouri farmers formed armed bands at the border to turn back Texas drovers.

The result was inevitable. The "commercial Thebans of the New World" assembled herds to drive through Indian Territory to northern shipping points on the railroads building westward through Kansas and Nebraska. A number of cattle trails developed; the Texas Road was a favorite.

Along the way, some of the drovers willfully or carelessly accumulated cattle belonging to the Creek and Choctaw Indians, precipitating conflict between armed Indians and cowboys, each trying to protect their herds.

Conditions along the road were not ideal. In 1866 a drover recorded his experiences in a journal:

> May 31st. Swimming Cattle is the order. We worked all day in the River & at dusk got the last Beefe over—& am now out of Texas—This day will long be remembered by me—There was one of our party Drowned today & Several narrow escapes & I among the no.
>
> [June] 5th. Oh! what a night—Thunder Lightning & rain—we followed our Beeves all night as they wandered about—put them on the road at day break. found 90 Beeves of another mans Herd. traveled 18 Miles over the worst road I ever saw & came to Boggy Depot & crossed four rivers. It is well Known by that name.

Meanwhile, the railroads were striving to get treaties amended to extend lines through Indian lands and acquire property upon which to build towns along the way. In October 1867, a United States peace commission met on Medicine Lodge Creek, near present-day Medicine Lodge, Kansas, with some five thousand representatives of various Plains tribes. High-ranking United States officials, army officers, and press representatives attended. Satanta, a Kiowa chief, delivered a speech that won him the title "Orator of the Plains." It was recorded by a *New York Times* correspondent:

> All the land south of the Arkansas belongs to the Kiowas and Comanches, and I don't want to give away any of it. I love the land and the buffalo and will not part with it. I want you to understand well what I say. Write it on paper. Let the Great Father see it, and let me hear what he has to say.... I hear a great deal of good talk from the gentlemen whom the Great Father sends us, but they never do what they say. ... I have heard that you intend to settle us on a reservation near the mountains. I don't want to settle. I love to roam over the prairies. There I feel free and happy, but when we settle down we grow pale and die.... A long time ago this land belonged to our fathers; but when I go up to the river I see camps of soldiers on its banks. These soldiers cut down my timber; they kill my buffalo; and when I see that my heart feels like bursting; I feel sorry. I have spoken.

In the long run, Satanta's oratory was of no avail. The Medicine Lodge treaty ended the view of the Great Plains as "one big reservation" where the Indians could continue their traditional way of life. The new treaty embodied principles of Indian assimilation and cultural elimination which would shape United States policy for three-quarters of a century.

By 1870, the Union Pacific—soon to be known as the Missouri-Kansas-Texas—reached Indian Territory. During 1871-72 the railroad forged across the Cherokee Nation and followed the Texas Road into Creek territory. Construction workers were lawless and disorderly.

Satanta, "White Bear," a leading Kiowa chief who won the title "Orator of the Plains." —Fort Sill Museum

Gamblers and criminals came along to prey upon the workers. When the railroad was completed it brought land-hungry adventurers and entrepreneurs, determined to fasten themselves upon Indian Territory and turn it into a white man's land.

US 69 closely follows the old Texas Road from near Vinita to the Red River, the route trod by Indians, trappers, fur traders, missionaries, freighters, emigrants, and pioneer settlers. From the Kansas line to Muskogee, in the Three Forks district, it follows the old Osage Trace, along which Osage Indians sent hunting parties into the wilderness before the white man's encroachment.

—*Picher* - US 69———

This community started in 1916 as a mining camp. The Eagle-Picher Company leased the heavily mineralized lands from the Quapaw Indians and scattered drill derricks helter-skelter, puncturing the earth in search of lead and zinc. Miners erected tents and built shacks by the mine openings.

Lead and zinc mining began in northeastern Oklahoma in 1890, but production was insignificant until the outbreak of World War I. In 1917 the *Daily Oklahoman* told about the tumult created by wartime demand:

> This is the story of gold. Fifty square miles of gold. That is what . . . the Oklahoma zinc and lead mining district is today. . . . Drill derricks are sprouting up multitudinously. . . . And they are finding ore with astonishing, electrifying regularity.
>
> The town of Picher has sprung up from the prairie. Its forced growth has necessarily been of the shack character. There it sprawls on the open plain, a gangling, awkward, disheveled creature, hot as an inferno under its noon sun, and treeless as a desert.

Following the war, the furor died down, but World War II brought another boom. Employment in the mines reached 5,000. Caverns as large as football fields were scooped out. Tunnels crisscrossed from two to four hundred feet deep; one underground road was a hundred miles long. Buildings were interspersed with sprawling piles of chat.

Picher's business district, 1936.
—Western History Collections, University of Oklahoma Library

Limestone pillars supported the earth above most of the caverns, but in 1950 a four-block area around Picher's Second and Main streets showed signs of collapse. The area was fenced off and converted into a bird sanctuary. Mining activity dwindled to nothing through the 1960s, leaving abandoned ruins to serve as a powerful advertisement for exercising environmental control over mining operations.

HISTORICAL HIGHLIGHT

The Miner's Life

Around the mine openings, hoists, mills, shops, offices, and storage bins awaited raw ore-bearing dirt in the midst of a cluster of sludge ponds and piles of chat. Shacks and tents sprawled in wavering rows. Boardwalks provided precarious footing along streets ankle-deep in mud. Honky-tonk music blared from dance halls to attract miners coming out of the ground, places with names like The Big Red Apple, Bucket of Blood, and Beaver's Flats; and bootleggers sold liquor out of covered wagons.

Men rode down into the earth in a can which dropped silently through a dark, narrow shaft where water dripped down slimy cribbing. The "hoisterman" held their lives in his hands. The can slowed and was guided to a loading platform by a tub-hooker in a large chamber lighted by sputtering paraffin torches. The miners wore "sunshine" lamps on soft caps that offered no protection from falling boulders. The smoking lamps exuded a rank smell, but they would go out in the presence of a gas pocket, giving the miners sufficient warning to escape asphyxiation.

Typical scene underground in a lead and zinc mine in eastern Oklahoma.
—Western History Collections, University of Oklahoma Library

The miner's language was sprinkled with words like *stope, sump, spile, drifting, squibbing, tramming,* and *hoisting.* He knew about a "number two scoop" and what a "bruno" should do to properly "pop a boulder." He knew that a "screen ape" wore a wire mask for protection from flint fragments as he broke up boulders. "Cokey herders," "bruno paddles," and "roof trimmers" were a familiar part of his underworld. The area in which he dug was not a tunnel but a "drift."

He stood in two or three inches of water to work with more water dripping from the roof. If he was lucky, when he came out of the shaft, gasping for fresh air and squinting against the light, there would be a "dog house," a change house in which he could put on dry clothing.

Mining was a chancy occupation. In the early days there were no hard hats, safety goggles, or hard-toed shoes. There were no compensation laws. Mine operators were not rewarded by lower insurance rates for complying with safety precautions. When there was an accident, a whistle shrieked. Each mine's whistle had a distinctive tone, and women at home listened in fear, hoping they would not have to bring sheets to wrap the mutilated bodies often brought up from the depths. Deaths from pneumonia and tuberculosis were common, and silicosis or "miner's con" was accepted as an occupational hazard.

—*Cardin* - US 69———

The settlement initially named Tar River, after nearby Tar Creek, in 1920 was changed to Cardin because Oscar Cardin promised to construct a half-mile of sidewalk if the town would perpetuate his name. It grew to be a city of mills. There were dozens of concentrating plants, separating waste chert and limestone from ore, preparing "concentrate" for shipment to smelters.

By 1918 the town boasted three theaters and three banks. Mines within the town limits had names such as Dorothy Bill, Blue Goose, Woodchuck, and Anna Beaver Number One and Number Two. Cardin was incorporated that year, illegally including 1,040 acres of restricted Quapaw Indian lands. In 1923 the land was released and the townsite shrunk to forty acres.

There was a boom in 1932 when the Eagle-Picher Central Mill was constructed. Capable of milling as much as 17,500 tons of ore in a day, it replaced more than 250 smaller mills. Unemployment followed, and in 1938 Cardin found itself with only 125 taxpayers. The citizens voted to disincorporate. Today the Eagle-Picher mill is a vast ruin in the midst of chat piles.

—*Quapaw* - US 69 Alt.————————

In 1818 the United States government negotiated a treaty with the Quapaw Indians by which they abandoned claim to lands south of the Arkansas River. The tribe, some 200 strong, went to live among the Caddoes on the Red River. The Stokes Commission had been charged with preparing the "wild" natives of Indian Territory to receive the "civilized" tribes from the east as neighbors.

In 1833 the Stokes Commission investigated a claim that the Quapaws were destitute and needed help. Quapaw chiefs agreed to move to a 96,000-acre reserve in the northeast corner of the territory, present Ottawa County. After the Civil War a portion of the reservation extending into Kansas was taken away from them, and the western portion of their "homeland" was given to the Peoria Indians.

Between 1889 and 1892, tribes within jurisdiction of the Quapaw Agency began receiving allotted lands in severalty (to individual owners), 80-acre allotments. The Quapaw tribe held out for more, and in 1893 received 200 acres each.

In 1896 the Kansas City, Ft. Scott, and Gulf Railway built a line across the Quapaw reservation to connect Baxter Springs, Kansas, and Miami, Indian Territory. The line slashed across individual allotments. Minutes of the Quapaw National Council reveal that the railroad paid a total of $365.25 for the right of way on a share-and-share-alike basis. Each Quapaw received $1.56.

At that time, the site of present-day Quapaw was in the midst of 2,000 acres of rich prairie-hay land. John Quapaw made a portion of his allotment available for a railroad depot and school site. A building was moved from the old Quapaw Boarding School, established in 1872, to serve as a depot. Other buildings were moved from the school and lined up along the railroad track; Quapaw became a town. In 1904 Quapaw farmers shipped 1,000 cars of hay, 800 cars of corn, and 25 cars of flax to market.

That same year lead and zinc was discovered on the Quapaws' land, and the Old Dark Horse Mine opened three miles east of town. Most Quapaw farmers became miners. The Quapaws were considered the most backward tribe in the agency because they adhered tenaciously to ancestral ways. They did not like to plow the land because it injured Mother Earth. Grass had been put there to feed buffalo and, later, longhorn cattle.

When the town was incorporated in 1917 the population was 3,000. Eighteen passenger trains stopped every day. The newspaper listed seventeen businesses; three lumberyards furnished materials for local construction. Now the mines have closed down, and Quapaw has reverted to rural ways.

Commerce: Early-day photograph of Commerce Street looking west.
—Western History Collections, University of Oklahoma Library

—*Commerce* - US 69————

With development of the Emma Gordon Mine in 1906, this community became one of the earliest mining camps in the Tri-State mining area. Rival post offices were called Hattonville and Geneva. In 1913 the town was named North Miami, then changed to Commerce the following year after the Commerce Mining and Royalty Company.

Commerce developed as a financial center for the mining district but, like other communities in the area, suffered with decline of the mining industry. However, the town was successful in attracting small businesses. Commerce became nationally known as the boyhood home of Yankee baseball slugger Mickey Mantle. In 1959, Mickey's mother cut a ribbon to open Glenn Berry Manufacturers, Inc. The plant manufactured Mickey Mantle work clothes.

—*Miami* - US 69————

Three Indians and a group of white entrepreneurs from Kansas banded into the Miami Town Company to form a town on the bank of the Neosho River in Indian Territory. They got the Ottawa Indians to sell 588 acres. The Ottawas agreed ten dollars an acre would be a fair price for a portion of tribal land they didn't use.

Then the Bureau of Indian Affairs had to agree, and Congress had to pass a special act because, to date, no towns had been allowed to build on Indian reservations. A patent was issued on May 19, 1891. A handbill advertised a Grand Auction Sale to be held June 25-26, 1891:

A tourist park in Miami during the 1920s.
—Western History Collections, University of Oklahoma Library.

> This is the chance of your life to secure a home in the Indian Territory and a fee simple title. It is located in one of the best agricultural districts, in close proximity of lead and zinc mines, is underlaid with coal and possesses one of the finest water powers in the west. . . . Remember, no such chance will ever exist again during your lifetime.

At first the sale of lots was slow, but in 1895 Miami incorporated with a population of 800.

By 1902 Miami had five attorneys, three dentists, six physicians and surgeons, two banks, four barber shops, seven blacksmith and wagon shops, two boarding houses and three hotels, seven restaurants, and four newspapers. It took nine grocery stores and four general merchandise establishments to serve the community. Three millinery stores featured ladies' hats. Two wagon and carriage manufacturers supplied transportation.

The first real boom came with lead and zinc mining to the north and the community became a financial center for the Tri-State mining area. At the height of the demand for metals during World War I, the population was estimated at 15,000. In 1919 establishment of the Miami School of Mines, now Northeastern Oklahoma A. & M., made the town an educational center. Following World War II, the construction of a large Goodrich plant cushioned the economic effect caused by decline of demand for metals.

—*Twin Bridges State Park* - US 60————

East from Miami, OK 10 leads to the northern end of Grand Lake O' the Cherokees, at the juncture of the Neosho and Spring rivers.

—*Ottawa* - OK 137————

In January 1909, the tiny community of Ottawa petitioned to be put on the ballot among those vying to become county seat of Ottawa County. Even though its post office closed down the year before, Ottawa had been a town for over twenty years.

Ottawa's action was inspired by the fact that Hilburn, another contender, was not even a town yet. A banker, a well-to-do Indian farmer, and a hay merchant were promoting Hilburn, a speculative real-estate venture with nothing but a plat on paper to back the promises of its promoters. Hilburn's developers promised two public squares for county buildings. They maintained the change would constitute moral progress because Miami, with its many saloons, had been known as a "Whiskey Town" during territorial days. The promoters managed to get twenty-five percent of the voters in Ottawa County to sign a petition to make Hilburn the county seat instead of Miami.

Ottawa dropped by the wayside. The final contest was between Miami and nonexistent Hilburn, with Miami receiving 1,544 votes and 1,072 for Hilburn. Hilburn never made it off paper; however, Ottawa continued to hang on as a town, despite having no post office and losing the battle to become county seat.

—*Peoria*————

In September 1877, John Patrick McNaughton heard a tale about an old mine from a Shawnee Indian. The Shawnee said Spaniards had loaded many caravans of pack animals with shiny rocks out of the ground. The Indian's directions led McNaughton to the Peoria reservation in far northeastern Oklahoma.

He found crude shafts and tunnels scattered over about forty acres, round in typical Spanish fashion. Remains indicated from 500 to 1,000 men had participated in the mining venture, but there was no trace of gold or silver. The area was littered with flint chips.

Archaeologists and historians have debated the theory that this was a lost Spanish mine. In 1884 a Smithsonian investigator believed the "mines" were Indian quarries where arrowheads were manufactured. Some historians maintain the work was done by eighteenth-century French explorers searching for gold and silver. Later, a shaft

*"Chicken ladders"
commonly used by the
Spaniards in early
mining operations.*
—William Ritch, 1885

was found containing tree limbs with notches hacked in the sides, like the "chicken ladders" used by the Spaniards in their mines at Santa Rita, New Mexico.

McNaughton persisted. In 1879 he obtained leases to prospect. It was 1889 before he was able to organize the Peoria Mining Company and haul in equipment. He sunk a shaft and hit pay dirt, not gold but lead.

The Peoria shafts were shallow, fifty to seventy-five feet deep. Women and girls worked the ore-bearing earth after it was brought from the mines. Clara Potter, who was fourteen at the time, told about it: "We broke the rocks with an implement something like a churn dash." Ore had to be taken to Galena, Kansas, or Joplin, Missouri, for processing.

By 1891 Peoria had a post office, a hotel, a blacksmith shop, and a schoolhouse. The population swelled to 800. There were no saloons, since whiskey could not be sold on an Indian reservation. But the inevitable bootleggers came in.

"Due to numerous copperhead snakes in the area, miners insisted that some whiskey should be kept on hand in the case of snake bite!" explained Clara Potter.

The boom was short-lived as richer strikes developed in Commerce, Cardin, Quapaw, and Picher. The post office finally closed in 1941, and the community, located north of OK 10C, deteriorated to virtual ghost-town status.

—Wyandotte - US 60———

In 1872 this community began as Prairie City. However, in 1876 it moved three miles east to be on the Atlantic and Pacific Railroad, which was pushing through Indian Territory, and the name was changed to Grand River. The post office was a shack on the bank of Lost Creek. Beside the post office, a small boy drove a blind horse around and around to pump water into the railroad's water tank. Most of the town's activities revolved around the Seneca Indian Boarding School which had been established by Quaker missionaries in 1869. It grew from a log cabin to a dozen brick and frame buildings.

The post office was renamed Wyandotte in October 1894, city ordinances were written, and the official plat of the town was filed in 1896. Among the laws were those prescribing where privies were to be located and levying a fine upon anyone operating a "bawdy house of ill fame." Persons under eighteen years were subject to an 8 o'clock curfew from December 1 until April 30. Another ordinance assessed a fine of $20 for tying a pony under a shade tree if the pony ate the tree.

In 1926 Wyandotte received national publicity as "The Petticoat City of Oklahoma" because all of its city officials were women. Anyone with bobbed hair was barred from office. The report read:

All city officials and board members are women and the city is run from a woman's point of view in spite of long opposition from the men.

It seems the city marshal had not been sufficiently active. Unsavory characters made a practice of riding up and down the boardwalks, shooting up the town, and interrupting church services. Women's suffrage wrought changes. The article reported that Mrs. Mamie Foster, prominent in church and social affairs, had been mayor for five years. "No opposition can force her to resign, nor is any power strong enough to oust her." The city marshal was Mrs. Rosa Rakes, "who can rake any dive with a .45." Miss Westline Lietzman, pastor of the Friends Church, was the alderman. She "stands with Mrs. Foster and helps balk the men."

13

After the Pensacola Dam Project was completed in 1940 on the Neosho and Grand rivers, much agricultural land was flooded. The local economy began to revolve around catering to resort visitors.

—*Fairland* - US 60————

This community had its beginning in 1888 as an agricultural trading center on the Saint Louis-San Francisco Railway. The Fairland post office was established in 1891. The town incorporated in 1896 under Indian Territory laws prohibiting those other than Cherokees from holding office. To encourage development, settlers who bought one town lot received another free. By 1897 the population numbered 700.

Brick buildings were the only structures to escape "the big fire," which swept Main Street in 1903. Less than a year later disaster struck again in the form of a tornado. Four people were killed and a dozen injured, but Fairland persevered.

Until development of resorts on nearby Grand Lake, the base of the economy was cattle, which thrived on the rich bluestem grass surrounding the town.

—*Afton* - US 60————

This town began as a Cherokee settlement in the early 1800s. With the coming of the Missouri-Kansas-Texas Railroad in 1871, Anton Aires, a railroad surveyor, named it for his daughter, who had been baptized in memory of a river in Aires' native Scotland.

The village grew into a division point on the Frisco. Twenty-two passenger trains came through every day. There were coal chutes, a roundhouse, and a water tower. Trains changed crews; hotels, rooming houses, and restaurants did a thriving business. In 1912, the *Afton American* took pride in "the fact that Afton is the smallest town in the state of Oklahoma having day and night electric power."

In the late 1940s, Afton declined as diesel engines replaced steam locomotives. However, the town benefited from the development of recreational facilities around the Grand Lake O' the Cherokees.

———— EXCURSION

—*Pyramid Corners* - OK 2-25————

Located on the old Jefferson Highway and the Ozark Trail, this community took its name from a large pyramid-shaped directional marker located at the highway intersection.

—Bluejacket - OK 25————

This town was formed when the Katy railroad pushed south from Kansas through the Cherokee Nation in 1871. "Uncle" Charley Bluejacket, a Methodist minister, and his brother "Shawnee Tom" Bluejacket brought their families from Johnson County, Kansas, and settled in the tent town that mushroomed around the railroad depot. Shawnee Indians who sold their land in Kansas to the government and moved to Indian Territory were given full rights in the Cherokee Nation.

Railroad workers, opportunists who followed the railroad looking for land to buy along the right of way, and white "intruders" who had no right to be in the Cherokee Nation populated the tent settlement. The Bluejacket brothers began work to improve the town, and it was named in their honor.

Agriculture was the main source of income. Hay and grain were prime cash crops because transportation depended upon horse- and mulepower. The population peaked at about 800 in 1907.

—Welch - OK 2-10————

Welch was settled about 1888 by D. B. Nigh, who leased the townsite from Frank Craig. The Katy railroad built a switch in 1891, and the town became a hay and grain center for the north end of Craig County. The *Welch Watchman*, a weekly, billed itself as the "official city newspaper." A telephone directory filled two of its columns. In 1905 it was serializing *Peck's Bad Boy With the Circus* by George W. Peck.

HISTORICAL HIGHLIGHT

Brangus Cattle

Raymond Pope created Brangus cattle, a cross between Brahman and Angus, on the Clear Creek Ranch west of Welch. With a background of ranching under severe climatic conditions in Louisiana, Pope determined that a blend of three-eighths Brahman and five-eighths Angus was an ideal combination.

Pope advertised Brangus cattle heavily in trade publications for the cattle industry, and he made trips to Central and South American countries to explain the breed. His most effective promotional coup came in the mid-1950s when King Tut, one of his Brangus bulls, was selected to co-star with Elizabeth Taylor and Rock Hudson in the movie *Giant*. King Tut was a worthy representative of the new breed. He was a 2,360-pound grand champion from the San Antonio stock show.

15

—*Vinita* - US 69————————

In July 1866, the Cherokee Nation made an agreement with the United States Department of the Interior that the first railroad to cross the Kansas border into Indian Territory would have exclusive rights across their land. The Missouri-Kansas-Texas Railroad reached the border June 6, 1870, and began laying rails along the Texas Road.

Meanwhile, the Atlantic and Pacific Railroad was building from the east. The resulting controversy was typical of railroad shenanigans in Indian Territory. Col. Elias C. Boudinot, a self-seeking, part-Cherokee lawyer, knew that a town would develop where the two lines crossed. The Katy railroad had already designated a site for the station. In company with some cohorts, Boudinot secretly arranged with the A & P to veer southward to a new crossing.

Using heavy posts and lumber, Boudinot and his friends fenced off two square miles at the new crossing. They planned to develop a townsite and sell lots. Katy officials insisted the A & P should follow the original survey; however, A & P workers laid the new crossing during the dark of night. The next morning Katy forces tore up the track and slowly ran boxcars back and forth over the crossing so the A & P workers could not make headway on construction.

The dispute was finally settled by a court injunction which left Boudinot and his friends in possession of the townsite, a hollow victory. A new faction gained control of the Cherokee Nation, a faction unfriendly to Boudinot. They tore down the fence, appointed town commissioners, platted the townsite, and called the place Downingville after Lewis Downing, then chief of the Cherokees. Town leaders tried to get the railroads to build a union station, but each insisted upon a station of its own.

Boudinot went to Washington, D.C., where he practiced law, for the most part on behalf of railroad interests. His only victory in the situation was getting the name of the town changed to Vinita commemorating his friend, sculptress Vinnie Ream, who had created the life-sized statue of Abraham Lincoln in the Capitol at Washington.

Cattle trails between Texas and rail links to northern and eastern markets had long passed the vicinity, and Vinita took on importance as a shipping center. In 1941 completion of the Pensacola Dam on the Grand River gave Vinita an economic shot in the arm.

—*Grand Lake O' the Cherokees* - US 60———

The idea of damming Grand River to generate electrical power was first suggested in 1891. In 1935 the Oklahoma legislature created the Grand River Dam Authority, and construction of the $22.75 million Pensacola Dam began. When completed in 1941, the dam stretched 5,680 feet, the longest multiple-arch dam in the world.

The massive reservoir holds 59,200 surface acres of water. It has 1,300 miles of shore line and stretches 66 miles through the Ozark foothills. It serves primarily for production of electrical power and flood control; however, surrounding resorts and recreational facilities are its most visible aspects.

—*Bernice* - OK 85A———

The town was established in 1894 with the name Needmore, presumably in reference to the economic status of its inhabitants. In 1913 the name was changed to Bernice, for Bernice Lundy, the daughter of a prominent local family. Initially, its lifeline was the Kansas, Oklahoma and Gulf Railway, extending across the northwest corner of Delaware County. The route of the old Texas Road was nearby. An early highway map showed a road known as the Ozark Trail, from St. Louis to New Mexico, going through Bernice westward to Vinita.

HISTORICAL HIGHLIGHT

The Ozark Trails

In 1916 plans were under way to promote a road network through Oklahoma called the Ozark Trail. Col. W. H. Harvey of Monte Ne, Arkansas, was president of the Ozark Trails Association. Early plans were grandiose. Colonel Harvey said, "The Ozark Trail is to be a link in an ocean-to-ocean road. It will run from St. Louis to New Mexico and is intended to be above high water, hardsurfaced and later oiled."

Over the years the organization held meetings in Arkansas, Missouri, Oklahoma, Texas, and New Mexico. Plans were made to mark the route with impressive pyramids and concrete mileage posts. Old-timers remember that the markers sometimes consisted of green paint on telephone poles. Proposed routes proliferated as towns competed to be included on the trail.

In 1990, David Lopez, systems supervisor of the Oklahoma Department of Transportation, traced the Ozark Trails through yellowed newspaper files and fragile maps, coming up with a variety of routes.

17

The northern route was proposed from Coffeyville, Kansas, to Bartlesville and through Ramona, Collinsville, Tulsa, Fisher, Keystone, Cushing, and Guthrie. On November 5, 1916, the *Daily Oklahoman* reported citizens along the central route were actively preparing for a road from Galena, Kansas, to Miami, Nowata, Collinsville, Tulsa, Sapulpa, Bristow, Stroud, Chandler, Wellston, Luther, Jones, and Oklahoma City. The southern route was planned from Joplin, Missouri, through Miami, Afton, Vinita, Chelsea, Claremore, Tulsa, Glen Pool, Okmulgee, Henryetta, Okemah, Prague, and Oklahoma City.

By 1926, Rand McNally maps showed roads as "Ozark Trails." Such plans generated the name Ozark for the rural crossroads village just east of Altus on US 62, still on some present-day highway maps. A newspaper reported that towns wishing to be on the route "worked like fury for the Ozark Trail. This resulted in the overnight improvement of long stretches of highway."

Over intervening years, memories and memoirs have named various highways as having been *the* Ozark Trail—US 60, US 62, US 66, OK 9, and others. All of those memories may be correct, because during that early effort to promote tourism in Oklahoma, people in many areas were running to catch the bandwagon on Colonel Harvey's "national highway."

—Grove - OK 59—OK 25————

Established prior to 1888, this community took its name from Round Grove, a nearby landmark and Civil War site. It was the county seat of Delaware County from statehood in 1907 until 1912. For a time a railroad branch line ran from Southwest City, Missouri, to Grove, a distance of about thirty miles. Grove had the dubious distinction of being a railroad town with a railroad that did not reach any other part of the state.

After 1912 Grove struggled as an agricultural trade area. Since construction of the Pensacola Dam it has become an increasingly important resort center appealing to tourists.

—Cleora - OK 85————

Originally, the principal purpose of this community was to provide ferry service. When the post office was established in 1896, it was named Klaus for Robert H. Klaus, the ferry operator. The name was changed to Cleora in 1900. Today the town has a seaplane base and serves fishermen.

18

—Ketchum - OK 85———————

This community was established in 1899 about a mile north of the home of Rev. James and Elizabeth Ketchum. Reverend Ketchum was an outstanding leader of the Delaware tribe, an orator, and a Methodist minister. The town was moved in 1912 to be on the Kansas, Oklahoma and Gulf Railway. It is located adjacent to the Old Military Road, a branch of the Texas Road.

During its early days the town's principal source of income was from agricultural products, cotton, corn, and other grains.

—Disney - OK 85———————

Construction of the Pensacola Dam spawned this town in 1939 by way of a promoter named C. D. Armstrong. In 1940 the Tyler Boat Works dredged a channel, built a 12-foot seawall, and prepared for a booming boat business. Train trips were scheduled to Disney for excursions of the dam site, boat rides, refreshments, and entertainment. Fox Pictures came to film a movie. The town is named for Wesley E. Disney, a congressman from Oklahoma, rather than for the creator of Mickey Mouse, as many visitors assume.

—Langley - OK 28———————

Langley got its start with the construction of the Pensacola Dam. In 1937 Cliff Bogle divided the area at the west end of the dam into lots, and staged a dedication ceremony with a drawing for free lots to attract visitors. Initially a ferry from Spavinaw was the only access to Langley. The town got off to a flying start, but tourist trade slowed during World War II because of tire and gasoline rationing.

—Pensacola - OK 28———————

In December 1823, Hopefield Mission was established near the present site of Pensacola. The agricultural settlement remained active for several years. The growth of Pensacola as a community began in the 1890s, taking its name from the nearby Pensacola Ranch of a prominent Cherokee named Joseph Martin. The post office, located in the Martin home, was approved May 23, 1896.

A monument marking the Second Battle of Cabin Creek is a half-mile north of Pensacola. This Civil War battle took place along the Old Military Road on September 19, 1864.

—Big Cabin—Pryor - US 69————————

This small town on the Missouri-Kansas-Texas Railroad got its name from a large plank cabin built by Indians near the Texas Road. After the coming of the railroad, one of the first buildings in town was a large hay barn, built in 1888. Loose hay was cured in the barn prior to shipment. So much hay was shipped from Big Cabin between 1883 and 1910 that the area became known as "The Hay Capital of the World."

Historically the area is more noted for two Civil War battles fought near Cabin Creek, which parallels US 69 between Big Cabin and Patton. On July 1-2, 1863, Cherokee Confederate General Stand Watie attacked a southbound Union supply train of two hundred wagons where the Texas Road crossed Cabin Creek, but the Northern troops repelled the aggressors and continued shipments to Fort Gibson.

A year later at the same spot, in the second battle of Cabin Creek, General Stand Watie and Confederate General R. M. Gano captured a Union supply train valued at $1.5 million. In addition to food, clothing, and military supplies the wagons contained whiskey. The victorious Confederate troops embarked on an orgy lasting until Stand Watie ordered the remaining whiskey poured into Cabin Creek.

—Adair - US 69—OK 28————————

This town was established with the coming of the Missouri-Kansas-Texas Railroad in 1872 and named for William Penn Adair, of a prominent Cherokee family. The bullet-pocked night of July 14, 1892, provided the most exciting day in Adair's history.

That night the Daltons robbed a train in Adair. Actually, the gang intended to stage the robbery at Pryor Creek, nine miles to the south; but, rightly suspecting that their plans were known, they moved the operation to Adair. When the train passed Pryor Creek, the posse aboard the smoking car relaxed and bragged to each other about what they would have done had the outlaws showed up.

As the train whistle sounded for Adair, the Dalton gang appeared on the depot platform, rifles in hand. Two subdued the station agent and loungers who had come to watch the express go through. Two more covered the engine crew. Three forced open the express car to get the loot, while two others went farther down the platform to prevent interference from the remainder of the crew and passengers. An estimated two hundred shots rang out in a blistering five-minute exchange of gunfire. Two local doctors were shot during the fray; one died. Three members of the posse were wounded. The Dalton gang rode away unharmed with an estimated $17,000 in currency.

Bill Powers, Bob Dalton, Grat Dalton, and Dick Broadwell—four of the five outlaws killed during the Dalton gang's attempt to rob two banks at once. —Western History Collections, University of Oklahoma Library

The Dalton Gang

Grattan, Robert, and Emmett Dalton were the heart of a gang that scourged Oklahoma during the 1890s. For a while they served as law officers in the Osage Nation, but it soon became evident that they were stealing horses as a side line. Grat went to California, where he was convicted on a charge of train robbery. He escaped and returned to Oklahoma in September 1891.

Upon his return, Grat joined his brothers in a rampage of robbery and murder until they tried to rob two banks at once in Coffeyville, Kansas, on October 5, 1892. In part, the Coffeyville caper was an attempt at one-upmanship: Robbing two banks in broad daylight on the same day would top anything Jesse James had done. Bill Powers and Dick Broadwell accompanied the three brothers. They drew lots; Grat Dalton, Powers, and Broadwell would take the Condon Bank while Bob and Emmett went across the street to the First National. Then the alarm sounded.

"The Daltons are robbing the bank!"

Armed citizens poured into the streets. The shooting lasted twelve minutes. When it stopped, Grat and Bob Dalton lay dead, as did Bill Powers and Dick Broadwell. Emmett Dalton was sorely wounded. Four of Coffeyville's citizens were dead or dying, and three more were wounded.

Emmett Dalton recovered and was sentenced to life imprisonment. Pardoned after fourteen and a half years, he married Julia Johnson, who had waited for him through his imprisonment. Some say he went to an old hide-out near Sand Springs and dug up loot the gang had buried after the Adair train robbery. He moved to California and went into business as a building contractor. Emmett wrote a book, *When the Daltons Rode*, which was made into a movie.

—*Pryor*- US 69—OK 20————

The first settlement in the area was called Coo-Y-Yah, meaning "huckleberry" in the Cherokee tongue. It developed slowly until the Katy railroad arrived in 1871.

Coo-Y-Yah proved too difficult for English speakers, and on April 23, 1887, postal authorities changed the name to Pryor Creek. In 1909 the Post Office Department dropped the word "creek"; however, Pryor Creek continued as the legal name.

The name honors Nathaniel Pryor, a scout with the Lewis and Clark expedition of 1804-06. After discharge from the army, he married an Osage woman and established a trading post on Pryor Creek. He died in 1831. One of the first veterans of United States wars interred in Oklahoma, his grave is in the Fairview Cemetery east of Pryor.

The town's economy was based upon farming and ranching until 1941, when the federal government announced plans for a munitions plant about five miles from Pryor. Not all residents welcomed the addition until after the attack on Pearl Harbor; in the meantime, the Pryor Ordnance Works wrought changes.

Every available house was rented to DuPont workers. Homeowners fixed up the chicken coops in their backyards and had no trouble finding tenants. Farmers pitched large tents and rented space in them. Surrounding towns swelled. Each morning and evening, trains brought and returned workers from their homes in Muskogee and Parsons, Kansas. Roads jammed between 4:30 and 6:00 P.M. in all directions from Pryor.

Then, on the afternoon of April 27, 1942, what appeared to be a typical thunderstorm approached from the west. A truck driver who was on OK 20 between Pryor and Claremore told about it:

> There wasn't time to think. I just slammed the car against a bank of earth and Leonard Wallace and I jumped out. From where we were standing we could see automobiles being picked up off the road and carried a quarter mile over the fields. Some that were dumped all around us were just twisted masses of junk.

The storm struck Pryor without warning, cutting a swathe two blocks wide. A clock on the front of the Post Office Book Store stopped at 4:45 P.M. to mark the time. Windows exploded from houses and buildings. Roofs collapsed. A locomotive and twelve cars of a shuttle train carrying munitions plant workers were lifted and thrown to the ground.

The typical early-day storm cellar was always built close to the homesteader's sod house.

A pilot who witnessed the storm radioed the Tulsa airport and help arrived from surrounding communities. After the final count, 52 were dead and 402 injured. Property damage exceeded $2 million. It took eight months to erase the physical scars; mental anguish lasted longer. Most Oklahomans automatically look for the nearest cellar when a storm darkens the sky; residents of Pryor are particularly vigilant.

After the war, the munitions plant closed and was converted into the Mid-America Industrial District, a complex of mills and plants for the production of paper, cement, fertilizer, and other products; old Coo-Y-Yah became an industrial city.

EXCURSION

A circle tour east of Pryor, starting on OK 20 and returning to US 69 by way of US 412 at Chouteau takes one through a number of the earliest and most historically significant communities in Oklahoma.

—*Salina* - OK 20——

This town is recognized as the oldest continuing white settlement in Oklahoma. During the latter part of the eighteenth century, the Chouteau family of St. Louis obtained a license from the Spanish government to trade with the Osage Indians.

Historical documentation is scarce, but according to Chouteau family recollections, in 1794 the trade monopoly in the area around St. Louis was threatened. In March 1796 Jean Pierre Chouteau organized an expedition to extend farther west. About a dozen traders and some Osage Indians followed the Osage Trace. They came to a river the Osages called Ne-o-zho (Neosho), carved a *pirogue* out of a large cottonwood tree, and followed the stream Chouteau called *grande riviere*.

The spot chosen by Jean Pierre Chouteau is now within the city limits of Salina. Jean Pierre's son, Auguste Pierre Chouteau, returned early in the nineteenth century to establish a post for trade in furs, fowl, wild honey, and other marketable items.

Travelers on the Texas Road found gracious hospitality at a pretentious two-story log home in which Chouteau lived the life of a feudal baron with his numerous children and an Osage wife named Rosalie. A piazza extended across the front of the house with buffalo and bear skins draped over the railing. In A *Tour on the Prairies*, Washington Irving recorded a visit in 1832.

When Irving arrived, a number of Indians were roasting venison under a tree in front of the house. Negro slaves, half-breeds, and squaws welcomed the visitors. Negro girls ran about giggling. Dogs, pigs, hens, turkeys, geese, and ducks sounded their welcome. The meal consisted of venison steak, roast beef, fricasseed wild turkey, bread, cake, wild honey, and coffee, served by Masina, the half-breed sister of Chouteau's wife.

Auguste P. Chouteau died December 25, 1838. John Ross, chief of the Cherokees, acquired many of Chouteau's holdings. A Cherokee Orphan Asylum established in 1874 became the designation of the first post office. The name was changed to Salina in 1884, after the nearby salt works.

—*Spavinaw* - OK 20————

After coming over the Trail of Tears, many Cherokees settled in the area. In 1829 John Rogers came to Spavinaw Creek from Arkansas. He built a dam and erected a mill and a distillery at the site of Spavinaw.

In 1846 a group of Mormons were forced from their homes in Illinois and Missouri. They began a long westward trek in search of land. Some camped on Spavinaw Creek for a night and decided to stay. They repaired Rogers' old mill and used it to grind grain and saw wood. After a few years, the Mormons moved on to join others in the promised land.

Later the mill was operated by a Joseph M. Lynch, and on May 9, 1878, the post office was registered as Lynch's Prairie. The name was changed to Spavina Mills later that same year. The present spelling was adopted in 1892.

In 1922 Tulsa wanted to dam Spavinaw Creek to supply the city with water. In the face of protest, Tulsa bought the town. Most of the buildings and the cemetery were moved to higher ground. The dam was completed in 1924. Spavinaw Lake became the first man-made lake in northeastern Oklahoma, and Spavinaw embarked upon a career as a resort town. Wealthy Tulsans came to build summer homes and clubs.

During Prohibition, Spavinaw catered to the new residents with open saloons and earned a reputation as a wild town. Newspapermen dubbed it "Little Chicago."

—Strang ———

Located five miles northwest of Spavinaw, this rural community on the east bank of Markham Ferry Reservoir was known as Lynch from 1905 until 1913. Two ferries operated on the Grand River, one serving Salina, Chouteau, and Muskogee, and the other going to Adair and Vinita.

In 1913 the Missouri, Oklahoma and Gulf Railway came, and the railroad developer renamed the town after his wife's maiden name. The line extended from Neosho, Missouri, to Denison, Texas. The last spike was driven in Strang, connecting the two ends of the line with a "golden spike" ceremony.

On February 14, 1913, a crowd of several thousand gathered to watch an engineer ease a steaming engine onto the new section of track. The crowd besieged the locomotive. Finally, the engineer stuck his head out of the engine, swept the crowd with a stern look, and yelled: "Look out, everybody. We're going to turn 'round!"

Then he gave two shrill toots on the whistle. The panic-stricken crowd stampeded before anybody realized that the track-bound locomotive could not turn around.

Strang's population peaked during construction of the Pensacola Dam.

—Jay - OK 20———

This community got its start from a fight to become county seat of Delaware County, an affair with the makings of a comic opera. In 1908 a campaign started to locate the county seat in the geographical center of the county. That site turned out to be in a woods with no inhabitants within a mile.

Promoters got busy. They cleared timber from a ten-acre plot, platted it into lots, and named it Jay for Jay Washington, a Cherokee whose land allotment included the townsite. The election to select the county seat was bitterly fought. To the chagrin of the citizens of other communities, they were outvoted by Indians living in the southern part of the county.

Immediately, the disappointed communities appealed to the courts. This upstart town had no houses, no railroads, and no conveniences. The Oklahoma Supreme Court found in favor of Jay and the governor declared it the county seat. During the interim a few store buildings, houses, and a frame courthouse were erected.

The trouble did not end. W. J. Creekmore platted a forty-acre area next to the original ten acres and erected a large frame building. He offered it to the county commissioners as a courthouse. The commissioners accepted, but the newcomers who had settled the original ten-acre plot would not relinquish the courthouse.

Again, the issue went to court as residents of the ten-acre plot dug a trench around their courthouse and guarded it with shotguns. Firing broke out; the only casualty was a mule. The state militia was called in to quell the disturbance. The governor issued another proclamation: Jay, with its original ten-acre plot, was still the county seat of Delaware County.

Jay now serves as a supply center for the recreation industry. East of Jay, for 5.4 miles, OK 20 runs on the boundary between Oklahoma and Arkansas. From the south, highway signs read OK 20; from the north they designate Arkansas State Highway 43. At the Missouri line motorists can have their pictures taken beside a marker showing that they are in three states at the same time.

—*Flint* - US 412————

Today, one is likely to pass Flint without noticing it. Shortly after the Cherokee removal, a community grew up around a gristmill and sawmill established on Flint Creek in 1838. The millstones from France came to Flint via Van Buren, Arkansas, by water and ox team. In 1872, Polly Chesterton, the Cherokee wife of the miller, was killed by an Indian named Ezekiel Proctor. Proctor intended the shot for her husband. Proctor's trial precipitated the Going Snake District Courthouse Massacre.

Cherokees were incensed with federal officers operating out of Van Buren or Fort Smith, Arkansas, who would come into Indian Territory, arrest Indians charged with crimes, and take them back where they were obliged to make bond, if they could, among strange people. The Indians resented this invasion of their rights; they wanted trial in their own courts.

Proctor was being tried in a Cherokee court. A posse of deputy marshals from Fort Smith arrived with a warrant for his arrest on another charge. They invaded the courtroom to take the prisoner into custody. During the ensuing gunfight, eleven men were killed. The judge, a juror, and several spectators were wounded. The affair grew to such proportions that the United States Senate demanded a report, which was submitted to President Grant.

Ruins of the business district of Flint, including the old mill building, are north of the highway.

—*Twin Oaks—Oaks* - OK 412A————

From Twin Oaks, at the intersection of US 412 and OK 412A, one can visit Oaks, the site of a historic Cherokee mission. In 1842, Moravian missionaries to the Cherokees built the New Springplace Moravian Mission, a combination log schoolhouse and church. During the Civil War, James Ward, Jr., a Cherokee missionary, was killed by a band of "Cherokee Pins" and the mission closed until after the war.

Cherokee Pins were full blood Cherokees who sided with Union forces. They identified themselves by wearing crossed pins on their lapels. The mission reopened after the war and operated until 1898. Only a few ruins remain.

—*Rose* - US 412————

This small community contains the only one of the nine original district courthouses of the Cherokee Nation. It was built during the first half of the nineteenth century on the road between Tahlequah and Siloam Springs. It is now maintained as a museum by the state of Oklahoma. Exhibits include the old springhouse, which also served as a jail, the execution tree, gravestones, and foundations of other buildings.

The post office was named Rose in 1891, a corruption of nearby Rowe's Prairie, which had been named for David Rowe, an early resident.

—*Locust Grove* - US 412————

This old town in the Cherokee Nation was established in 1872 and named for a nearby grove of locust trees. It had been the site of a Civil War battle in 1862. With the coming of the Kansas, Oklahoma and Gulf Railway, the present town was established by O. W. Killam in 1912.

Killam bought the Elzina Ross Indian allotment for $3,000 and platted the town. Auction of lots started at 10:00 A.M. on May 12, 1912; all were sold by 4:00 P.M. Killam made arrangements for a friend to offer double the price to create a market and put added value on the development.

On the first Christmas in the new town, Killam purchased a hundred turkeys, turned them loose, and invited the citizenry to try their luck at catching one. Those not lucky enough to catch their Christmas dinners were invited to be guests of the Killam family at the Montgomery Hotel. Two hundred guests ate turkey with all the trimmings for 25 cents each. The turkey chase became a yearly affair, known as Locust Grove's Annual Goose Grab. The name was changed when sponsoring merchants added geese, ducks, guineas, and chickens to the flock because of a shortage of turkeys. The event was discontinued after the Society for Prevention of Cruelty to Animals brought pressure to bear.

—Chouteau—Wagoner - US 69-412————

The site of Chouteau was relatively insignificant until the arrival of the Missouri-Kansas-Texas Railroad in 1871. It was prairie land, sparsely occupied by a few hardy settlers who raised cattle. A fence around the town kept cattle out, and parents escorted their children through the gates. Many early citizens lived in tents outside town. Some raised hogs and sold pork to travelers on the Texas Road. When the railroad came, the Texas Road lost its importance.

Shortly after 1900 a number of Amish farmers arrived in the area. Their buggies and wagons still frequent the business district.

The town was named Chouteau, after Jean Pierre Chouteau. The post office was established October 18, 1871, with the name officially misspelled "Choteau." The error was corrected in 1941.

The "Old Iron Post" is located about 2.5 miles southeast of Chouteau. This marker was implanted in 1849 during a survey to determine the boundary of Indian lands. It marked the northeast corner of the Creek Nation. Since 1849 it has been used as a reference point for all land surveys in the area.

HISTORICAL HIGHLIGHT

Union Mission

In 1819 the United Foreign Missionary Society of New York obtained permission from the Osage Indians to establish a mission in their country. In April 1820, twenty-two men, women, and children departed from New York. They arrived at a site in the remote wilderness five miles southeast of what is now Chouteau on February 18, 1821. Along the way they suffered hardship, disease, and two deaths.

The missionaries cultivated a hundred acres of surrounding land. They built about twenty buildings and established a school for Osage and

Creek Indians that operated until 1832-33. Unfortunately, the missionaries were not entirely successful.

They had hoped to take Indian children from their parents, board them at the school, educate them to "civilized" lifestyle, and "Christianize" their "heathen worship." The Indians, skeptical of Europeans because of past contacts, failed to realize the new arrivals meant well. Yet, the missionaries failed to realize that chants to "heathen gods" were just as much prayers to the Indians' Maker as the formal worship conducted each morning at the mission. Most of their pupils belonged to white missionaries or were mixed-breed children of local traders.

In 1828 the Osage Indians were removed from the surrounding country and the land was given to the Cherokees. The mission was abandoned. In 1835 the Reverend Samuel Austin Worcester, a missionary to the Cherokees, arrived from Georgia. He brought a printing press.

Worcester hurried to print the first book to be published in what is now Oklahoma. He wanted material evidence to show the Cherokee Council what he intended to do if he were allowed to remain. His printer was ill, so Worcester set type for the book and printed two hundred copies himself. He described it as "merely a little book of eight pages, filled chiefly with pictures, but containing the alphabet and a little more."

After about a year, Worcester moved to Park Hill, near the capital of the Cherokee Nation at Tahlequah, and continued his work. Today, all that remains of the old Union Mission are a few foundation stones and a lonely cemetery containing the grave of Epaphras Chapman, who founded Union Mission. He died in 1825.

—*Mazie* - US 69————

In 1871, the Katy railroad had planned to cross the Cherokee Nation to Fort Gibson. However, the Cherokees charged $1.75 per head for shipping cattle from the Cherokee Nation. So the railroad built a 2,000-foot switch at the present site of Mazie as a loading point for Texas cattle.

One of the largest stockyards along the Katy developed. In a day, as many as six trainloads of Texas longhorns could be unloaded and dipped into vats to control Texas tick fever. Before shipment to northern and eastern markets, the cattle grazed on the lush stand of bluestem grass surrounding the area.

It was thirty-three years before the town was platted. One of the developers from Fort Smith had a small daughter named Mazie, hence the name of the town.

—*Wagoner* - US 69—OK 51————————

The Texas Road ran just east of present-day Wagoner, and Texas drovers herded cattle northward over the East Shawnee Cattle Trail through the prairie that became the townsite. The town was founded in 1887, when a station house and lunchroom was established at the juncture of the Missouri-Kansas-Texas and the Kansas and Arkansas Valley railroads.

Henry "Bigfoot" Wagoner, a train dispatcher from Parsons, Kansas, saw need for a switch for loading logs and cattle. When the switch was completed, a telegram was sent: "Wagoner's Switch is ready." And that became the name of the town. In the beginning Wagoner's Switch was used to load walnut logs from the Verdigris River valley for shipment to northern furniture factories.

When the post office was established in 1888, the word "Switch" was dropped. The town prospered as a shipping point with as many as thirty-eight freight trains a day passing through. Local ranchers and businessmen began to build fine homes, and Wagoner was dubbed "The Queen City of the Prairies." Today historical plaques mark the old residences and buildings, and many can be visited.

———— EXCURSION

US 69 is the shortest distance south to Muskogee, but by taking a leisurely drive east through the former Cherokee Nation you can join hands with history while enjoying woods, streams, and manmade lakes. OK 51 leads past Sequoyah State Park and through Hulbert to Tahlequah, which became the permanent capital of the Cherokee Nation in 1839.

—*Tahlequah* - OK 51————————

After the bitter experience of losing its eastern homelands to white expansionism, the council of the Cherokee Nation passed a "perpetual law" imposing the death penalty against any member of the nation who should propose the sale or exchange of their lands. Chief Doublehead had already been assassinated for his part in succumbing to bribery during treaty negotiations in 1805. In 1839 Major Ridge, who participated in the Doublehead assassination, suffered the same fate for his part in negotiating an 1835 treaty.

After their removal from the East, conflicting factions reunited into the Cherokee Nation on September 6, 1839, with Tahlequah as the capital. It remained the seat of government until 1906 when Oklahoma statehood obliterated the Cherokee Nation. Despite a national

Cherokee National Capitol, Tahlequah, circa 1898. ——Western
History Collections, University of Oklahoma Library

policy toward expunging the Indians' culture by assimilation, the Cherokees still celebrate September 6 as a tribal holiday. Dedicated members of the tribe still fight for the land and rights granted by solemn treaty.

In 1844 the Cherokees established the *Cherokee Advocate* as their official newspaper, a successor to the *Cherokee Phoenix* that had been published in Georgia since 1822. Invention of the Cherokee alphabet by Sequoyah in 1821 enabled full-bloods who could not speak or read the English language to keep posted on events and progress of their tribal affairs. For the benefit of mixed-bloods who never mastered the alphabet, the newspaper was published in both Cherokee and English. Publication continued for about sixty years. Today many signs in the business district of Tahlequah are printed in the Cherokee language. Tahlequah continues as a tribal capital, in spirit if not in fact.

In Tahlequah you can experience a feeling for the colorful past by visiting historical landmarks: the old Cherokee National Capitol, completed in 1870; the Cherokee National Supreme Court building; the Cherokee National Prison; and many historic homes. Libraries at Bacone College and Northeastern State University provide books and documents for those who wish to pursue the past.

—*Cherokee Heritage Center* - US 62——

The Cherokee Heritage Center is located three miles south of Tahlequah just off US 62. It includes the Cherokee National Museum, presenting the Cherokee story from man's arrival on the North

31

The McSpadden Grist and Flour Mill on Spring Branch Creek, Tahlequah, built about 1886, was typical of early construction in the Cherokee Nation. It is no longer in existence. —Western History Collections, University of Oklahoma Library

American continent to the present. Tsa-La-Gi Ancient Village portrays Cherokee tribal life in the 1700s. Adams Corner is a detailed reconstruction of a small crossroads community during 1875-90, the final years of the Cherokee Nation.

In the fall and winter of 1838-39, the Cherokees were driven from their homes and pushed along a dreary march westward. Of 16,000 who started that miserable journey, more than 4,000 died from disease, hunger, and exposure. From the first Saturday in June through Labor Day weekend, the *Trail of Tears* drama unfolds the bittersweet story of the Cherokees' immigration to the strange and foreboding wilderness that would become the state of Oklahoma.

—Park Hill - US 62————

Little remains of Park Hill, once "The Athens of Indian Territory." In 1836, Presbyterian missionary Samuel Austin Worcester established the Park Hill Mission. It included homes for missionaries and teachers, a boarding hall, gristmill, shops, stables, and a printing office and book bindery.

In 1846 the Cherokee National Council authorized the creation of two seminaries or high schools, the female seminary at Park Hill and a male seminary a little closer to Tahlequah. Both three-story brick structures opened on May 7, 1851. Cherokees were studying Greek and Latin while many whites in Indian Territory could not sign their own names.

The mission was the scene of retribution for the Trail of Tears. Elias Boudinot, who played an active role in shaping the Treaty of New Echota, which agreed to removal of the Cherokees to the West, was tried by a secret meeting and condemned to death. He was killed on June 22, 1839, at the Park Hill Mission.

Park Hill never recovered from the raiding and pillaging during the Civil War. The Cherokee Female Seminary opened after the war, but it was destroyed by fire in 1887. Today, only ruins remain.

The Worcester Mission Cemetery has been restored by the Oklahoma State Historical Society. It contains the grave of Samuel A. Worcester with the inscription: "To his labors, the Cherokees are indebted for their Bible and hymn book."

George Michael Murrell, a white man, was a business partner in Tennessee with Lewis Ross, brother of Chief John Ross. Murrell married Lewis Ross's daughter, Minerva, and came to Indian Territory with the Ross family in 1840. In 1844 he built the Murrell House. Murrell kept a kennel of fox hounds and entertained lavishly. Young

Cherokee leader Elias Boudinot was killed at Park Hill for his part in negotiating an unfavorable treaty. —Western History Collections, University of Oklahoma Library

military officers from Fort Gibson came to meet belles from the Cherokee Female Seminary. Murrell drove back and forth to his business in Tahlequah in a carriage drawn by a "fiery team of four." When the Civil War broke out, Murrell returned to his Virginia home to raise a cavalry troop. He never returned to Indian Territory.

The Murrell House survived the carnage of the Civil War, and ownership passed to the Ross family. Now owned by the state, it has been restored as a historical monument.

—*Proctor* - US 62————

This small community was named for Ezekiel Proctor, a leading participant in the Going Snake Massacre that resulted from federal meddling in tribal affairs. As Proctor awaited trial by the Cherokee tribal court on a murder charge, word came that United States law officers were coming from Fort Smith to arrest him on another charge. The Going Snake schoolhouse on the bank of Baron Creek, south of present-day Proctor, was chosen as the site for the trial because it could be more easily defended than the Going Snake Courthouse.

Everyone in the schoolhouse was armed to repel the attack. Seven U.S. officers were killed, the prisoner and the judge were wounded, and the clerk was killed at his desk. A federal grand jury at Fort Smith issued indictments against twenty Cherokee citizens who had been present at the trial. Later, all charges were dropped.

Ezekiel Proctor recovered from his wounds. He lived a law-abiding life and, eventually, was elected sheriff of the Flint District of the Cherokee Nation and a member of the Cherokee Council. The name of this tiny rural community keeps his memory green.

—*Westville* - US 59—US 62————

This lumbering town was established in 1895 soon after the Kansas City Southern Railway reached the vicinity. It was named for Samuel West, a local resident. The Frisco railroad arrived in 1905 and Westville aspired to become a city. When Oklahoma became a state in 1907, Westville was designated the county seat of Adair County but lost out to Stilwell in 1910.

Before the use of numbered highways in Oklahoma, when the Ozark Trails road was headed toward Westville, the entire population turned out to cut down a hill to conform to requirements of the Ozark Trails' Association. Businessmen donned overalls and took up picks and shovels beside laborers; women followed with baskets of food.

In addition to lumbering, Westville's economy has revolved around fruit-raising. One hundred fifty carloads of apples were shipped from Westville in 1920. During 1921 more than 500 acres were planted in berries and grapes.

34

—*Watts* - US 59————

Perched on a wooded hill, Watts became a rendezvous for hunters and fishermen and has long served as a starting point for float trips on the Illinois River. With establishment of the post office in 1912, it was named for John Watts, a Cherokee chief.

The site of the Cherokee Baptist Mission, commonly known as Breadtown, is nearby. In 1838 Rev. Evan Jones led a contingent of Cherokees from North Carolina to their new home in Indian Territory. His mission was called Breadtown because it was one of the places where rations were issued to the newly arrived exiles.

He established the Baptist Mission Press, the second printing press in the Cherokee Nation. The output consisted of the book of Genesis and about half of the New Testament, schoolbooks, tracts, an English hymn book, a Creek hymn book, the Cherokee alphabet, and two of the messages of the Principal Chief John Ross. In addition, the *Cherokee Messenger* was published every other month.

—*Stilwell* - US 59—OK 51————

Stilwell had its beginning in 1896 when the Flint post office was moved from three miles to the north. The name was changed to honor Arthur E. Stilwell, developer of the Kansas City Southern Railway. The community drew its sustenance from timber and agriculture.

Strawberries became the mainstay, and by 1956 some 1,200 acres were dedicated to growing them. A local processing plant can handle 8,000 crates a day. In mid-May, the Strawberry Festival attracts visitors from throughout the state. During the rest of the year the plant processes green beans, spinach, peas, potatoes, and other locally grown vegetables.

The Bitting Springs Mill, one of the state's few remaining water-powered gristmills, is a nearby point of interest. It was built in the late 1830s or early 1840s. It is still turning out stone-ground corn meal.

—*Fort Gibson Stockade* - US 62—OK 10————

In October 1806, Lt. James B. Wilkinson, second in command of the Zebulon M. Pike expedition, was sent to explore the Arkansas River. As winter set in, the river froze over, and Wilkinson and his party of five enlisted men had to walk the bank. At last they reached the mouth of the Verdigris River. Then, on December 6, they came to an Osage village on the east bank of the Grand River where it joins the Arkansas and the Verdigris, the site recommended by Lieutenant Wilkinson for a fort. Thus Three Forks was born, the cradle of Oklahoma history.

The area became a trading center before the United States got around to building a fort. Auguste P. Chouteau had a shipyard at the

The original Fort Gibson stockade has been restored and reconstructed. It is furnished with period memorabilia and operated as a museum by the Oklahoma Historical Society.

mouth of the Verdigris. On April 2, 1824, he shipped a barge destined for New Orleans loaded with 38,757 pounds of furs and skins—387 packs made up of hides from 300 female bears, 160 bear cubs, 387 beavers, 67 otters, 720 cats, and 364 deer. Some two thousand French, American, Cherokee, and Delaware hunters were scattered through the area. The Osages maintained that the animals in this region belonged to them. In November 1823, Mad Buffalo led 200 Osage warriors on a foray along the Blue River and wiped out a party of French trappers.

On April 21, 1824, Gen. Matthew Arbuckle arrived in long boats with 121 officers and men of the 7th Infantry. His mission was to establish a fort to protect Cherokee emigrants and wandering whites from the Osages. The troops set about clearing land and building a frontier post. Log stables made up two sides of a large quadrangle. The other two sides contained quarters for men and supplies. Blockhouses at the corners provided observation points for lookouts.

Garrison life at Cantonment Gibson, as it was first called, was harsh. Enlisted men received five dollars a month, ate salt pork and beans, and performed monotonous duties. Hard labor, heat, flies, mosquitoes, malaria, fever, and bad liquor took their toll. During the first eleven and a half years 570 men died, earning the fort the label "Graveyard of the West."

Intemperance flourished and desertions were frequent. Degrading punishments were inflicted. Offenders did extra duty in stocks or astride a wooden horse and suffered teeth-chattering duckings in the river. Drunkards stood for days on a barrelhead, an empty bottle in each hand.

Fort Gibson was a testing ground for West Point graduates. As nearby communities grew, many young ladies came from the East to visit relatives and ended up marrying young officers. Attractive Cherokee maidens were always welcome at military dances. The post was a frequent conference site for negotiation of treaties, an outfitting point for military and exploratory expeditions, and a rendezvous point for army officers, government commissioners, writers, artists, missionaries, traders, and adventurers.

In 1844 Inspector General George Croghan complained of "buildings scattered about amidst weeds, gardens, patches of corn, old hay stacks, etc." He recommended relocation on a hill to the east and work began on permanent stone buildings in 1845, but only one was finished when the fort was abandoned to the Cherokees in September 1857. Reconstruction was completed during the Civil War when Union forces reoccupied the post. Activity during the 1870s and '80s was limited to curbing lawless elements that accompanied construction of the Katy railroad, ousting squatters from Cherokee land, and aiding civilian authorities in chasing thieves and desperadoes. Final abandonment came in 1890.

HISTORICAL HIGHLIGHT

Washington Irving: Early Oklahoma Tourist

In May 1832, Washington Irving, of Rip Van Winkle fame, returned to the United States after spending seventeen years in Europe as a highly successful writer and a minor diplomat. Before the year ended he joined an excursion to the Indian lands of the West.

The purpose of the expedition was to interview wild Indians in an effort to make friends in anticipation of peaceful settlement of the "Civilized Indians" emigrating from the East. Irving's group arrived at Fort Gibson on October 8.

Washington Irving had been promised a buffalo hunt. The tour lasted almost a month over a roughly circular route that brought the party to the vicinity of present-day Oklahoma City and Norman, where Irving killed a buffalo. It did not afford the triumph he had anticipated:

> Now that the excitement was over, I could not but look with commiseration upon the poor animal that lay struggling and bleeding at my feet. His very size and importance, which had before inspired me with eagerness, now increased my compunction. It seemed as if I had inflicted pain in proportion to the bulk of my victim, and as if there were a hundred-fold greater waste of life than there would have been in the destruction of an animal of inferior size.

Washington Irving kept a journal during his travels—factual, day-to-day notes concerning the people and conditions he encountered on the Oklahoma prairies. Were it not for his journals and the subsequent book, *A Tour on the Prairies* (1835), the early 1830s in that area would be a much blanker page in history. His journal captured pictures of Indian life:

Indian we met to-day in mourning—dirt on his face—does not eat till sunset. The dead are painted white & other colours when buried—
A chief lately deceased was buried sitting up under a mound.

—*Fort Gibson* - US 62—OK 10————

The town of Fort Gibson is an agricultural community adjacent to the Fort Gibson Stockade Historical Area. The later fort was composed of stone buildings constructed during the Civil War. Some are impressive ruins, others have been restored. Historical markers guide visitors.

The Fort Gibson National Cemetery is located a mile east of town off US 62. A plot previously used by Fort Gibson for burial purposes was converted into a national cemetery in 1868. The first soldiers laid to rest in the plot prior to 1850 were "Old Dragoons," members of the first regiment stationed at Fort Gibson in 1824. Representatives of all the major wars in which the United States has participated are buried in the cemetery.

HISTORICAL HIGHLIGHT

Vivia: First Woman in the Army

In the Fort Gibson National Cemetery Officers' Circle, among the wives and daughters of military men who manned the fort, is a grave marked "VIVIA THOMAS—JANUARY 1870."

As the story goes, Vivia was a Boston girl from a good family. Shortly after her betrothal, her fiance broke off the engagement and went west in search of adventure. Eventually, Vivia heard that her lover had joined the army and was stationed at Fort Gibson. She cut her hair, dressed as a man, and made the long trek to Fort Gibson where she requested enlistment.

Sure enough, her erstwhile lover was there. He had risen to the rank of lieutenant. Vivia was not assigned to his company, and he did not recognize her. At night she trailed the lieutenant as he left the fort and found that he was visiting an Indian sweetheart.

A short time later the lieutenant was mysteriously murdered, shot through the head. His killer was never found, and Vivia continued to serve at the frontier post. Her disguise became known only as she lay on her death bed several years later. It was then she confessed to the chaplain that she had killed her faithless lover.

While there are those who maintain that a woman could not have posed as a man in the frontier army, the legend has persisted for more than a century, and the grave marker gives mute testimony.

—*Okay* - OK 251A————

This is one of the oldest white settlements in Oklahoma. In 1819, George W. Brand, a Tennessean who had married a Cherokee, and a merchant from New Orleans named Henry Barbour established a trading post. In 1822 the firm of Brand and Barbour sold out to Auguste P. Chouteau. Chouteau brought in Creole carpenters to build keelboats for the shipment of furs down the Arkansas and Mississippi rivers to New Orleans.

In 1828 the Chouteau holdings were bought by the government for use as a Creek agency. The area was devastated during the Civil War. With the coming of the railroad in 1871, the community moved north to the present site and became known as Coretta Switch, North Muskogee, and Rex. Finally, in 1919, the name Okay came from the OK Truck Manufacturing Co.

—*Muskogee* - US 69-64-62————

Muskogee was nothing but prairie until 1872, when the Missouri Pacific Railroad (now the Katy) came to the Arkansas River three miles north of present-day Muskogee. It took three months to bridge the river, and a colony gathered in tents and shacks, waiting to see where the railroad would locate the next town. There were bridge builders, railroad employees, excursionists, homeseekers, freighters, hucksters, boarding-house keepers, gamblers, liquor peddlers, loafers, and outlaws.

On January 1, 1872, the bridge was completed, and the railroad announced the next town would be a mile and a half south of the river. The colony moved across the bridge and the new station was christened "Muskogee" in honor of the Muskogee or Creek Tribe of Indians.

As the new town was established, still in tents and shacks, the colonists noticed that the quality of bread, meat, coffee, and canned goods provided by the crude boardinghouses and restaurants was much better than had been served north of the river. They discovered that two guards from Fort Gibson had sold a large amount of the military provisions to gamblers for a trifling sum. In 1874 the Union Agency of the Five Civilized Tribes was established, and the town (officially spelled Muscogee) was incorporated in 1898. In 1904 the opening of gas and oil fields brought three more railroads, and the subsequent opening of the Arkansas River Navigation System made it an important manufacturing, wholesale, and distribution point.

McClellan-Kerr Arkansas River Navigation System

Port of Muskogee! They must be kidding.

Out-of-state visitors, particularly from salt-water ports such as Houston or San Francisco, tend to view a highway sign designating the Port of Muskogee with skepticism or outright disbelief. But it is for real.

River navigation in what is now Oklahoma began with Indian dugouts and rafts floating downstream on the Arkansas River. The Arkansas flows from the Rocky Mountains in Colorado through Kansas; it meanders across northern Oklahoma and leaves the state at Fort Smith, Arkansas. As early as 1833, steamboats regularly docked at the far-western military post of Fort Gibson.

But the Arkansas was a contentious stream. It could turn into a raging torrent, wreaking havoc and destruction. River boats often ran aground on sandbars. The development of railroads abated the problem. In 1884 a railroad was completed between Little Rock and Fort Smith. The completion of other railroads in the late 1890s sounded the death knell for steamboat traffic on the Arkansas. The river was left pretty much to itself for half a century, during which time it went on periodic rampages, ravaging farms and towns along its banks.

By the River and Harbor Act of July 14, 1946, Congress authorized the U.S. Army Corps of Engineers to develop the Arkansas River for navigation, additional flood control, hydroelectric power generation, and other purposes—the largest civil works project ever undertaken by the Corps of Engineers. Construction began in 1957. The 445-mile shipping channel originated at the confluence of the White and Mississippi rivers. By December 1970, ships could reach the upper end of the system at the Port of Catoosa near Tulsa.

The system utilizes seven lakes, as well as the Arkansas and Verdigris rivers in Oklahoma, to store potential floodwaters. Locks lift and lower vessels at dam sites. Four dams, two in Arkansas and two in Oklahoma, generate electrical power. Banks were stabilized as the wandering river was straightened.

And, yes, there are honest-to-goodness ports at Muskogee and other places. Upstream barges carry bauxite, grain, chemicals, fertilizer, butyl rubber, hemp, soda ash, newsprint, petroleum products, and miscellaneous commodities. Downstream cargoes include soybeans, wheat, coal, gypsum, acid, lumber, scrap iron, rock, and peanuts.

—*Oktaha—Rentiesville* - US 69————

The Battle of Honey Springs—the climactic engagement of the Civil War in Indian Territory—was fought on July 17, 1863, on a field straddling the Texas Road between Oktaha and Rentiesville.

More than two years earlier the United States government had withdrawn its peace-keeping forces from Indian Territory. In April 1863, Col. William A. Phillips reoccupied Fort Gibson and prepared to challenge Confederate authority. The Confederates were making plans to drive the Union troops from Fort Gibson.

Brig. Gen. Douglas H. Cooper, a former Choctaw-Chickasaw Indian Agent and a veteran of the Mexican War, commanded the Confederate forces. About 6,000 soldiers, mostly Indians, were martialed. Supplies were brought from Fort Smith, Arkansas, as well as from Boggy Depot, Fort Cobb, Fort Arbuckle, and Fort Washita in Indian Territory.

Maj. Gen. James G. Blunt arrived to lead the Union troop. The battle took place along the Texas Road. Union forces drove the Confederates back to their supply depot at Honey Springs, about a mile north of present-day Rentiesville, where the rebels held long enough to evacuate virtually all their forces, artillery, and baggage train. Then they torched the buildings and supplies at Honey Springs. The Federals arrived in time to extinguish some of the flames and save the stores of bacon, dried beef, flour, sorghum, and salt.

Cooper reported Confederate losses as 134 killed and wounded, with 47 taken prisoner. He maintained Union losses exceeded 200 killed and wounded. However, Blunt reported his losses at 17 killed and 60 wounded. He said he buried 150 Confederates, wounded 400 of their men, and took 77 prisoners. The exact numbers will never be known. Later, General Cooper sent Blunt a letter of appreciation for his burial of the Confederate dead.

The settlement at Honey Springs disappeared with construction of the Katy railroad in 1872. The farming community of Oktaha was named for Oktarharsars Harjo, a prominent Creek leader.

Rentiesville, dating from 1904, was predominately a black settlement, named for William Rentie, the townsite developer.

—*Checotah* - US 69-266————

Before organization of the community, the Checotah area was a ranching center. In 1872 the Katy railroad brought settlers from the cotton-producing states. Later, farmers practiced crop diversification as they planted wheat, oats, barley, and alfalfa.

The town was named after Samuel Checote, last full-blood chief of the Creeks. Checote introduced constitutional procedures modeled after those of the white man, and conservative elements objected. A traditionalist, Oktarharsars Harjo, opposed the displacement of old tribal ways and led a series of insurrections against the tribal government known as the Green Peach War.

The new constitution was adopted in 1867, and the Katy railroad decided not to play favorites: They named Checotah, originally called Checote Switch, after the peacemaker Checote and Oktaha after the insurrectionist.

——— EXCURSION

—*Webbers Falls* - US 64———

When removal of the Cherokees got under way in 1829, they came up the Arkansas River, and many settled in the vicinity of the falls named for Walter Webber, one of the early emigrants. Webber operated a salt works and a trading post and accumulated considerable wealth.

The falls cascaded six feet in 1806; however, erosion soon reduced them to a mere ripple. Nevertheless, in the nineteenth century they blocked travel for river steamers. Smaller craft were towed over the riffle by a rawhide line stretched to the shore and pulled by oxen. Today the Webbers Falls Lock and Dam eases barges over the shallows.

The Webbers Falls post office was established in 1856. On April 26, 1863, Union forces attacked the Confederate forces of General Stand Watie at Webbers Falls. They burned a considerable portion of the town.

Brig. Gen. Stand Watie was the first Indian to be commissioned a general officer. At the close of the Civil War he commanded all Confederate troops in Indian Territory. Most of his troops had been sent home before the end of the war; however, Watie was the last Confederate general to surrender. He laid down his arms on June 23, 1865.

—*Cookson* - OK 82———

This isolated community was established in 1895 and gained fame from three things: the scenic beauty of the Cookson Hills, the quality of hunting and fishing, and the outlaws who haunted the area. For a number of years, life was pretty bleak and outlaws were sanctioned, if not approved. As one old-timer put it, "They were about the only ones who had money to spend."

Brig. Gen. Stand Watie was the first Indian to be commissioned a general officer in the Confederate army and the last Confederate general to surrender. —Western History Collections, University of Oklahoma Library

HISTORICAL HIGHLIGHT

Pretty Boy Floyd: Oklahoma Robin Hood

Charles Arthur Floyd grew up in the Cookson Hills listening to stories of how Jesse James, Bill Doolin, and the Daltons had outwitted the law by hiding out in the hills around him. Local residents had an inborn dislike of law officers; some families had been moonshiners for several generations.

Floyd liked Choctaw beer and young women. At the age of eighteen he got married, but farm life did not agree with him. In 1925 he went to St. Louis, committed his first robbery, and returned to the Cookson hills with $12,500 to spend. He was caught and sentenced to five years in the Missouri State Penitentiary. During the three years before his parole he received a liberal education from fellow inmates.

In 1930 Floyd was caught again and sentenced to fifteen years for robbing a bank, but he escaped. Thereafter he employed techniques he

43

This picture of Charles Arthur Floyd, alias "Pretty Boy," was taken in 1932.
—Western History Collections, University of Oklahoma Library

had learned in prison: fast cars, submachine guns, bullet-proof vests, and a steel skullcap. Within the next two years he shot his way out of scrapes as he robbed more than a dozen small banks; law officers organized a posse rumored to number 500.

In 1931 Floyd wrote a postcard to the governor of Oklahoma: "I have robbed no one but moneyed men." Radio stations in the Cookson Hills played a tune called "Pretty Boy Floyd, the Phantom Terror." On November 1, 1932, he robbed the Sallisaw State Bank, shaking hands with and greeting friends in the process.

Floyd was generous with his proceeds, earning a Robin Hood-type reputation, which made the $7,000 bounty the governor put on his head laughable in the Cookson Hills. His end came in Ohio on October 24, 1934, when his body was riddled with bullets. The news made the front page of the *New York Times*, which described him as "the most dangerous man alive." J. Edgar Hoover said he was "just a yellow rat who needed extermination."

The people in the Cookson Hills disagreed. Charles Arthur Floyd's funeral in Sallisaw drew a throng estimated at 20,000. Many recalled his largesse, some named their children after him.

In 1960 advertisement for a movie entitled *Pretty Boy Floyd* billed him as a "sagebrush Robin Hood." Today the stories of his exploits are still related in the Cookson Hills, particularly by the grandparents of children named Floyd.

—*Vian* - US 64—OK 82——————

This community took its name from the nearby creek. There are two theories regarding origin of the name. One holds it came from the French word for meat, *viande*. The other points out that Hernando De Soto explored the area in 1541-42; a member of his party was named Viana.

The town began as a trading post in the 1880s, when the Saint Louis, Iron Mountain and Southern Railway (later the Missouri Pacific) came through. The Vian *Sun* began publication in 1899. In 1907 a four-page weekly called the *Indian Sentinel* claimed a circulation of 350. At that time the town had a population of 276.

Vian became renowned for a three-day picnic. People came from miles around. As many as twelve cattle were barbecued for the event. There were balloon ascensions and parachutists.

—*Gore* - US 64——————

A community at this location on the east bank of the Arkansas River first appeared on a map drawn in 1718 by Guillaume de Lille, a French explorer. The name was Mentos or Les Mentous. In 1888 the town was called Campbell, after Dr. W. W. Campbell, owner of the ferry at Webbers Falls. It was a stop on the stage line between Fort Smith and Fort Gibson. When the railroad came through in 1888, the name was changed to Illinois. After statehood, it finally became Gore to honor United States Senator Thomas P. Gore.

About 1829, Cherokee Chief John Jolly (Oo-loo-te-ka) ascended the Arkansas River and built a house near the mouth of the Illinois. Tahlonteeskee, the western Cherokee capital, was established. Here Sam Houston was formally adopted by the Cherokee tribe and given the name "The Raven" by Chief Jolly. Tahlonteeskee served until tribal courts were abolished in 1839 by the Curtis Act. The site is about two and a half miles east of Gore.

The community began about 1870 as a stage station and trading post on the military road between Fort Smith and Fort Gibson. It was called Childer's Station after a prominent Cherokee who provided food and lodging for travelers. A post office established in 1879 operated until 1888 when the name was changed to Sallisaw. The name derives from the French *salliseau*, referring to salted meat.

The Cherokees began to settle in the area in the 1820s. Sequoyah, inventor of the Cherokee syllabary, was among those who came. The area became an educational center for Cherokees in 1829 when Dwight Mission, operated by the Presbyterian Mission Board, was moved from Arkansas to a location seven miles northeast of Sallisaw. The school closed before the Civil War and reopened in 1884. It continued until 1948.

Today Sallisaw is a prosperous city benefiting economically from traffic on the Arkansas River Navigation Channel; from visitors to recreational facilities on nearby lakes and rivers; and from Blue Ribbon Downs, a quarter-horse racetrack which opened in 1985.

Sequoyah's home site is located seven miles from town (north on US 58, then east on OK 101). The historic landmark is operated by the Oklahoma Historical Society. The original cabin has been enclosed in a rock house to prevent further deterioration.

HISTORICAL HIGHLIGHT

Sequoyah: Cherokee Genius

The only American Indian to conceive and perfect an entire alphabet was Sequoyah, an unlettered Cherokee who could neither understand nor speak English.

Born in the Cherokee village of Tuskegee, Tennessee, about 1770, Sequoyah became a silversmith. One day, about 1809, he was discussing the superiority of the white people with other young men. One of the group said it was because they could put "talk" on paper and send it any distance and it would be understood by those who received it.

Sequoyah boasted that he could do that. He set about trying to convert the Cherokee language to writing.

Prejudice immediately reared its head. The Cherokees told Sequoyah of an ancient tradition which had relegated the Indians to their present state. In the beginning, the Great Father created the Indian and gave him a book. Later, He created the white man and gave him a bow and arrow. The Indian was indifferent to the book, so the white man stole it from him. Since the Indian forfeited his right to the book, he was then given the bow and arrow and from then on had to gain his subsistence by hunting.

Undaunted, Sequoyah continued his efforts. First he tried to make a symbol for each word, but after about a year he had several thousand characters with no end in sight. Then he tried to use sounds, but by the time he had recorded symbols for more than 200 sounds, it was obvious this was also too unwieldy for practical use.

All of this took some nine years, during which no one was supportive of his work. Not only was Sequoyah ridiculed, fellow tribesmen looked upon him as a poor provider for his family because he spent so little time working his farmland. His wife berated him, and he moved into a small cabin to pursue his studies. Apparently at the instigation of his wife, neighbors burned the cabin, destroying all his work. It was generally felt Sequoyah was conniving with evil spirits.

After three more years, he hit upon the idea of dividing words into syllables. With the help of his daughter, he reduced the Cherokee

Sequoyah or George Guess, inventor of the Cherokee alphabet.
—Western History Collections, University of Oklahoma Library

language to eighty-six syllables, and by 1821 he had created the Cherokee alphabet. He took English letters for symbols, copying them from a newspaper he could not read. He even used some Greek letters he found in a book, and added designs of his own making.

His next problem was getting skeptical Cherokees to accept his invention. He taught his syllabary to some people in Arkansas. They wrote a letter to friends in the Cherokee Nation east of the Mississippi. Sequoyah took the letter to Tennessee and read it. The miracle of the "talking leaves" was unveiled: Here was a message all the way from Arkansas, sealed in paper, which could be spoken from the paper precisely as it had been written.

The alphabet gained acceptance. Sequoyah could teach his system to others in a week or less. Use of the alphabet spread. By 1828, the *Cherokee Advocate*, was being printed, partially in Cherokee and partially in English.

The Cherokee Alphabet.
—Western History Collections, University of Oklahoma Library

Sequoyah's cabin, believed to have been constructed in 1828, has been enclosed in a building to prevent further deterioration.

Now, Sequoyah was honored instead of ridiculed. He journeyed to Washington as a member of the Arkansas Treaty delegation. A medal was struck in his honor; his portrait was painted by Charles Bird King.

He moved to a permanent home near Sallisaw in modern Sequoyah County, Oklahoma. There he spent many years teaching his alphabet to anybody who would come to learn. He died in northern Mexico in 1843 while visiting a group of Cherokees who had moved there.

—*Brushy* - US 59————

In 1900, when it was big enough to warrant a post office, the village was called Brushy because of thick undergrowth on the nearby mountain. Times were hard in Brushy during the early days. Some residents lived in tents or log cabins. The houses were papered with old newspapers, and children later said they learned to read by studying the "wallpaper." The few who made money grazed cattle on the open range. The land on Brushy Mountain resisted crops, and farmers had to make and haul ties for the railroad between "laying-by" and "gathering."

—*Muldrow* - US 64—OK 64B————

In 1887 a group of men in the village that would become Muldrow struck a deal with the railroad. They agreed to raise $300 if the railroad would locate a switch and a station at the site. The *Muldrow Register* was established in 1890. In 1892 the paper's circulation was advertised as "exceeding 100." In 1896 Muldrow's population topped 600.

Cotton and potatoes gave way to truck crops: spinach, green beans, sweet corn, and soy beans. Located within commuting distance of both Sallisaw and Fort Smith, Arkansas, Muldrow escaped the fate of many small rural towns as it became a bedroom community.

—*Roland* - I-40————

This community had its inception in Civil War times when the first white settlers from Missouri and Arkansas came to clear land for homesites. A town did not exist until the railroad arrived during the early 1890s. The whistle-stop depot was called Garrison Creek Station. The post office was named Garrison in 1902 but changed to Roland in 1904.

Settlers from the surrounding area came by horseback, buggies, and wagons. They left their horses and wagons and caught the train into Fort Smith to do their trading. Roland experienced a boom after statehood, when cotton became king. A newly built cotton gin saved farmers the long haul to Fort Smith. During harvest season the gin operated day and night.

After World War I a lively cross-tie business developed, and surrounding roads were crowded with wagon trains hauling railroad ties from the cutters in the hills. Restaurants sprang up to feed the tie hackers. More recently, like Muldrow, Roland has profited from its proximity to Fort Smith.

—*Moffett* - US 64————

This border town came into being about 1908. It gained notoriety because of laxity of law enforcement. Numerous drinking and gambling establishments sprang up, operated and patronized by people from out of town.

The first bridge between Moffett and Fort Smith was built by the Missouri Pacific Railroad. There was a toll booth at each end. When the bridge was not in use by trains the railroad collected tolls: five cents for pedestrians (one way), forty-five cents round trip for a buggy, and sixty-five cents for a wagon. In 1922 a "free bridge" opened.

—*Eufala* - US 69—OK 9———————

The confluence of the North and South forks of the Canadian River was the end of the trail for the Creek Indians when they were moved from Alabama to Indian Territory in 1836. A large settlement developed. It was called North Fork Town, and the trading post was a stop on the Texas Road. In 1849, during the California gold rush, North Fork Town became a crossroads as emigrants by the thousands traveled the road from Fort Smith.

At North Fork Town they stopped to organize and equip California companies, elect officers, and adopt regulations. It became such a busy place that a post office called Micco was established. The site, east of present-day Eufaula, was inundated by Lake Eufaula.

The Missouri-Kansas-Texas Railroad built to the present site of Eufaula in 1871, and the next year five residents of North Fork Town paid $1,000 for railroad property upon which to found a town. The Eufala post office was established in 1874.

According to old-timers, Eufaula lost out in obtaining the Union Agency for the Five Civilized Tribes because of dirty-dealing by someone from Muskogee. The year was 1874. Muskogee and Eufaula were running neck-and-neck. An inspector came from Washington to determine which of the two towns was better suited to care for employees of the agency. The night before his arrival, some scoundrel from Muskogee emptied a barrel of salt into Eufaula's municipal well. After one taste of the water, the inspector decided upon Muskogee as the administrative headquarters for Indian Territory.

Today, Eufaula is virtually surrounded by Lake Eufaula, created by the dam which was completed in 1964. The town, draws a considerable amount of its economic sustenance therefrom.

The grave of Belle Starr, "the Bandit Queen," is about a mile from the dam at Younger's Bend, near Porum and Briartown, where Belle lived with her husband Sam Starr. A cave, a canyon, and other historical sites in the Eufaula area are named for her. Eufaula does its part with the Belle Starr Amusement Park.

HISTORICAL HIGHLIGHT
Belle Starr: Queen of the Bandits

The folklore surrounding Belle Starr was generated largely by an article in the *National Police Gazette*. She was characterized as a dazzling beauty who headed a following of male outlaws. According to the article, they garnered thousands from train, stagecoach, and bank robberies. The *Gazette* dubbed her "The Petticoat Terror." Hanging Judge Isaac Parker was closer to the truth when he charged her with being "the leader of a band of notorious horse thieves."

Photographs belie the description of her as a beauty; however, there is no doubt that she was a superb horsewoman, and she dressed well. Velvet dresses and plumed hats were her favorite attire, topped by a pair of six-shooters hanging from a cartridge belt about her waist. She rode a black mare named Venus and carried a Winchester in her saddle holster. With a flair for the theatrical, she was fond of parading up and down main streets on horseback and visiting saloons to gamble and drink.

Myra Belle Shirley was born in Missouri in February 1848. At the age of sixteen she was riding with the Jameses, the Youngers, the Reeds, and the Daltons in Quantrill's renegade guerilla band. She was smitten by Cole Younger and bore a daughter by him. As Cole Younger went his way, she took up with an outlaw named Jim Reed and was "married" in a ceremony during which a member of the outlaw band is reputed to have played the role of preacher.

By Jim Reed she had a son named Edward. In 1874 Reed was killed by a member of his own gang. Belle went on to head up a band of horse and cattle thieves that operated between Fort Smith and Eufaula. For a while she consorted with an Indian named Blue Duck, but eventually

Belle Starr: "I regard myself as a woman who has seen much of life." —Western History Collections, University of Oklahoma Library

settled down in common-law marriage with a Cherokee named Sam Starr at Younger's Bend near Briartown on the Canadian River.

Despite her rough ways and profane language, Belle did not let her riders forget that she was "a lady." On one occasion her hat blew off. She pulled up her horse, stared at her companions, and waited. They stared back. Belle drew her Colt and aimed it at Blue Duck.

"Get down there and pick up that hat, you ignorant bastard!"

In February 1883, Belle and Sam were brought to trial in Judge Parker's court in Fort Smith. The *Fort Smith Era* said:

> The very idea of a woman being charged with an offense of this kind, and that she was the leader of a band of horse thieves, and wielding a power over them as their queen and guiding spirit, was sufficient to fill the courtroom.

For the sentencing, Belle showed up in her finest velvet gown. She had a new ostrich plume flowing from her hat. The "hanging judge," who had sent eighty-six men to the gallows, sentenced her to only six months on two counts and Sam to one year on one count. They served time in the federal prison in Detroit. Good behavior reduced their sentences to three months.

After their return to Indian Territory, Belle is said to have taken part in a "Wild West" show in Fort Smith, during which she played the part of an outlaw holding up a stagecoach. A passenger in the coach was none other than Judge Isaac Parker.

In 1885, back at Younger's Bend, it was business as usual. Belle Starr ran away with John Middleton, a young outlaw from Missouri who was wanted on assorted charges; he drowned while crossing a creek, and Belle went back to Sam Starr.

Belle made another appearance in the Fort Smith court in 1886. Released on bond, she spent the remainder of the day shopping. Two Colt revolvers were among her purchases.

After Sam Starr was killed, Belle took up with a young Creek Indian named Jim July, Sam's cousin. She insisted that Jim take the name Starr. In 1889 Belle accompanied him to court to face a charge of rustling. On her way back to Younger's Bend she was shot in the back and head with a shotgun. The murder was never solved. The suspects included Jim Middleton, John Middleton's brother; a neighbor; Belle's son, Eddie Reed; and a jealous Jim July Starr. Historians are still speculating.

About a year before her death, Belle Starr neatly summed up her past to a reporter for the *Fort Smith Elevator*: "I regard myself as a woman who has seen much of life."

—Canadian - US 69—OK 113——————

During the Civil War, this small settlement on the Texas Road was an important supply point known as Canadian Depot. It was called South Canadian when a post office was established in 1873, but the "South" was dropped in 1899. The *Canadian Advertiser* began publication on September 2, 1898.

In 1972 Canadian had its day in the sun when Hollywood came to town. An old territorial jail and a livery stable were incorporated into a movie set for the filming of a couple of Westerns. Canadian is convenient to Arrowhead State Park on Lake Eufaula.

—Indianola - OK 113——————

George Choate, a leader of the Choctaw Nation, was the first settler in this tiny community seven miles west of Canadian on the south shore of Eufaula Lake. Choate's log cabin is still standing, furnished with pre-statehood items. It is open by appointment.

The community got its post office in 1891. The name is "Indian" plus Choctaw *olah*, meaning "this side of." During the late 1890s and just after the turn of the century, four newspapers were published in Indianola at various times. In 1897 the editor of the *Indianola Herald* was greatly concerned over talk among a group of Indians who were thinking about emigrating to Mexico.

—Bugtussle - US 69——————

Yes, the name is for real! It was also called Flowery Mound, but it won fame as Bugtussle, the boyhood home of Carl Albert, Speaker of the House of Representatives from 1971 until 1977.

—McAlester - US 69-270——————

The town was founded by James J. McAlester, a native of Arkansas who learned of coal deposits in the area while serving in the Confederate army. After the Civil War, to get to Indian Territory, he hired out to a party hauling sawmill equipment from Fort Smith to Fort Sill.

McAlester married a Chickasaw woman, which made him a citizen of the Choctaw Nation. He opened a store; the date of the town's origin is generally fixed at 1872 when the tracks of the Missouri-Kansas-Texas Railroad reached McAlester's store.

With the coming of the railroad, McAlester and other Choctaw citizens began mining coal under a Choctaw constitutional provision allowing a citizen to mine any mineral discovered by him for a mile in every direction.

The Choctaw government wanted the royalties; so did the operators of the mines. Coleman Cole, principal chief of the Choctaws, ordered

McAlester and three co-owners arrested. The Choctaw Light Horse, military force of the Choctaw Nation, captured McAlester and two of the operators. McAlester was informed he would be shot. While the Light Horse was looking for the fourth man, McAlester and his friends escaped. A compromise finally settled the affair by giving half the royalties to the Choctaw Nation. McAlester later became lieutenant governor of Oklahoma.

The town grew into a stable commercial and industrial city. Its growth was aided by the Oklahoma State Penitentiary, locally known as "Big Mac" but called "Gatsville" by the inmates. In 1942 the United States Naval Ammunition Depot was established southwest of McAlester with a wartime high of 8,000 employees. Nearby Eufaula Lake has added variety to McAlester's economic base.

—Perryville ————

Only a historical marker remains about four miles south of McAlester to designate the site of this once important settlement. A trading post and stage station was established on the Texas Road about 1838 by James Perry, member of a prominent Choctaw-Chickasaw family. A post office opened in 1841. During the California gold rush, parties heading for California from Fort Smith, Arkansas, crossed the Canadian River and turned west at Perryville.

During the Civil War the Confederates used Perryville as a supply depot. The Confederate forces retreated from the Battle of Honey Springs to Perryville. Despite reinforcements, the Union forces were victorious and Confederate General Douglas H. Cooper realized the futility of further resistance. Before evacuating the town, he dumped salt in the water wells. The Union soldiers confiscated what they could find and completed the destruction of Perryville by burning the buildings.

—Savanna - US 69————

In 1880 this coal-mining town in the Choctaw Nation thrived. In 1887 an explosion killed eighteen miners, and the mine operators closed the mines and removed their machinery. The post office was established in 1876. The name of the community was taken from the private railroad car used by the general manager of the Katy railroad.

—Chockie - US 69————

This old Choctaw village was originally named Chickiechockie for the two daughters of Captain Charles LeFlore, member of a prominent Choctaw family who operated a toll bridge on the old Texas Road across nearby Buck Creek. The girls had been named Chickie and Chockie for the respective Chickasaw and Choctaw nationalities of their mother and father.

Chickie, who became the wife of Lee Cruce, Oklahoma's second governor, died early in the twentieth century and her name was removed from the sign on the railroad depot. Railroaders dreaded this lonely stretch of track because bandits favored it. Mounted gangs would block the track and hold up the train, then take shelter in the nearby hills.

—*Stringtown* - US 69—OK43————

This community owes its economic success to the coming of the railroad about 1871-72. Lumbering and limestone quarrying were the mainstays of the community. The town was originally intended to be named Springtown, because of nearby springs, but in designating the place on a timetable a Missouri-Kansas-Texas Railroad official spelled the name with a "t" and it remains Stringtown to this day.

Boogaboo Canyon, east of Stringtown, has an intriguing buried-treasure mystery in its past. According to the story, when Maximilian saw difficult times looming in Mexico, he sent his treasure—gold and silver coins, gold bars, artwork, and jewelry—out of Mexico toward Kansas for shipment to the East Coast. Sometime about 1864, the mule train ran into a smallpox epidemic near Boogaboo Canyon. The survivors hid the treasure and went back to Mexico.

In 1909 a cart appeared in the vicinity. A group of dark-complexioned strangers set up camp at an abandoned sawmill and began to dig near some strange markings which had long been the subject of local discussion.

Their only part in community life was to purchase supplies. For two years this went on. Then, suddenly, the camp was deserted. The team, still hooked to the cart, was left behind in a meadow. There was no trace of the party. The farmer who owned the land where the cart was found appropriated both cart and team. The mystery remained unsolved: Did the party find treasure? Were they murdered and buried? Did they abandon the cart and take a train to Mexico?

—*Atoka* - US 69-75—OK 3-7————

This town was founded in 1867 by Rev. J. S. Murrow, a Baptist missionary, who founded the Atoka Baptist Academy the following year. The name honors Captain Atoka, a Choctaw subchief. The Atoka Agreement was signed in Atoka, ultimately resulting in the break up of tribal government by the Five Civilized Tribes.

Following the Civil War, in 1866, the nations of the Five Civilized Tribes finally consented to railroads being built across Indian Territory. However, there was protest. In his diary, Rev. J. S. Murrow captured the argument of an elderly full-blooded Indian as he explained to a crowd why the railroad would be a detriment:

"I've ridden on those railroads east of the Mississippi. They have little houses on wheels—whole strings of them. One string can carry several hundred people. Those little houses can be shut up and the doors locked. If we allow that railroad to come, the white man will give a picnic sometime by the side of their iron road, and will invite all the full-bloods to attend. They will get the men to play ball, off a piece. Then, they will get our women to go into the little houses on wheels and will lock them up and run off with them into Texas or Missouri. Then what will we do for women?"

Nevertheless, the railroad came, probing down along the Texas Road and across the Red River into Texas.

Choctaw and Chickasaw Indians registering for their government allotments of land, circa 1900.
—Western History Collections, University of Oklahoma Library

EXCURSION

—*Boggy Depot State Park* - OK 7———

The site of Old Boggy Depot is located about eleven miles west of Atoka on OK 7. An important Choctaw-Chickasaw town grew from an Indian log cabin built in 1837 to a flourishing trade center and Civil War army post. The name of the town came from Clear Boggy Creek, about a mile west. Early French traders called the Muddy Boggy and Clear Boggy creeks Vazzures (from *vaseuse*, "miry" or "boggy").

"Depot" was added in 1837, when annuities were paid to the Chickasaws emigrating from the east at the "depot on the Boggy."

The post office at Boggy Depot was established in 1849. Located at the junction of the Texas Road and a trail from Fort Smith to California, the town soon became important.

Rev. Cyrus Kingsbury, "Father of the Choctaw Nation," built a church in 1840. The community served as the Choctaw capital in 1858. The Confederates made Boggy Depot a military post during the Civil War. Indian troops fighting for the South rode around the flagpole bearing the Stars and Bars, whooping and yelling, and singing the Choctaw war song.

The Missouri-Kansas-Texas Railroad bypassed Boggy Depot in 1872, and the town deteriorated rapidly. Today a 630-acre state park encloses the old cemetery, and historical markers tell of the past.

Boggy Depot State Park. —Oklahoma Tourism & Recreation, Fred W. Marvel

—*Tushka* - US 69————

This area between Muddy Boggy and Clear Boggy was once the heavily timbered hunting ground of the Choctaw Indians. In 1872 the Katy railroad laid a short siding alongside the main line and called it Peck Switch. By 1903 enough people had come and bought lots to warrant a post office; they shortened the name to Peck. The railroad brought in a boxcar to serve as a depot.

Residents in the area harvested timber to make ties for the railroad, pit ties and beams for the coal mines at Lehigh and Coalgate, and *bois d'arc* posts for farmers. In 1905 the name of the town was changed to Lewis to honor Charles S. Lewis, who opened the first store. In addition to the usual staples, he sold candy, calico, china-head dolls, and hoop cheese.

The railroad wanted the town's name changed to Dayton, but the Post Office Department said there were already too many Daytons. Finally, a Choctaw Indian suggested Tushka ("warrior"), and both the railroad and the Post Office Department agreed.

After the timber was harvested, the community depended upon cotton. During the 1920s, droughts and boll weevils dealt agriculture a blow; by 1935 the last cotton gin had folded. The Planters State Bank moved to Atoka, stores closed, the stock market crashed, and, like many other rural communities, Tushka suffered hard times.

—*Caddo* - US 69—OK 22————

This town is named for the Caddo Indians who occupied the area long before the coming of the Choctaws. The Caddoes and the Choctaws were traditional enemies. While still living in Mississippi, Choctaw hunting parties made long trips to the plains in this area. In 1806 a Choctaw hunting party was surprised by Caddoes. The ensuing battle left the hills south of present-day Caddo seeded with arrows and sun-bleached bones. When the Choctaw chief Pushmataha was making a treaty with General Andrew Jackson at Doak's Stand, he agreed to exchange land in Mississippi for land he knew in Indian Territory from his "big hunts." The Washita River gained its name from these expeditions; the Choctaw words *owa chito* mean "big hunt."

When the Choctaws arrived, they began raising horses and cattle, and the Caddoes made periodic raids. The Choctaws took a dim view of their depredations. The last raid took place about 1840. Some 400 Caddoes staged a foray into the Choctaw Nation, burning houses, destroying property, and gathering a large herd of horses and cattle. They returned to their camp to celebrate the victory. The Choctaw Minute Men, organized to protect the Choctaw Nation, charged the camp. So many Caddoes were killed or wounded that those who could fled to the timbered hills. The Choctaws pursued. It is believed that the last Caddo Indian was killed near the only spring where water could be gotten.

The Katy railroad arrived in 1872. As a Choctaw court town, the community grew rapidly. The official publication of the Choctaw Nation, the *Oklahoma Star,* was first printed at Caddo January 14, 1874. This newspaper was first to use the Choctaw word *Oklahoma* in its title.

In 1890 Caddo was the largest cotton market in Indian Territory; that was the first year of the federal census. Caddo counted 2,170, second only to Muskogee, in all of Indian Territory.

The Choctaw Code Talkers

During the closing days of World War I, eight Choctaws were instrumental in helping the American Expeditionary Forces prevail over the Germans in the Meuse-Argonne campaign, the Germans' final push of the war.

The Germans had broken the Americans' code and tapped their telephone lines. They were capturing one out of four American messengers who served as runners between various companies on the battle line. The commander of a company overheard two Choctaws conversing in their native language.

"How many of you Choctaw boys do we have in this battalion?" he asked.

There were eight, two in headquarters company. The company commander got the two Choctaws in headquarters company to stand by to translate while he wrote messages to be transmitted in Choctaw over the field telephone. The operation was successful; within hours the Choctaws were distributed with one at each field company headquarters.

They handled field communications, translating messages into Choctaw and back to English. They wrote messages in Choctaw to be carried by runners. No longer were Allied operations known to the Germans. Within twenty-four hours the tide of battle turned; in less than seventy-two hours the Germans were retreating with the Allies on the attack, guided by messages delivered through the Choctaw Code Talkers.

—*Durant* - US 69-70————

The community was first settled about 1870 by a Choctaw family named Durant. When the Katy railroad came through, it built a station on land owned by Dixon Durant and called it Durant Station. Ten years later "Station" was dropped from the name. Initially, cotton was the principal crop, but that gave way to peanuts, and by the 1940s some

20,000 acres were being harvested annually. Today, Durant is virtually dedicated to the peanut. A 36-inch aluminum peanut is mounted on a granite base in front of the City Hall, and signs in the business district point visitors toward "the big peanut."

Settlers in Durant developed an early interest in education. The 1830 Treaty of Dancing Rabbit Creek required government-paid education for forty Choctaw youths a year. For a while Armstrong Academy, northeast of Bokchito, was the closest school. In 1894 the Presbyterian church established the Calvin Institute as an effort toward higher education, eventually to become Oklahoma Presbyterian College. It closed as an educational institution in 1966 and the building became a home for the Choctaw National Tribal Headquarters.

In 1909 Southeastern Oklahoma State University began as Southeastern Normal School. The institution has kept pace with population growth by expanding to a campus that covers more than fifty acres.

Durant has long called itself the City of Magnolias; its streets are lined with the fragrant trees. Many fine old galleried homes with high ceilings and big windows reflect influence of plantation architecture from the Old South.

HISTORICAL HIGHLIGHT

The Marriage Mill

Between 1928 and 1931, when the state passed a law against marriage solicitors, Durant established a reputation as the Gretna Green for Texas couples seeking quick marriages. Texas had a three-day cooling off period between license and marriage. In Oklahoma there was no waiting, no age requirement, no blood test; all that was needed were two warm bodies, a wedding license, and a minister, a judge, or a justice of the peace.

Business boomed in Durant as couples came from Fort Worth, Houston, Waco, and Dallas at the rate of 200 or more a month. As a likely looking couple drove down Main Street, a marriage solicitor would hop on the running board and ask: "Are you young folks looking to get married?"

If the answer was affirmative, the helpful solicitor would guide the couple to the courthouse to get a license; then he would find a judge, minister, or justice of the peace to perform the nuptials.

Competition was stiff among marriage solicitors. On one occasion two arrived at a car simultaneously. One dragged the groom-to-be from under the steering wheel; the other took the bride-elect through the door on the passenger side.

When he found the state was abolishing the post, one justice of the peace became an ordained minister. Before he was through, he tied the knot for more than 15,000 couples.

Business was good during the war years—1942-46—when young soldiers were anxious to enjoy themselves as much as possible before shipping overseas. And there were avaricious women. After recognizing the same woman with a succession of different soldiers, a justice of the peace did not have much trouble figuring out that he had a customer who was seeing how many allotment checks she could get.

There was a slump after Oklahoma began requiring juveniles to have parental consent to get married, but the marriage mill continued to be a major financial asset. One Durant judge's business picked up after it was publicized that he had married Rosemary Clooney and Jose Ferrar.

—Calera - US 69————

In the opening chapter of *Hell and High Water*, a novel about the Indian Territory of 1870-80, William McLeod Raine had his hero ride into Cale, Indian Territory, leave his horse at Merritt's livery stable, and eat a scanty supper at the country store before bedding down for the night.

The Katy railroad called its depot Cale Switch, for a railroad official named George W. Cale. The first post office was established as Cale in 1899. Cale was one of the first townsites in Indian Territory that allowed white men to purchase lots and get titles directly from an Indian tribe.

The post office was changed to Sterrett in 1897 because Dr. John A. Sterrett of Troy, Ohio, was a member of the Choctaw Townsite Commission, but the railroad timetable still called it Cale. In 1910 the city fathers and railroad officials compromised on Calera.

—Colbert - US 69————

In 1846 Benjamin Franklin Colbert came from Mississippi with the Chickasaw tribe. Colbert was not one to sit around in a teepee. Within seven years after he got to Indian Territory and pitched camp at what is now Colbert, he had a sawmill, a gristmill, and a cotton gin in operation. Since he owned about everything in town, people called the place Colbert.

In 1853 the Chickasaw Council granted Colbert a franchise to operate a ferry across the Red River. By council stipulations, he was obliged to keep the roads leading to the ferry in excellent order. In return he was allowed to charge $1.25 for a four-horse team, wagon, or stage. There was a cattle crossing nearby. With traffic on the Texas Road and the Butterfield Overland Mail route from 1858 until 1861, Colbert profited greatly.

After completion of the Katy railroad line in 1875, ferry business dropped off. Colbert built a $40,000 wagon bridge across the Red River. It was 577 feet long and 16 feet wide with a turnout in the center for passing teams. In 1931, construction of a free bridge precipitated the "Red River Bridge War."

For many years the Texas Toll Bridge Company, successor to Colbert, had operated a toll bridge. In 1929, with the consent of Congress, Texas and Oklahoma began building a free bridge. Stockholders in the toll bridge company secured an injunction from the United States District Court to prevent opening of the free bridge. The governor of Texas then ordered barricades erected at the south end of the bridge.

By July 23, 1931, Oklahoma Governor William H. "Alfalfa Bill" Murray discovered a previous Supreme Court decision placing both banks of the river under Oklahoma jurisdiction. He ordered the Oklahoma National Guard to clear the bridge and let traffic flow. The toll bridge company was granted an injunction against Oklahoma, but the Federal Circuit Court of Appeals reversed the decision and the Red River Bridge War came to an end.

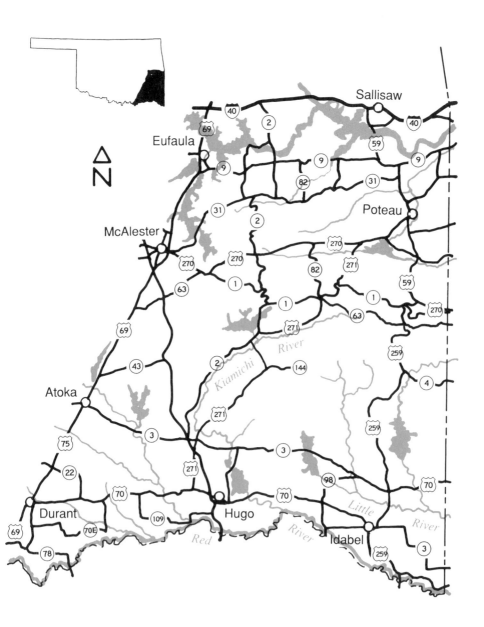

II. Butterfield Overland Mail and Kiamichi Country

In 1845, Congress turned its attention to establishing postal communication with newly acquired territories in California and Oregon. Ocean traffic was painfully slow. A ship carrying mail by way of the Strait of Magellan cleared New York harbor on October 8, 1848; it did not arrive in San Francisco until February 28, 1849.

On September 16, 1857, the Post Office Department inked a contract with John Butterfield and his associates to provide service for six years at $600,000 a year, the largest contract for land mail service to date. Routes started at St. Louis and Memphis, and converged into one route at Fort Smith, Arkansas. It crossed the southeastern corner of Indian Territory and continued across Texas and New Mexico to San Francisco.

Service was to be provided "twice a week in good four-horse post-coaches or spring wagons, suitable for the conveyance of passengers as well as the safety and security of the mails." Butterfield spent a year and approximately $1 million in preparation. He laid out his route over existing trails and opened new ones. He placed orders for two hundred fifty coaches and special mail wagons, harness sets and accessories, as well as a fleet of freight wagons and specially constructed tank wagons for water. The operating force consisted of conductors, drivers, station keepers, blacksmiths, mechanics, helpers, and herders. More than 1,800 horses and mules were distributed along the route.

The first westbound stage left St. Louis on the morning of September 16, 1858. Early Sunday morning on September 19, it crossed the Poteau River into Indian Territory "on a shaky ferry" and stopped at Walker's Station, the first stop in Indian Territory. The stage arrived in San Francisco at 7:30 Sunday morning, October 10: twenty-three days, twenty-three hours, and thirty minutes from St. Louis—the fastest time yet recorded for the overland journey.

Mail delivery on the Butterfield Trail. Harper's Weekly commented: "In the Eastern States the old-fashioned stagecoach is remembered as a thing of the past . . . but in the West it may be called the advance-guard of invading civilization."
—Harper's Weekly, 1874

Fare was $200 from St. Louis to San Francisco and $100 from San Francisco to St. Louis. Passengers were allowed forty pounds of baggage free; additional weight cost a dollar a pound. All passengers were encouraged to bring along rifles; they were expected to fight Indians, if necessary, and to help push the stage when it became stuck in the mud or mired down at river crossings. The postal rate was ten cents for each letter.

John Butterfield laid down a maxim: *"Remember boys, nothing on God's earth must stop the United States mail!"*

The coaches rolled along day and night. Any attempt to sleep in them was fraught by jolting on rough roads since they were cushioned by leather thoroughbraces instead of springs. The coaches had three seats designed for nine passengers, but some rode on the outside, preferring dust and open air to the crowded interior.

Understandably, there were complaints: the most common included lack of toilet and bathing facilities, extensive use of whiskey by fellow passengers and stage attendants, drunken and profane stage drivers, and "miserable and expensive food." (The price of meals varied from forty cents to a dollar.) Some reported a fixed menu of jerked beef, mesquite beans, corn cake baked in hot ashes, black coffee, and a mysterious concoction known as "slumgullion."

Service continued until the advent of the Civil War in 1861. In Indian Territory the route crossed the Choctaw Nation with a series of "meal and change" stations, most of which were named after the station keepers: Walker's, Trayhern's, Holloway's, Riddle's, Pusley's, Blackburn's, Waddell's, Geary's, Boggy Depot, Nail's, Fisher's, and Colbert's Ferry.

Station keepers were Choctaw citizens. Many had been granted charters to operate tollgates or toll bridges. The rate for a four-wheeled wagon and four or more horses was fifty cents. If the vehicle was pulled by two horses the fee dropped to twenty-five cents. A man with a horse paid ten cents, and one cent was charged for each animal in a drove.

The Butterfield Overland Mail route ran through the area of southeastern Oklahoma today known as the Kiamichi Country, six counties renowned for mountain forests and sparkling streams.

Historically, the Kiamichi Country has a rich Indian heritage reaching back more than 1,000 years to prehistoric mound builders. The area was claimed by Spain following exploration by Hernando De Soto. During the early eighteenth century French traders and trappers traveled through it. After the Indian removal it became the Choctaw Nation. Its rugged hills concealed outlaws such as the James brothers, the Doolins, the Younger brothers, Machine Gun Kelly, Pretty Boy Floyd, and, of course, Belle Starr.

Modern-day highways OK 9 and OK 31 come closest to following the route of the Butterfield Overland Mail from the Arkansas border to the vicinity of McAlester; there the road intersected the Texas Road (US 69) and followed it to the Red River crossing at Colbert's Ferry.

OK 9-9A
Arkoma—Enterprise

—*Arkoma* - OK 9A————

This town was platted by Capt. James E. Reynolds as a "bedroom" community for Fort Smith, Arkansas, just across the state line to the east. The name was coined from Arkansas and Oklahoma, and the post office was established April 8, 1914.

Reynolds helped establish a streetcar line between Arkoma and Fort Smith. Most of the residents of Arkoma are still employed in Fort Smith. Although Arkoma has its own city administration, including a fire and police department, it draws upon Fort Smith for water and sewer service.

—Skullyville - OK 9————

Also known as Old Town and Oak Lodge, this once-thriving community was established by Choctaw Indians in 1832 after they were removed from their ancestral homes in the southeastern United States. The town was the subject of several paintings by George Catlin, an early Western artist.

As capital of the Choctaw Nation, Skullyville was an important trade and political center. Choctaws received their tribal allowances here, thus giving the community its name. From the Choctaw word *iscully* (small money), the place became known as Skullyville—sometimes spelled Scullyville (Moneytown).

The Butterfield Overland Mail made its first stop inside Indian Territory at the station in the home of the Choctaw governor, Tandy Walker. During the initial westbound trip, early Sunday morning, September 19, 1858, New York *Herald* reporter Waterman L. Ormsby noted that the governor came out to help hitch the horses. In September 1859, another reporter, Albert Richardson, had a left-handed compliment for the governor: "He was educated in Kentucky, intelligent and agreeable; nearly as white as myself, with no betrayal of Indian origin in speech or features."

Capt. Randolph B. Marcy stopped here in 1849 during his reconnaissance for a wagon road between Fort Smith, Arkansas, and Santa Fe, New Mexico. The Skullyville Cemetery is one of the oldest cemeteries in Oklahoma and contains the graves of some of the most influential individuals in its early history.

—Spiro - OK 9————

The community was founded about 1895 when the Kansas City Southern Railway was built through the region. At that time, the few remaining residents of Skullyville moved to the new town. Today the economy of Spiro is agriculturally based with several small and medium industries. It is best known for the nearby Spiro Mounds.

The Spiro Mounds Archaeological State Park encompasses twelve earthen mounds, remnants of an Indian culture that flourished from A.D. 850 to 1450. Thousands of grave goods have been excavated. Exhibits include beads; pearls; wooden, stone, and copper-covered earspools; T-shaped pipes; effigy pipes in the shapes of human beings and birds; cedar and shell masks; baskets; textiles and blankets; pottery; arrowheads; spear points; axes and tools; knives; headdress plates; conch-shell ornaments; and bowls. One decorative piece portrays a hand with an object in the position used to this day by magicians to conceal by palming, indicating that priests may have used magic in exercising control over their congregations.

Indian mounds at Spiro Mounds Archaeological State Park date from A.D. *850-1450.* —Oklahoma Tourism & Recreation, Fred W. Marvel

—*Cowlington* - US 59————

Nine miles off OK 9 on US 59, Cowlington dates from 1884. A. Cowling was an early-day settler whose house, built in the 1870s, is still standing. In 1890, Thomas George Overstreet developed a 3,000-acre plantation overlooking the Arkansas River. The 15-room house was given to the Kerr Foundation in 1988 as a monument to the Overstreet family.

The village was well on its way to becoming a ghost town in the 1960s when construction began on the Robert S. Kerr Reservoir, part of the Arkansas River Navigation System. The Robert S. Kerr Dam and Locks allow boats and barges to move through a 48-foot change in the channel's elevation, the second highest lift on the system.

—*Keota* - OK 9————

Keota began in the early 1900s as a tent-town trading post. In 1903, pioneers Al Jennings and Chad Sewell staked lots and hitched teams of horses and mules to plows and drags to make streets. The Midland Valley Railroad, later the Texas and Pacific, arrived in 1904 with Major W. C. Wells as a "townsite man." The orator William Jennings Bryan was brought in to speak at a picnic on July 4, 1904, to promote and sell the community as an ideal place to live and establish businesses.

For a while Keota prospered from coal mining. Today, location on the Robert S. Kerr Reservoir is its most profitable asset.

—Kanima - OK 9————

Originally this community was called Ironbridge, after a bridge that spanned San Bois Creek before the Civil War. The footings of the old bridge are still visible. A Civil War engagement was fought at this site. The name of the town was changed to Kanima August 24, 1910. Kanima is Choctaw for "somewhere" or "someplace." The Kanima post office closed in 1940.

—Stigler - OK 9-82————

Joseph S. Stigler came to the area in 1887, married a Choctaw named May Folsom, and began to farm. He built a home in a fledgling community called King's Prairie. He platted a townsite called Newman, but a year later the Post Office Department requested the name changed because of confusion with Norman. On May 3, 1893, the town was renamed for its founder.

When Stigler learned that C. N. Haskell was building a railroad from Muskogee to Fort Smith, he approached Haskell to have the line routed through Stigler. It cost $1,000 and half the town lots, but Haskell joined Stigler in promoting the town and they opened a bank together. After statehood, Haskell was elected Oklahoma's first governor.

Stigler really did not begin to thrive until two college students came to town selling books door-to-door. L. J. Lantz and H. C. Dobyns were roommates at Emporia State College. During the summer they peddled a book called *Century Book of Facts* through Kansas, Texas, and Oklahoma. They had such good luck in Oklahoma that they decided to devote all their time to selling books there.

Before his college days, Dobyns had worked in his uncle's hardware store in Kansas. He and Lantz saw the need for a hardware store and struck a deal. They rented space and opened a store in a building Joseph Stigler had recently built. Over the years, this pair of college dropouts helped develop many other businesses in Stigler.

The community suffered economically for many years after the decline of the coal industry. However, its location between Eufaula Lake to the west and the Arkansas River Navigation System to the north and east has stimulated both recreation-related activities and coal mining.

Tamaha

Tamaha is northeast of Stigler; it can be reached by a county road. Before the Civil War this picturesque town, located on a bluff overlooking the Robert S. Kerr Reservoir, was a steamboat landing on the Arkansas

River. As early as 1838 it began taking on the appearance of a Choctaw village and was called Pleasant Bluff. When it got a post office, in 1884, it was renamed Tamaha ("town" in Choctaw).

This was the scene of the farthest inland naval battle of the Civil War. On June 15, 1864, at Pleasant Bluff, just below the mouth of the Canadian River in the shallows, Confederate General Stand Watie swept from ambush with a cavalry charge and captured the Union steamboat *J. R. Williams*, which was on its way to deliver provisions, uniforms, and medical supplies to Fort Gibson.

—*Whitefield* - OK 2-9————

This community is one of the oldest towns in Haskell County, having been the site of a village since 1860. It was the first town in Indian Territory to be called "Oklahoma." The post office was established with that name on December 21, 1881. However, the name had to be changed in 1887 at the request of the Post Office Department to avoid confusion with Oklahoma Station, which eventually became Oklahoma City. The present name honors George Whitefield, an early-day Methodist bishop.

EXCURSION ————

—*Porum* - OK 2————

This town originated because of the Midland Valley Railroad. Its post office, established March 25, 1890, was named for J. Porum Davis, a prominent Indian. The community grew to an agricultural trading center with general stores and two cotton gins.

Porum was the home of Tom Starr, a participant in the bitter conflict between two factions of the Cherokee Nation: the "Old Settlers" and the "Newcomers." Tom's father, James Starr, had signed the Treaty of Dancing Rabbit Creek, resulting in the removal of the Cherokees from their homes in the East. James Starr was among those assassinated for having signed the treaty, and Tom Starr dedicated himself to killing members of the antitreaty faction to avenge the death of his father.

The Cherokee government was unsuccessful in killing or capturing Tom Starr. To stop his rampage, the government agreed to grant him complete amnesty and $100,000 if he would stop the bloody feud. Starr complied, then moved to nearby Briartown and became a model citizen. Sam Starr, one of Tom's sons, became the husband of Belle Starr.

Porum's principal claim to fame is the site of Belle Starr's grave southeast of town near Eufaula Lake. The once-elaborate tombstone has been badly damaged by vandals. The stone was engraved with a picture of Belle's horse and a verse:

"Shed not for her the bitter tear,

Nor give the heart to vain regret

Tis but the casket that lies here,

The gem that filled it sparkles yet."

—*Enterprise* - OK 9-71————

This crossroads community provides access via OK 71 to the Eufaula Dam on the Canadian River. The powerhouse is open to visitors. The town, founded in 1890, took its name from the USS *Enterprise*. This Navy vessel, the fifth of that name, was commissioned in 1877.

Belle Starr's tombstone has been damaged by vandals. —Western History Collections, University of Oklahoma Library

—*Bokoshe*————

This coal-mining town was established in 1886. Its name is Choctaw for "little creek." The underground mining operation produced an excellent quality of coal and the town grew. Its first newspaper was the *Bokoshe Chronicle*. Editor Andrew Allen Veatch labored to elevate the cultural level of his readers by writing and publishing poetry in his newspaper.

—*McCurtain* - OK 26-31————

The first settlement was called Panther. Located just west of present-day McCurtain, its post office was opened in 1890. Harry Chant had established another nearby community in 1889, duly called Chant by the Post Office Department. McCurtain's townsite was surveyed in 1903 and the two towns merged. The amalgam was named McCurtain to honor Green McCurtain, governor of the Choctaw Nation.

The discovery of coal precipitated the settlements. McCurtain became a company town with 400 company houses and the ubiquitous company store. By statehood, in 1907, McCurtain was experiencing boom times, supporting two banks and four hotels. The *McCurtain American* began publication in November 1903, followed by the *Sans Bois News* in 1904 and the *McCurtain Statesman* in 1906.

—*Kinta* - OK 2-31————

In 1900 old San Bois Town, about four miles east of present-day Kinta, was the home and headquarters of Green McCurtain, the last principal chief of the Choctaw Nation. The Fort Smith and Western Railroad bypassed the town. Businessmen began to move nearer to the railroad; Green McCurtain followed suit and San Bois faded. Today, a cemetery containing graves of members of the McCurtain family, ruins of a jail, and the restored McCurtain mansion are all that remain of San Bois.

Kinta, "beaver" in the Choctaw language, reached its peak while the railroad was operating. When the *Kinta Enterprise* began publication in 1905 there were two hotels, three stores, three cotton gins, four churches, a barrel-stave factory, a drugstore, and a theater. Around 1912, after the death of Green McCurtain and cessation of Choctaw Nation activities, the community began to deteriorate as businesses moved to Stigler, the county seat.

—Quinton - OK 31-71————

Settled shortly after 1900, Quinton drew its sustenance from a large zinc smelter that employed about 400 people. The town was named for Martha E. Quinton, a prominent Choctaw. When the Fort Smith and Western Railroad was abandoned in 1939, the smelter closed down as did the mines northwest of town.

During the early twentieth century, as statehood grew nearer, people became passionate about politics. The skirmish between Andrew Carter, editor of the *Quinton Pioneer*, and Virgil Winn, editor of the *Eufaula Republican*, was a typical example of the verbal warfare frequently carried on between rival newspaper editors with differing political affiliations. Winn launched his paper in 1906 with a salvo at Carter: "The living, breathing, brainless wonder who for the past several years has unsuccessfully attempted to edit the *Quinton Pioneer*, to the detriment of the people and the Democratic party . . . emitted another streak of venom at the stockholders of the *Eufaula Republican*."

—Krebs - OK 31————

The area was rich in veins of coal, and Krebs was settled in 1871 upon arrival of the Katy railroad. During its early days, Krebs was ruled by Choctaw law, United States courts, and the Indian agent. Confusion of laws regarding the importation, sale, and manufacture of alcoholic beverages provided many loopholes, and Krebs became known for the production of "choc beer," a concoction made of hops, tobacco, fishberries, barley, and alcohol.

Employment in the coal mines attracted an influx of Italian miners. By 1900, a dozen mines were operating in the vicinity, and the population soared to 7,000. There were no hospitals, and mining accidents were frequent, particularly gas burns and explosions. The local drugstore stocked Vaseline in 500-pound quantities, raw linseed oil in 50-barrel lots, and iodoform in 10-pound packages. On January 7, 1892, an explosion caused by blackdamp killed a hundred miners, and the drugstore stayed open day and night for two weeks.

As the mining boom died down, many of the Italian miners turned to farming. They have retained their ethnic heritage and Krebs is still renowned for Italian food. An annual Italian Festival is celebrated in September.

US 59-259-271
Panama—Harris

—*Panama* - US 59-271————

This former coal-mining center came into being with the arrival of the Kansas City Southern Railway about 1895. Construction of the Panama Canal during that period inspired the town's name. A newspaper was published twice a month, mostly ready-print interspersed with local happenings. The newspaper was called the *Panama Canal*; its motto was "We Live for Those Who Love Us."

As coal mining declined in the area, farming and stock raising became increasingly important. The community has an abandoned stone jail dating back to the Choctaw Nation.

—*Shady Point* - US 59-271————

Originally named Harrison, this town's name was changed to Shady Point December 11, 1894. This small agricultural community was once a way station on the military road between Fort Smith and Fort Towson as well as a stop known as Brazil Station on the Butterfield stage route.

—*Poteau* - US 59-271————

In 1719, Bérnard de la Harpe explored northward out of New Orleans to eastern Oklahoma. He opened the way for subsequent French traders. Although La Harpe's journal does not specifically identify the Poteau area, French names for surrounding geographical features leave little doubt of French presence.

In 1887, Poteau, a Choctaw Nation record town, took its name from the nearby Poteau River. In French *poteau* means "post." Some historians maintain that the reference was to a post or stake that marked a trading area.

The Frisco railroad in 1888 and the Kansas City Southern a few years later were the stimuli for Poteau's growth. Agriculture took a back seat to coal mining as rail transportation stretched from the coal fields of western Arkansas and eastern Oklahoma to Muskogee. With the decline of coal mining, Poteau's economy depended upon lumbering, truck farming, and small industries.

Poteau's greatest asset may have been Senator Robert S. Kerr. He built a palatial mountainside mansion just south of town. After Kerr's death the family donated the mansion to the town for educational purposes. It now serves as a conference center and museum.

"The World's Highest Hill"

For people who like to participate in superlatives, Cavanal Hill is waiting near Poteau, "The World's Highest Hill." No one is quite sure how the designation came about.

Before World War II, members of an English class in a LeFlore County high school exchanged letters with students in a similar class in England. The British class discovered from a Boy Scout manual that Cavanal Hill, near Poteau, was "The World's Highest Hill." Subsequent investigation revealed that the British Geological Society defined a hill as less than 2,000 feet above the surrounding terrain, and a mountain as 2,000 feet or more. Cavanal Hill measures 1,999 feet above the local area.

From US 59 at the north edge of Poteau, Witteville Road leads to the top of Cavanal Hill. It is approximately five miles, and there is an additional five miles of road in the park on top of the hill. The road leads past the site of Witteville, a thriving coal-mining town now shriveled to only a few houses.

—Heavener - US 59-270————

This community began in 1896 with the arrival of the Kansas City Southern Railway. It became a division point in 1910. The village was named for Joseph Heavener, a white man who lived among the Choctaws and owned the land on which the townsite was platted.

Did Norsemen Get to Oklahoma?

The subject is still being debated; but, in the meantime, Heavener Runestone State Park has been set aside to display the evidence upon which the controversy is based.

Gloria Farley grew up in Heavener. Years later, while living in Ohio, she read of the Kensington Runestone in Minnesota, saw a runic alphabet, and remembered "Indian Rock," which she had seen near Heavener in 1913. She returned to Oklahoma in 1951, found the stone with its mysterious carvings, and launched an investigation to determine its authenticity.

The stone is a great slab of sandstone twelve feet high, ten feet wide, and sixteen inches thick. Eight weathered symbols, six to nine inches tall, are incised in its west face. They match the runic alphabet. Mrs. Farley contacted the Smithsonian Institution; yes, they had heard about the inscription and were of the opinion the carving had been done "by someone with a knowledge of Scandinavian grammar."

The Heavener Runestone offers mute testimony that Norsemen may have visited Oklahoma in November 1012.
—Oklahoma Tourism & Recreation, Fred W. Marvel

Mrs. Farley was not satisfied. Her investigation finally led to Frederick J. Pohl, an authority on Viking exploration in America. Pohl visited the runestone in 1959 and determined that the inscription was authentic. In 1967 Alf Monge, native of Norway and a retired U.S. Army cryptographer, and Dr. O. G. Landsverk, a Scandinavian history specialist, decoded the inscription: It read, "November 11, 1012."

Monge and Landsverk believed the inscription had been coded by a Benedictine monk. The Benedictines were in Greenland in A.D. 1000, and monks of the order accompanied exploratory expeditions.

Monge and Landsverk predicted that their translation would be challenged. Indeed it has, but no one has yet produced evidence to damn the carving as a hoax, and Mrs. Farley tracked down two more stones in Oklahoma inscribed with the same alphabet. One was translated as reading "November 24, 1024."

—Conser - US 59————

The town once located six miles southwest of Heavener has disappeared; however, its remains merit a visit. Conser was established in 1894 with Jane Conser as the postmistress.

Conser was the home of Peter Conser, a well-known Choctaw Lighthorseman. He came to the area after the Civil War with a small amount of seed corn and began farming. Through hard work and careful planning, he accumulated considerable wealth. Affluence brought social

77

recognition and in 1877, at age twenty-five, he became a deputy sheriff in the Choctaw Nation.

Later, he was appointed a captain in the Choctaw Lighthorse, the mounted police of the Five Civilized Tribes. Initially, in the 1820s, the Lighthorse served as sheriff, judge, jury, and executioner. By the 1870s, the organization had been stripped of its judicial power. It was a peace-keeping force. Peter Conser was responsible for preserving order and discipline among his men and seeing that each was properly armed, equipped, and mounted.

Peter later served as a representative and then a senator to the Choctaw Council. In addition, he ran a large farm, a gristmill, and a sawmill. He kept a general store. He died in 1934, but his two-story nineteenth-century home has been restored and furnished with items reflective of the Conser family's wealth and social position. It is operated as a museum by the Oklahoma Historical Society.

—Hodgen - US 59————

The town was named Houston at its founding in 1896 for Texan Sam Houston. The name was changed to Hodgen in 1910, misspelling the name of J. W. Hodgens, a timber buyer for the Kansas City Southern Railway; and there has been trouble ever since. The Post Office Department gives it the official correct spelling on the post office, but maps, highway signs, and residents frequently spell it "Hodgins."

—Big Cedar - US 259—OK 63————

A monument to President John F. Kennedy marks memory of a day in the sun for this small crossroads village. On October 29, 1961, two years before his assassination, Kennedy spoke here at a highway dedication as the guest of Senator Robert S. Kerr. As US 259 tops Kiamichi Mountain there is a scenic overlook as well as a monument to those responsible for the highway.

—Smithville - US 259—OK 4————

Smithville, an isolated village at the junction of US 259 and OK 4, is in the heart of a sportsman's paradise. According to pioneer settlers, the Choctaws found game and fish most plentiful in this area. It was said they could fish when "the rabbit hollers" or "the Peter bird sang," using as bait anything from bread dough to foot-long fishworms. One of the latter was judged ample for catching twenty fish.

Smithville was founded in 1886 as Hatobi (Choctaw for "warrior man"). The name was changed in 1890 to honor Joshua M. Smith, a local resident.

From Smithville, US 259 follows Mountain Fork River and crosses Boktukolo Creek, an excellent fishing stream. On the east bank of the creek is a cut or "narrows," the route of a pre-Civil War trail. During the 1870s, this trail was used by prospectors who searched vainly for silver and copper in the Kiamichi Mountains.

—*Harris* - US 259—OK 87————

W. B. Harris and his family came to the Red River valley with the Choctaw migration of the 1830s and settled at Pecan Point, near present-day Harris. Henry Harris, for whom the town would be named, was the son of W. B. Harris. Henry operated a ferry across the Red River at Pecan Point. In 1867, he built an impressive home four miles north of Harris. It has been restored by family descendants. Open to the public by appointment, it is filled with family furniture, documents, and artifacts dating back to the American Revolution.

OK 112
Pocola—Cameron

—*Pocola*————

Pocola ("ten" in Choctaw) was so named in 1881 because it is ten miles from Fort Smith, Arkansas. Like other border towns in the area, it has profited from proximity to Fort Smith. During the 1980s Pocola's population jumped seventy-seven percent, resuscitating its post office by the latter part of the decade.

At the outbreak of the Civil War, in 1861, most of the inhabitants of LeFlore County aligned with the South. Military action in the area was limited, but two battles were fought at Backbone Mountain near Pocola. On September 1, 1863, Confederates under Brig. Gen. W. L. Cabell ambushed a Union force commanded by Maj. Gen. J. G. Blunt. They were driven off after a three-hour engagement. Nearly eleven months later a Choctaw battalion commanded by Capt. Jackson McCurtain defeated a federal cavalry force.

In 1886, a 1,288-foot railroad tunnel was built through Backbone Mountain, the only railroad tunnel in Oklahoma.

—Cameron———

This community celebrated its centennial in 1986. Confederate Capt. James E. Reynolds came to Indian Territory in 1867 and married a Choctaw. He came to Cameron in 1890 and built an impressive stone "castle" on a hill.

Cameron was named for J. D. Cameron, the contractor who graded the railroad bed through the town in 1886. When the Indian Territorial Court was closed at Fort Smith in 1896, Cameron became a federal court town until the court was moved to Poteau in 1900.

US 270
Wister—Alderson

—Wister———

Wister started as a railroad junction in 1890. The construction of a dam to form Wister Lake in 1949 and the dedication of Wister State Park in 1953 rescued the town from nonentity. When plans for flooding the area became known, archaeologists began to explore. The extensive Garner Collection of artifacts from prehistoric hunters and gatherers who lived in the Fourche Maline Creek valley some 2,000 years ago can now be seen at the Wister Lake Project Office.

—Red Oak - US 270—OK 82———

Between Wister and Red Oak, US 270 is punctuated by tiny rural communities, remains of the railroad's passing and of coal-mining activities: Victor, Caston, Fanshawe, Hughes, and Denman. Of these, Fanshawe, a railroad siding from the early 1890s, has fared best, largely because of its reputation as a mecca for hunters.

Red Oak was established in 1868, named for a large oak tree in the center of town; it was used as a whipping post for punishment handed down by the district court of the Choctaw Nation. The last legal execution under Choctaw tribal law was carried out near Red Oak on November 5, 1894.

From Red Oak one can visit several stops on the Butterfield Overland Mail route. Holloway's Station was located about two miles northeast of Red Oak on the gravel road leading to Shady Point. William Holloway operated a tollgate at a scenic pass known as "The Narrows." Choctaw citizens were exempt from toll tariff. For whites, "beating around" a tollgate was a serious offense.

The most famous stop is the Edwards Store, about eight miles northeast of Red Oak. The log cabin, built in 1850, is still standing. This was the original site of the Red Oak post office. Thomas Edwards was postmaster. He furnished meals to stage passengers at forty-five cents per person. Ailing passengers could buy "lung balm" at seventy-five cents a bottle. A fever and ague specific at sixty cents a bottle was another bestseller.

HISTORICAL HIGHLIGHT

The Man Who Would Rather Die Than Lie

In the early 1890s, as Indian Territory moved toward statehood, bitter controversy developed between the Progressive and Nationalist parties in the Choctaw Nation. The Progressives favored statehood and allotment of lands for the Choctaws; the Nationals fought the plan. In 1892, the conflict erupted into gunfire, assassinations, and the execution of a man whom some viewed as a murderer and others as a scapegoat.

On September 11, 1892, Silon Lewis and Simeon Wade set out in separate parties to execute a number of their Progressive tribesmen. Lewis and his men rode to Hartshorne, found Joe Haklotybbi asleep on his front porch, and killed him before he could get to his feet. At the same time, Wade and his men killed three other Progressives. Then the two parties joined and rode toward McAlester where other Nationalists were

Silon Lewis kept his word: He voluntarily kept a date to meet his death by execution. —Western History Collections, University of Oklahoma Library

supposed to be carrying out assassinations. However, the others had not put the plan into effect. Lewis and Wade gave up their plans for further killings.

The Choctaw militia caught up with the guilty Nationalists. Nine were tried and sentenced to be killed by rifle fire, a single bullet for each. As a result of legal actions, only Lewis and Wade were ordered to be executed. Finally, Wade was released.

The delays lasted until 1894, at which time Silon Lewis was given his freedom according to Choctaw law—under the condition that he return to the courthouse southwest of Red Oak for his execution on November 5, 1894.

Family and friends urged Lewis to flee, but Lewis refused because he had given his word. The day before the scheduled execution, he hitched up his team and rode with his wife Sally to the appointed site. He camped for the night and wrote out his last will and testament.

The following day, a crowd gathered. Sheriff Tecumseh Moore stood by with deputies because of rumors that Lewis might be rescued. At high noon Lewis walked out to keep his date with death. He took off his coat and sat on a blanket. A Choctaw official unbuttoned Lewis's shirt and somebody else placed a spot of white powder on his chest. Another pulled Lewis's feet out in front of him; two more stretched his arms to his sides.

Sheriff Moore refused to commit the execution. He said Lewis was a friend. He turned the task over to Deputy Lyman Pusley. Pusley walked up, aimed a Winchester at Lewis's chest, and pulled the trigger. Lewis jerked; blood stained his white shirt. He fell back on the blanket, but he did not die.

For thirty minutes, Lewis lay jerking while Choctaw officials wrestled with a quandary. Lewis was supposed to be executed by a single bullet. Finally, Sheriff Moore pulled out his handkerchief and smothered his friend to end his misery.

—Wilburton - US 270—OK 2————

John Riddle's Station on the Butterfield Overland Mail route was three miles east of present-day Wilburton. In October 1858, Riddle was granted a concession to operate a toll bridge on the Fourche Maline Creek near his home. In 1873, Riddle's Station was referred to as Big Fourche Maline post office, and George Riddle, John's son, was appointed postmaster.

The present town had its beginning with shafts to reach the rich, underlying bed of coal. The Choctaw Coal and Railway Company sank a shaft west of Wilburton. Dr. E. M. Bond, who had Indian rights by marriage, contested the claim. In those days, when an Indian found coal he took a mile-long rope and stretched it around as much land as it would encompass, thus laying out his claim. Dr. Bond's claim held up, and he leased the land to James Degnan and James McConnell in 1895.

On October 27, 1905, the *Wilburton News* headlined: "Buried Treasure is Found by Negroes." Three blacks, Robert and Elmo Randolph and Tim Casey, had been out hunting. They found five-, ten-, twenty-, and fifty-dollar gold pieces embedded in a clay bank. They rushed back to Wilburton to announce that they were "Rockefellers and Vanderbilts." The Degnan-McConnell Coal Company gave the men a day off, and they went back to probe for more treasure. They returned with some $400; one coin was dated 1821. They remained tight-lipped regarding the location of their bonanza.

In 1909, Eastern Oklahoma State College was established in Wilburton as a School of Mines and Metallurgy. With the demise of mining, Wilburton focused on other economic resources, and the college shifted direction to become a state junior college awarding associate degrees in a variety of academic and occupational fields.

Wilburton keeps Belle Starr's memory green with an annual Belle Starr Festival featuring a shootout between Belle Starr's gang and the law. At noon each day someone is "hung," and robberies are staged every day.

In 1987, the Wilburton Chamber of Commerce established the Wilburton College of Loafing. It is a coeducational "institution"; tuition is $2.00. To earn a Bachelor of Loafing, students must admit to being part-time or full-time loafers. Resulting publicity has dubbed Wilburton "The Loafing Capital of the World."

EXCURSION ⎯⎯⎯⎯

—*Robbers Cave State Park* - OK 2⎯⎯⎯

Robbers Cave, located five miles north of Wilburton on OK 2, was first used during the early eighteenth century by French traders and trappers to store provisions, furs, hides, and trade goods. During the Civil War it served as a haven for both Union and Confederate deserters. The renegade Cherokee Black Jack is the first outlaw credited with using the cave as a hideout. Later Ned Christie, another Cherokee outlaw, frequented the cave.

A path along Fourche Maline Creek became known as "Robbers Trail" as gangs of outlaws used it on the way to the cave between raids on stores, stagecoaches, agency payrolls, and law-abiding farmers. The Younger brothers, Frank and Jesse James, and Belle Starr made it a rendezvous.

Once the haunt of Frank and Jesse James, the Younger brothers, and Belle Starr, Robbers Cave is now part of Robbers Cave State Park, a popular recreational area.

The cave is built into a shelf of sandstone in the San Bois Mountains, protected by a maze of boulders. The narrow entrance was easily guarded by a single sentry. The cave extends into the cliff about forty feet. A cool, freshwater stream provided water. A hidden exit allowed outlaws to escape when cornered by Judge Parker's deputies.

Deputy U.S. Marshall Heck Brunner is credited with spoiling the effectiveness of Robbers Cave. One night while the outlaws were away he found the secret exit. A short time later, a group of deputies cornered a gang in the cave while others in the posse covered the secret exit. All were captured except for one, who was killed while trying to escape.

There were many stories of hidden treasure connected with the cave. In 1931, three men came from Texas to search. They departed abruptly, thus spreading the rumor among locals that they had found what they came for.

Subsequently, the area became a Boy Scout camp. In 1935, it was developed as a state park and is now a recreational area with a variety of camping and entertainment facilities.

—*Gowen* - US 270————

Established during the early 1890s, the town was named for Francis I. Gowen, a Philadelphia lawyer. Gowen was the home of Lincoln Perry, a popular black actor whose screen name was Step'n Fetchit. According to the local story, the one-mile walk from his home to school was "jes too much," and he rarely attended school. However, he capitalized on his laziness by rising from a $3-a-week job with a medicine show to long-time status as a well-known, well-paid character actor. His screen name evolved from his consistent answer to requests for action: "I'll step'n fetchit purty soon."

—Hartshorne—Haileyville - US 270—OK 1-63————

The French explorer Bérnard de la Harpe camped three miles east of Hartshorne on August 25, 1719, during his expedition to the Arkansas River. He hoped to make treaties and open trade with the Indian tribes he encountered.

Hartshorne and Haileyville were once known as the Twin Cities of Pittsburg County. Both were established about 1890 and platted in 1902. Hartshorne was named for Dr. Charles Hartshorne, a railroad official; Dr. David Morris Hailey lent his name to Haileyville. He was instrumental in opening the district's first coal mine. Lumbering, farming, and ranching took up the slack after the mines closed down.

—Bache—Dow—Alderson - US 270————

These three coal-producing communities clung to the umbilical cord of the Choctaw Coal and Railway Company during the late 1890s. Alderson was the scene of a unique labor dispute in 1894. The Choctaw Nation required mining corporations to pay a small monthly tax for each employee. A strike over a twenty-five percent wage reduction idled most of the employees, and the company refused to pay the tax on people who were not working.

The Choctaw chief countered by insisting that the miners be removed from his nation; nonpayment of the head tax made them intruders. The dispute was appealed to the commissioner of Indian affairs, then to the secretary of the interior, and finally to President Grover Cleveland. The Indians' position was held to be valid.

Three companies of infantry and two troops of cavalry arrived to deport the idle miners. Alderson was designated as troop headquarters. The miners were arrested and brought in. Along with their families, they were loaded into boxcars and taken to Jenson, Arkansas, the nearest town outside of Indian Territory.

The governor of Arkansas protested. So did the governments of Italy and Great Britain, since many of the miners were citizens of those countries. After the strike was broken, the mines reopened and royalties once more began to flow into the Choctaw treasury.

—*Talihina* - US 271—OK 1-63————

Talimena Drive (OK 1) between Talihina and Mena, Arkansas, is one of the most scenic drives in the state. From Talihina, it passes historical sites on the old Fort Towson Military Road. After Horsethief Springs, it snakes along the spine of Winding Stair Mountain. This is where John Wayne caught the outlaws in *True Grit*.

There was a small missionary settlement in this valley of the Winding Stair Mountains in 1888 when the Frisco railroad built across the mountains from Fort Smith, Arkansas, to Paris, Texas. Talihina took its name from this event; in Choctaw the word means "iron road." The town remained virtually inaccessible except by rail until 1919, when convict labor was used to build a highway through the mountains.

—*Higgins* - OK 1-63

This community started in 1903 as Caminet and within a month changed its name to Higgins to honor a territorial jurist. Higgins flourished briefly, but there is hardly a trace left.

From 1858 to 1861 Pusley's Station, located two miles southwest of Higgins, served passengers on the Butterfield Overland Mail. Waterman L. Ormsby, a reporter for the New York *Herald*, had been assigned to ride the stage on its first trip. He reached the station on September 19, 1858:

"Here," Ormsby wrote, "I gave an Indian boy a paper of tobacco to give me water enough to wash my face, put on a blue flannel shirt, and considered myself pretty well out west.

OK 43
Daisy—Redden

—*Daisy* - OK 43————

Before there was a settlement large enough to be called a town, the vicinity around present-day Daisy was called Many Springs. By 1906 Daisy had several stores, a sawmill, a cotton gin, a drugstore, a blacksmith, and other enterprises. The town continued as a trade center for many years, but when county lines were redrawn, Daisy no longer had a courthouse, and businesses began to move away. Today Daisy is a quiet rural town on the Indian Nation Turnpike.

Cotton was the principal crop and there were a number of sawmills in the area when Redden was established. The post office opened June 1, 1903, with John A. Redden as postmaster.

Redden's most exciting night occurred during the 1930s when Clyde Barrow visited the area. Barrow and a companion wounded the sheriff and killed his deputy. The outlaws were believed to have headed for Redden. Citizens loaded their guns and the search was on, but they were too late. Barrow had already been to John Redden's home. Redden's son Hack, the rural mail carrier, owned one of the few automobiles in town. Barrow and his companion kidnapped Hack Redden, took his car, and headed east. They left Hack handcuffed to a tree east of Daisy.

OK 2
Damon—Moyers

OK 2, stretching more than eighty miles between OK 31 on the north to OK 3 on the south, is not listed as a scenic drive without reason. It passes through the Potato Hills Recreation Area, past Sardis Lake, and along the Kiamichi River. The highway is sprinkled with small ranching and lumbering communities: Damon, Yanush, Clayton, Stanley, Eubanks, Wadena, Kosoma, and Moyers. Most came into being during the first decade of the twentieth century immediately following statehood and the opening of Indian Territory to all comers.

The Clayton area attracted a rough and tough breed of loggers and lumbermen, ranchers and farmers, followed by shrewd merchants and businessmen, eager to tap the wealth of an undeveloped area. The roughness of the area provided hideouts for outlaws, and bootleg whiskey became big business during the Prohibition era. During Depression days, many people moved away; others survived off the land and on WPA projects; still others converted corn crops into moonshine whiskey. The lumber industry struggled.

Today, the timber industry is thriving. The beauty of the area is preserved by replanting. Clayton Lake, Sardis Reservoir, Lake Nanih Waiya, and the Kiamichi River attract tourists, hunters, and fishermen.

Moonshiners

By the time Prohibition was put into effect in 1920, Oklahoma had already been "dry" for many years. Federal and Indian laws forbid the sale of "firewater" to the Five Civilized Tribes. Moonshiners and bootleggers were well-practiced in their trades.

The moonshiner usually conducted business at night, thus the name. Bootleggers were so called because on small deliveries they would stick a bottle into their loose-fitting cowboy boots.

Moonshine whiskey was made from ground corn, hops, malt, and sugar. The ingredients were allowed to ferment until a thick cap formed on top. When the cap fell, much as a cake might, the sour mash was ready to run through the still. In warm weather the mash would be ready to cook in three to five days. The main parts of the still were the cooker, the thumper keg, and a condenser. Fifty gallons of mash made about five gallons of whiskey.

The mash vaporized and left the cooker through a pipe into the thumper keg. From the thumper keg, a line went to the condenser—a series of water-cooled copper coils. The vapor condensed and the liquor was strained, usually through a hat stuffed with cotton. Frequently the hat was the one the moonshiner wore.

The whiskey was stored in vessels ranging from half-pint bottles to kegs. Fruit jars were the most common. Some moonshiners were so proud of their products that they sold their whiskey in custom-made bottles or jars bearing their names.

Stills were artfully concealed, and moonshiners were careful about obtaining their supplies. The overt purchase of 500 pounds of sugar was bound to arouse suspicion. Most were on friendly terms with county law officers and simply paid a monthly bribe as a cost of doing business. If caught, it was preferable to be arrested by county officials. The minimum sentence was usually thirty days, with fines from $50 to $500. If caught by revenuers (federal agents), the guilty party could end up busting rocks at Leavenworth, Kansas, for a year and a day.

Most customers went to a moonshiner's or a bootlegger's house, paid money, and obtained liquor. In some cases there was delivery service, and in a few cases one went up to a hollow stump and found a can and a cowbell. The system was to put money in the can, ring the cowbell, and leave for a while. When the customer returned he would find a jar of cat in the hollow stump.

—Albion—Kiamichi - US 271————

Southwestward from Talihina, US 271 skirts the southern slopes of the heavily wooded Potato Hills to Albion, a lumbering town dating from 1887 when the Frisco railroad built a line from Fort Smith, Arkansas, to Paris, Texas. It was given the Roman name for England by an Englishman named John T. Bailey.

Five miles farther along US 271 is Kiamichi, another community that developed on the railroad in 1887. It took its name from the river that roughly parallels this section of the highway. *Kamichi* is a French word meaning "horned screamer," probably for the shrike—once a common bird in the area. Many of the residents are descendants of black slaves of Choctaw Indians, freedmen who settled upon allotments they received from the Indians following the Civil War.

—Tuskahoma - US 271————

The town came into existence with the arrival of the railroad; however, long before that it had been the political capital of the Choctaws. Near here in 1834, the first constitution written in what is now Oklahoma was adopted by the Choctaw Nation.

Only scattered stones remain of the once-splendid Tuskahoma Female Academy near Tuskahoma. —Western History Collections, University of Oklahoma Library

The Treaty of Dancing Rabbit Creek promised the Choctaws many things in return for their homelands farther east. One of those things was money to erect a new council house in the approximate center of the land they were to occupy in Indian Territory. That site was about a mile and a half northwest of present Tuskahoma. They called the new capital Nunih Wayah, the name of a sacred mound in Mississippi prominent in ancient Choctaw legends.

The old Choctaw Council House is still used for meetings of the Choctaw tribal council; it also serves as a museum for Choctaw artifacts, paintings, and photographs. During Labor Day weekend, the grounds come alive for the Annual Choctaw Festival. Among the events is Kabucha Tolih, the "stick ball game," which is being revived as a cultural sport.

HISTORICAL HIGHLIGHT

Stick Ball Game

Tolih, the Choctaw stick ball game, is perhaps the oldest competetive game on the North American continent; lacrosse is nearest to a modern counterpart, tennis is a close relative, and any game in which the object is to move a ball along a field or court against an opposing team or individual has ancestral ties.

In 1832, the American artist George Catlin was first to document stick ball among the Choctaws. He was a true fan. "I have made it a uniform rule, whilst in the Indian country, to attend every ball-play I could hear of, if I could do it by riding a distance of twenty or thirty miles," Catlin wrote.

Each team had a goal consisting of two upright posts about twenty-five feet high and six feet apart with a crossbar across the top. The goals were forty or fifty rods apart, more than twice the length of today's football field. Each player had two sticks with oblong hoops at the end covered with netting. A ball was thrown up in the center of the field, and players vied to catch it between the nettings on their sticks and throw it. Players could not use their hands to catch or strike the ball.

The objective was to throw the ball home between the stakes on the goal line. A game consisted of a hundred goals, and it was not uncommon for a game to start by mid-morning and continue until sundown, the only stops being intervals of approximately one minute after each goal while judges prepared to start play again.

The games inspired spirited betting that began as soon as the field was marked off. Catlin told about it:

> The betting was all done across this line, and seemed to be chiefly left to the women, who seemed to have martialed out a little of everything

Western artist George Catlin captured the Choctaw stick ball player on his sketch pad. —Catlin, 1841

that their houses and their fields possessed. Goods and chattels—knives, dresses, blankets, pots and kettles, dogs and horses, and guns—and all were placed in the possession of stake-holders, who sat by them and watched them all night, preparatory to the play.

The melee continued unabated from mid-morning until sundown. Players went barefoot and wore only breechclothes with beaded belts and flowing tails made of white horsehair or quills. No player was allowed to carry a weapon other than his sticks onto the field of play, but few players left the field without battered shins and bloodied noses.

During later years competition developed between the counties of the Choctaw Nation. Teams were much smaller, but there was no less betting, and encounters on the field of play were no less violent.

A body of superstitions was handed down through the years. One was the belief that water containing the scrapings of dried bones of carcasses

Haileyville was the scene of spirited stick ball games. —Western History Collections, University of Oklahoma Library

would cause fatigue in the person who drank it. Each team would attempt to treat the opponent's water. The conjurer for each county made the ball for the county's team. They believed that if the heart of a red-headed woodpecker was in the ball's center, the ball would be repelled when it was thrown toward the opponent's goal.

US 271—OK 144
Honobia—Goodland

—*Honobia* - OK 144————

This tiny community is scattered about in one of the most isolated scenic areas of Oklahoma. The name came from an early Choctaw settler. The post office was established in 1919. A nearby religious retreat, Christ's 40 Acres, attracts religious leaders from all over the world.

—*Antlers* - US 271—OK 3————

The early settlement got its name from the Indian custom of fastening a set of antlers to a tree to mark the site of a spring. For years before the Civil War, hunters and stock traders stopped at the spring within the city limits of present-day Antlers. When the Frisco railroad came in 1887, Antlers Station was shortened to Antlers.

During the winter of 1892-93, Antlers was the scene of a political insurrection known locally as the "Locke War." Congress had voted to pay $2.9 million to the Choctaw Nation in settlement of a land claim. Strife developed between the Nationalist and Progressive parties over how the money was handled.

The Progressives were declared winners in a close election, and the Nationalists formed armed bands to march against the capital and seize the government. Most were dispersed with little bloodshed by the tribal militia, but 150 men barricaded themselves within a log stockade in Antlers under the leadership of Victor M. Locke, an intermarried white man, and prepared to defy the administration. The Choctaw militia was called out to persuade the two factions to make peace.

—*Hugo* - US 70-271————

Hugo sprang into being with the coming of the Arkansas and Choctaw Railroad in 1901. The name of the first post office was Raymond, but Victor Hugo was the favorite author of Mrs. W. H. Darrough, wife of the townsite surveyor. His name was inscribed on the plat of the townsite.

By 1912, more than a thousand Hugo residents were employed on the Frisco line. Agriculture flourished in the area during and following World I, and so did Hugo. As with most agricultural communities in Oklahoma, the 1930s took an economic toll. Following World War II,

The old Frisco railroad depot at Hugo is now a museum, complete with a restored Harvey House. —Courtesy Smith Luton, Jr.

Hugo suffered a loss of population. The town launched a highly successful drive for industrial development. First prize was the Wells-Lamont
Glove Plant; other firms followed.

As a "circus town," Hugo is unique to Oklahoma. For many years, the
community has provided winter quarters for the Carson & Barnes Circus
(formerly Al G. Kelly & Miller Bros. Circus) as well as other outfits.
Passing motorists see gayly painted circus vans and, occasionally,
vacationing elephants or camels.

The gemstone of Hugo's collection is the old Frisco railroad depot. The
depot was built in 1914, at that time the third largest in the state. It had
a Harvey House restaurant. Passenger service was abandoned in 1956;
a few months later Railway Express discontinued service. The depot
endured progressive deterioration until it was rescued by the Choctaw
County Historical Society. The building was restored and now operates
as a museum, displaying railroad memorabilia and historical artifacts.

HISTORICAL HIGHLIGHT

Harvey Houses

Frederick Henry Harvey has frequently been credited with civilizing
the West. Before Harvey began opening restaurants in Santa Fe stations
through the West, eating while traveling by railroad was grim business
unless one packed a lunch. Dining cars had not yet made their appearance;
meals were served at railroad depots during stops that frequently lasted
only ten minutes.

Passengers paid about 50 cents in advance for a lunch or supper of
rancid bacon, canned beans, eggs, bitter coffee, and biscuits so heavy
they were called "sinkers." The restaurants were often in league with the
train crews. As soon as dinners were served, the train whistle blew and
the conductor called "All aboard!" Passengers ran to catch the train,
often leaving their meals uneaten. The restaurants reheated the leftover
food and served it to the next victims. They customarily paid the train
crew 10 cents per passenger.

That changed with the arrival of Fred Harvey, an Englishman with an
appreciation for good food and pleasant surroundings. When Fred
Harvey opened his first railroad restaurant in 1876 in the Santa Fe depot
in Topeka, Kansas, he laid down strict regulations for the dress and
behavior of waitresses. Soon he had a long waiting list of job applicants.

Applicants promised not to marry for a year, a pledge frequently
broken. The girls were furnished uniforms: black shirtwaist dresses with
crisp white bib aprons and black bow ties. No wrinkles or spots were
allowed. They were furnished meals and a room. A housemother watched
over them. Mr. Harvey allowed them to have a dance every Friday night.

94

*Country boys came to
the Harvey House in
Hugo "to get a gawk
and giggle at the
Harvey Queens."*
—Courtesy Smith Luton, Jr.

Passengers enjoyed a leisurely, complete meal for fifty cents—all they could eat! Signals and split-second timing were necessary. Orders were telegraphed ahead. When the train was about a mile away, a blast on the whistle alerted restaurant employees to get the first course on the table. As the train slowed for the meal stop, a gong announced that the food was ready. Five minutes before departure, the engineer sounded a warning blast of the whistle.

In addition to providing service to railroad passengers, Harvey House refinements—starched linen tablecloths, Sheffield silverware, and a rule requiring gentlemen to wear coats—attracted members of the local social set to dabble their hands in finger bowls.

—*Goodland* - US 271————

The community was originally located four miles north of Hugo, but it was bypassed by the railroad. Residents moved the town piecemeal to Hugo, and then to its location three miles southwest of Hugo. Its identity has survived, despite the loss of its post office in 1944, because it is the location of the Goodland children's home, said to be the nation's oldest protestant Indian orphanage. A church built in 1852 on the campus of the children's home claims to be "Oklahoma's oldest continuously used church."

———— EXCURSION

—*Wright City* - OK 98————

Wright City was established in 1910 by the Dierks Lumber Company and named Bismark to honor the German chancellor. World War I called for a new name, and Wright City was chosen to honor William W. Wright, the first soldier from Pushmataha County to lose his life in the war. In 1966, Wright City became the location for part of the Dierks Division of the Weyerhaeuser Company, and the lumber mill was expanded.

OK 3
Glover—Lane

Scenic OK 3 between Broken Bow and Antlers crosses southern Pushmataha County through Glover, Corinne, Oleta, Rattan, and Dela, small lumbering and ranching communities established between 1900 and 1920. Timber from these places was processed at the lumber mill in Wright City.

—*Farris* - OK 3————

This rural settlement dates from 1902. The experiences of Smith Butler, proprietor of the Farris General Store, are typical of survival tactics practiced by small-town retailers in rural Oklahoma during the depression of the 1930s.

Most people did business on credit then and paid as soon as they could or when the proprietor caught up with them. Some "worked out" their bills. Some traded for groceries; a dozen eggs would get a pound of coffee. A storekeeper had to be ready to barter for everything from fence posts to chickens. On one occasion, Butler had a problem with a "homing chicken." Every Saturday, a man came in to trade a chicken. Butler finally discovered that he was buying the same chicken every week; when he let his chickens out of their pen, this one would go back home.

Smith Butler also operated a sawmill and a gristmill. During the 1940s, he opened a dance hall behind his store and had as many as a hundred patrons on a good Saturday night. In 1947, a minister borrowed the dance hall for church services. While waiting for the preacher to finish so he could lock up, Butler listened to the sermon and was converted. He then changed the dance hall to a church; for a year the building served as a church, community hall, and justice of the peace court.

—*Lane* - OK 3————

Like many communities of early Indian Territory days, Lane traces its beginning to the Treaty of Dancing Rabbit Creek, which allotted this part of Oklahoma to the Choctaw tribe in 1830. Tradition has it that in 1843, a Choctaw named Katiotubbi built a cabin in the rolling hills between Muddy Boggy Creek on the north and Clear Boggy to the south. It came to be known as the "settlement in the fork of the Boggies."

The official name of Lane was selected by T. H. Thomas, in 1904, when he built a two-room trading post with space for a post office. He called it Lane because the trading post was located on a lane. Mail was delivered three times a week by horseback from Atoka.

The first school in Lane was a one-room frame structure. There were no desks; homemade benches with backs served the children, who kept their books under the bench and wrote on tablets held on their knees. The first teacher arrived in 1905. She was paid $35 a year by the Bureau of Indian Affairs and another $15 from donations by residents of Lane.

School was held seven or eight months of the year because children had to help with farm work. Classes were conducted in July and August, then dismissed for the months of September, October, and November. They resumed in December and continued until spring planting.

US 70
Eagletown—Blue

—*Eagletown* - US 70————

Located east of Broken Bow on US 70, this historic community is one of the oldest in Oklahoma. Settlers began arriving about 1820 when the area was still part of Arkansas Territory. Rev. Cyrus Byington established the Stockbridge Mission in 1837 and produced his monumental *Dictionary of the Choctaw Language*. In 1842, the Choctaw General Council founded the Iyanubbee Seminary for Girls at the mission.

The community was also the site of Bethabara Mission, established by Presbyterians in 1832. Loring S. Williams, the Presbyterian missionary, became the first postmaster. The post office was established July 1, 1834. Eagle Town, as it was officially designated until 1892, was the first station west of the Arkansas border on the military road from Little Rock to Fort Towson.

On the mission grounds at the Bethabara crossing of the Mountain Fork River stood a log courthouse that served as the seat of Eagle County in the Choctaw Nation from 1850 until statehood in 1907. The town was moved to its present location in 1892.

None of the "Old Town" buildings remain; however, a two-story house built in 1884 by Jefferson Gardner, principal chief of the Choctaws, is maintained as a museum. A 2,000-year-old cypress tree stands on the grounds, reputed to be the largest tree in the state of Oklahoma.

—*Broken Bow* - US 70-259————

The town was established in 1911 by the Dierks brothers, pioneer lumbermen, and named for their home in Nebraska. It became the hub of the state's lumber industry. In 1966, the Dierks' operations merged with the Weyerhaeuser corporation, and a new mill was constructed.

Choctaw Indians came to the area during the 1830s, but Caddoan Indians had lived in the area for centuries before that. The Memorial Indian Museum depicts the Caddoan culture.

The Forest Heritage Center at nearby Beavers Bend State Park portrays the history of forestry research through a series of dioramas. The entrance is decorated by a 22-foot hand-carved wooden Indian.

—*Idabel* - US 70—OK 3-37-87————

The modern city of Idabel had its beginning in 1902 when it was platted on what was then the Arkansas and Choctaw Railroad being built across the southern portion of the Choctaw Nation. The community was named for Ida and Belle, daughters of a railroad official.

98

Jones Sawmill at Idabel 1916. —Western History Collections, University of Oklahoma Library

In 1907, when designated as the county seat of McCurtain County, Idabel was a little village with dirt streets huddling beside the railroad track. Farming and lumbering became the principal economic supports. Today it is the location of the headquarters of the Dierks Division of the Weyerhaeuser Company's lumbering operation in the state of Oklahoma.

Shawneetown was located about three miles southwest of Idabel. This is believed to have been the site of the first "farm" in Oklahoma, cultivated as early as 1804. Shawnee Indians broke ground, planted crops, and built fences. During the 1830s, Col. Robert M. Jones, a Choctaw farmer, acquired the land and expanded it into one of Oklahoma's largest plantations.

Oklahoma's first post office, Miller Court House, stood about five miles south of Shawneetown. On April 1, 1820, the territorial government of Arkansas created Miller County, which included a large area of southeastern Oklahoma. The Miller Court House post office was established September 7, 1824.

By a treaty signed on January 20, 1825, the area was ceded to the Choctaw Nation. White residents made an unsuccessful effort to be exempted from provisions of the treaty. Arkansas abolished that part of Miller County within the Choctaw Nation, and the settlers burned the courthouse in protest.

—America—Tom - OK 3——————

Settled in 1903 when cotton and lumber were booming local industries, the town had some 2,000 inhabitants at its peak. It was not called America in a fit of patriotic fervor. The name came from Mrs. America Stewart, the wife of Tom Stewart. America was the home of William Spencer, a storekeeper who billed himself as "the richest man in America."

The nearby community of Tom, also a virtual ghost town, was named for Tom Stewart in 1916. The historic Garland Cemetery is four miles east of Tom, near the Arkansas line. It is on the antebellum plantation of Samuel Garland, a principal chief of the Choctaw Nation. Graves date from the early 1830s. One bearing the inscription "David Crockett, husband of Cynthia Ellen Garland," is believed to be the grave of a relative of Davy Crockett of Alamo fame. The monument inscribed "Sophia, wife of Major John Pitchlynn" gives her birth as December 27, 1773, the earliest known birth date on a grave in Oklahoma.

—Garvin - US 70——————

This community began as a railroad siding in the mid-1880s. Garvin was named for Isaac Garvin, Choctaw principal chief (1878-80). The present village gives no hint of the town's past. Subscribers paid a dollar a year for the *Garvin Graphic* when it started publication in 1903, and the first bank in McCurtain County opened immediately after statehood. The first U.S. Commissioner's Court in southern Oklahoma sat in Garvin.

—Millerton - US 70——————

Settlement dates from 1832 when the missionary Rev. Alfred Wright organized a congregation. About a mile and half north of US 70, the Wheelock Mission Church still stands, a handsome stone structure erected in 1846, said to be the oldest standing church in Oklahoma. This church was the only Indian Territory subject ever used for a Currier and Ives print. The Wheelock Cemetery across the road contains the graves of Alfred Wright and others who played important roles in development of the Choctaw Nation.

Reverend Wright, frail though he was, labored at translating the New Testament and other books into Choctaw. In August 1835, he sent the manuscript for *Chahta Nolisso*, a spelling book, to Boston for publication. In September 1837, he completed translation of the Gospels and Epistles of St. John and had to stop work because he had no more money to pay his translator.

The difficulties under which missionaries labored are illustrated by the fact that it took two years for a box of books sent from the mission at Park Hill, five miles south of Tahlequah, to reach Wheelock. They went by way of New Orleans. In 1841, Mrs. Wright wrote the mission board in far-away Boston, begging them to raise the Wrights' annual allowance from $450 to $600 so they could take more Choctaw orphan girls into their home for education.

In 1844, the Choctaw Council established Wheelock Academy, a seminary for Indian girls. The academy operated until 1955. The buildings are still standing not far from the Wheelock Mission Church. The name Wheelock honors Eleazer Wheelock, founder and first president of Dartmouth College.

—*Valliant* - US 70————

The town began as Fowlerville in the 1890s. As the community began to boom because of the railroad, the name was changed to match that of F. W. Valliant, chief engineer of the Arkansas and Choctaw Railroad. Initially the town's economy depended upon agriculture, and hunting and fishing in the nearby hills and streams.

Today, Valliant is home of one of the nation's largest containerboard mills. Weyerhaeuser opened the installation in 1971. The $100-million plant boasts the world's largest paper-making machine.

The old water-powered Clear Creek gristmill is located three miles southwest of Valliant. It operated until the 1950s, and much of its original equipment remains.

—*Swink* - US 70————

This village also owes its existence to the Arkansas and Choctaw Railroad. The post office was established in 1902 and named for D. R. Swink, a local merchant.

The "Old Chief's House," believed to be the oldest house in Oklahoma, is two miles northeast of US 70 at Swink. The two-story log house was built for Thomas LeFlore, chief of the Apukshenubbee district of the Choctaw Nation. Specifications for the house were published in the *Arkansas Gazette* (Little Rock) in 1836. The contract completion date was set for September 1, 1837. The house has been restored by the Oklahoma Historical Society, which operates it as a museum.

—*Fort Towson* - US 70————

The village of Fort Towson took its name from Old Fort Towson, the ruins of which are located a mile east and three-quarters of a mile north of the community. The post office of the present town was established in 1903.

Fort Towson was born as Camp Phoenix "on the banks of the Red River" in 1824. The exact site is unknown. Initially the garrison consisted of wooden shacks and tents. Its small contingent of troops was relatively ineffective. Indians killed soldiers, and the soldiers could not pursue the raiders. The *Arkansas Gazette* summed up the situation: "Fort Towson has ceased to give a feeling of security to the whites; the post was reduced to forty men, and—it is likely to need protection from citizens instead of giving them protection."

In 1829, the government abandoned the installation. Residents in the region immediately protested that they had been "left to the mercy of merciless savages." The Indians set fire to the buildings as soon as the troops were gone.

The garrison was designated as a permanent fort in 1830 and built on its present site. By 1837, Dr. Cyrus Kingsbury, a missionary to the Choctaws, was complimenting the post for the high moral character and piety of the personnel stationed there. Dr. Kingsbury may have caught the troops on a good day.

On July 25, 1838, the *Arkansas Gazette* described the Fourth of July dinner. After the banquet, the men drank thirteen formal toasts "with hearty good cheer and good feeling." The reporter noted, "Those who had survived up to this point" participated in ten additional "volunteer toasts."

The largest number of troops known to have been stationed at the fort was 800 immediately before the Mexican War. The contingent shrunk to a skeleton force of fourteen to maintain the buildings after the companies had been removed to fight against Mexico.

As the frontier moved westward, Fort Towson lost its military importance. It was abandoned June 8, 1854. During the Civil War, Confederate troops used the fort. In June 1865, two months after Appomattox, Gen. Stand Watie surrendered his Indian troops—said to have been the last organized Confederate force to surrender—at Fort Towson. The fort fell into ruins soon after.

The ruins have been stabilized, and the sutler's store has been reconstructed in accordance with the only written description of the building, found in 1851 editions of the *Doaksville Choctaw Intelligencer*. The fort is operated as a museum by the Oklahoma Historical Society.

Doaksville

The site of Doaksville is close to old Fort Towson. Established in 1821 by the Doaks brothers, two fur traders, the settlement became an important center for trappers, Indians, and white settlers as the frontier pushed farther and farther west. Shallow-draft Red River steamers and overland freight served the village. In 1833, seventeen boats discharged cargoes for Doaksville, such items as powder and shot, churns, and cloth. Furs and cotton were loaded for the return trips.

By a treaty made at Doaksville in 1837, the Choctaw Nation agreed, for $530,000, to grant equal rights in their country to the Chickasaws, and the boundaries of the Chickasaw district were defined. In 1855, the tribes agreed to formal separation and the Chickasaw district became the Chickasaw Nation.

The Reverend William H. Goode, writing in *Outposts of Zion* (1836), described the scene on annuity day as Chickasaws gathered to receive rations and annuity payments from the government:

> Some thousands of Indians are scattered over a tract of nearly if not quite a mile square around the payhouse. Here are cabins, tents, booths, stores, shanties; wagons, carts, campfires; ponies, mules, oxen and dogs; men, women and children; white, red, black and mixed in every imaginable shade and proportion and dressed in every conceivable style from the tasty American fop to the wild costume of the savage; buying, selling, swapping, betting, shooting, strutting, sauntering, talking, laughing, fiddling, eating, drinking, smoking, sleeping, seeing and being seen—all huddled together in one promiscuous and undistinguishable mass.

From 1850 until 1863, Doaksville was the Choctaw capital. The Choctaw Convention of 1860 was held at Doaksville; the constitution under which the Choctaw Nation operated was drafted at that convention. The first Masonic Lodge in Indian Territory was instituted at Doaksville—Doaksville Lodge No. 279—under jurisdiction of the Grand Lodge of Arkansas; many army officers and missionaries belonged to it.

The town's decline and eventual disappearance were due to war, discontinuance of river traffic, and finally the removal of the capital. Today only a cemetery and crumbling stones remain of the community.

—*Sawyer* - US 70————

This small town on the east bank of the Kiamichi River near the Lake Hugo spillway was called Miah in 1902. It was a product of the Arkansas and Choctaw Railroad. In 1903, the name of the post office was changed to Sawyer to honor Charles H. Sawyer, attorney for the Dawes Commission.

The site of Spencer Academy is approximately eight miles north. The academy was established in 1841 by the Choctaw Nation. It was long noted as a school for Choctaw boys. Students wore military uniforms and engaged in drills. Teachers were employed by the Presbyterian Board of Missions.

It was here that the well-known spirituals "Swing Low, Sweet Chariot," "Steal Away to Jesus," and "Roll, Jordan, Roll" were created. "Uncle Wallace" and "Aunt Minerva" Willis were slaves who belonged to Britt Willis. As was the custom, they took their master's surname. The slaves were on loan to Spencer Academy.

Uncle Wallace had created the words to the spirituals, and Aunt Minerva joined him in singing them. While in New York, Rev. Alexander Reid, superintendent of Spencer Academy, gave the words and melodies of the spirituals to the Jubilee Singers from Fisk University. The Jubilee Singers popularized them.

—Soper - US 70————

This is another rural town born of the Arkansas and Choctaw Railroad. The post office was established April 2, 1903, and named for P. L. Soper, a United States attorney. The story goes that Mr. Soper designated a sum of money to be paid by his estate to the town of Soper to erect a monument in his memory. However, after his death, by the time all of his debts were satisfied, the fund was depleted and there is no monument to P. L. Soper.

—Boswell - US 70—OK 109————

Originally established as Mayhew, a name taken from the old Mayhew Presbyterian Mission in Mississippi, the community was located two miles south of present-day Boswell. With the coming of the railroad in 1902, the town moved north and was renamed Boswell after a local merchant.

Boswell was strongly Indian in character. In a nearby cemetery there are Choctaw burials protected by the traditional grave houses. The custom of the "funeral cry" was long-practiced in Boswell.

HISTORICAL HIGHLIGHT
Choctaw Funeral Cry

A "funeral cry" was held twenty-eight days after the burial of a Choctaw. On the day of the burial, the surviving head of the family cut twenty-eight small sticks representing the duration of the lunar month. Each morning one stick was taken from the bundle and broken.

When only seven sticks remained, he sent invitations to kinsmen and friends to come for the cry on the day the last stick was broken. Each family brought its own provisions of corn meal, flour, beef, and vegetables and camped near the burying ground. The cry began with the recital by a close relative of the good qualities of the deceased. As he proceeded, the mourners gathered around the grave with covered heads and started to cry. This ceremony sometimes lasted for several days. In inclement weather, it was held in a church, lighted at night by candles.

EXCURSION

—Bennington—Roberta - OK 70E

OK 70E offers a relaxing drive through the rich farming area between Blue River and Island Bayou by way of five small rural communities: Bennington, Wade, Albany, Utica, and Roberta. The post office at Wade was established in 1890 and named for a prominent Choctaw. The other three towns were founded in 1894. Someone from New York obviously had a hand in selecting names for Albany and Utica. Roberta's name was a mistake. The town was to have been named for James Roberts, the first postmaster, but someone in the Post Office Department made it Roberta instead, and so it has been ever since.

—Bokchito - US 70

The post office dates from 1894. The community was incorporated April 27, 1901, with two hundred people living in what is now called "Old Town." The village moved to its present location when the railroad came through.

Bokchito was a progressive town: three banks, four doctors, a drugstore, grocery stores, and a stable. The first sidewalks were planks. The *Bokchito Times* began publication in 1905, claiming a "guaranteed circulation one-half thousand." Even in those days, allergies were a problem. On August 17, 1905, a banner across the top of the front page demanded: "Are you going to wait for Jack Frost to cut those weeds, or the fever to cut you down?"

The site of Armstrong Academy is located about two miles northeast of Bokchito. The institution opened in 1845, operated by the Baptist Mission Society for the Choctaw Nation to serve the western portion of the Pushmataha district. The school for Indian boys had thirty-five students the first year.

Eighteen students began with the alphabet, four with "easy reading," three in McGuffey's First Reader, and two in the Second Reader. During fall and winter, the first bell rang at four o'clock in the morning for those who had the tasks of building fires and sweeping out the sitting room. At five o'clock all students rose. Roll call was at 5:15, breakfast at 6:00. Classes started immediately after breakfast.

The Choctaw National Council held its sessions in the main hall of Armstrong Academy for twenty years. From 1863 until 1883 the site was renamed Chata Tamaha (Choctaw Town), and it served as the capital of the Choctaw Nation.

Armstrong Academy carried on an adult education program until 1921 when the school was destroyed by fire. Toward sunset on Friday evenings wagons bearing families began arriving at the campground in the clearing around the building. From Saturday morning to Sunday evening, classes for men and women were held in reading, writing, and arithmetic, along with religious instruction. Today nothing is left but a weedy cemetery and a few crumbling ruins.

—*Blue* - US 70————

This scattered, dwindling community on the Frisco railroad started in the middle 1800s as a Choctaw trading post at a survey marker, an iron stob. The year was probably 1846; at least the Philadelphia Baptist Church was established that year.

The site was about two miles southeast of its present location. The town moved to the railroad when it was completed in 1903. Its name derives from the nearby Blue River. Between 1890 and 1920 there were from 300 to 400 residents. The town burned in the early 1920s and was never rebuilt.

The first official reference to a school was to a log schoolhouse that existed in 1894. Today's visitor cannot help being impressed by the bright blue color of the high school. Members of the athletic teams are called Blue Warriors. "We do not paint our faces except on 'Spirit Day' or for support of our athletic teams," a teacher explained.

OK 78
Achille—Kemp

—*Achille* - OK 78————

A group of Cherokee refugees settled in the area during the Civil War. They called their community *atsila* (fire).

When the Kansas, Oklahoma and Gulf Railway (now Missouri Pacific) came past, a post office was established and named Achilla, but the name was shortly changed to Achille. When the railroad line was abandoned the town began to shrink.

The Bloomfield Methodist mission was located about three miles to the south. The missions brought men and women of superior character and intellectual achievement to the Indians. Missions served as inns for travelers and their locations often determined the routes of roads.

Bloomfield Academy for girls was established by the Chickasaw Council in 1853 under John H. Carr. Mission schools introduced the study of music and chromatic art, areas in which the Indians displayed natural talent. An extensive building was erected for Bloomfield Academy in 1896; it burned in 1914. All that remains today are footings of the building and gravestones marking the burial sites of prominent Chickasaws and missionaries. In 1917 Bloomfield Academy was moved to Ardmore and reopened under the name Carter Seminary.

—Yuba—Karma - OK 78———

Yuba is a rural town which was established during the late 1890s. It now serves as a trade and school center for various small communities in this bend of the Red River. Its post office was designated in 1898 and remained in service until 1932.

A post office in the neighboring town of Karma had been in business since 1929. In 1950, the residents of Karma requested that the name of their post office be changed to Eagle Lake; however, the Post Office Department arbitrarily assigned the name Yuba.

—Kemp———

Located in the southwest corner of the Chickasaw Nation, Kemp was settled in the 1880s with the name Warner Springs. The springs were located on a creek west of Main Street, and people came in wagons from around the country to haul water and do their washing. In 1890, the community was renamed Kemp, after Jackson Kemp.

Jackson Kemp was a prominent Chickasaw who resided in the area. In 1830, he had been an interpreter for the Chickasaw agency in western Alabama. He was one of three hundred Indians who arrived in Doaksville in 1838 during the Indian removal. At that time, according to the census, he owned 52 slaves, 17 horses, 90 cattle, 200 hogs, 47 sheep, 1 wagon, and 1 pleasure carriage. He was president of the Chickasaw Constitutional Convention in 1856, and senate president in 1869 and 1870. He became sheriff of Panola County, in which Kemp was located, in 1887. Various members of the Kemp family were granted charters to operate ferries across the Red River from 1876 to 1898.

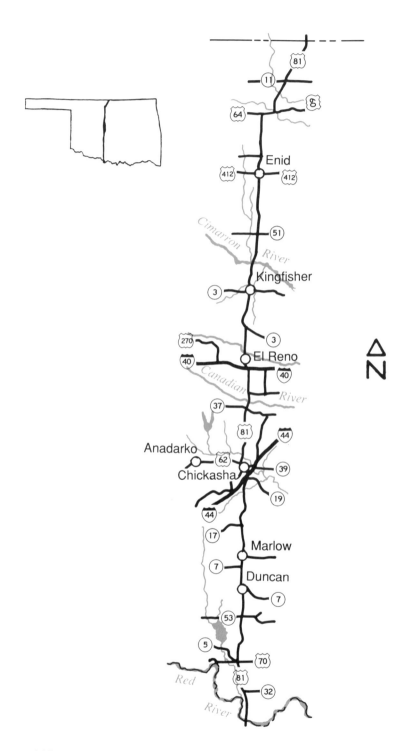

III. The Chisholm Trail

The route that eventually became known as the Chisholm Trail was first used by Jesse Chisholm, an Indian trader. His father was of Scottish descent; his mother was a Cherokee Indian. When the Civil War broke out, Chisholm and a number of other Indians left their homes in south-central Oklahoma and moved to a site near present-day Wichita, Kansas.

After the war, probably in the fall of 1865, Chisholm loaded wagons and headed south to Indian country on a trading expedition. He chose the most direct route allowing plenty of wood for campfires and water for both camping and cattle. These were essentials for freighters and, later, for cattle drovers.

Chisholm's route had been previously blazed by a Delaware Indian named Black Beaver, a guide for various army expeditions. Black Beaver knew of a dim path from water hole to water hole followed by buffalo in their annual migration from winter to summer feeding grounds. This was the route Chisholm traveled south to the North Canadian River. He returned in the spring of 1866 with buffalo robes and furs.

Jesse Chisholm died on March 4, 1868, before his name was associated with the route then becoming known as a cattle trail. The exact date of its use by Texas drovers is uncertain, but it is generally believed herds were driven over the trail as early as 1867. On September 5, 1867, the Kansas Pacific Railway loaded twenty carloads of bawling Texas longhorns at Abilene, Kansas, on a train destined for Chicago. This was the forerunner of the livestock traffic that swelled to fantastic proportions within a decade.

As soon as grass began to "green up" in South Texas, herds started moving north. Cattle were driven through Texas as quickly as possible because ranchers along the way did not want them eating their grass and drinking their water. Beyond the Red River, grass and water were free to the Kansas line. Cattle usually gained weight during the drive.

Between 1867 and 1871, almost a million and a half longhorns went up the Chisholm Trail, but Abilene's heyday was short-lived. Farmers' fears of Texas fever forced the drovers farther west as laws and hot lead pushed the "Dead Line" to the west of agricultural areas. Also, thanks to the recent and rapid development of barbed wire, Kansas ranchers and farmers south of Abilene began fencing off the trail and charging fees for allowing cattle to cross their lands.

Competition entered the picture when the Atchison, Topeka and Santa Fe crossed the Chisholm Trail at Newton in July 1871. Within a year the new railroad offered service direct to Chicago. The Kansas Pacific Railway sought to meet this serious threat to its most lucrative freight traffic by attracting drovers to newly developed stockyards at Ellsworth, Kansas.

The railroad published a *Guide Map of the Great Texas Cattle Trail from Red River Crossing to the Old Reliable Kansas Pacific Railway*. It was a pocket-sized booklet to be used by drovers on the trail. It described streams, camping grounds, wood, water, grass, trading posts, and other facts concerning thirty-three stops along the 328 miles of trail through sparsely populated Indian Territory, from the Red River to the grazing grounds at Ellsworth:

Names of Points	Distance Between Points	Total Distance	Description of Trail
Beaver Creek branch of . . .	15	15	Trail from Red River follows the divide through an open prairie, with an abundance of wood and water on the tributaries of the Beaver. The stream being small, the crossing is always good and safe. Good camping ground.
Monument Rocks or Stinking Creek	15	30	Trail from Beaver Creek over high rolling prairie; supply of wood and water abundant for camping purposes; small stream with good crossing. Good camping ground.

A typical herd of longhorns on the Chisholm Trail as illustrated in the Kansas Pacific Railway's guide map published in 1874 for the use of drovers on the trail.

Turkey Creek camp was noted as "Good camping ground, with plenty wood and water." But drovers were warned, "Take wood from here for camping purposes. No wood at Hackberry." At Pond Creek, where Sewell's Store was located, the guide noted: "At this point the route, opened last year, known as 'Cox's Trail,' diverges from the old trail and is the only route drovers can take and avoid trouble with settlers in Sumner, Sedgwick, and Reno counties, Kansas."

Settlers may not have been the principal offenders. Writing in 1874, Joseph G. McCoy laid blame on "outlaws and thieves" who used the fear of disease as "an excuse to pillage, kill, and steal." McCoy wrote:

> The practice was to go in force and armed to the teeth, surround the drover, insult him by words such as a cowardly bully only knows how to use, spit in his face, snatch handfuls of beard out of the drover's face, tie him to a tree and whip him with anything they could lay their hands on, tie a rope around his neck and choke him; in short, provoke him to a demonstration of resistance or self-defense, then kill him, and straightway proceed to appropriate his herd.

As a trail herd was made up in Texas, the animals passed through a chute and each received a "road brand." Cowboys furnished their own saddles and bedding; horses were usually supplied by the owner of the cattle. Bedding, food, and camp equipment was loaded in a chuck wagon driven by the cook; a "horse wrangler" handled the "remuda" or herd of horses. Cowboys received $25 to $40 a month and the cook $5 more. The trail boss, who was responsible for the herd, earned about $125 a month.

Jesse Chisholm.
—Western History Collections,
University of Oklahoma Library

Owners figured one man to each 300 cattle, plus the cook, wrangler, and trail boss.

The cattle were moved slowly until they were "road broken." After a few days—or weeks—they could be pushed along more rapidly. Two men at a time were usually sufficient to stand night guard in three shifts. Night guards soothed restless cattle by singing to them, and most cowhands of the day had a goodly repertoire of religious hymns at their command. A writer commented wryly: "Singing hymns to Texan steers is the peculiar forte of a genuine cowboy, but the spirit of true piety does not abound in the sentiment."

As the herd moved, a "point" consisting of two experienced hands directed the herd, prevented mixups with other herds, and checked any tendency to run. Swing riders rode about a third of the way back on each side to keep cattle from straying. Flank riders were about two-thirds of the way back for the same purpose. Drag riders, usually young and inexperienced, brought up the rear, hazing slow, lame, and lazy cattle along.

After cattle got trail wise, the stronger steers took the lead and usually held it to the end of the drive. A pecking order developed with the strong at the point and old cows and small calves at the drag. There are stories of old steers who were natural leaders; they were driven back to Texas to lead other herds to market. One old steer was such a favorite that cowboys had silver balls made for the tips of his horns.

A herd of 2,500 longhorns would cover the trail about fifty feet wide and stretch out for a mile. The cook drove the chuck wagon ahead to an agreed upon spot for dinner. When the herd arrived it was loose herded along a stream for a couple of hours before moving on to the place previously selected as a camp ground for the night. One vast herd of 25,000 head, belonging to several ranches, was driven only a few miles a day. It stretched five miles wide and twenty miles from point to drag.

The trail varied in width at stream crossings from fifty to a hundred yards. In other areas it spread from a mile to two miles in width. A day's drive would average between eight and twelve miles. Time on the trail between Texas and Abilene or Ellsworth, Kansas, was from sixty to ninety days, depending on the size of the herd and how much the cattle were allowed to graze along the way.

Thunderstorms were the bane of the trail driver's life, particularly if there were other herds in the vicinity. S. H. Woods, the horse wrangler with a herd of 3,000 head in July 1881, told of running into a storm:

> That night we had a terrible storm. Talk about thunder and lightning! [That was when] you could see phosphorescence (fox fire) on our horse's ears and smell sulphur. We saw the storm approaching and every man, including the rustler, was out on duty. About 10 o'clock at night we were greeted with a terribly loud clap of thunder and a flash of lightning which killed one of our lead steers just behind me.

Driving cattle across a river was tricky business. —Bartlesville Public Library

That started the ball rolling. . . . Finally so many herds had run together that it was impossible to tell our cattle from others. When lightning flashed we could see thousands of cattle and hundreds of men all over the prairie, so we turned everything loose and waited patiently for daybreak. The next morning all the different outfits got together and we had a general round-up. It took about a week to get everything all straightened out and trim up the herds.

Once across the Red River into Indian Territory, Indians became a problem. The usual demand was "Wohaw," their word for a steer, and the drovers could prevent their cattle from being stampeded or horses stolen by donating a lame steer. Some herd bosses would send one man ahead to keep buffaloes out of the herd and scout for Indians.

Col. Ike T. Pryor, a San Antonio cattleman, supplied information on the cost of driving cattle from Texas to markets in the northwestern states:

> To illustrate, I drove fifteen herds in 1884 from South Texas to the Northwestern States. . . . These cattle were driven in droves of 3,000 to each herd, with eleven men, including the boss, and each man was furnished with six horses.
>
> The salaries of these eleven men, including the boss, were $30.00 each for the ten men, including the cook, and $100.00 a month for the boss. This gave an outlay of $400.00 a month, and estimating $100.00 for provisions, there was an expense of $500.00 a month to move a herd of 3,000 cattle 450 to 500 miles. Briefly speaking, in those days it was possible to drive 3,000 cattle 3,000 miles for $3,000.00, or, in other words, from South Texas to Montana a herd could be driven of 3,000 head for not to exceed $3,000.00.

Literally millions of cattle were driven up the Chisholm Trail during the time it was in use. One authority estimated that more than a quarter of a million cattle crossed the Red River in 1867. The year 1871 was probably the peak. During that year, 600,000 head followed the route in herds varying between 2,000 and 3,000. By 1880 fences increasingly stretched across what had once been open ranges. By 1884 the trail was virtually blocked, strangled in barbed wire.

The traveler interested in retracing this historic route should take US 81 north from the Texas border to Kansas. Along the way, on most jukeboxes, one can find the familiar cowboy song that opens with the couplet:

> Come along, boys, and listen to my tale,
> I'll tell you a story of the old Chisholm Trail.

The Chisholm Trail entered Indian Territory at Red River Station and passed through the present sites of Waurika, Duncan, Chickasha, El Reno, Kingfisher, Enid, Pond Creek, and Medford.

—*Fleetwood—Fletcher* - US 81————

The Chisholm Trail crossed the Red River at Red River Station, on the Texas side of the river. It passed through Fleetwood and Fletcher. Fletcher faded long ago. Fleetwood—named for H. H. Fleetwood, who operated a ferry across the Red River—hung on as a small rural community.

—*Ryan* - US 81—OK 32————

Settlement of this struggling crossroads community dates from 1881, when it was called Baldwin. From 1888 until 1890 it was called Sugg; then the name was changed back to Baldwin. In 1893 the post office became Ryan, after an early-day resident.

In 1892, the Rock Island railroad arrived. Two years later, Ryan was awarded a federal court and a stone courthouse was built. At statehood, it became the temporary county seat of Jefferson County. During year-long political machinations, Ryan lost out in a bitter fight to retain its status as county seat. Since that time, the community has struggled.

—*Sugden* - US 81————

Sugden began as the IS Ranch, established by the Suggs Brothers, Carl and Ikard, during the late 1870s. Four miles east of present-day US 81, the Suggs Camp Ground was located on the Chisholm Trail. Reid's Store, on the trail two miles to the north, furnished supplies to drovers.

Sugg was the name of the post office at nearby Ryan until 1890. In 1892, when the railroad built across the IS Ranch, the ranch headquarters became the post office for Sugden. In 1907, the community had 160 citizens, and the Sugden *Leader* reached out to 175 families. The *Sugden Signal* began publication in 1906. In spite of valiant efforts on the part of the newspaper, the town lost out in its bid to become the county seat. It began a slide toward ghost-town status.

—*Waurika* - US 70-81————

The main route of the Chisholm Trail was five miles east of present-day Waurika, but the rich grassland surrounding Waurika was a favorite area to fatten cattle during the drives. As a community began to grow, its post office was named Peery in 1890. The Rock Island railroad came in 1892, and in 1895 the name was changed to Moneka. The town became a crew-changing point on the railroad with shops to boost the economy.

In 1901, the surrounding country, which had been part of the Kiowa-Comanche reservation, was opened to white settlement by land lottery. In 1902, a Rock Island official suggested a name-change: Waurika (Indian for "good water"). Soon stretches of alkali-whitened land alternated with pastures, wheat and cotton fields, and thin borders of timber along small creeks.

As farming and railroading dwindled, Waurika reached out to attract small industry. Raising parakeets was among the industries. With more than 300 residents producing birds for market, one dealer handled 850,000 a year, valued at $2 million. The state legislature issued a proclamation dubbing Waurika "Parakeet Capital of the World."

The town exploited a local pest—rattlesnakes—by organizing the annual Waurika Rattlesnake Hunt, attracting as many as 10,000 visitors to comb the surrounding countryside, join in a street carnival, and watch the crowning of a Rattlesnake Queen.

—Hastings - OK 5————

Hastings was established in 1902 on a branch of the Enid and Anadarko (now Rock Island) Railroad. The Hastings *Free Lance* began publication in 1904. Editor Willa Huser must have been a student of Shakespeare. A quotation from *Hamlet* appeared under the newspaper's title: "The friends thou hast, and their adoption tried, grapple them to thy soul with hoops of steel." By 1908, Hastings boasted a population of 1,000. However, the "hoops of steel" were apparently not strong enough; the community began to losing "friends" when its Southwest Academy moved to join the Oklahoma Baptist University in Shawnee, and shoppers and businesses gravitated to nearby Waurika.

—Addington - US 81————

This ranching community dates from 1896. It took its lifeblood from the 18,000-acre Price Ranch, established by J. C. Price three miles to the east in 1886. The Chisholm Trail ran through the middle of the ranch. Price had driven herds over the trail before settling down to ranching.

Monument Hill, more frequently called "Monument Rocks," is located three miles east of Addington. This was a well-known landmark on the Chisholm Trail. A nearby spring made it a popular camping spot, and over the years drovers added rocks to the pile until a substantial monument was created.

116

—Comanche - US 81—OK 53————

Before the coming of the railroad, Comanche's post office was called Tucker. The town started as a trading center for the surrounding ranching area in the Chickasaw Nation and the Kiowa-Comanche reservation. Stockmen leased ranges for their cattle at the rate of twenty-five cents per head. The Chisholm Trail was three miles to the east. In 1893, the name was changed to Comanche.

The land lottery in 1901. brought many new settlers, primarily farmers. Corn, wheat, and cotton became the principal crops. At one time Comanche had five cotton gins. An oil boom began in 1918, resulting in the construction of a refinery and a tremendous boost to the local economy.

—*Beckett* (Sunray) - US 81————

This "company town" was a product of the oil boom. Some 4,500 producing wells were drilled in the county, and Stephens County referred to itself with considerable pride as "The Buckle on the Oil Belt." Much farm land was given over to oil production, and many farmers gravitated to work in the oil fields.

—*Duncan* - US 81—OK 7————

Between Comanche and Duncan, US 81 crosses the trail followed by Capt. Randolph B. Marcy in 1852 during his search for the source of the Red River. The Chisholm Trail is only two miles east of the highway at Duncan.

In 1872, William Duncan, a former tailor at Fort Sill, married a citizen of the Chickasaw Nation and became a trader. He bought a store alongside the Chisholm Trail. When it was learned the Rock Island Railroad was coming through from the north, Duncan moved his store west. Mrs. Duncan acted under her tribal rights to select a 500-acre tract in the path of the railroad. The first train came through June 27, 1892.

A depot was built and a townsite was platted on Mrs. Duncan's land; a furrow was plowed around the site to mark the limits. As the railroad brought newcomers, Mrs. Duncan sold lots with the understanding that when it became possible to give legal title she would do so. The promise was carried out after allotment.

In 1920 Duncan was a town of about 3,000, largely dependent on agriculture. In 1921 oil gushed from the earth, and Duncan was absorbed by the oil industry. Erle P. Halliburton developed his oil well cementing business, an industry which would spread around the world from Duncan.

By 1940 Duncan had grown to 9,000. In 1947 new oil discoveries sparked additional growth, and by 1956 four large refineries operated in the area. Though it has become an industrial city, Duncan still celebrates its agricultural and ranching heritage with an annual livestock show, the Championship All Girls Rodeo, and a county fair.

—Marlow - US 81—OK 29————————

The town took its name from Dr. Williamson Marlow, father of the infamous Marlow brothers. According to local reports, the five brothers—Boone, Alfred, Epp, George, and Charles—spent their nights raiding herds coming up from Texas on the Chisholm Trail. They would drive longhorns into the timber east of the trail, then, a day or so later, drive them back to the herd and claim they had found them straying or in the possession of cattle thieves. Such deeds earned the brothers a reward.

Downfall of the Marlow brothers began when the sheriff of Young County came to arrest Boone Marlow for rustling. Boone killed the sheriff. A posse captured the five brothers. While in jail, they were attacked by a mob. Alfred and Epp were killed; the three remaining brothers escaped. Boone was later killed; George and Charley were captured and held for trial, but the charges were dropped and they left the county.

They turned up in Ouray, Colorado, where they served as law officers. In their seventies they wrote a lurid account of the affair back in Indian Territory. As might be expected, in *Life of the Marlows* they placed themselves in the best light. They wrote that Boone had been poisoned by people who were hiding him, and his body traded for the $1,500 price on his head. The other four brothers were greatly misunderstood.

Marlow began as a tent town in 1892, when the Rock Island laid tracks through the area. Holding pens and loading chutes were built to process cattle off the Chisholm Trail.

In the triangle formed by the junction of US 81 and OK 29 stands a pear-shaped, pink granite Monument to All Oklahoma Peace Officers. The killing of Sheriff W. A. Williams near this spot in 1930 inspired it.

—Rush Springs - US 81—OK 17————————

Rush Springs took its name from the flowing springs that formed the headwaters of Rush Creek. It was a favorite camping spot on the Chisholm Trail. One of those springs is in the center of the community's Municipal Park.

In 1892 a village known as Parr moved six miles west to the railroad, and the post office changed its name to Rush Springs. Parr was the site of the tragic Battle of the Wichita Village on October 1, 1858.

Battle of the Wichita Village

In late September 1858, Buffalo Hump and a band of Comanches were camped at a Wichita Indian village near present-day Rush Springs. Through the Wichitas, who were friendly to whites, they had been communicating with authorities at Fort Arbuckle regarding a treaty talk to settle intertribal differences. Buffalo Hump had been advised to bring his three leading chiefs to meet with the commandant at Fort Arbuckle. He had every reason to believe he was safe. Buffalo Hump's camp consisted of about 120 lodges.

On the morning of October 1, Major Earl Van Dorn led a cavalry force through the Comanche camp in a devastating surprise attack. The troops burned the lodges, killed fifty-six warriors and two squaws, and captured more than 300 horses. The army lost one lieutenant, one sergeant, and three privates, plus a number wounded.

Van Dorn's defense was that he was unaware of the peaceful nature of the Comanches' mission; he was under orders to pursue Indian trails without regard to the boundary between Texas and Indian Territory and exterminate Comanches in retaliation for their recent raids into Texas. It is small wonder that the Comanches continued to be avowed enemies of the Texans.

After service in the U.S. Army, Major Earl Van Dorn became a general officer in the Confederate Army. —Fort Sill Museum

—*East Ninnekah* - US 81————

This community on the railroad was established in 1892 by the Choctaw-Chickasaw Townsite Commission under direction of the Department of the Interior. The plat was not filed until 1902. The name came from Choctaw *ninek*, referring to night or darkness. The Chisholm Trail was only a mile east of the railroad track. At this point on the trail, the Cook Brothers Store was established in 1874 to serve drovers. Its post office, named Fred for Franklin L. Fred, an Indian trader, operated from 1884 until 1894. The Boggy Depot to Fort Sill road crossed the Chisholm Trail at this point, and there was a stage station about three miles east of Chickasha.

—*Chickasha* - US 81-62————

On the Chisholm Trail, the Rock Crossing of the Washita River was just east of present-day Chickasha. In 1890 a French-Canadian named Jacob Descombs built a store on the north bank of the river. He named the post office Waco. That was a mistake: Mail addressed to Waco, Indian Territory, ended up in Waco, Texas. People said they should change the name of the post office.

"*Pensée*," said Monsieur Descombs, meaning in French that he thought it was a good idea.

Listeners thought he was suggesting a name, and on September 11, 1891, Waco officially became Pensee, Indian Territory. The Pensee settlement did not last. Residents and businessmen moved south to be at the division point of the Rock Island. The railroad called the station Chickasaw, but the Post Office Department misread the application and the town has been Chickasha since June 22, 1892.

Prior to the coming of the Rock Island that year, the townsite was part of the Swinging Ring Ranch, owned by James L. Speed, an intermarried citizen of the Chickasaw Nation. The ranch house was near the corner of 11th Street and Kansas Avenue.

The first industrial development was a cottonseed oil mill. Cattle feeding pens used "cake," the residue from the cottonseed oil mill, to fatten the thousands of steers that were shipped out every month. By 1902, Chickasha had become a "city of the first class" with a population of 6,370. It supported two daily and two weekly newspapers.

Not all of Chickasha's early citizens were progressive in their attitudes toward modern innovations. In 1904 a doctor and a couple of others brought automobiles to town. Protest precipitated an injunction issued in federal court against driving cars on Chickasha Avenue between Sixth Street and the Rock Island Depot "for the reason they frightened horses and were therefore dangerous."

Street scene on Chickasha Avenue, about 1897. The photograph may have been taken during a Fourth of July celebration. —Western History Collections, University of Oklahoma Library

After statehood, growth of the city was slow but steady. The establishment of a railroad division point, agricultural diversification, and development of local industry broadened Chickasha's economic base. The city was less dependent than most communities on the peaks and valleys of the oil business. In 1908, establishment of the Oklahoma College for Women (now the co-educational University of Science and Arts of Oklahoma) assured a lasting intellectual and cultural atmosphere.

EXCURSION

—*Tuttle* - OK 37-92

This prosperous community also dates from the arrival of the Frisco railroad. It was named after James H. Tuttle, a local rancher. A 12-ton boulder beside OK 37 on the east edge of town marks the course of the Chisholm Trail. Bearing the names of 112 pioneers, the marker is "Dedicated to Ranchmen, cowboys, early settlers, and their descendants." Tuttle has fared better than most central Oklahoma agricultural towns. Due to its proximity to Oklahoma City, it has grown as a bedroom community.

The land Tuttle sits on was the subject of lengthy court litigation. The question was whether the secretary of the interior could cancel the original allotment and segregate the land for townsite use. Ownership was in limbo until 1915.

Main Street, Tuttle, 1908, on the occasion of the sale of lots.
—Western History Collections, University of Oklahoma Library

Early ranchers in the area had to ride herd on their cattle and horses at night or keep them in pens to prevent them from joining buffalo herds and drifting away. Blacks and Indians were hired as herders because Kiowa and Comanche raiders preferred white scalps.

—*Pocasset* - US 81————

This small agricultural village was established shortly after the Rock Island railroad built its line in 1890. It was named for an Indian village of the same name in Massachusetts. The town was the scene of a bizarre train robbery. Al Jennings—who was successively a lawyer, train robber, convict, candidate for governor of Oklahoma, amateur evangelist, and author—led a gang in a badly bungled holdup. They tried to dynamite a safe in the baggage and express car and blew up the whole car. The frustrated outlaws then robbed passengers of jewelry and some $400 in cash. From the wrecked car they salvaged a bunch of bananas and a two-gallon jug of whiskey before riding away into the night.

—*Minco* - US 81—OK 37————

The Chisholm Trail passed seven miles east of Minco. The trail crossed the South Canadian River by way of the Bond Crossing. Settlement began in 1889 and the railroad arrived the following year, but construction was delayed during 1890-91. Later, Minco became a busy cattle shipping point and attracted herds and trade from a wide area. Today, grain elevators signify the importance of wheat to the economy of the area.

122

—*Mustang—Piedmont* - OK 4———

To the north of the South Canadian River, the Chisholm Trail divided: the east fork went through the present-day communities of Yukon and Piedmont in the outskirts of Oklahoma City; the west fork was used principally as a wagon and stage road. Most of the cattle were driven north through Yukon and Piedmont, at which point the trail angled northwest to Red Fork (Dover). To follow the east fork, take OK 152 from Union City east to Mustang and OK 4 north to Piedmont. Mustang dates from 1895. Yukon was founded in 1891. It became an agricultural and milling center with a concentration of Czechoslovakian families. Piedmont started as an agricultural trade center in 1903. All three are now residential satellites of Oklahoma City.

—Union City - US 81———

This small trading point for farmers and ranchers was established as Sherman, four miles west of the Chisholm Trail, in 1881. On the western edge of the Chickasaw Nation, some of the white residents married Chickasaw women and became adopted citizens, some operated small ranches on leased lands, and others were intruders defying tribal laws.

When the area opened for settlement in 1889, the official name of the post office was changed to Union. Locally, the town was called Union City, and it made its way onto highway maps by that name.

—*El Reno* - US 81-270—I-40—OK 66———

First there was Reno City, across the Canadian River from present-day El Reno. With a population of 1,500 two months after the run of April 22, 1889, and tracks of the Choctaw, Oklahoma and Gulf Railroad (later Rock Island) heading its way, Reno City looked forward to having a railroad connection. Railroad officials announced the customary levy of cash plus a substantial number of town lots for the privilege of having the railroad come through town. The people of Reno City refused to pay.

Railroad officials found El Reno more cooperative and swung the line south. Most of the residents of Reno City then loaded their household goods on wagons and moved across the river to El Reno. Buildings, even a three-story hotel, were mounted on crude rollers and scooted across the bed of the shallow river. El Reno profited from its investment in the railroad, becoming one of the state's largest rail centers as the Rock Island built repair and maintenance shops and opened division offices.

In 1892 the Cheyenne and Arapaho reservation was opened to settlement by a land run. In 1901 a lottery was held for claims in the vast

The crowd at the El Reno land lottery in 1901 was estimated at
145,000. —Western History Collections, University of Oklahoma Library

Kiowa-Apache-Comanche reservation, the last area in the territory
opened to white settlement. On both occasions, El Reno was inundated
by homeseekers. The crowd during the 1901 lottery was estimated at
145,000, most of whom left as soon as the drawing was completed.

HISTORICAL HIGHLIGHT
Fort Reno

Five miles west of El Reno, about two miles north of I-40, old Fort Reno
is now an agricultural research station operated by the U.S. Department
of Agriculture and Oklahoma A&M University.

Fort Reno was established in 1874 to protect the Cheyenne-Arapaho
Agency at nearby Darlington during and following the Cheyenne uprising
of 1874. By March 1875, the rebellious Cheyennes were subdued. The
leaders were put in irons and sent to Fort Marion, Florida, for imprisonment. The commissioner of Indian affairs predicted this unnecessary
cruelty would stimulate further resistance and more bloodshed.

While the Arapahoes were glad to have their children attend the
mission school at Darlington, the Cheyennes viewed the school with
disdain; Cheyennes did not need a school to learn how to hunt buffalo.
In October 1876, a detachment of soldiers from Fort Reno accompanied
the Cheyennes on their annual buffalo hunt. About 7,000 animals were
killed. Additionally, Indians in the neighborhood of Fort Reno tanned
15,000 skins for traders who paid them two dollars each.

The following year, the buffalo hunt was a dismal failure. The Indians brought back only 219 robes to sell and received only 640 skins to tan. The Indian agent's report for 1879 stated that the buffalo were all gone; the government must prepare to furnish subsistence to the Indians 365 days of the year.

From 1880 until 1885, the principal occupation of the garrison at Fort Reno was trying to keep David L. Payne and his Boomers out of Oklahoma Territory. On one occasion, a party of about sixty illegal settlers headed for Council Grove, not far from present-day Oklahoma City.

Lieutenant Taylor, with a detachment of troopers from Fort Reno, captured the party, but Payne was away on a hunting expedition. Taylor sent two troopers to bring him in. The wily Boomer saw the soldiers coming, got the drop on them, disarmed them, and marched them back to the military camp. He informed Lieutenant Taylor that he had a couple of deserters for him. Having been informed it was "not prudent" to arrest Payne, Lieutenant Taylor escorted the Boomers back to the Kansas line.

During the opening and settlement of Oklahoma Territory in 1889, soldiers from Fort Reno were assigned to guard the boundaries, keep order among the homeseekers camped along the border, and prevent the encroachment of Sooners. At noon on April 22, 1889, they fired the shots that signaled the beginning of the race for homesites in Oklahoma.

Troops from Fort Reno officiated at putting down an inner-tribal rebellion during the winter of 1900-01. By that time, the Five Civilized Tribes had agreed, albeit reluctantly, to break up their tribal governments and accept allotment of their lands. There was a holdout, Chitto Harjo (Crazy Snake), a Creek traditionalist also known as Wilson Jones.

Fort Reno, I.T., looking northeast.
—Western History Collections, University of Oklahoma Library

Chitto Harjo ("Crazy Snake") leader of the Crazy Snake Creek Rebellion. —Western History Collections, University of Oklahoma Library

Chitto Harjo led a protest movement to establish a new Creek government. Based upon old tribal law and custom, he and his followers arrested people who accepted allotments and whipped them in public. Creek Chief Pleasant Porter called for help, and soldiers from Fort Reno rounded up the rebels. They were convicted in federal court at Muskogee and paroled on the condition that they reconcile themselves to the new conditions.

This was the last stand of the Five Civilized Tribes for their treaty rights. Chitto Harjo was their last hero.

The Fort Reno, I.T., to Caldwell, Kansas, stagecoach, ready to start the 120-mile run. —Western History Collections, University of Oklahoma Library

Fort Reno was abandoned as a military post on February 24, 1908. After service as a remount depot, it became an agricultural research station.

—*Concho* - US 81————

The Cheyenne-Arapaho Agency was established in 1869 about five miles northwest of El Reno on the bank of the Canadian River. Generally called the Darlington Agency, it was opened by Brinton Darlington, a Quaker Indian agent appointed by President Grant. With stage lines connecting it to various points in Texas, Kansas, and Oklahoma Territory, it became an important community. A school and a Mennonite mission were established there.

By 1897, the Cheyennes no longer wanted to share the Darlington Agency with the Arapahoes. Separate facilities were established for them at Caddo Springs. The Darlington Agency was abandoned in 1909, and the Cheyennes and Arapahos were again united at Caddo Springs. The agency continues to this day in some of the same brick and frame buildings. Caddo Springs, however, was renamed Concho in 1915. The word is Spanish for "shell"; Charles E. Shell was the Indian agent at the time. Caddo Springs is still flowing.

—*Okarche* - US 81————

Okarche grew around a cattle-loading station on the Rock Island railroad following the opening of the Cheyenne-Arapaho reservation by a run on April 19, 1892. The name was coined from the first syllables of OK(lahoma), AR(apaho), and CHE(yenne).

The surrounding lands were farmed by German-speaking Catholics, Lutherans, Evangelicals, and Mennonites. The town once had a German-language newspaper. The German heritage is still an important part of community life.

—*Kingfisher* - US 81—OK 33————

Prior to the land opening in 1889, King Fisher Station was a stage stop on the Chisholm Trail. In April, people planning to participate in the run for homesteads were allowed to assemble in the Cherokee Outlet on the north side of the unassigned lands, in the Cheyenne and Arapaho country on the west line, and along the South Canadian River to the south.

After a pistol started the race at noon on April 22, some 2,500 "West Liners" occupied choice lots at King Fisher Station. They named their town Lisbon. About two hours later, "North Liners" arrived and staked lots north of the earlier group and called their town Kingfisher.

Ruts of the Chishom Trail are still clearly visible from the air.
This photograph was taken a few miles northeast of Kingfisher,
east of US 81. —Robert L. Klemme

The deep, narrow ruts of the Chisholm Trail in the vicinity of the townsite had overgrown with grass. During the mad rush, horses broke their legs and vehicles were wrecked. The countryside was so dry that sand blew from the creek beds, and water sold for five cents a bucket. Two weeks later the drought broke. Kingfisher Creek flooded, and the northern part of town was inundated to a depth of seven or eight feet.

Lisbon and Kingfisher joined, and the growing town became known locally as "The Golden Buckle of the Wheat Belt."

—Dover - US 81————

A small agricultural community today, Dover was known long before the area opened to settlement as Red Fork Station. Freighters hauling supplies to Indian agencies and forts in Indian Territory followed the Chisholm Trail. Red Fork served as a supply depot and change-station from the late 1860s to the 1890s.

During the Cheyenne uprising in 1874, it was fortified with troops from Fort Sill so teamsters could safely change horses. Freighters often had to detour to avoid delays by the massive northbound herds.

—Hennessey - US 81—OK 51————

On July 4, 1874, Pat Hennessey escorted a train of three wagons southward over the Chisholm Trail to the Kiowa-Comanche agency. Indians attacked, presumably Cheyennes, killing and scalping the three teamsters who were with Hennessey, then tied him to a wagon wheel and burned him alive. From 1874 until the opening of Oklahoma on April 22, 1889, passing freighters on the Chisholm Trail paid homage to Pat Hennessey by leaving stones at his grave with their initials and the dates of their visit. During the run on April 22, 1889, tents blossomed around the grave and a town grew, named Hennessey in honor of the freighter.

Initially, Hennessey was an agricultural community surrounded by wheat and diversified farming. It experienced boom times with the discovery of oil and gas, and it still keeps Pat Hennessey's memory green with an annual community celebration.

HISTORICAL HIGHLIGHT
Mail-Order Brides

Hennessey was the scene of a marriage resulting from advertising for a bride, not uncommon on the western frontier where men far outnumbered women. In 1893, a 24-year-old German emigrant had a sod house and a bedroll; he had planted an orchard on his claim. He had land but he had no wife. His friends suggested he place an advertisement in one of the matrimonial newspapers that flourished during that period:

> I have a good income, own improved acres, a German, Methodist faith; age is 24, height 5 ft. 4 in., weight 158; brown hair, blue eyes, most amiable disposition. Want to correspond with some good, kind hearted lady (not wealthy) with view to marriage.

In Illinois, the advertisement was read by a 26-year-old woman whose first marriage had not lasted. She had a 4-year-old daughter. Alwina Bush and August F. Yuhnke exchanged letters and photographs. Six months later Alwina went to Hennessey, Oklahoma Territory, for the wedding and they lived happily ever after.

Ranchers called mail-order brides "catalog women." Ramon F. Adams, in *Western Words: A Dictionary of the Range, Cow Camp and Trail*, quoted Alibi Allison's definition: "One o' them widders that wants 'er weeds plowed under."

—Bison - US 81——————

During the heyday of the Chisholm Trail, a popular camping spot near present-day Bison was known as Buffalo Springs. The springs are about a mile north of Bison and they still flow. This was Pat Hennessey's last campsite before the Indians killed him.

It was also a camping place for home seekers waiting to engage in the Run of April 22, 1889, for unassigned lands. A military escort accompanied wagon trains from Caldwell, Kansas. The crowd was said to have numbered 10,000, putting a considerable strain on the water supply at Buffalo Springs.

A 160-acre claim was staked by Abraham R. Roseboom. His widow sold the claim and it was acquired by J. C. Ward on August 8, 1901. The plat for Bison was laid out on this land, and by August 31 a post office was established. Wheat assured Bison's early prosperity.

—*Waukomis* - US 81———

This small agricultural community was established in November 1893, just after the opening of the Cherokee Outlet. Its name is supposed to be a modification of the phrase "walk home us," tracing back to a time when a railroad official missed a train and had to walk back to Enid. At this point, the old Chisholm Trail is synonymous with Main Street in Waukomis.

—*Enid—North Enid* - US 81-412———

An apocryphal story credits the origin of Enid's name to a sign advertising a restaurant—DINE—having been accidentally turned upside down. The truth is more mundane. The first official train carrying M. A. Low, vice-president and general council of the Rock Island, arrived at the end of the line in August 1889.

"What's the name of this place?" asked Low.

The business section of Enid in 1902.
—Western History Collections, University of Oklahoma Library

"Skeleton," was the reply. That was the name of the ranch and stagecoach stop on the nearby Chisholm Trail.

"We'll not have that name. Nobody would want to live in a town with such a name. We will name it Enid."

Enid became one of Oklahoma's "instant towns," springing from raw prairie to a tent city teeming with thousands of homeseekers in a single day. It had a head start. The government had chosen the site for a land office. Surveyors and troops had already run section lines and platted townsites. The Rock Island railroad had built a depot and was furnishing service.

Interior Secretary Hoke Smith discovered that some shrewd Cherokees had chosen allotments within the area planned for the town, so he ordered the townsite—including the government land office, county courthouse, and post office—moved three miles south of the original settlement around the railroad station.

A feud developed between the two communities. Each claimed the name Enid and dubbed the other a suburb. People at the north site called the government town "South Town"; people at the south site called the railroad settlement "Tank Town." Travelers leaving the train at what they thought was Enid had to hire a rig to get to the business section; those in the south had to go to North Enid to get their freight. The Rock Island railroad adopted a high-handed attitude:

WE INTEND TO DESTROY
THE CITIES OF SOUTH ENID AND SOUTH POND CREEK

These cities were created without our permission or consent; and while the cities may be better than those which we selected, and may be the choice of the people, yet the precedent is such that we cannot permit it to exist.

On July 13, 1894, a Rock Island freight train stopped in Enid, but not because the railroad had had a change of heart. Skilled hands had been at work with saws on the underpinnings of a bridge at the south edge of Enid. The engine and two cars of a northbound train made it across the bridge before it crumpled.

Enid's first celebration of the town's founding and the opening of the Cherokee Outlet came one year later, in 1894. Fifteen thousand came to watch a reenactment of the race, and 150 Cheyennes entertained the crowd with tribal dances and ceremonies. But it was not a happy time. Wheat was bringing 35 cents a bushel, eggs sold for 8 cents a dozen, extra fine salmon 5 cents a can. A three-year drought was beginning.

In 1897 the rains came, and better times were ahead. Wheat shot to a dollar a bushel. Ringling Brothers' circus came to help the town celebrate, and 30,000 people attempted to squeeze into a big top that would hold only 20,000.

Today, Enid is blessed with a healthy economy and numerous cultural and social assets.

HISTORICAL HIGHLIGHT

John Wilkes Booth: Dead or Alive?

In Enid, on January 13, 1903, David E. George, a house painter, a drifter who drank a lot and quoted Shakespeare when he was in his cups, committed suicide. The incident attracted little attention until the man's body was being embalmed. The Rev. E. D. Harper, a Methodist minister, walked into the funeral parlor and told the embalmer that the body was that of John Wilkes Booth, Abraham Lincoln's assassin. After a previous attempted suicide he had confessed to the minister's wife and another woman.

"I believe I am going to die," George had told Mrs. Harper. "I'm not an ordinary painter. I killed the best man that ever lived."

The embalming process turned the corpse into a mummy. The mortician tied the body into a chair, opened its eyes, placed a newspaper on its lap, and Enid had a new tourist attraction. It also sparked a national controversy.

Shortly after "John Wilkes Booth's" death, the undertaker dressed the mummified body, placed him in a chair, put a newspaper in his hands, opened his eyes, and took this photograph. The body was displayed at carnivals for many years. —Robert L. Klemme

Everybody knew that an army sergeant named Boston Corbett had killed Booth in a burning tobacco barn near Bowling Green, Virginia. On the other hand, doctors examined the mummified body and reported that everything matched John Wilkes Booth including a broken leg Booth suffered when he jumped from Lincoln's theater box after the assassination. Other telltale marks were scars on the back of the neck and in the right eyebrow and a deformed right thumb.

Finis L. Bates, a Memphis attorney, appeared to identify the body as that of John St. Helen, who had been his client when he practiced law in Granbury, Texas, in 1872. St. Helen had also confessed to Bates on what he thought was his deathbed that he was John Wilkes Booth. John St. Helen—or Booth—recovered, and Bates forthwith wrote to the War Department in an effort to collect the $100,000 reward offered for John Wilkes Booth. The War Department informed Bates that they took "no interest" in the matter. After all, they had already paid the men who cornered Booth in the tobacco barn.

Bates acquired the mummified corpse. He wrote a book entitled *The Escape and Suicide of John Wilkes Booth* with the subtitle *Written for the Correction of History*. He rented the mummy out to carnivals and finally sold it. The mummy passed from hand to hand. It was last heard of in a cellar in Philadelphia in the 1950s, held as security from a roomer who died owing rent. R. K. Verbeck, of Ohio, paid $15 for it, but when he went to pick it up in 1958 the neighborhood had been demolished in a slum-clearance project.

Was David E. George, itinerant house painter, John Wilkes Booth? Much has been written pro and con, but the question has never been answered to a certainty and the evidence has disappeared.

—*Pond Creek* - US 60-81————

The site of this agricultural community was called Round Pond in April 1889, when the race for homesites was scheduled to take place. It was the southern terminus of the Rock Island. It was also the Pond Creek station on the old stage route from Kansas to Fort Sill.

As April 22—opening day—drew near, the Rock Island engaged D. R. Green, owner of half a dozen rickety stagecoaches, to carry Rock Island passengers who intended to make the run to the border. Green waited in his "Leadville Cannon Ball" stagecoach with a caravan of coaches, wagons, hacks, buggies, and buckboards strung out behind him. As soon as the train was unloaded, Green started his rush to the border. It must have been a memorable experience over forty miles of rutted prairie.

Round Pond was named for a natural lake on the Chisholm Trail. Shortly after the run, a group of farmers plowed a furrow from the Round

Pond lake to Pond Creek until the furrow was deep enough to partially drain the lake. They took out several wagon loads of fish by spearing them with pitchforks. Water still accumulates in the lake.

—Jefferson - US 81————

Just south of town a grove of elms and cottonwoods marks the site of Rock Island Park, once planned as a townsite. But when the railroad came through, it was too far away to be of value, and its few residents moved to Jefferson. Jefferson was the site of Sewell's Ranch on the Chisholm Trail, now located about a half-mile south of Jefferson. During the 1870s, Sewell built a stockade to protect drovers from Osage Indian mourning parties and raiders.

It was an Osage custom to bury a tribesman with the scalps he had taken. It was unthinkable to send a warrior to the next world without at least one scalp. However, as warfare between tribes waned, scalp-taking became more and more uncommon and the problem of getting a trophy to bury with the dead was increasingly acute. And so arose the custom of sending out a secret "mourning party" to bring in a scalp. Since the killing of a Pawnee or other Indian could lead to intertribal warfare, the scalps of isolated white men were in steady demand.

In 1873, Ed Chambers came north with a Texas herd; as he searched for strayed cattle near where the Black Dog Trail crossed Pond Creek, an

Troopers find a victim of a "mourning party," Indians who had collected a scalp to bury with a dead warrior. —Western History Collections, University of Oklahoma Library

Osage mourning party in search of a scalp found him. His grave is about a mile south of Jefferson.

—*Medford* - US 81—OK 11————

This community on the northern edge of Oklahoma's most productive wheat-growing region was established with the opening of the Cherokee Outlet in 1893. It was named for Medford, Massachusetts, and it became the county seat of Grant County in 1908, a year after statehood.

—*Renfrow* - US 81————

This tiny agricultural community is dominated by its grain elevators. It was established on the Rock Island railroad in 1894, a year after the opening of the Cherokee Outlet. It is named for W. C. Renfrow, the third governor of Oklahoma Territory. The Chisholm Trail passed a little less than a mile east of Renfrow.

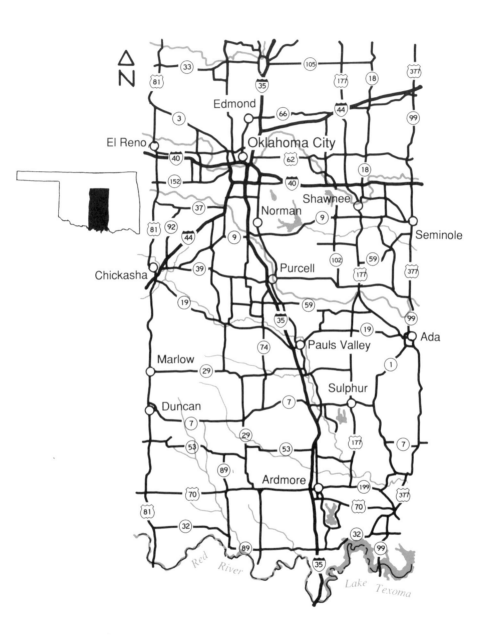

IV. Boomers and Sooners:
The Settlement of Oklahoma

Immediately after the Civil War, present-day Oklahoma was Indian Territory, a thinly populated checkerboard of tribal nations and reservations, and "such other tribes of Indians as the Government may desire to locate therein." Each tribe held the "unrestricted right of self-government, and full jurisdiction over persons and property within their respective limits."

As cattlemen drove herds through the area to railheads in Kansas they noticed its prime pasture land. During their drives north, drovers began to linger for weeks or even months to let their cattle fatten. Unwittingly, the cattlemen were paving the way for white settlement of Indian lands.

Viewing the area as a source of investments and markets, bankers and merchants in Missouri and Kansas joined the railroads in the campaign to usurp the area. The railroads hired land promoters called Boomers to whip up enthusiasm among homeseekers. T. C. Sears, a lawyer for the Missouri-Kansas-Texas Railroad, announced that he and Elias C. Boudinot, a Cherokee attorney, had found 14 million acres of public land in Indian Territory that could be filed on by qualified settlers.

"These lands are among the richest in the world," declared Sears. "Public attention is being called to them and my opinion is that, if Congress shall fail to make suitable provision for the opening of the Territory within a very short time, the people will take matters into their own hands and go down there and occupy and cultivate those lands."

True to Sears' prediction, Boomers gathered on the Kansas border to organize colonial expeditions into Indian Territory. The first was launched in May 1879 by Charles C. Carpenter. Carpenter was characterized by an official of the Indian service as a "bragging, lying nuisance." The entrepreneur was warned by a presidential proclamation, and troops appeared to block incursion. Carpenter's following evaporated, but the idea did not die.

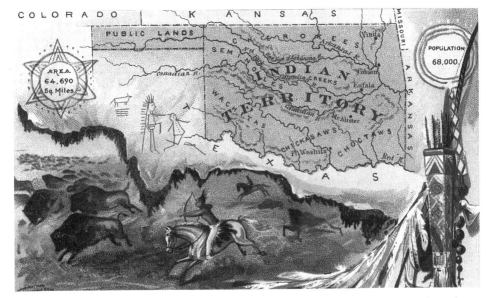

This Arbuckles' Coffee premium card, published shortly prior to the opening of Oklahoma to white settlement portrayed the area as belonging exclusively to Indians.

David L. Payne was next to take up the cause. On May 15, 1880, Payne and eleven companions were arrested about forty miles east of Fort Reno in a heart-shaped stretch of "unassigned lands" in the middle of Indian Territory. Payne maintained that soldiers had driven him from his "home" on public domain. A fine of $1,000 was assessed but never collected, and Payne went back to recruiting potential homesteaders.

Payne organized Payne's Oklahoma Colony. He exhorted his followers with a biblical paraphrase: "And the Lord commandedeth unto Moses to go forth and possess the promised land.'" He called the unassigned lands "New Canaan," and adopted "On to Beulah Land" as his colony's marching song.

Payne led seven expeditions into Oklahoma. He was arrested for the last time in August 1884. He died on the morning of November 28 in Wellington, Kansas, while making plans for his eighth invasion. His motives and reputation notwithstanding, Payne's activities on behalf of the settlement of Oklahoma were commemorated by a county named after him.

After Payne's death, the Boomers' cause was carried on by his associates. By 1885 more than a thousand court cases were pending against Boomers, but the laws in effect did not authorize criminal prosecution for trespass upon Indian lands.

The Boomers won.

On March 3, 1889, just before Congress adjourned, a rider was attached to the Indian Appropriations Bill providing for opening the unassigned lands to settlement. On March 23, President Benjamin Harrison issued a proclamation for the opening to take place at noon on April 22. Eastern newspapers called it "Harrison's Horse Race."

Any man or single woman twenty-one or over could claim 160 acres by being the first person to place a stake on the property. Within a few days, the claimant had to go to a government land office in Kingfisher or Guthrie to file a claim. The filing fee was $20. The government required homesteaders to "prove up" on land in five years by living on the premises six months of each year, building a house, and planting a portion of the farmland. After that, they could apply for homestead certificates and be granted ownership.

By the opening date, thousands of people had congregated along the Kansas border. At Arkansas City, the crowd swelled to 10,000; others gathered at Caldwell, Hunnewell, and elsewhere. Similarly, eager homeseekers were poised on the bank of the South Canadian River at

GRAND RUSH

FOR THE

INDIAN

In 1879, Charles C. Carpenter was recruiting Boomers for an illegal colonizing expedition into Indian Territory. The movement was blocked by presidential proclamation and troops. —H. Dick Clarke

TERRITORY !

NOW IS THE CHANCE
—TO—

PROCURE A HOME

In this Beautiful Country!

Over 15,000,000 Acres of Land
NOW OPEN FOR SETTLEMENT !

Being part of the Land bought by the Government in 1866 from the Indians for the Freedmen.

THE FINEST TIMBER !
THE RICHEST LAND !
THE FINEST WATERED !
WEST OF THE MISSISSIPPI RIVER.

Every person over 21 years of age is entitled to 160 acres, either by pre-emption or homestead, who wishes to settle in the Indian Territory. It is estimated that over Fifty Thousand will move to this Territory in the next ninety days. The Indians are anxious to have the whites settle up this country.

The Grand Expedition will Leave Independence May 7, 1879

Independence is situated at the terminus of the Kansas City, Lawrence & Southern Railroad. The citizens of Independence have laid out and made a splendid road to those lands, and they are prepared to furnish emigrants with complete outfits, such as wagons, agricultural implements, dry goods, groceries, lumber and stock. They have also opened an office there for general information to those wishing to go to the Territory. IT COSTS NOTHING TO BECOME A MEMBER OF THIS COLONY. Persons passing through Kansas City will apply at the office of K. C. L. & S R R, opposite Union Depot, for Tickets.

ABOUT THE LANDS.

In answer to inquiries concerning these government lands in the Indian Territory, Col. E. C. Boudinot sends the following from Washington:

FIRST—In reply I will say that the United States by treaties made in 1866, purchased from Indian tribes, in the Indian Territory, about 14,000,000 acres of land.

SECOND—These lands were bought from the Creeks, Seminoles, Choctaws and Chickasaws, by their treaty of 1866.

The Creeks, by their treaty of 1866, sold to the United States the sum of $975,168. The Seminoles, by their treaty of 1866, sold to the United States 2,169,080 acres, for the sum of $325,362.

The Choctaws and Chickasaws, by their treaty of 1866, sold to the United States the "leased lands" lying west of 98 degrees of west longitude, for the sum of $300,000. This number of acres in this tract is not specified in the treaty, but it contains about 7,000,000 acres.

Of these ceded lands the United States has since appropriated for the use of the Pac and Foxes 479,667 acres and for the Pottawatomies 575,877 acres, making a total of 1,055,542 acres. These Indians occupy these lands by virtue of treaties and acts of Congress. By an unsettled agreement, the Wichita Indians are now occupying 743,610 acres of these ceded lands. A previous act acting some action will be taken by the United States government to permanently locate the Wichitas upon the land they now occupy. The title, however, to these lands is still in the United States.

By executive order, Kiowa, Comanche, Arrapahoe, and other wild Indians, have been brought upon a portion of the ceded lands, but such lands are a part of the public domain of the United States, and have all been surveyed and sectionized. A portion of these 14,000,000 acres of land, however, has not been appropriated for the use of either Indians and all probability never will be.

THIRD—These unappropriated lands are situated immediately west of the 98th degree of west longitude and south of the Cherokee Territory. The soil is well adapted for the production of corn, wheat, and other cereals. It is unsurpassed for grazing, and is well watered and timbered.

FOURTH—The United States have an absolute and unembarrassed title to every acre of these 14,000,000 acres, unless it be to the 1,054,544 now occupied by the Sac and Fox and Pottawatomie Indians. The Indian title has been extinguished. The articles of the treaties with the Creeks and Seminoles, by which they sold their lands, begin with the statement that the lands are ceded "in compliance with the desire of the United States to locate other Indians and freedmen thereon." By the express terms of these treaties the lands bought by the United States were not intended for the exclusive use of either Indians nor has one been so often asserted. They may be made as much for the negroes of this country as for Indians.

ADDRESS

WM. C. BRANHAM,
Independence, Kansas.

To parties accompanying my Colony, I would advise them to purchase their Outfit at Independence, Kas., I have examined Stock and Prices of Goods, such as Wagons, Plows, Lumber, Dry Goods, Groceries, and, in fact, everything that is needed by Parties settling upon new Land, and find them as cheap as they can be bought in the East.
RESPECTFULLY YOURS,

Col. C. C. CARPENTER.

P. S.—Parties will have no trouble getting transportation at Independence for hauling their goods into the Territory. G. G. G.

Captain David L. Payne and the leaders of the Boomer movement. —Western History
Collections, University of Oklahoma Library

Purcell. The total number of participants may have reached 100,000, but 50,000 is probably realistic.

At precisely noon on April 22, 1889, a signal officer raised a bugle to his lips and gave a long, loud blast while waving a flag. Shots rang out, and the race began. A mass of humanity, on foot and in every available mode of conveyance from bicycles to trains, surged into New Canaan.

There are hundreds of descriptions of the run by participants and eyewitnesses. Perhaps the best at capturing the spirit of the occasion is a composite assembled forty years later by Edna Ferber in her novel, *Cimarron,* as Yancey Cravat told of his experience:

> "Folks, there's never been anything like it since Creation. Creation! Hell! That took six days. This was done in one. It was History made in an hour—and I helped make it. Thousands and thousands of people from all over this vast commonwealth of ours. . . . As I got nearer the line it was like ants swarming on sugar. Over the little hills they came, and out of the scrub-oak woods and across the prairie. They came from Texas, and Arkansas and Colorado and Missouri. They came on foot, by God, all the way from Iowa and Nebraska! They came in buggies and wagons and on horseback and muleback. In prairie schooners and ox carts and carriages. . . ."

The movie version of *Cimarron* was introduced in 1930. Its opening portrays the frenzy of the run as the bigger-than-life hero Yancey Cravat participated in the race.

140

Few photographs of the 1889 land run exist; the reporters in attendance were too busy staking their own plots to take pictures. Eyewitnesses testified that 10,000 people camped the night of April 22 on the present site of Oklahoma City. Within a few days, Guthrie, which was to become the state's first capital, had approximately 30,000 people camped among a sea of tents.

There were not enough home sites for all of the participants. Fewer than 12,000 quarter-section claims were available. The shortage was exacerbated by "Sooners" who surreptitiously entered the district and staked claims in advance of the opening. Initially these early birds were called "Moonshiners" because they slipped in the night before "by the light of the moon." The term Sooners did not come into use until five or six months after the run. Today, the opprobrium is used with pride by residents who designate Oklahoma as the Sooner State.

Other portions of Oklahoma were opened later as the Indians lands were systematically turned over to white settlers by clauses such as "whereas, it appears that said land is no longer used or required for use by said Indian agency" and so on. But none was as dramatic as the Run of April 22, 1889.

On May 2, 1890, Congress created the Territory of Oklahoma, consisting of all of Indian Territory except that occupied by the Five Civilized Tribes and Greer County, which was still claimed by Texas. By June 1906, all of the Indians had been coerced into giving up their tribal governments. On June 16, 1907, President Theodore Roosevelt issued a proclamation declaring Oklahoma a state. Indian Territory existed no more.

I-35—US 77
Orlando—Oklahoma City

I-35 bypasses the majority of the communities on US 77. Exit numbers are included for the benefit of travelers who use the freeway but want to get off and visit some of the historic communities along the way.

—*Orlando* (Exit 180) - US 77————

Orlando is built on land that was homesteaded on April 22, 1889, the day of the opening, by Warren—or Orlando—Hysell (sources differ as to his name). Hysell paid the government $1,600, or $10 per acre, to have his land proved up at once for a townsite. The town was laid out around the railroad station called Cherokee until the Orlando post office was established in July 1889.

The town pursued its rural ways until the opening of the Cherokee Outlet. Almost overnight, Orlando grew to a tent city with a population of about 60,000. On September 15, 1893, hopeful homeseekers headed into the Cherokee Outlet, leaving Orlando to return to normal.

Orlando's next period of excitement came in 1896 when a group of swindlers "salted" a farm southwest of town. The "pay dirt" assayed $185 to the ton. Gold fever infected the town and a number of local businessmen invested, only to discover that gold did not naturally occur there.

—*Mulhall* (Exit 170) - US 77————————

On April 22, 1889, the day of the opening of unassigned lands to settlement, present-day Mulhall consisted of a depot and stockyards on the Santa Fe Railway. It was called Alfred. The train bearing homesteaders arrived shortly after noon. Col. Zack Mulhall, a livestock agent for the railroad, also arrived. Mulhall donated lots upon which to build a town, as did two other homesteaders with adjacent claims. The Santa Fe Railway changed the name to Mulhall.

During the days of "Uncle Zack" Mulhall, the town prospered as headquarters for his 80,000-acre ranch, which stretched north into the Cherokee Outlet. Colonel Mulhall entertained visitors by staging rodeos. In 1900 he hosted Theodore Roosevelt with a show that featured his daughter, Lucille, as "the world's first cowgirl." Will Rogers started performing with Mulhall's show and went on to twirl his rope into the limelight on a worldwide basis.

In 1901 Carrie Nation came to Mulhall. She visited the two local saloons in town and issued warnings that she would be back. The citizenry forthwith voted the saloons into oblivion.

—*Guthrie* (Exits 157 & 153) - US 77—OK 33————————

Prior to the opening on April 22, 1889, Guthrie was a reddish-brown Santa Fe depot. A post office had been established April 4. During the run, Guthrie attracted more people than any other community in the new territory. It was the site of one of the two land offices in the area; it was a station on the railroad; it was the projected capital of the new territory.

Before sundown on April 22, fully 15,000 homeseekers were swarming about the Guthrie station. Existing statutes said no townsite set aside from the public domain should include more than 320 acres, a space a half-mile wide and a mile long. Before the dust from the land rush settled, claimants to lots covered a space approximately four times the size permitted by law. The people had a solution to the legal problem. They laid out four townsites—Guthrie, East Guthrie, Capitol Hill, and West Guthrie.

142

U.S. Land Office and army troops in Guthrie during the survey of townsite streets for the opening. —Western History Collections, University of Oklahoma Library

A "Committee of Thirty-two" was established and its first act was to decide that each of the four townsites should organize separately. In Guthrie three candidates for mayor emerged, and political rivalry threatened to turn into physical combat. The chairman halted the attempt to elect by voice vote and devised a new method of balloting.

Three farm wagons were lined up, and a candidate got into each wagon. Voters formed lines to pass the wagons of their favorite candidate with a teller in each wagon counting heads as they passed. But "ballot stuffing" became apparent. After passing a wagon, voters were returning to the rear of the line and coming around to be counted again. The convention adjourned until the following day.

By compromise between candidates, on April 25, Col. D. B. Dyer, of Missouri, became the unanimous choice for mayor. A tent was designated as City Hall. Most beginning communities in Oklahoma had city councils composed of four or eight members. Guthrie elected seventeen to the ruling body.

Fights, shootings, and killings were common between multiple claimants for lots, but a tent was hardly a suitable jail. Besides, the councilmen were unsure of their legal authority; they left the settlement of brawls to U.S. marshals. The city fathers were more interested in municipal income.

*Lawyers quickly set up offices in Guthrie. George M. DeGroff was
ready to assist in filing claims. He would also buy and sell land
claims and town lots.* —Western History Collections, University of Oklahoma Library

Their first acts were to establish licensing power and decree "that no
games of chance be permitted on the grounds of the City used as Public
Highways." On April 27, the city treasurer collected twenty-seven fines
of $5.00 each for operating such activities as "Chuck Luck," "Dice Case,"
"Prize Soap," "Spindle Game," and "Stud Poker."

The council established an arbitration board to settle contests over
building lots and charged 50 cents for title certificates. Similar activities
were underway in the other three adjacent townsites. On August 4, 1890,
East Guthrie allowed itself to be annexed by the "Village of Guthrie."
Shortly afterward Capitol Hill and West Guthrie followed suit and the
city was consolidated.

After staking a town lot in Guthrie, the next problem was to occupy it.
—Western History Collections, University of Oklahoma Library

By May 1889, Guthrie was a sea of tents and shacks. —Western History Collections, University of Oklahoma Library

Guthrie was the capital of Oklahoma Territory from 1890 to 1907. After statehood, it was the capital of the state of Oklahoma until 1910. Then disaster struck; a black Republican from Guthrie, A.C. Hamlin, won a seat in the Oklahoma House of Representatives.

Already shaken by widespread Republican victories in the 1908 elections, Hamlin's election inspired the Democrats to draft a bill in August 1910 that limited the voting power of blacks. Despite the efforts of Republicans and blacks to defeat it, the bill passed. In opposition to the Oklahoma Enabling Act, which decreed the capital would remain at Guthrie until at least 1913, Democratic governor Charles N. Haskell took steps to move the capital to Oklahoma City, declaring Guthrie a "Republican nest."

Guthrie's saloons did a thriving business during the early days.
—Western History Collections, University of Oklahoma Library

On June 11, 1910, the matter was put to public vote with Guthrie, Oklahoma City, and Shawnee vying for designation as the capital. Oklahoma City won. On the night of June 11, Governor Haskell sent his secretary to Guthrie to get the state seal. The next morning he proclaimed that the Lee Huckins Hotel in Oklahoma City was the new capitol.

Guthrie displays a historical marker that maintains the capital of Oklahoma was "stolen" by Oklahoma City.

Guthrie revels in its past and has done a monumental job of historical restoration and preservation. It boasts one of the largest districts on the National Register of Historic Places, 400 blocks containing more than 2,000 buildings. It has a "collection" of more than 1,300 Victorian homes built before 1910. Visitors should obtain a map from the Guthrie Chamber of Commerce to the city's historical sites and museums.

Annually, Guthrie stages a three-day '89ers Day Celebration, which includes street dancing, a rodeo, a carnival, and a historical parade known to attract as many as 100,000 spectators.

—*Meridian* (Exit 157) - OK 105————

East of Guthrie on OK 105, Meridian was named because it sat astride the Indian Meridian, the line which formed the eastern boundary of the unassigned lands. When the town was platted, the meridian became the main street with a township on either side. A post office was established in a store in 1894. The townsite was not laid out until 1902 when the Missouri-Kansas-Texas Railroad built through town.

Soon after, the Fort Smith and Western branch line to Guthrie came through. Two cotton gins were built and H. A. Booth thought the town showed enough promise to support a newspaper. The *Meridian Eagle*'s motto was "The Eagle Screams for a Greater Meridian." Apparently the *Eagle* did not scream loud enough; the paper began publication in March 1905, and ceased in July.

—*Seward* (Exit 151)————

West of US 77 on Seward Road, the community of Seward traces its beginning to high noon on April 22, 1889. Frank Cooper, a Santa Fe Railway engineer, stopped his train here and staked 160 acres of land while his passengers waited on board. Cooper and his family moved onto the land. Two years later he sold lots and started a town.

There was already a sign—SEWARD—where an east-west cattle trail crossed the railroad. It was where cattlemen who wanted to go to Texas or Kansas City flagged the train. Cooper adopted the name. Seward was one of several rural communities in Oklahoma that had a sizeable black population.

—*Edmond* (Exit 141) - US 77————

The community began in 1887 as a coal-and-water stop and a cattle shipping point on the Santa Fe Railway. According to the story, during the Run of '89, Nanitta Daisey of the *Dallas Morning News*, convinced the engineer to allow her to ride on the cowcatcher of the engine. As the train neared Edmond, she jumped off the engine, ran to a nearby plot, planted her stakes, fired a pistol to emphasize her ownership, and then raced back to the train where admiring spectators pulled her aboard.

With Central State University, Edmond is primarily a college town. The institution was established as a "normal school" in 1891 with twenty-three students, the first institution of higher learning in Oklahoma Territory. The school was sixty years ahead of its time. In 1895 an attempt was made to enroll black students, six decades before the United States Supreme Court decreed it mandatory.

—*Oklahoma City* - I-35—I-40————

The site that became Oklahoma City had several buildings prior to the land opening on April 22, 1889. The Santa Fe Railway had a depot, a section house, and a home for the station agent. The federal government had built a shack for a post office called Oklahoma Station. A stage company with a line passing through the area had built a stockade, and a family operated a boardinghouse.

The area had a generous allotment of brazen Sooners. The Sooners justified their illegal entry prior to the opening on the grounds that the

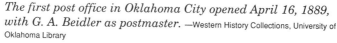

The first post office in Oklahoma City opened April 16, 1889, with G. A. Beidler as postmaster. —Western History Collections, University of Oklahoma Library

railroad right of way was private property and not public domain. They proceeded to lay out Main Street running westward at a right angle to the railroad tracks and to stake out lots on both sides of the street—the principal business section of present-day Oklahoma City. Since the direction of streets was controlled by the railroad and not by points of the compass, the so-called Seminole townsite lay at an angle to accepted surveying procedure.

When legal settlers began to arrive an hour or so later they found the choice lots had already been claimed by people who were willing to sell at the going rate of $25 each. A later group surveyed an additional townsite on cardinal points of the compass. Their "main street" is present-day Reno Avenue. This accounts for the jogs in streets and the odd-shaped lots that exist between Grand Avenue and Main Street.

As rival townsite organizations developed, warfare broke out between the Seminole Townsite Company and those who arrived later. The "Seminoles" won by threat of bloodshed and became the constituted authority. Certificates issued by the Seminole Townsite Company were declared as evidence of ownership. Later, Dan W. Peery told how it was:

> This Seminole Land Company claimed that they were a duly orga-
> nized and incorporated company, and that it was their townsite and
> they had a right to issue these certificates and charge the lot holders
> for them. Of course the town government upheld the company in this
> contention. Many lot holders got these certificates but some refused
> to contribute to the company and were promptly evicted by the city
> officials. If objections were made, the lot holder was brought at once
> before Judge [O. H.] Violet and either paid a fine or was thrown into
> the bastile.

Oklahoma City just northwest of the Santa Fe Depot shortly after the Run of 1889. —Western History Collections, University of Oklahoma Library

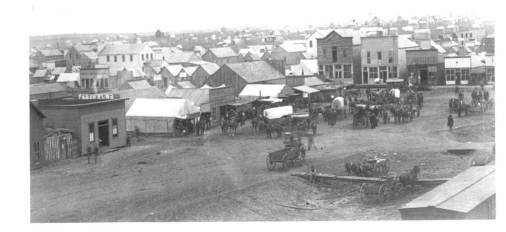

The city jail filled with indignant claimants who refused to pay tribute to the Seminole company or to recognize their certificates. Others refused to pay the fines assessed by the police judge. Many were forced to work out their fines through hard labor in the city streets.

It was obvious the Seminoles had the upper hand. When the opposition proposed a new charter, Mayor Couch succeeded in getting the commander of a company of United States infantry stationed in the city to use his troops to disperse voters who came to the ballot boxes. Finally, a United States marshal replaced the provisional government with his deputies. The contention was not resolved until May 2, 1890, when President Harrison approved the Organic Act of Congress providing for the establishment of Oklahoma's territorial government. The first legal city election was held August 9, 1890.

Oklahoma City became the permanent capital of the state in 1910. The first capitol building was the Lee Huckins Hotel. Governor Charles N. Haskell checked into the hotel with the state seal in his hand and posted a hand-lettered sign proclaiming the hotel as the official Capitol. Ground was broken for the beginning of construction of the present Capitol Complex on July 20, 1914.

On December 4, 1928, the Oklahoma City Oil Field was discovered, changing the city's image forever. The well came in a gusher, producing 6,500 barrels of oil every twenty-four hours, and the race for black gold was on. Oklahoma City became a sea of derricks. Before it was over, there were twenty-four wells pumping on the grounds of the state capitol.

Petunia Number One, in front of the capitol building, is the most obvious. Its legal description is Capitol Site #1. It got its nickname because drilling was started on November 10, 1941, in the middle of a flower bed. The well was completed 172 days later, and it produced for forty-four years. It was plugged on July 11, 1986, in such a way that it could maintain the appearance of a working well. Ownership was transferred to the Oklahoma Historical Society.

The most rambunctious well was Mary Sudik, which came in with a roar in the mid-1930s. It was a deep, uncased hole. The force of the gusher spewed drill pipe through the derrick. For eleven days, 10,000 barrels of black crude every twenty-four hour spread about the country-side in oily globules, spattering homes, Oklahoma City buildings, live-stock, automobiles, and people as far as fifteen miles away. Radio newscaster Floyd Gibbons gave twice-daily reports on "Wild Mary's" belligerence until the well was tamed. Today she flows no more; she is merely a deep hole in the ground in the southeast industrial area of Oklahoma City.

Over the years, Oklahoma City has grown to a lusty metropolis by absorbing outlying settlements. Real estate developers and entrepreneurs have created adjoining subdivisions and communities that have

Oklahoma City oil fields with Mary Sudik No. 1 blowing wild. —Western History
Collections, University of Oklahoma Library

incorporated to preserve their individuality against the expansion of Oklahoma City. Subsequently they were encircled by the sprawling metropolitan area. The following treatment of these communities begins with Bethany, to the west of Oklahoma City, and proceeds clockwise around the city.

—Bethany - OK 66————

Upon casual inspection it is difficult to distinguish the dividing line between Oklahoma City and Bethany, but it is there, a moral dividing line. Bethany began in 1908 when the Bethany Nazarene College was moved from Oklahoma City. Under influence of the Nazarene church, theaters, pool rooms, and dance halls were forbidden, as was the sale of beer and cigarettes. Urban sprawl has slightly diluted the influence of the church, but Bethany is still a highly religious community.

—The Village—Nichols Hills—Warr Acres————

These three suburban communities are now a part of the Oklahoma City metropolitan complex, hardly distinguishable as separate entities. The Village was incorporated as a separate municipality in 1950. Its name comes from Euclid Village, a Cleveland, Ohio, suburb.

Developed and incorporated in 1929 by G. A. Nichols, Nichols Hills was Oklahoma City's first exclusive and highly fashionable suburb. It is a mile-square area limited by North Western and Pennsylvania avenues and Northwest 63rd Street and West Wilshire Boulevard.

Warr Acres, on OK 66, was incorporated in 1948 by C. B. Warr as a separate suburban community. The name of the school system—Putnam City—reflects the earlier history of the area. In 1909, as Oklahoma City campaigned to have the capital moved from Guthrie, a real estate promoter named I. M. Putnam acquired the land, filed a townsite plat, and built a large structure he hoped would become the capitol of Oklahoma. The building was partially destroyed by fire and remodeled several times. It now serves as part of the Putnam City school plant.

—*Lake Aluma—Forest Park*—————

Lake Aluma is a posh municipality on the northeastern outskirts, created from a game preserve. The corporate name is Aluma Chulosa, a Choctaw phrase generally translated as "peaceful retreat." That translation is somewhat bowdlerized. A Choctaw will tell you that the phrase actually refers to a place in the bushes used as a comfort station.

Incorporated in 1956, Forest Park is situated within the western edge of the Cross Timbers. The name derived from the growth of blackjack and other oak within the townsite.

—*Spencer* - US 62—————

Spencer began as a town called Munger on the Frisco railroad in 1899. In 1903, the name was changed to honor A. M. Spencer, a railroad developer. It has since become a haven for people seeking refuge from the pace of city life.

Jones, on the North Canadian River, was originally called Glaze. In 1898, the name was changed to Jones for C. G. Jones, an Oklahoma City industrialist and railroad promoter who, in 1907, served as "groom" in a symbolic wedding ceremony uniting Oklahoma and Indian territories to create the state.

Nicoma Park was established in 1929 by developer G. A. Nichols. The name of the community was coined from the developer's name and Oklahoma.

A town started as Choctaw City in 1890, the year following the opening of the territory to settlement. The word "City" was dropped from the name in 1896, after the arrival of the Choctaw Coal and Railway Company. The town has been virtually swallowed by the suburban sprawl of Oklahoma City.

—Midwest City - US 270————

Midwest City was established in 1943 to serve Tinker Air Force Base, which was activated on March 1, 1942, as Midwest Air Depot. During its early days, the community was called "Mudwest City" by the airbase employees who lived there. It has grown with the aviation facility, which remains the largest employer in the area. Its boundaries are scarcely distinguishable from Oklahoma City.

—Tinker Air Force Base - US 270————

This military installation is a city within itself, complete with bus service and a golf course. It draws 25,000 employees from a wide area. There are more than 200 miles of runways and roads. During World War II it was used for the repair of B-24 and B-17 bombers. As the war progressed, services were expanded to include fitting B-29s for combat. One special B-29, the Enola Gay, was processed in hushed secrecy. She had a date with destiny to bring the war to an end by dropping an atomic bomb.

—Del City - US 70————

Casual motorists may not distinguish Del City from Midwest City or from Oklahoma City, but there is a difference. As late as 1946 there were only two families living in the area that is Del City. George Irvin Epperly owned a 160-acre wheat field at what is now 29th Street and Epperly Drive. The community started with fifty low-cost, pre-cut, pre-subassembled homes. By 1948 there were 582 living units. That was the year the community was incorporated, taking its name from George Epperly's daughter Delaphene. By thirty-five years later, in 1983, Del City had grown to a thriving community of 36,000, the eighth largest in the state.

I-35—US 77
Moore—Texas Border

—Moore (Exit 117) - I-35—US 77————

Present-day Moore is believed to have been the site of a camp occupied by Washington Irving in 1832 while his party participated in a buffalo hunt.

As a community, Moore had its beginning as one of thirteen water stops on the Santa Fe Railway south of the Kansas border. If the railroad had its way, Moore would be called Verbeck. However, before the Run of '89, Al Moore, a conductor, had trouble getting his mail delivered. He painted his name on the side of his boxcar-home, and when the town was incorporated it was called Moore.

At the time, a town seeking incorporation had to have a population of at least a hundred. A man named William Jury was assigned to take a census. According to the family story, he could find only ninety-nine men, women, and children. This included five or six business owners and some thirty homeowners. As he and others discussed the bleak prospects for incorporation, Bud Cottrell's jackass brayed out in the street.

"Let's count him and make it an even hundred," Jury suggested.

Thus, Moore's application for incorporation was submitted listing the population as "an even 100."

At first Moore grew slowly, but its location between Norman and Oklahoma City resulted in a growth rate officially measured in the 1960s at 952.2 percent. Today it is a commuter community with most of its residents employed in Oklahoma City, Tinker Air Force Base, and Norman.

—Norman (Exits 110A-B & 106) - I-35—US 77————

In 1870 the U.S. Land Office initiated a survey of land west of the "Indian Meridian" between the Red River and the Canadian. Abner E. Norman, of Kentucky, was in charge of a party that established a camp three-eighths of a mile south of the intersection of Classen Boulevard and Lindsey Street in present-day Norman. To taunt the young supervisor of their crew, members of the party removed the bark from a large elm and burned the words "Norman's Camp" into the tree.

On July 4, 1884, the Southern Kansas Railway, a construction subsidiary of the Santa Fe, received authorization to build a railroad across Indian Territory. The railroad got a 100-foot right of way plus an additional 100 feet for cuts and fills where needed. At ten-mile intervals, 13.5-acre plots were granted for station grounds.

By April 15, 1887, the track went past Norman's Camp, and a boxcar was emblazoned Norman's Switch. The first train came by on June 13. Prior to the land run of April 22, 1889, only four townsites had been designated in the unassigned lands: Guthrie, Oklahoma City, Kingfisher, and Norman. During the race for land, Norman did not attract as many settlers as Guthrie, Oklahoma City, and Kingfisher.

By nightfall of the first day of the run, Norman had an estimated 500 residents compared to 15,000 in Guthrie and 10,000 in Oklahoma City. At the first meeting of the town council, on May 20, 1889, the townsite plat was adopted. Problems developed with "lot jumpers." The second ordinance required registration or re-registration of all lots at a fee of 75 cents. The town marshal deputized twenty men to pick up a building erected on the wrong lot and move it.

By January 25, 1890, *The Norman Transcript* boasted of the community's two newspapers, four churches and "twenty-nine business houses of importance." Liquor could be sold only for "medicinal, chemical or mechanical" purposes by dispensers approved by the county commissioners. Five drugstores were authorized to sell liquor to a population of less than a 1,000. It was reported that immediately after the licenses were approved there was an outbreak of sickness, and mechanics and chemistry became popular hobbies.

The first attempt at higher education in Norman failed. In June 1893, High Gate College for girls opened under auspices of the Methodist Episcopal Church. Promotional brochures may have appealed to parents, but it is doubtful if the students were thrilled by their promise: "Young ladies desiring to have a good time will not find this institution to their liking."

High Gate's students were not allowed to "attend places of amusement." All correspondence from students was censored. Male faculty members were required to wear silk neckties and Prince Albert coats when appearing on the street to promote the dignity of the institution. Before Christmas 1894, both teachers and students were gone from High Gate.

Although Norman's economy would eventually derive almost exclusively from higher education, a century ago it was principally a center for marketing cotton. During the harvest, Main Street was literally paved with cotton as farmers brought their crops to town to have them ginned and baled. Buyers would cut handfuls of cotton from the bales, examine them, and throw the samples on the ground as they made their bids to the farmers.

East Main Street, Norman, during cotton-ginning season, circa 1900. —Western History Collections, University of Oklahoma Library

Football game in 1889, University of Oklahoma vs. Arkansas City.
—Western History Collections, University of Oklahoma Library

A bill establishing a university at Norman was signed on December 19, 1890, by George W. Steele, the first territorial governor, but there was a catch. Cleveland County residents had to approve $10,000 in bonds to assist in the construction of a building, and the town of Norman had to donate forty acres of land as a site. *The Norman Transcript* reported "much rejoicing" on May 19, 1891, when the bond issue passed. *Transcript* editor Ed Engle dubbed Norman the "Athens of Oklahoma."

A contract was let for the university's first building in March 1892. When finished, it stood three stories high with a basement the entire length; it was "the largest public building in Oklahoma." The cost was $15,739. David Ross Boyd became its first president at a salary of $2,000 per year.

However, the building was not ready for the September 15 opening. Classes were held on the second floor of a business building on West Main Street. The teaching staff consisted of President Boyd and two faculty members. By 1893, enrollment reached "approximately 100 students." The new building was completed in 1893, sitting in the midst of a barren prairie where Evans Hall stands today at the end of the North Oval. The building burned on January 6, 1903.

Football assumed early importance. On Thanksgiving Day 1899, the Sooners were in their fourth season as an undefeated team when they met the Railroaders of Arkansas City. Ark City took an early 17-5 lead, but an OU runner tore off a run of 70 yards to score; a touchdown and a goal kick tied the game. With minutes remaining, an OU player broke through the Railroaders' line and made for the end zone. It looked like a sure win until an enthusiastic fan jumped out on the field to get a better view. The runner slowed to avoid the spectator, a Railroader tackled him, and the Sooners went down to their first defeat.

In 1964, Clyde Bogle, who had been a student and football player in 1899, reminisced about the game:

> The rules were different. We had five yards, three downs. Now you have 10 yards and four downs. There was no passing whatever. We didn't have huddles, you waited for him [the runner] to get up, and as soon as you could get hold of the ball, it was time to play again. . . . Sometimes we'd have to stop the game and shoo them [spectators] off the field. . . . [Players wore long hair] in order to protect their heads. If you didn't have any other piece of equipment, you had shin guards. They kicked in those days. . . . We wore anything we could get hold of. . . . There was no standard uniform.

EXCURSION

—*Little Axe* - OK 9————

This small community east of Norman off OK 9 was formerly the location of Friends Mission, established in 1897 to serve the Absentee Shawnees. About 1845, this division of the Shawnees left the rest of the tribe, then in Kansas, and moved to Indian Territory. Some of the group sought greener pastures in Mexico and returned with an infusion of Mexican blood. Little Axe was named for Mexican Billy Little Axe, an early-day store owner. The Friends Mission is gone, but Little Axe has an impressive school facility.

—*Brendle Corner* - OK 9————

Rumor contends that during the heyday of gangsterism in Chicago, Brendle Corner was a vacation hideout for members of "the mob." One Chicago attorney was wont to catch a Friday evening train out of Chicago, spend two days relaxing in the rural quiet of Brendle Corner, and return on Sunday evening to courtroom rigors in the Windy City.

—*Noble* - US 77————

This community was founded in 1889 at the opening of Oklahoma Territory. It was originally designated as Walker by the Santa Fe Railway, but the name was changed when Albert Rennie, the founder, drew up the townsite. Rennie established the town with high hopes, but Noble stood in the shadow of nearby Norman. A college was organized in Noble in 1891, a year before Oklahoma University opened its doors. Until 1895 Noble Academy was the largest institution of higher learning in the county, drawing more than two hundred students from all over Oklahoma Territory and Texas. The influx created a housing shortage, and some students had to live in dugouts. However, financial troubles beset the school's backers, and their problems were compounded when Oklahoma University began to provide tuition-free education. The academy closed in 1895.

Noble now prospers as a bedroom community for Oklahoma City and Norman. On May 22, 1990, residents of Noble voted in a new charter to convert the statutory township to a home-rule city. Thus, after more than a century, Noble officially became a city.

—Slaughterville————

The community consists of some twenty-five sections of land about five miles east of US 77. Residents incorporated in 1970 to avoid annexation by nearby Norman. The town was named for a popular local blacksmith and merchant. Some residents believe the name should be changed because "slaughter" has an unpleasant connotation. What is reputed to be the largest rose rock quarry in the world is located in Slaughterville.

—Lexington - US 77-OK 39————

Late in the summer of 1835, a short distance northeast of present-day Lexington at a place called Camp Mason, a council was held between the Five Civilized Tribes and several Plains tribes. Some 5,000 attended and worked out a peace treaty that lasted until the Civil War. Also in 1835, the Chouteau family established a trading post at Camp Mason. In 1849, Chouteau's post was the last stop where gold-seekers en route to

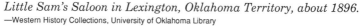

Little Sam's Saloon in Lexington, Oklahoma Territory, about 1896.
—Western History Collections, University of Oklahoma Library

California could buy supplies. Jesse Chisholm patronized the post during his trips through Indian Territory.

Before the land run of 1889, five Kentuckians selected a site for a town on the north side of the Canadian River. They prepared the necessary documentation and on April 22 took a train to Guthrie where they filed the papers, naming the community Lexington after a town in their home state. Thus, Lexington has the distinction of being the oldest town in Oklahoma Territory.

Its citizens immediately dedicated themselves to slaking the alcoholic thirsts of nearby Indian Territory residents. The town was variously called "Booze Capital of Southern Oklahoma Territory," "Fun City," and "Sand Bar Town."

Estimates of the number of saloons have varied between twenty-one and thirty. Prostitution and gambling thrived. The bubble burst in 1907, when Oklahoma was granted statehood. It came into the Union as a dry state on November 16.

Lexington has survived fire, flood, and Prohibition. Today an active chamber of commerce advertises, "We Have Room To Grow."

—*Purcell* (Exit 91) - I-35-US 77-OK 39————

According to an early issue of *Sturm's Oklahoma Magazine*, four settlements in the Purcell area anxiously awaited the arrival of the Santa Fe Railway. They knew that somewhere on the high ground just out of the Canadian River bottom a town would be built on the Chickasaw side of the river.

Two ranchers named Love and Sparks had hay pens and a corral on the present site of Purcell. They employed an engineer to lay out a town. He platted the first four blocks on a piece of wrapping paper. Love and Sparks plowed furrows to mark streets and alleys. They gave away lots to Indian citizens—two free lots to each applicant if he or she was a Chickasaw citizen.

On April 21, 1887, the post office was officially established, named for E. B. Purcell, a Santa Fe director. On November 23, 1887, the *Purcell Register* boasted:

> Six months ago Purcell was nothing, but with the advent of the Texas line of the "Santa Fe" came a change. Heretofore the only visitors here were an occasional ranchman, a straggling hunting party, or band of Indians; now we have a town of 1000 inhabitants, with nearly every line of business represented.

Purcell, located in Indian Territory, was dry. In Lexington, just across the Canadian River in Oklahoma Territory, liquor was as plentiful as water. A number of enterprising barmen of Purcell were loathe to let money escape to Lexington. They built saloons on stilts in the river.

The famous Sand Bar Saloon in the Canadian River between Lexington, Oklahoma Territory, and Purcell, Indian Territory.
—Western History Collections, University of Oklahoma Library

The most famous was known as the Sand Bar Saloon. Initially, it was constructed on piling and connected to the shore by a rickety catwalk, but several rises of the river prompted the owners to set the saloon on a flat-bottomed boat. The saloon became known as the "Ark." Another floating saloon was dubbed the "City of Purcell." Periodically a saloon would be washed down river, and at least one tippler lost his life as a result. One two-story structure had a saloon and dance hall on the first floor and "accommodation rooms" upstairs.

—*Paoli* (Exit 79) - US 77-OK 145————

This small agricultural community was established in 1888 as the Santa Fe forged north. Its name echoed a town of the same name in Pennsylvania. In 1899 there were three hundred inhabitants, and the *Paoli Times* kept them abreast of news.

More recently, archaeologists have unearthed the remains of ancient Indian villages southwest of Paoli, most likely ancestors of the Wichitas who farmed, hunted, and fished along the banks of the Washita River about A.D. 1200. Finds include agricultural and cooking tools made from bison and deer bones, arrow points, and pottery shards. Charred seeds are believed to be leftovers from meals prepared some 800 years ago.

—*Pauls Valley* (Exit 72) - US 77-OK19————

Smith Paul was the first white man to come to this valley. As a boy, Smith ran away from home and lived with the Chickasaw Indians in northwestern Mississippi. He came west with them over the Trail of Tears. He worked for a Scotsman named McClure who had married a Chickasaw. After McClure died, Smith Paul married his widow.

Paul came to the valley about 1847 and farmed the rich bottom land. The settlement became known as Smith Paul's Valley. In 1871, when a post office was established, the name was shortened to Pauls Valley.

A newspaper, the *Chickasaw Enterprise*, was established in 1887, before the railroad came to that part of Indian Territory. The press and supplies were hauled overland from Caddo. A formal townsite was laid out in 1892, and the town was incorporated in 1897. Despite pressure for modernization, local citizens interested in preserving the community's territorial flavor have managed to retain the original brick streets in the downtown area. Principal crops have been alfalfa, cotton, broomcorn, grain sorghums, corn, and pecans. During World War I, Pauls Valley was a major market for supplying mules to the U.S. Army.

—*Wynnewood* (Exit 66) - US 77-OK 29————

This community began in 1886 as Walner, named for John H. Walner, an early settler. With the coming of the Santa Fe, in 1887, railroad officials changed the name to Wynnewood, after a town in Pennsylvania. In 1892 the community had a population of 500. It was a shipping point for cotton, alfalfa, livestock, and poultry. It became one of Oklahoma's largest pecan markets. With the coming of the oil industry, a Kerr-McGee industrial complex spread south of town, including a tank farm and asphalt plants.

———— EXCURSION

—*Fort Arbuckle* (Exit 55) - OK 7————

The site of Fort Arbuckle is located off OK 7 five miles west of I-35. This fort was the fourth and last military installation in Oklahoma to be named after Brig. Gen. Matthew Arbuckle, who founded Fort Gibson. Fort Arbuckle was established in April 1851 to keep order among Plains Indians, to protect immigrant Chickasaws from raids, and to provide assistance to California-bound travelers.

The following year, captains Randolph B. Marcy and George B. McClellan set out from Fort Arbuckle to explore the source of the Red River. At its height there were thirty or forty buildings at Fort Arbuckle, including a hospital, livery stable, sutler's store, quarters for the troops, a guardhouse, school, church, blacksmith shop, library, and parade ground. Boredom was the greatest problem; hunting rattlesnakes and racing horses were standard diversions.

The fort became a trade center for Chickasaw farmers and ranchers who sold their produce there. There was room for four companies; but, like many western forts, the installation was never heavily garrisoned. In April 1861, the War Department abandoned the military posts in Indian Territory, and Confederate troops moved in immediately. After the Civil War, federal troops were again stationed at Fort Arbuckle. Among the soldiers were 200 members of the newly formed 10th Cavalry, a unit made up of blacks. The troopers were primarily farmers and ex-slaves. The Indians called them "Buffalo Soldiers," a term that spread through the West.

Fort Arbuckle served as a site for treaty discussions and the ransom of captives. On one occasion, the fort was visited by a group of Plains Indians, and the commander decided to impress them with a show of military strength. He brought out a big gun and explained its operation through Horace Jones, the interpreter. In the process of firing a few rounds, a cow belonging to the post dairyman was killed. The Indians ran to butcher the animal; when they returned they asked the commander to repeat the display of fire power. The incident cost the government $7 for the cow.

The post was abandoned in 1870, when the need for military eminence farther west brought Fort Sill into prominence. Today all that remains of Fort Arbuckle are a few chimneys and the outlines of foundations. The site is located on private land.

—Davis—Turner Falls (Exit 51) - US 77————

Davis originated when the Santa Fe built north from Ardmore through the Arbuckle Mountains in 1887-88. Samuel H. Davis had a store near the Washita River. He built another on the railroad and the new town was named for him. During the 1890s the town served as a gateway to the health resorts at Sulphur. It now profits from its proximity to the Arbuckle Wilderness and the Chickasaw National Recreation Area.

Davis has the good fortune to own Turner Falls, claimed to be the oldest park in Oklahoma. Mazeppa Thomas Turner was born of Scottish parentage in Virginia. He married Laura J. Johnson, of Chickasaw lineage. Acquiring Indian rights through his marriage, he moved to Stringtown in the Choctaw Nation, where he engaged in farming.

In 1878 Turner moved to a cabin on the bank of Honey Creek in the foothills of the Arbuckle Mountains. Nearby he found a fall where Honey

Turner Falls prior to development as a recreation area.
—Western History Collections, University of Oklahoma Library

Turner Falls as it appears today.

Creek cascaded in a 77-foot drop—the tallest waterfall in Oklahoma—to form a natural swimming pool below. Over the years the area has developed into an 850-acre family amusement park, now operated by the town of Davis.

—*Dougherty* - OK 110———————

According to old-timers, this area off OK 7 southeast of Davis was first called Strawberry Flat because of an extensive field of wild strawberries along the Washita River bank. Later it was locally known as Henderson Flat; however, in 1887 when the railroad came through, it was formally named for banker William Dougherty of Gainesville, Texas. For many years it thrived as a shipping point for cattle.

Besides ranching, the area supplied sand, gravel, rock, and asphalt on a commercial basis. In 1905 the Santa Fe ran Sunday excursion trains from Texas to Dougherty. People brought picnic lunches and spent the day exploring mountains in the area. Burning Mountain was a popular attraction; it was a mountain in John Easley's pasture that emitted mysterious plumes of smoke. It is believed that gas seeping from crevasses had been ignited by lightning. The fire eventually burned itself out.

—*Ardmore* (Exits 31A & 31B) - US 77—OK 199———————

Before arrival of the Santa Fe Railway in 1887, the headquarters of the 700 Ranch was the only building within the limits of present-day Ardmore. The ranch began operations in the Chickasaw Nation in 1880. The ranch house consisted of two log cabins connected by a "dogtrot" or breezeway. The old building has been restored and presently serves as a pioneer museum on the grounds of the Hardy Murphy Coliseum.

Before the railroad came, ranchers grazed their cattle on the open range. Any Chickasaw citizen could build a house wherever he pleased as long as it was at least a quarter of a mile from his nearest neighbor. With the coming of the railroad in 1887, a townsite meant lots to sell, land to lease, and money to be made. Richard McLish, a prominent Chickasaw citizen, acquired title to much of the land that later became Ardmore.

Railroad construction was funded by Philadelphia financiers. The directors of the bonding house named new towns along the railroad after towns along the main line of the Pennsylvania Railroad running west out of Philadelphia: Wayne, Paoli, Wynnewood, Berwyn, Ardmore, and Overbrook.

Stores opened around the railroad, at first in tents, to supply provisions to laborers and crewmen working on the roadbed. On the afternoon of July 28, 1887, the first train arrived, bringing a boxcar filled with

North Washington Street from Main Street in Ardmore about 1895.
—Western History Collections, University of Oklahoma Library

lumber. It was Ardmore's birthday; the lumber was used to build Bob and Frank Frensley's general store. The depot moved from a tent into a boxcar. A town was born.

During its early days, Ardmore was a notoriously tough town with bootleggers, cattle thieves, gamblers, and outlaws haunting the saloons along Caddo Street. The jail population usually numbered about a hundred. From 1895 to 1897 there was a jail whipping post for punishment of insubordinates. This practice was stopped and recalcitrant prisoners were incarcerated in a stone dungeon beneath the jail on a two-day bread-and-water diet.

On one occasion an attempted escape was self-defeating. Prisoners burned a hole in the wooden floor of their cell and spent several days digging a tunnel to freedom. Unfortunately, the tunnel ended up in the backyard of the man next-door who had a contract to feed the prisoners.

The most common offense was "introducing" intoxicating liquor into the Chickasaw Nation. Large fines and extended jail sentences did little to stem the flow. Up to $200 worth of whiskey came into Ardmore every twenty-four hours. A favorite method was to ride the Santa Fe to Gainesville, Texas, and return with a bottle in a shoe box. On Sunday afternoons Ardmorites passed the time by going to the railroad station to count debarking passengers carrying "Gainesville shoes" under their arms.

As early as 1890 Ardmore had some ten "saloons," not openly selling liquor but advertising oat beer, hop ale, malt mead, malt tonic, Schlitz fizz, hokey-pokey, and Pablo. The Farmers and Traders Saloon advertised "Kind Treatment to Customers." The Court Street Billiard Hall featured "Special Attention to Orderly Conduct." Gainesville saloons advertised in the *Daily Ardmoreite*. Alongside their ads was the notice: "Wherrell Whisky Cure: Bi-chloride of Gold preparation endorsed by the United States Government." U.S. marshals regularly raided Ardmore's five gambling houses and burned their equipment, only to have them reopen in a few days.

Ardmore had plenty of saloons and a jail, but no city government, no police department, and no fire department. Wells and cisterns were the only source of water, and this led to disaster on April 19, 1895. Fire broke out in a livery stable, and within a few hours eighty-two business buildings and residences were destroyed. The town was practically wiped out.

However, the community arose from the ashes, organized a volunteer fire department, and bought a horse-drawn steam pumper fire engine. The Ardmore Board of Trade, Ardmore's first civic organization, raised money to hire a night watchman to help deter burglars.

In 1913, with the discovery of oil, Ardmore became a boom town. The boom was followed by a period of stagnation, which lasted until the 1960s when new local industries and growing payrolls were crowned by a $75 million Uniroyal tire plant.

HISTORICAL HIGHLIGHT

Law Enforcement in the Chickasaw Nation

Indian Territory was a popular hideout for Texas outlaws. The United States court at Paris, Texas, had criminal jurisdiction over the area. Periodically the judge would issue fifty or sixty "John Doe" warrants to deputy marshals and instruct them to go into Indian Territory and clean out the whiskey peddlers, horse thieves, murderers, and other criminals that infested the area.

The marshals traveled the country in a wagon, following cow trails and wagon roads. They searched old shacks and isolated ranch houses. As miscreants were identified they were arrested and chained to the wagon. When the wagon was full, the marshals would take them to Paris where charges were filed and the prisoners tried.

Law officers from Texas did not always get their man. R. L. Nichols, who lived near Gainesville, Texas, in the 1870s and 1880s, told about a recurring problem:

> . . . in those days it was no uncommon thing for a bunch of from ten to twenty cowboys from the Washington and McLish ranches in the Indian Territory to come to Gainesville on horseback and have a big time, such as riding in saloons and ordering drinks, sitting on their

horses, and sometimes throwing a rope on any policeman who happened to show up, or maybe leading him around the square with possibly ten or fifteen cowboys shooting in the ground near his feet to see him jump. They would do those tricks just before they were ready to leave town, and generally a posse was gotten together to arrest the cowboys, but the Indian Territory cowhands would always outrun the officers on the south bank of the river.

For weeks during the spring of 1894 deputy marshals were aware that a band of thieves was in the vicinity of Healdton to the west of Ardmore. They became particularly watchful after the robbery of a bank at Longview, Texas.

On June 7, Houston Wallace and two women—Mrs. Brown and Miss Pruitt—appeared in Ardmore. The party spent more than $200 on pistol and rifle ammunition, dress goods, jewelry, groceries, and a camping outfit. This attracted considerable attention but was not cause for arrest until Wallace went to the Wells-Fargo office and picked up a large package containing whiskey.

Wallace was arrested and jailed for "introducing," and the two women were held for questioning. Nobody admitted anything, and Deputy U.S. Marshal S. T. Lindsay organized a posse to investigate the Wallace farm, about twenty miles northwest of Ardmore.

Early the next morning, a woman gave the alarm as the posse was sneaking up on the farmhouse. Bill Dalton was inside. He escaped through a small window in the rear and was met by C. L. "Los" Hart, who ordered him to halt. Dalton broke for the timber a short distance away. Hart fired and Dalton fell to the ground. He died in one convulsive movement as he turned face-up.

A money sack from the Longview bank was found in the farmhouse, along with about $1,700. Dalton had $285 in his pocket. Dalton's body was loaded into a wagon. En route to Ardmore the posse met Mrs. Brown and Miss Pruitt making their way back to the Wallace farm. At first they denied any knowledge of Dalton and the bank robbery, but when "Mrs. Brown" saw Dalton's body she admitted that he was her husband.

She said: "This is the seventh time I have been told that my husband was dead, but this is the first time his body has been cold."

The undertaker embalmed Dalton's body, then placed it on a plank for display in front of the funeral parlor. Hundreds of people filed past to view the corpse.

In consideration of her grief, Mrs. Dalton was quartered at the Sherman Hotel and guards stood outside her door to see that no one molested or annoyed her. No charges were brought against her and within a week she accompanied Dalton's body to California for burial. Deputy Marshal Lindsay and the eight members of his posse divided a $25,000 reward for killing Bill Dalton.

—*Lake Murray State Park* (Exit 24) - OK 77S————

Lake Murray State Park, covering 12,496 acres, is Oklahoma's largest state park. The park started in 1933 during the Depression. Fifteen hundred Works Progress Administration workers manned axes, saws, and grubbing hoes. They received $1.25 for six hours work each day and were required to furnish their own tools and camping equipment. The facility was named for William H. "Alfalfa Bill" Murray, one of Oklahoma's most colorful governors.

Lookout Rock rising from one arm of the lake is said to have been used by outlaws during territorial days. They hid out nearby in the thick brush along Anadarche Creek now inundated by the lake.

—*Marietta* (Exit 15) - US 77—OK 32————

Marietta is the county seat of Love County. The community grew around the Santa Fe depot when the railroad built north out of Texas in 1887. Most of the land in the area was owned or leased by two ranchers, Jerry and Bill Washington, who married Chickasaw women and thus got shares of allotted land. The town was named after Jerry Washington's wife.

William E. Washington ran his cattle empire from a Victorian mansion still standing about four miles southwest of Marietta. When Bill Washington built his house a century ago, he had the walls filled with fine gravel to above head height, not for insulation but as protection from bullets.

Bill was a millionaire at thirty-eight. His cattle roamed the range for miles around, and he grew cotton. He operated a commissary and a store. When he got mad at his brother Jerry, who owned a bank, Bill Washington had his own money printed and pewter coins cast. Washington's money was good at his enterprises and virtually legal tender in the surrounding area.

The Washingtons—Bill, Jerry, and another member of the clan named Claude—were known throughout the area. The story is told of a Texas rancher who, like many early pioneers, was unable to read. He arrived at a bank in Gainesville, Texas, and found it closed. A sign hung from the doorknob. The rancher asked a passerby what the sign said.

"It's a holiday," was the reply, "Washington's birthday."

The Texan started toward his horse, then stopped long enough to ask, "Which one—Bill, Jerry, or Claude?"

—*Thackerville* (Exit 5) - US 77————

This small farming community nearly surrounded by the Red River dates back to 1882, when it was in the Chickasaw Nation. The community was named after Zachariah Thacker, one of the original settlers. Refuge

Spring, a burial ground for early Texas outlaws, is hidden away among a clump of white cedar trees about a mile west of US 77 near the river. The trees, planted in 1840, formed an approximate boundary between Texas and Indian Territory. When an outlaw fleeing Texas reached this spot he felt safe from his pursuers, but for some who were sorely wounded it became a final resting place.

OK 74-74D-74E-74F
Marshall—Navina

—Marshall - OK 74E————

Like so many towns, Marshall moved from its original site in 1903 to be on a newly established railroad. The community was established during the Run of '89 when Sylvan Rice and his uncle, Miles Rice, staked adjoining claims. They built a crossroads store to serve surrounding homesteaders and cowboys from the nearby Cherokee Outlet. Sylvan Rice petitioned for a post office named Marshall, after his hometown of Marshalltown, Iowa. The petition was granted March 1, 1890, but people still called the place "Rice's Corner."

With the opening of the Cherokee Outlet on September 16, 1893, Marshall's trade territory doubled in a day. On June 28, 1927, a wildcat oil gusher came in six miles west of town, and Marshall prospered until the Depression, when oil prices dropped to 10 cents a barrel. Business activities declined in Marshall as automobiles and trucks allowed people to shop in surrounding cities.

—Lovell - OK 74D————

Originally established as Perth in May 1889, Lovell moved in 1904 to be on the Denver, Enid, and Gulf Railroad. James W. Lovell purchased land for the townsite from homesteaders. To celebrate filing the plat for the new town, settlers filled the cavity between two anvils with gunpowder and lit a fuse. The explosion was heard for miles around. The name was officially changed from Perth to Lovell in 1906.

During its heyday, Lovell had two grain elevators, a cotton gin, a bank, and numerous business establishments. In the early 1920s most of the land owners in the vicinity benefited from the frenzied trade in oil and gas leases. In more recent years business in the community has suffered from the availability of nearby cities.

—Crescent - OK 74-74C————

Crescent, situated on the edge of the Cimarron River basin, erupted from the Run of '89. There are two stories of how it got its name. One says the name came from a nearby crescent-shaped stand of oak timber. The other version claims that early settlers believed their community would prosper and grow just as a crescent moon grows to a full moon.

The early settlers were right. Crescent became a prosperous agricultural trading center serving a large section of western Logan County. The local economy was aided by the oil industry and the nearby Kerr-McGee nuclear research facility.

—Cashion - OK 74F————

The town was originally called Downs. A product of the opening of the territory to settlement, it was located about a mile north of present-day Cashion. Downs was bypassed by the railroad, and a new town was platted in 1900. At the time, there was a campaign to build a monument to Roy V. Cashion of Hennessey, a member of Teddy Roosevelt's Rough Riders who died during the charge up San Juan Hill. Cashion commemorates the first Oklahoma Territory soldier killed during the Spanish-American War.

Cashion fulfilled the hopes of A. L. Willhoit, publisher of the *Cashion Advance*, who started his newspaper in 1900. Soon there was a bank, four grain elevators, three cotton gins, a hotel, two lumberyards, hardware and drygoods stores, a drugstore, and a livery stable. During the 1930s, Cashion lost its railroad connection; most of the businesses and much of the population moved away. Recently, it has experienced a comeback as people who work in Oklahoma City moved to Cashion to enjoy "country living."

—*Navina*————

Located east of OK 74, the town was established by John Berg, of Leavenworth, Kansas, on a farm he had purchased in 1890. Berg platted a town and opened a store on the east side of his property. He applied for a post office to be called Berg, but there was already a town of that name in the territory. Next he tried Alvina, but that too was turned down, and the blossoming town became Navina.

Navina's most exciting day was August 28, 1925. Three masked men appeared in the bank. The cashier was out. Albert Kinney, a clerk, was on duty. The robbers scooped up as much money as they could find and took Kinney as a hostage. Kinney was finally released after the outlaws spent a long time driving about through woods between Kingfisher and Guthrie. Before starting the walk back to Navina, Kinney grabbed a stick and wrote the license number of the car in the dust. Two of the robbers were killed at a roadblock near Kingfisher and the third was sent to prison.

—*Stillwater* - US 177—OK 51—————

Stillwater was the scene of the most ambitious attempt on the part of Payne's Oklahoma Colony to occupy land in Oklahoma Territory prior to the opening. A week after Payne's death, William L. Couch assumed command of the Boomer organization and organized an incursion into the forbidden territory. On December 12, 1884, he settled some two hundred would-be homesteaders just southeast of present-day Stillwater.

A small detachment of troops under Lt. Matthias W. Day confronted the Boomers on December 24. He was met by two hundred men armed with double-barreled shotguns and Winchesters. Day wrote his superior:

> They refused to submit to an arrest without a resort to arms: though I had about 30 men on a skirmish line, as they were densely massed I hesitated to give the command to fire as the slaughter would have been great.

Day went on to request reinforcements if he was expected to arrest the Boomers without opening fire upon them. In the issue of January 21, 1885, the *Oklahoma Boomer*, a newspaper published by the colonists, gave a somewhat different report:

> On the 24th of December, Lieut. Day came to our camp with forty cavalrymen and two bags of handcuffs. He first ordered the colonists to lay down their arms and surrender; this they refused to do, Couch asking Day for his authority to which Day replied:
> "I have only one authority, the carbine."
> "That is an authority we do not recognize," replied Couch.
> Lieut. Day then ordered eight of his soldiers to tie Couch, who was about thirty feet in advance of a hastily formed line. When they advanced to execute this order, Couch, who was armed with a Winchester told them that if they laid a hand on him he would consider it an assault and treat it as such. The soldiers then were ordered back to the line, were commanded to load, and Lieut. Day gave the colonists five minutes to surrender or he should open fire. The colonists didn't surrender nor did the troops open fire, but soon after went into camp near the colonists under a truce not to molest the colonists going or coming in any way. Lieut. Day is a gentleman, and he did his duty in every way, but he could not bluff the colonists and was too weak to fight them.

A festering thorn in the side of the military, the Boomers remained in the community, which they called Stillwater after the nearby creek that flowed into the Cimarron River. Col. Edward Hatch arrived on the scene. The Boomers dug rifle pits to fortify their position. Hatch sent for reinforcements, including artillery. Hatch won by cutting off the colonists' supplies. On January 26, 1885, with rations for only five days, Couch capitulated and said he was ready to withdraw.

Frank Leslie's Illustrated Newspaper, published in New York, reported on the affair on February 7, 1885, in anything but complimentary terms:

> The Oklahoma squatters and tramps who, under the name of "boomers," "settlers," "patriots," etc., have for two years invaded the Indian lands of Indian Territory, have at last surrendered to [Colonel] Hatch with a detachment of soldiers. The Government has been put in a rather humiliating attitude by the whole proceeding. It ought long ago to have driven out these impudent invaders at the point of the bayonet, ... It has been a wanton defiance of law all through, not at all calculated to reassure the hardy settlers who have pre-empted their homes where they had a right to. Now let the Indian Territory be protected.

Couch and sixty-seven other leaders were indicted. Plea bargaining resulted in dismissal of the charges if the Boomers refrained from further invasion of Indian Territory. The military patrolled the area just to be sure, and most of the Boomers went to work on the railroads then building across Indian Territory.

On April 22, 1889, the territory was opened to settlement, and the Stillwater Town Company laid out a town on the present site of Stillwater. In the beginning, $5 would buy one business or two residential lots. On April 7, 1891, the citizens of Stillwater voted unanimously to incorporate their city. The second act of the newly elected officials was to call for a vote on whether the town should issue $10,000 in bonds to aid in the construction of the Agricultural and Mechanical College, which Oklahoma Territory's first legislature had just authorized. Again, the vote was unanimous, and Stillwater was on the way to fulfilling its destiny as a college town.

Since that time, the city and the college—now Oklahoma State University—have grown together. Stillwater has become "Aggieland."

—*Perkins* - US 177—OK 33———————

The town was established with the opening of the territory in 1889. It was named for B. W. Perkins, a United States senator from Kansas who participated in the run. During the summer of 1889, even before the post office was officially approved, between forty and fifty men from Perkins attempted to steal the county records and move the county seat to Perkins. They were met by a force twice their size and retreated. In 1891 Perkins made an unsuccessful bid for the Agricultural and Mechanical College by offering an 80-acre tract of land.

Perkins was the home of Frank "Pistol Pete" Eaton, a United States deputy marshal under "hanging Judge" Parker out of Fort Smith,

Arkansas. At the age of fifteen, Eaton was judged to wear the "fastest guns" in Indian Territory. He served in various capacities as a peace officer for more than sixty years. He died in Perkins at the age of ninety-seven.

EXCURSION

—*Coyle* - OK 33——

This agricultural village was established in 1899 two miles north-west of its present site. The townsite plat was filed as Iowa City. The town moved the following year to be on the Santa Fe Railway and the post office was named Coyle honoring William Coyle of Guthrie. Cotton gins processed crops from the area. A cotton carnival in the fall capped the season, and businessmen offered a prize to any couple who would consent to a public wedding. Today most of Coyle's visitors come to attend Camp Cimarron, a nearby recreational facility for Camp Fire Girls that overlooks the Cimarron River.

—*Langston* - OK 33——

This all-black town was founded in 1890 by E. B. McCabe, who had been state auditor of Kansas. It was named for John M. Langston of Virginia, a black educator and a member of Congress. As early as 1885, a movement to establish an all-black community—possibly a state—was started by S. H. Scott, a black attorney in Fort Smith, Arkansas.

Worshipers in front of the Catholic Church in Langston. —Western History Collections, University of Oklahoma Library

After the opening of 1889, McCabe promoted the town as a new "Eldorado" where the black man would prosper and rule supreme in his own community, "the only distinctly Negro city in America." His newspaper, the *Langston Herald*, circulated through the South. The paper pictured buildings to show how the town was expected to look in the future. McCabe's enthusiasm attracted some 2,000 who found a scattering of tents rather than buildings. Job opportunities were so limited that many were forced to leave after they had exhausted their savings on living expenses. McCabe moved to Guthrie, the territorial capital, and served for a time as deputy state auditor. The population quickly shrank to less than a 1,000.

In 1897, the territorial legislature authorized Langston University. Over the years it developed into a four-year coeducational institution comparing favorably with other state-supported colleges of comparable size. Then, 1954, the U.S. Supreme Court ordered desegregation of all schools. Despite desegregation, the enrollment at Langston University is still predominately black.

HISTORICAL HIGHLIGHT

Black Communities in Oklahoma

The first blacks in Oklahoma came as slaves owned by members of the Five Civilized Tribes. One Choctaw planter owned more than five hundred. Each of the five tribes adopted a slave code to control its black chattels. The Cherokee, Choctaw, Chickasaw, and Creek laws were quite severe, particularly regarding runaways.

The Seminoles were more lenient. Many of their slaves were literate, serving as clerks and interpreters. Usually they lived in separate villages and were free to come and go, but they were obligated to furnish an annual tribute of grain, meat, or services to their owners, similar to a share-cropper arrangement.

In 1842 there was an uprising among slaves in the Cherokee and Creek nations. The leaders were apparently slaves who had emigrated to Oklahoma with the Seminoles. The plot centered in Webbers Falls. At four o'clock in the morning, slaves in that area locked the sleeping overseers in their cabins and took horses, mules, guns, and food. Some say two hundred were involved; others put the figure as high as six hundred. They headed southwest with the intention of reaching colonies of free blacks in Mexico. The rebels were captured and punished.

Sometime after this insurrection, the Creek tribal council adopted its slave code. If a slave killed an Indian, he suffered the death penalty. If an Indian killed a slave, he had to pay the owner the value of the slave or suffer death. A slave who killed another slave received a hundred

When the artist Frederic Remington toured the West he entitled this painting the Buffalo Soldiers "Watering Horses." —Fort Sill Museum

lashes and his owner had to pay the owner of the murdered slave half the value of the dead black.

On July 28, 1866, Congress passed an act providing for six black regiments in the U.S. Army. The 9th and 10th Cavalry regiments were assigned to frontier duty. The white troops called them "brunettes" and sometimes less complimentary names, but the Plains Indians dubbed them "Buffalo Soldiers," a name that stuck.

Col. Benjamin Grierson commanded the 10th Cavalry, and he was their champion. He raged against discrimination in the issuance of inferior horses, supplies, and food. He ordered his company commanders not to use the word "colored" in their reports; his men were "simply the 10th Regiment of Cavalry, United States Army." The Buffalo Soldiers repaid Grierson with yeoman service. They built the original Fort Sill.

During territorial days and the early years of statehood, there were many all-black communities in Oklahoma. Black sociologist Mozell Hill maintained these towns represented an attempt to escape the "caste system" imposed by whites, in which the blacks were treated as social subordinates.

174

Black immigration into Oklahoma Territory was not welcomed by all the freedmen. They called the newcomers "State Negroes" and expressed resentment toward those who came from the South. The freedmen were proud and independent. They objected to the servility displayed by some of the immigrants toward whites.

Gradually, the inner-racial friction faded as blacks banded into towns to counter the dissatisfaction toward biracial communities. On November 29, 1902, the *Beaver Journal* reported: "A vigilance committee of citizens of Waurika posted notices to the negroes to vacate the community within 24 hours." Blacks instituted their own brand of segregation. The *Daily Oklahoman* of July 5, 1904, reported that a white man was not allowed to stop in Wybark after sunset.

Bvt. Maj. Gen.
Benjamin H. Grierson.
—Fort Sill Museum

Frederic Remington entitled this encounter between an Indian and a Buffalo Soldier "The Sign Language." —Fort Sill Museum

The 1954 U.S. Supreme Court decision barring school segregation and subsequent civil rights legislation turned the all-black communities into a historical study rather than an ongoing activity.

—*Jacktown* - US 62-177————

This crossroads community at the intersection of US 62 and US 177 is now a scattering of houses. Once on a branch of the Ozark Trail across Oklahoma, Jacktown had service stations on all four corners. Now only one convenience store with gasoline pumps is sufficient to serve local customers and passing motorists.

—*Shawnee* - US 177————

This city had its beginning in 1872 as a trading post on the West Shawnee Cattle Trail from Texas to Kansas. The trading post stood on the south bank of the North Canadian River southwest of the present city. It was known as Shawneetown, and a post office by that name operated from 1876 to 1892. It served both drovers on the cattle trail and Indians from the nearby reservation.

The area—including reservations of the Sac and Fox, Iowa, and Shawnee-Potawatomie Indians—was opened to white settlement on September 22, 1891. About 20,000 persons raced for 7,000 quarter-sections, and all of the land was occupied in one afternoon.

According to the story, on the day of the opening two young women from Oklahoma City stood in Kickapoo land with their toes touching the border of the territory to be opened. When the gun sounded, they stepped across the line and staked claims in what became Shawnee south of Highland Street and east of Kickapoo Street.

The town of Shawnee already had a start from the nearby Shawnee Indian Agency and the Shawnee Mission Church, which had been established by the Society of Friends in 1872. The townsite was laid out the following spring, and railroads arrived in 1895, 1902, and 1904.

Shawnee prospered from shops for two of the three railroads that ran through town. It lost out in competition for the state capital, but finally, in 1930, won the county seat away from Tecumseh. The city swelled to 30,000 during the oil boom and survived the subsequent decline by industrial diversification.

The author of "Home on the Range," a favorite song among cowboys on the cattle trails to Kansas, lived in Shawnee. Dr. Brewster Higley wrote the song while living in Kansas, and the words were printed in a local newspaper in 1873. Night riders had soothed many a herd with it before it was finally published in 1910. In the meantime, Higley had

The Shawnee railroad yards looking north from Main Street during Shawnee's heyday as a railroad center. —Western History Collections, University of Oklahoma Library

The unique Santa Fe Depot in Shawnee now houses a historical museum.

moved to Shawnee in 1886. Higley died in 1911 without ever seeing a copy of his song or receiving a cent of royalty.

The highly photogenic Santa Fe depot was completed in 1903, an outstanding example of Romanesque Revival architecture popular in the late nineteenth century. The walls are of Bedford rock from Indiana. A tower rises forty feet above the roof line. It houses the Shawnee Museum.

—Bethel Acres———————

This area to the west of Shawnee was homesteaded during the run of September 22, 1891. Cotton was the primary crop; until the Depression, when many residents left the area. Bethel Acres remained a somewhat isolated rural area until the middle of the 1960s, when I-40 was completed and connecting state highways were opened. Bethel Acres developed from Lucile B. Walker's 320-acre farm, and she was elected mayor of Bethel Acres in 1973. It is now a prosperous residential community.

—Tecumseh - US 177—OK 9———————

Tecumseh had been predetermined by the government as the county seat of County "B," and the date for the opening was September 22, 1891. However, the surveyors had not finished their work, and homeseekers waited on the outskirts of the site until September 23. At high noon the rush started. The only recorded casualty was a Dr. Roundtree, who jumped off his horse to stake a town lot and was trampled to death by a rider following close behind.

The first business was a restaurant that served meals in a tent. Two young men knocked together a frame building where they baked bread, which they sold as quickly as they could take loaves from the oven. The first school opened in the spring of 1892 and was taught by Miss Lela Hendry. She rented a building on Main Street for $3 a month and taught twenty-five pupils whose parents paid $1.50 each per month.

When the Choctaw, Oklahoma and Gulf Railroad missed Tecumseh by three miles, civic leaders raised $30,000 to build a branch line to connect with the main line at Shawnee. In 1900, the branch line shipped more than 11,000 bales of cotton from Tecumseh. Choctaw railroad officials joined with Shawnee businessmen in an effort to wrest the county seat away from Tecumseh. The railroad offered free lots in Shawnee to businesses willing to move from Tecumseh.

By 1907, the year of statehood, Shawnee's population stood at 10,955 while Tecumseh registered only 1,621. In an election in 1909, Shawnee won the county seat from Tecumseh, only to have the supreme court nullify the results on a charge of bribery. In a 1911 election, Tecumseh won. Shawnee won the third election, held in October 1930. Tecumseh charged bribery, liquor at polling places, and counting the votes of college boys, but the supreme court ordered removal of the courthouse. Since that time, Tecumseh's economic well-being has been largely dependent upon a state industrial school for delinquent girls.

Looking north on Broadway in Tecumseh, 1907. —Western History Collections, University of Oklahoma Library

—*Brooksville* - US 177————

Dating from the early 1900s, Brooksville was the only all-black community in Pottawatomie County. Initially, the settlement now west of US 177 was called Lelian. Briefly, during 1905, after the Santa Fe Railway put in a switch, the name was changed to Sewell for a local white physician. Not long after, the name was changed to Brooksville to honor A. R. Brooks, a cotton buyer and farmer, the first black in the neighborhood. Surrounding land produced from 75 to 100 bales of cotton to the acre, keeping three cotton buyers and a gin busy. The population reached a peak of 400 before the boll weevil and the Depression caused an exodus to California and other places of apparent opportunity.

———— EXCURSION

—*Maud* - OK 59—OK 9A————

Founded in the 1890s, Maud grew from a general store and post office about a half-mile west of the present site. It was a one-store country town until the railroad came through in 1902. In 1898, Maud was the scene of a heinous example of mob violence.

A white woman, the wife of a Choctaw, was raped and murdered by two Indian youths in late December 1897. On January 8, 1898, with a hundred men watching, a Baptist minister prayed as he touched a match to a brush arbor to burn two Seminole boys alive. Since there was no trial, the guilt of the boys was never established. Congress appropriated $25,000 to hunt down members of the mob. Seventy-six men were arrested for participation in the orgy. Five were sentenced to prison for terms ranging from three to ten years. One of the five was gunned down on a Maud street after his release from prison.

During the oil boom, Maud mushroomed in size and ran wide open with saloons and gambling, crowded muddy streets, and flaming gas wells. The town has since resumed its small-town ways.

Asher - US 177—OK 39

The original townsite of Asher was an Indian allotment belonging to a man named Blackbird. The land was later acquired by George M. "Matt" Asher, of Lexington, Kentucky. Asher offered his land for a townsite, and it was named in his honor. Lots sold for $750.

Two miles north, a post office had been operating under the name Avoca since August 4, 1894, but when the Rock Island branch line began service to the new community, Postmaster George A. McCurry surreptitiously moved his store and post office without notice to or permission from Washington. His application to change the name to Asher was approved on November 26, 1901.

In 1848 Jesse Chisholm operated a trading post two miles east of present-day Asher to the north of OK 39. Chisholm Spring still flows. The site is on private land.

—*Stratford* - US 177—OK 19————

This community was laid out during the first decade of the twentieth century and named after Stratford-on-Avon for reasons obscured by the mists of time. Stratford's principal asset is a private collection of Indian, pioneer, and historic artifacts strung along the street. Displays include a pre-1900 barbershop, hardware store, doctor's office, telephone exchange, and Wells Fargo office.

Peaches have been a cash crop in Stratford since the town's founding in 1906. Development progressed from backyard trees and door-to-door sales during the 1930s to commercial orchards in the 1960s. Styling itself as the "Peach Capital of Oklahoma," Stratford staged its fourteenth annual Peach Festival and Rodeo in 1990.

—*Sulphur* - US 177-OK 7————

Prehistoric pottery reveals that Indians knew about the many mineral springs that bubbled from the earth in the vicinity of Sulphur long before a white man set foot in Oklahoma. The Indians called them "smelling waters." By 1895 a store housed a post office and the community was called Sulphur Springs.

During the Victorian era, visitors arrived by way of two railroads to "take the waters" in the hope of curing various afflictions. Hotels and rooming houses blossomed to tend their needs. The Artesian Hotel was the biggest and most elaborate. It boasted a French mirror from the St. Louis World's Fair.

In 1924 a travel guide pointed out Sulphur's attractions: Mystic Cave, six miles south of town, was "never fully explored; large subterranean river of clear water. Water falls, boating in the dark recesses of Mother Earth, stalactites, stalagmites and other interesting geological formations." . . . Oil Springs, "a spring flowing oil instead of water" was hidden away from "the nervous jars, jolts and strains of business life." Bromide Spring was "nationally known as a sure cure for nervous diseases and stomach troubles."

Improvements in medical knowledge and technology shifted the public's faith in natural healing to reliance upon medication and surgery. With automobiles at their command, tourists sought recreational resorts instead of health resorts, and Sulphur suffered a decline.

181

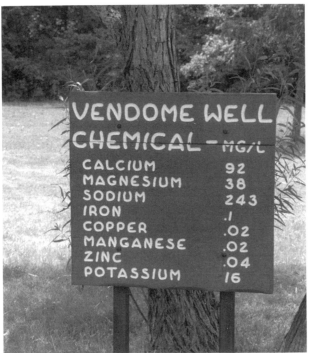

VENDOME WELL	
CHEMICAL - MG/L	
CALCIUM	92
MAGNESIUM	38
SODIUM	243
IRON	.1
COPPER	.02
MANGANESE	.02
ZINC	.04
POTASSIUM	16

Vendome Well is still flowing in Sulphur's city park. Indians called the springs "smelling waters." Visitors who sample the spring from a nearby fountain learn why.

Men waiting to fill their water jugs from Bromide Spring at Platt National Park in Sulphur. —Western History Collections, University of Oklahoma Library

Sulphur still has one spring bubbling up in a city park. A nearby spigot is available for sampling. One visitor stepped up and took a pull from the fountain. When asked "How is it?" he replied: "Everybody should taste that water *once.*"

Sulphur is bisected by Rock Creek. Today downtown includes both sides of the creek. In early days "East Sulphur" and "West Sulphur" were bitter rivals. When a bridge was built across Rock Creek a bloody hatchet was imbedded in the concrete as a symbol of settling the antagonism that divided the towns. A horseshoe was added for good luck, and the strife has apparently subsided.

—Nebo - US 177————

The trading post that later became Nebo originated in 1887. Hardel Wells was the self-appointed postmaster, operating from his house. Neighbors left notes for each other without benefit of postage. With the coming of the railroad, Wells applied for a commissioned post office and suggested naming the town Mount Nebo, from Deuteronomy 33:34. But the Post Office Department insisted upon shortening the name to Nebo.

There were three general stores, a pool hall and gambling house, two cotton gins, and two blacksmiths, but there was no bank. Banking was done on horseback. A "banker" rode about the country loaning money without the formality of notes. A man's word was sufficient collateral; no one dared tarnish his reputation by failing to pay a debt.

183

The general store at Gene Autry serves farmers and ranchers in the area and loudly proclaims the town's namesake.

—Gene Autry - OK 53——

This rural community just off OK 53 to the south has gone through a series of name changes and economic reversals. In the 1870s a store opened on the bank of the Washita River about a mile east of the present town. On July 11, 1883, a post office in the store was designated Lou, for Lou Henderson, wife of the merchant. On November 22 of that year the post office was moved and the name changed to Dresden for reasons not recorded. In 1887 the railroad came to within a mile of Dresden, and the post office and stores moved to the railroad. The name was then changed to Berwyn by a financier in faraway Philadelphia who probably never saw the village, and Berwyn became an agricultural "Saturday town."

All of that changed in November 1941. Gene Autry, one of Oklahoma's favorite sons, bought a 1,200-acre ranch some two miles west. Application was made to change the name again, and a celebration was scheduled for November 16; it was a Sunday, the thirty-fourth anniversary of Oklahoma's statehood.

An estimated 35,000 came to the party. A newspaper reporter wrote, "You couldn't see the town for the people." Both Governor Leon Phillips and Gene Autry spoke. Autry was planning to spend $250,000 in improvements on his ranch.

However, on December 7, 1941, Japan attacked Pearl Harbor and Gene Autry went into the armed services. He did not carry on with his plans for the ranch and later sold it. The town experienced a boom when the Ardmore Air Force Base was built closeby, but the community shrank after the airbase closed.

OK 18
Cushing—Aydelotte

—Cushing - OK 18-33———

Cushing is located at the junction of OK 33 and OK 18. The town began during the run of September 22, 1891, into the Sac and Fox Indian country as a settlement on the roundup grounds of the old Turkey Track Ranch. The ranch, owned by James Jerome and Leslie Combs, had been utilized during the trail drives to fatten cattle from Texas before they were taken to railheads in Kansas.

The town was established by William Rae Little, a former Indian trader who knew the Sac and Fox country from experience. He turned half of his 160-acre homestead into a town, named for Marshall Cushing, private secretary to Postmaster General John Wanamaker. The town remained an agricultural community of little significance until March 1912. Promise was in the air as oil prospectors drilled test wells nearby.

April 11 was the precursor to a forest of derricks and a maze of tank farms, refineries, and pipelines. On that day Wheeler No. 1 blew in

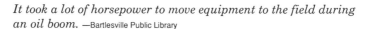

It took a lot of horsepower to move equipment to the field during an oil boom. —Bartlesville Public Library

twelve miles to the northeast. Almost overnight Cushing became a city, a brawling boomtown. By the end of 1915 there were 710 wells gushing out 72 million barrels of oil a year. *Pathe's Animated Weekly News* came to record the frenzied activity for theater audiences across the nation.

Business lots, which had sold for $100 six months before were bringing $1,200 and $1,500. The bountiful production lowered the price of oil to 19 cents a barrel and Eastern oil companies stepped in to limit production. The collapse of the oil boom left Cushing with only one refinery, but the city escaped the usual boom-and-bust fate by becoming the "Pipe Line Crossroads of the World."

HISTORICAL HIGHLIGHT
Hijackers Originated in Oklahoma

During the Prohibition era in 1921, highwaymen hid out in the blackjack oaks between Tulsa and Cushing to waylay incoming bootleggers. The press began to refer to them as hijackers. By 1926 the term was in such common usage that the *American Mercury* took notice. H. K. Croessman wrote:

> The first time I heard *hijacker* was from the lips of an Oklahoman. He explained it as coming from the command customary in hold-ups: "Stick 'em up high, Jack," Jack being the common generic term for any male person of unknown or uncertain identity. Thus, the Oklahoman explained, both *stick-up* and *hijack* originate from the same command. *To hijack*, is a verb, now apparently used exclusively in reference to road-robbery of illicit liquor.

H. L. Mencken, guru of the American language, heralded the word into American argot, including it among the "terms that threaten to be remembered." In subsequent usage it was spelled *hijack* or *highjack*, with reference to robbing bootleggers and rumrunners of their stock. Later use has expanded the term to include robbing truckers of their cargoes and comandeering airplanes.

Agra—Aydelotte - OK 18

South across Lincoln County, OK 18 leads through or past a series of rural settlements dating from homestead days and the coming of railroads. Before the advent of automotive transportation, Agra, Tryon, Kendrick, Sparks, Payson, and Aydelotte were agricultural trade centers that came alive on Saturday nights. Today the merchants are gone and the scattered residents do their shopping in nearby cities. Meeker will be of interest to baseball buffs. It was the hometown of Carl Hubbell, one-time New York Giant pitching star. As might be expected, there is a Carl Hubbell Museum.

—*Jennings* - OK 99————

The community just south of the Cimarron Turnpike dates from the opening of the Cherokee Outlet in 1893. The townsite was laid out on land allotted to George Jennings, hence the name. The tangled woods and rugged terrain at the junction of the Arkansas and Cimarron rivers east of Jennings were a favorite hideout for the Daltons, the Doolins, and other outlaws. Since the bank robbers refrained from plying their trade in Jennings, residents allowed them undisturbed access to the town.

Just west of Jennings, there are two knolls known as Twin Hills. There is "gold in them thar hills," according to a story periodically revived by the *Jennings Hummer* and the *Jennings News*. A patrol of soldiers escorting a government paymaster to Fort Sill camped between the two hills and was attacked by Indians. The paymaster buried $11,000 in gold while the soldiers tried to break through the circle of Indians. Only a few made it. When they returned with help, the rest were dead including the paymaster, the only one who knew where the gold was buried. There has been a lot of digging but no report of discovery.

EXCURSION ————

—*Yale* - OK 51————

The town was established in 1895. According to historian George H. Shirk, it was given its name by Postmaster Sterling F. Underwood because there was a Yale lock on the post office door.

Yale was the home of Jim Thorpe, Oklahoma's best-known athlete. The Thorpe house was acquired by the Oklahoma Historical Society, which now operates it as a museum in honor of the native son who called it home.

HISTORICAL HIGHLIGHT

Jim Thorpe: An Indian Legend

Some say he was the greatest all-around athlete in the history of sports.

Jim Thorpe was born May 22, 1887, near Prague, Indian Territory, northeast of Shawnee. He was almost half Pottawatomie and a quarter Sac and Fox, with Menonomie and Kickapoo rounding out his heritage. His Indian name was Wa-Tho-Huck, "Bright Path," because his mother looked out of a window following his birth and saw a reflection of the sun on the path to the house.

"Great athletes come and go but none ever topped the great Jim Thorpe."
—Western History Collections, University of Oklahoma Library

Jim Thorpe attended the Carlisle Indian school in Pennsylvania where he learned tailoring, but that was the least of his accomplishments. He also played football. He could punt 75 yards. He could drop kick or place kick 50 yards. But above all, he could run. In one season he scored 72 touchdowns.

Sports writer Bill Stern noted, "The Carlisle Indians were the only team in history to play simply for the pure pleasure of it." The squad seldom numbered more than sixteen players, so every man had to learn to play every position and be able to play sixty minutes in every game.

After he left Carlisle in 1910, Jim Thorpe played for the Anadarko baseball team. The manager fired him for breaking training rules, and Jim purportedly told him, "Okay, you're going to spend a nickel to read about me sometime."

The prediction came true. During the 1912 Olympics at Stockholm, Sweden, Thorpe won both the Pentathlon and the Decathlon. He was honored by Sweden and Russia for his accomplishments. However, in 1913 the Olympic committee forced Thorpe to return his medals because he had played semiprofessional baseball. The following year he began right field for the New York Giants in the World Series. His professional career lasted from 1913 until 1925. He became first president of the American Football League, predecessor to the National Football League.

Sports writer Gene Schoor named Thorpe the greatest football star and all-around athlete of the century. "Great athletes come and go but none ever topped the great Jim Thorpe."

In 1917, Thorpe acquired a house in Yale to free his family from the strenuous travel involved in his athletic career. The family resided in Yale until 1923, when Thorpe sold the house and moved. He drifted from job to job until his death in California in 1953. The Olympic committee restored his medals posthumously.

—Oilton - OK 99————

This town was a product of the boom during the development of the Cushing oil field. The town was platted in the middle of a cornfield in 1915. Initially lots were priced at $500; within a week a hundred houses were built. Developers boosted the asking price for lots on Main Street to $4,000. Businessmen refused to pay the price and moved a block north to develop the business district. Oklahoma's first "river-bed oil well" was drilled in the Cimarron River near Oilton.

—Drumright - OK 33-99————

This town was also a product of the Cushing field. Originally called Fulkerson, the town was renamed for Aaron Drumright, owner of the townsite. Laid out in 1913, the community spent its first three years as an accumulation of tents, lean-tos, and jerry-built wooden structures. It was a mecca for hijackers and gamblers. A half-blood Creek Indian named Creekmore was the leader of Drumright's criminal element. In 1916, aroused citizens appointed "Fighting Jack" Ary to clean up the situation. With Creekmore in prison, Drumright settled down to a more staid existence.

During boom days, Drumright's steep main street over Tiger Hill was alternately ankle-deep in dust and hub-deep in mud, a problem for mule-drawn wagons loaded with oilfield equipment.

—Shamrock - OK 16————

Seven miles southeast of Drumright on OK 16, Shamrock was—literally—one of the most colorful communities in Oklahoma. It was a product of the oil boom with an Irish flavor; the streets have names like Dublin, Cork, Kilarney, and Tipperary. As the town was on its way to its peak population of 10,000 in 1917, an official Blarney Stone was hauled in. Virtually everything in town was painted green for the 1917 St. Patrick's Day celebration.

—*Prague* - US 62—OK 99————

Established in 1902 and named for the capital of Czechoslovakia, Prague became the home of many Bohemian settlers who wanted to create a village like those in their homeland. They read the *Oklahomské Noviny*, which was printed in Chicago, and established the Sokol Society and the Western Bohemian Association. The annual Kolache Festival continues still. Visitors may join the residents in street dancing and eat the tasty fruit rolls for which the celebration is named.

The community has special significance for Catholics. In 1949, when the Communists took control of Czechoslovakia, the "Infant Jesus of Prague" disappeared from the St. Wenceslaus Church. A replica of the 19-inch, 350-year-old figurine was established in the Catholic church at Prague, Oklahoma. Pope Pius XII declared it a national shrine in 1955, and it is visited by thousands of Catholics each year.

———— EXCURSION

—*Paden* - US 62————

This agricultural community was established in 1903 with the Fort Smith and Western Railroad as its lifeline and named for U.S. Deputy Marshal Paden Tolbert. In 1907 it was a bustling town with two newspapers. The railroad was abandoned in 1939 and the community began to shrink.

—*Boley* - US 62————

Boley was one of Oklahoma's all-black communities. It was established in 1903 where much of the surrounding land had been allotted to black freedmen listed on the rolls of the Creek tribe at the time of the division of the Indian lands. The idea for the town was advanced by Lake Moore, president of the Fort Smith and Western Township Company. W. H. Boley, roadmaster of the Fort Smith and Western Railroad, was largely responsible for implementation of the plan.

Within a few years the town had a population of 2,500. A cotton gin and gristmill, a lumberyard, brick plant, bank, and a variety of stores served hundreds of families who raised cotton and corn. The motto of *The Boley Progress* was "All Men Up—Not Some Down." Editor O. H. Bradley wrote: "Nothing like her has ever happened before. Nothing like her will ever happen again. The birth of this town reads like a fairy story." In 1905 the editor advised readers outside the area:

. . . you should take advantage of these opportunities: What are you waiting for? If we do not look out for our own welfare, who is going to do so for us?

Hopes ran high in Okfuskee County that when statehood came Boley would be the county seat of an all-black county, but the white population would not let it happen. Reporting on the 1907 Republican convention in Okemah to elect a slate of county officers, the *Weleetka American* launched a vicious attack:

Is it any wonder that the self-respecting white voter has tabooed the Republican county ticket? A common water bucket on the platform from which both black and white drank, using the same dipper. Will any self-respecting white man cast a vote for anyone who is willing to place himself on the level with a thick-lipped son of Ham in an endeavor to secure a county job?

In 1907, the legislature passed a series of Jim Crow laws that effectively segregated and disenfranchised practically all blacks. Okemah became the county seat. Despite isolation by prejudice, Boley continued to prosper and grow. The depressed cotton market of 1913 and legal and terrorist pressure from the outside brought a sense of disillusionment. It was a sad development to Editor Bradley's fairy story.

Into the scene came Chief Alfred Charles Sam. He described himself as one of the chiefs of the Tribes of Akim on the Gold Coast of western Africa. He espoused a Back-to-Africa movement and urged people to sell their land and possessions and purchase stock in his Akim Trading Company, which would buy a ship to carry them to Africa.

Velma Dolphin Ashley, former superintendent of the Boley school system, pieced the story together as she researched her thesis on Boley: "He promised farms for the families, with easy prosperity. He promised the women they would be princesses and queens. He claimed food could be picked from trees and diamonds found on the ground." Mrs. Ashley charged Chief Sam with taking "a fair third of Boley's population and wealth."

This started Boley's decline. With cotton prices falling from forty cents to two cents a pound, the Fort Smith and Western Railroad pulled out in 1938. Cotton gins closed down. The town withered, but it did not die. Some residents commute to jobs outside of Boley, and some are retirees who have returned to their former homes hoping for a they-lived-happily-ever-after ending to the fairy story.

—*Seminole* - OK 9-99———

It all began in 1890 when the Mekusukey Indian Mission was built three miles southwest of the present city. Freight shipments for the mission were addressed to "Mr. Tidmore," and the community was

A burning oil well at Seminole. —Western History Collections, University of Oklahoma Library

known as Tidmore until 1907, when it was officially named Seminole for the Indians on whose allotted lands the town sat. The name means "wild" or, literally, "those who camp at a distance."

With a population of less than a thousand, the town was a trading center for cattlemen and farmers until 1926. On July 16 of that year, Fixico No. 1 blew in about a mile and a half east of what is today downtown Seminole. Within a year the population reached 35,000. At the height of the oil boom more than 100,000 persons received their mail at the Seminole post office.

People lived in shacks and covered wagons. Prices of everything, even drinking water, skyrocketed. A small basement rented for $400 a month, an old barn for $200, and a smokehouse for $50. Farm produce became scarce as farmers took to "roughnecking" on oil rigs. Rock Island freight income for six months in 1926 exceeded a million dollars.

Vice and corruption came with the oil boom. W. A. Bishop, a local attorney, sought to alleviate the housing shortage by platting a subdivision on the edge of the city. It became known as Bishop's Alley as establishments with names such as 49er's Dance Hall, the Big C, and the Palace opened for business. Bootlegging, dope-peddling, hijacking, brawling, and murder became common occurrences. A state peace officer was brought in to clean up the area.

Seminole recovered from the problems associated with the development of the Greater Seminole Field. Employment in refineries and petroleum service and supply companies is augmented by a variety of manufacturing companies. Fixico No. 1, which started it all, no longer pumps, but a replica of the rig is located in Municipal Park along with vintage pieces of drilling equipment from boom times.

—*Earlsboro* - OK 9————

This town, six miles west of Seminole on OK 9, was also affected by the oil boom. The community was established in 1894 as Loftus. There were many Seminole freedmen living in the area. One popular black named James Earls operated a barbershop for blacks. During the Civil War he had been the personal orderly for Confederate General Joe B. Wheeler. The town was named for the barber. Though the townsite plat read "Earlsborough" the Post Office Department spelled it Earlsboro.

The *Border Signal* began publication June 19, 1896. Its motto was "The Independent Voter is the Hope of the Nation." The editors advocated "free silver; free homes; single statehood and home rule and a tariff commission, an income tax and restrictive immigration laws for the nation."

—*Hotulkee—Harjo* - OK 9A————

These two rural communities reflect a strong Creek Indian heritage in their names. Hotulkee was platted in 1905 and named after Hotulke Martha, a prominent Creek. *Hutulka* means "wind people." Although on the Katy railroad with a station listed on timetables, Hotulkee never had a post office. Harjo, meaning "crazy" in the Creek language, the more recent of the two communities, had a post office from 1921 until 1954.

—*Wewoka* - US 270—OK 56————

The history of Wewoka reaches back to 1845 when conflict developed over the Seminoles' migration to Indian Territory. The United States government foolishly negotiated a treaty forcing the Seminoles to settle on Creek Indian land under Creek government. During the Seminole War in Florida, Creeks had been used to help defeat the Seminoles. Additionally, the comparatively free status of the Seminoles' slaves was distasteful to the Creeks, who held their slaves in strict bondage.

The Creeks who volunteered for service in Florida had been promised by Gen. Thomas S. Jessup that they could have all the Seminole slaves they could capture. In 1848 the attorney general of the United States ruled that the captive slaves must be returned. Accordingly, 286 blacks from Florida were delivered to a group of Seminole chiefs at Fort Gibson in January 1849. Resentful of the decision, the Creeks passed a law declaring that no town composed of free or limited-slavery Negroes could exist in the Creek Nation.

Wewoka Avenue, Wewoka. —Western History Collections, University of Oklahoma Library

The slaves, accustomed to living in their own communities apart from their Seminole masters, had already settled near Wewoka. Aware of the hostility of the Creeks, they armed themselves. On January 24, 1849, a party of Creeks along with some whites and Cherokees came to Wewoka to seize several slaves they claimed were theirs. Seminole Indians prepared to aid in defense of the Negro town, but troops from Fort Smith, Arkansas, intervened in time to stop the battle.

As an aftermath of the dispute, the Seminoles were assigned a separate reservation in 1856. In 1866, because of a surveying error, the Seminole capital was laid out astride the boundary between the Creek and Seminole nations. The Seminoles built schools on land later found to belong to the Creeks. Present-day Seminole Street, a half-block east of Main Street in Wewoka, was the final boundary between the two nations.

Today, except for museum displays, the only physical evidence of the Seminole capital is a pecan tree on the courthouse lawn. It was the tribal whipping post. It replaced an earlier execution tree that was cut down in 1902. The stump of the old tree is preserved in the Oklahoma Historical Society Building in Oklahoma City.

After conviction for a crime, such as thievery, a Seminole was stretched across the branches of a whipping tree to receive from 25 to 150 lashes with hickory withes. When a Seminole was convicted of a crime three times, he was executed.

The Rock Island railroad was constructed through Wewoka in 1899. A townsite was laid out, and white settlers began to arrive in 1902. The railroad made the town an important trading post for the some 3,400 Seminoles living in the area. Once a year each family head received $40, paid in silver dollars.

In 1926 the oil boom caused Wewoka's population to double within two months. Today the frenzy has passed and Wewoka's economy is supported primarily by diversified small industries.

HISTORICAL HIGHLIGHT

The Wewoka Switch

Visitors unversed in oil-field slang will be mystified by the name of the Wewoka Switch Motel. During the early days in Wewoka, telephone service was inadequate and railroad facilities were congested with freight. Lost items were frequently found in the siding known as the Wewoka Switch.

This became a ready excuse for almost any problem. When a merchant was unable to find an item wanted by a customer, he would say, "I've got it, but it's in the Wewoka Switch." During the oil boom, workers adopted and adapted the expression. To "get caught in a Wewoka Switch" grew to mean becoming involved in any trying situation.

The expression spread to oil fields around the world. It was finally immortalized in neon back at the site of its origin in the name of the Wewoka Switch Motel.

—Holdenville - US 270—OK 48————

This city began as a trading village called Echo, located two miles south of its present location. On May 24, 1895, it was officially designated as a post office named Fentress for J. Fentress Wisdom, the son of an Indian agent. The present site was surveyed in 1895 at the junction of the Choctaw, Oklahoma and Gulf and the Frisco railroads. Fentress moved to the new site in November and its name was changed to Holdenville, paying deference to J. F. Holden, general manager of the Choctaw Railroad. After the oil boom, the community's economic base became vested in light manufacturing.

—Bowlegs - OK 99————

The town, a product of the oil boom, was established in 1927 on an allotment of a Seminole named Bowlegs, a nephew of Chief Billy Bowlegs who had fought valiantly against removal of the tribe from Florida. The Bowlegs field to the east was discovered in 1922 and by 1955 had produced 135,000,000 barrels of oil.

EXCURSION

—*Konawa* - OK 39————

Four miles west of OK 99 on OK 39, this prosperous agricultural community was established in 1904. It subsequently benefited from activities of petroleum production in the area. Its name means "string of beads" in the Seminole language. Every August the community sponsors an All Night Singing in Veterans Memorial Park. Musical groups come from miles around to participate in this thirteen-hour program, the nation's largest all-night gospel sing.

—*Sasakwa* - OK 56————

This old Seminole Indian settlement developed around the home of John F. Brown, a wealthy Seminole chief. A church and a large camp-meeting ground were nearby. The Sasakwa post office was established in 1890. The town is best known as the locale of the so-called Green Corn Rebellion of 1917.

The affair was precipitated by left-wing extremist groups, socialists and International Workers of the World (commonly called Wobblies) who preached that the struggle in Europe was a "rich man's war and a poor man's fight." In August some five hundred whites, Indians, and blacks formed the Working Class Union and roamed the countryside burning railroad bridges, cutting fences, and turning livestock into fields. The abortive effort to take over or at least thwart the government was quelled by a posse and the leaders were arrested and punished. The name of the rebellion came from the participants' diet of barbecued beef and an Indian green-corn dish called "tomfuller." The timing of the disturbance also coincided with the annual green-corn dance of the neighboring Shawnees.

—*Francis*————

This small agricultural community on the Frisco railroad just south of the Canadian River is reached by a county road off OK 99. The settlement began in 1894 as Newton. The name was changed to Francis in 1902, honoring David R. Francis, secretary of the interior under President McKinley. During its heyday, Francis was a railroad division point with a roundhouse and shops. Today the roundhouse is gone and the business section has dwindled to a single block.

—*Ada* - US 377—OK 99————————

William J. Reed, better known as Jeff, founded Ada in 1890 by building a combination log store and dwelling. The following year a post office was approved, called Ada for Reed's daughter. The town grew rapidly, aided by the coming of the Frisco railroad in 1900. By 1910 its population was 4,349. Within the first decade of the twentieth century it had seven newspapers, one of which was a daily. The population almost doubled by 1920 and again by 1940.

Times were turbulent in Ada during the first few years after statehood. The town earned a reputation as one of the toughest places in the Southwest. In 1908 there were thirty-six murders in or near town, few of which received more than passing attention by the courts. It was an accepted fact that if a killer had friends and money he usually went free.

In 1909 an ex-lawman, A. A. "Gus" Bobbitt, died from a shotgun blast in an ambush. James P. Miller was in town. Miller was better known as "Killin' Jim" or "Deacon Jim." Miller attended church regularly; he never drank, cursed, or smoked, but he killed for money. Miller's favorite weapon was a shotgun.

When word spread that Miller was the hired assassin of an outlaw gang, a committee of townspeople formed. They tracked down Miller and brought him to jail, along with three others who had planned the murder. After Miller's examining trial, it appeared that justice might be tempered with money.

At 2:30 in the morning on April 14, some forty or fifty masked men opened the jail and took the four accused men to a livery barn a short distance away. They threw ropes over the rafters and, one at a time, hoisted the four outlaws to their doom and left them hanging as a message for all to see. Oklahoma courts tightened their procedures and outlaws learned that their era had ended.

There was a sequel to the affair. Jim Miller had been a suspect in the assassination of Pat Garrett, the slayer of Billy the Kid. There was a rumor that Miller had confessed to killing Garrett before he was hung. But the jailer, Walter Gayne, flatly denied that Miller had confessed to anything.

"I ought to know," Gayne said, "because I hung him."

Ada settled into a peaceful existence, economically nurtured by the oil industry and numerous manufacturing enterprises. The old Frisco passenger depot has been renovated to house the Ada Chamber of Commerce, which tells visitors that "Ada is proud to be small enough to offer that 'hometown' atmosphere."

—*Fittstown* - US 377—OK 99————

Named to honor John Fitts, the geologist who discovered the Fitts oil pool, Fittstown is a product of the oil boom. Its post office was established in 1935.

Byrd's Mill Spring is three miles southwest of Fittstown. It flows at a rate up to twenty million gallons a day and is the source of Ada's municipal water supply. The spring was known to Indians long before white men came to the area. The Choctaws and the Chickasaws used to camp here and Frank Byrd, a Chickasaw chief, operated a water-powered gristmill during the 1870s.

—*Pontotoc* - US 377—OK 99————

With a post office established in 1858, Pontotoc is one of the oldest communities in the area. Although now in Johnston County, it took its name from Pontotoc County in the Chickasaw Nation. Once a prosperous trading center for surrounding ranches, it is now a roadside community with no commercial services. Its name means "cattails growing on the prairie."

—*Tishomingo* - US 377—OK 99————

The roots of Tishomingo penetrate deep into Chickasaw history. Before the capital of the Chickasaw Nation was established here in 1856, the site was an Indian camp called Good Springs. In 1850 an Indian named Jackson Frazier built a house and soon two stores were in business. The *Chickasaw and Choctaw Herald* began publication in 1858. It promised its readers:

> . . . the *Herald* is intended to be, what a paper under the circumstances should be; but what no paper, heretofore established among the Indians, has been. It will be a record of the habits, customs, laws and usages amongst the indian [sic] tribes, that cannot fail to interest all persons desirous of obtaining information on this subject. It will, at the same time, convey to the red men the advanced state of the Arts and Sciences among the whites, and stimulate the Indians to the acquisition of knowledge and the pursuits of industry.

In 1856 the capital of the Chickasaw Nation was established at Tishomingo with a log cabin serving as the capitol. A brick building replaced the log cabin in 1858, but burned in 1890 and was replaced by a granite structure that has served as the Johnston County Courthouse since 1907. The old log cabin Chickasaw capitol has been restored. It now serves as a museum maintained by the Oklahoma Historical Society.

The former capitol of the Chickasaw Nation in Tishomingo is now the Johnston County Courthouse.

—*Madill* - US 70—OK 99————

Madill was established in 1901 with the coming of the Frisco railroad and named for George A. Madill, an attorney for the railroad. For years the economy of the community was dependent upon surrounding farm and ranch lands. The first bank was known locally as the "Cottonwood National" because it was built of boards sawed out of nearby cottonwood trees.

The discovery of the Cumberland oil field in 1939 brought a change in the local economy and started industrial diversification. However, the construction of Denison Dam and the formation of Lake Texoma in 1945 wrought the greatest change. Madill set out to become a recreational center for the vast new playground, and it has succeeded admirably.

EXCURSION ————

—*Little City* - OK 199————

Originally called Pure City, the community was a product of petroleum development from oil discovered during construction of Denison Dam. The Washita River was diverted to permit development of the oil field. The name of the town was changed to Little City for Ruel V. Little, a Madill lawyer and oilman.

199

—*Fort Washita* - OK 199————

In 1841, Choctaw and Chickasaw Indians began building schools and establishing law and order in southeastern Indian Territory. However, their prosperity was threatened by Comanches and other Plains Indians. To fulfill a treaty to provide protection to the recently removed "Civilized Tribes," Fort Washita was established April 23, 1842, on the Washita River near its confluence with the Red River (now the bank of Lake Texoma).

The post was never attacked by Indians. Its greatest importance came after the discovery of gold in California. On the main road from Fort Smith, Arkansas, to El Paso, Texas, Fort Washita became a rendezvous for emigrant parties preparing for the trip across the Texas desert.

The surge of gold-seekers prompted the construction of massive stone buildings, but they were not completed until the gold rush was nearly over. However, during the 1850s there was a flow of settlers into Texas. Fort Washita's importance decreased as new forts were opened farther west. On May 1, 1861, Confederate forces appeared at the gates, and four troops of U.S. Cavalry surrendered the post and rode away. Confederate forces used the installation until 1865. Fort Washita was never again occupied by U.S. troops.

Fort Washita, a popular stop on the tourist trail, dates from 1842.

Visitors have been coming ot Fort Washita since 1903. —Western History Collections, University of Oklahoma Library

The fort reverted to the Department of the Interior in 1870, and it was turned over to the Chickasaw family of Abbie Davis Colbert and her son. Many of the fort's structures served as farm buildings until well into the twentieth century. The Colbert family also used the fort's cemetery as a family burial ground.

In 1962 the Oklahoma Historical Society acquired the fort and appropriated money to restore it. The society operates the fort as a museum. On weekends, "military reenactors" frequently turn the old post into a living museum and cannons again belch smoke across the parade ground.

—*Oakland* - US 70————

Located just west of Madill on US 70, Oakland was the older of the two communities. Capt. Richard Wiggs, a Confederate army officer, was the first settler. He came in 1874 and built a house on Glasses Creek. He farmed for eight years and then built the Wiggs Hotel. A post office opened in 1881. However, the railroad bypassed the town and most of the action moved to Madill. Today Oakland prospers as a residential suburb of Madill.

—*Kingston* - OK 32-70A————

When Kingston was settled in 1894, its residents had no idea of what the future would bring. In 1907 D. R. Johnston, editor and publisher of the *Kingston Messenger*, noted that while the population of the town was 800, his paper had 1,500 subscribers. Today Kingston caters not to farmers and ranchers but to fishermen and pleasure seekers who come to the small resort areas that speckle the coves and inlets of Lake Texoma. US 70 between Kingston and Durant traverses the Roosevelt Memorial Bridge, almost a mile long.

—*New Woodville* - OK 70A————

New Woodville is "new" because the original townsite of Woodville was inundated by Lake Texoma. It had been established in 1888 and named for L. L. Wood, a prominent Chickasaw. Like other small communities in the area, New Woodville draws its sustenance from visitors to Lake Texoma and retirees who have settled in the small communities that surround the lake.

—*Willis* - OK 99————

At Willis a bridge carries traffic on OK 99 across the Red River arm of Lake Texoma into Texas. The bridge is relatively recent. In 1840 the Willis family came from Mississippi by wagon and settled on the fertile land beside the Red River. Much of the time the river ran shallow enough to ford, but a ferry was available when the river made one of its frequent unannounced rises. The ferry was operated by a windlass and cable. Passengers summoned the ferry by ringing a large bell on the Texas side. Mail came to Willis via Hagerman, Texas, by horseback until the community got its own post office in 1886.

—*Roff* - OK 1————

Established in 1890, Roff was named for Joseph P. Roff, a local rancher. The Frisco railroad built a line through the community in 1900 and 1901, creating a minor boom. In 1913, the mining and processing of silica in the area began to make a strong contribution to the local economy.

—*Hickory* - OK 1————

As early as November 15, 1893, there were enough people in the Hickory area to warrant a post office. Like many small towns along the railroad, Hickory suffered from transient criminals. The post office became a target of burglars. The first robbery netted $59.12 in money and stamps. In 1908 the post office safe was blown open; residents thought the noise was a thunderstorm. The thieves made off with $300 cash and $270 worth of stamps. In May 1923, burglars hit the bank, they got $113.99, of which $76.04 was in pennies.

—*Mill Creek* - OK 1-7————

In 1879 Mill Creek acquired a post office. The nearby creek was so named because Cyrus Harris, perennial governor of the Chickasaw Nation, operated a gristmill on it. In 1902 the editor of the *Wapanucka Press* issued a gratuitous insult to Mill Creek: "*The Mill Creek Times* says there are no vacant houses there. That is easy as there are very few houses in the town." Silica and magnesium carbonate mining and granite quarries have since contributed to Mill Creek's economy.

—*Ravia* - OK 1-78————

The present size of this late-nineteenth-century trading center belies the fact that three newspapers once vied for subscribers. The *Ravia Gazette* heralded itself as "published for the dissemination of information of a public character." The rival *Ravia Tribune* was "a free forum for the discussion of all subjects." Lydia E. Pinkham's Vegetable Compound was the most persistent advertiser in the *Tribune*.

—*Washington* - OK 24————

While the area was still part of the Chickasaw Nation, Montfort T. Johnson, son of an English actor and a Chickasaw woman, established a number of ranches in the region. Jack Brown, a black cowboy, became Johnson's partner on a ranch just northwest of present-day Washington. Brown was to receive every fourth calf. He has been dubbed Oklahoma's first sharecropper.

Washington's post office was established in 1904, named for "Little Boy" George Washington, a Caddo chief. Washington was a shipping point on the Oklahoma Central Railroad, but there was no depot or platform. Trains stopped at a lumberyard to take on and discharge passengers and freight. Cotton, corn, and cattle were the principal crops.

—Blanchard - OK 76————

Near the Washita River crossing of the Chisholm Trail, this site was a trading post known as Fred during the 1870s. In 1906 W. G. Blanchard laid out a town incorporated the following year. The Santa Fe Railway provided the impetus for the development of Blanchard. In March 1908, excursion trains brought between 4,000 and 5,000 people from Chickasha, Purcell, and Ada. Before the day was over the newcomers bought 700 lots. Blanchard had economic problems, but recovered as a bedroom community for nearby Norman.

—Cole - OK 74B————

A. E. Cunningham and his family came to the area in 1900. In 1905 the Oklahoma Central Railroad proposed to come across the Cunningham farm. The Cunninghams joined with Preslie B. Cole and each dedicated ten acres to the proposed town. The post office was established in the Cunningham home but named for Cole.

—Dibble————

Located on a county road east of OK 76 and north of OK 39, Dibble grew out of ranching country where "the grass was as high as a horse's back." Ranchers John and James Dibble gave their name to the post office when it was established in 1894.

Dibble suffered for want of adequate farm-to-market roads, but it was on a road known as the Colbert Highway, which was built through Blanchard to Lindsay in 1917. By 1936 the *Lindsay News* complained that the road "has been sadly neglected for many moons." Dibble profited from the development of oil fields in the area.

—Lindsay - OK 19-76————

Settled in 1902, Lindsay was eventually able to claim the title "Broomcorn Capital of the World." Over the years, prices of broomcorn on the world market were set by buyers in Lindsay. Black Spanish broomcorn grew 6 to 15 feet in height. In appearance it looks like corn, but it heads out like maize and other grain sorghums. The head, minus seed, was used in the manufacture of brooms. Fibers grew 10 to 24 inches long, depending upon weather and soil conditions. Broomcorn was harvested by hand. It was a fairly short-lived industry, done in by high cost and shortage of labor along with the advent of plastic brooms.

Hauling broomcorn to market. —Western History Collections, University of Oklahoma Library

The Healdton Oil Field

From Lindsay to Wilson, OK 76 passes through the fabulously rich Healdton oil field. Oil and gas have been found in sixty-five of Oklahoma's seventy-seven counties, but it was the Healdton discovery that helped Oklahoma achieve national leadership in the production of oil.

The first producing well in the field was brought in on August 4, 1913, just southwest of Wirt, now virtually a ghost town. But it was far from a ghost town after the discovery well came in. Wirt became a sprawling, brawling, littered boomtown of clapboard, corrugated iron, and tent houses. There were so many tents that the town was called Ragtown. Barkers stood on street corners in Ardmore day and night calling *"Ragtown, fifty cents!"* to fill busses with people who wanted to be taken to the hub of oil activities, and there was no dearth of passengers.

In addition to bona fide oilmen, roustabouts, geologists, and speculators, the oil boom attracted slick-tongued horse traders, clever-fingered gamblers, gunmen, and shady ladies. Fires frequently swept through the jerry-built shanties. A resident of Wirt told about one fire that raged through the business section:

A gambler walked out of his casino to assay the conflagration. "About three hours away," he remarked, as he strolled back into the bustling gambling house. He picked up a telephone and ordered lumber to build a new building. Then he rounded up a crew and, at the last minute before the fire swept through his casino, had them set his furnishings out in the street. After the fire passed, his crew raked the coals off the lot and worked all night putting up a new building. He reopened his gambling house at six o'clock the next morning.

Many communities along OK 76 and on sideroads to the east and west are farming and ranching trading centers that were established during

Bull Head No. 3, a burning oil well in the Healdton field.
—Western History Collections, University of Oklahoma Library

the last decades before and after the turn of the century. Their populations multiplied during the oil boom. After the frenzy subsided, some returned to their former status, some attracted small industries to diversify their economic resources, and some deteriorated to virtual ghost towns, now little more than names on the highway map.

—Healdton - OK 76————

In 1883 Elisha S. Mason established a post office a half-mile east of the present site of Healdton. There were a few houses, a general store, and a wagon yard. Charles H. Heald became postmaster in 1897 and the settlement's name was changed from Mason to Healdton.

At the start of the oil boom, John Ringling, one of the brothers of Ringling Brothers' Circus fame, and Jake L. Hamon, an oil-property speculator, decided to build a railroad to service the Healdton field. The railroad was surveyed a half-mile west of Healdton. There was a rumor that Wirt, the upstart oil camp to the west was planning to move to the railroad. Ben C. Heald, who had succeeded his father as postmaster, acted fast. He loaded his post office on a wagon and relocated it at the present site of Healdton. Major oil companies and their supporting operators and services soon established offices in the growing town. Oil well service and supply companies still provide the base of Healdton's economy.

—*Lone Grove* - US 70————

In 1883 Christopher Columbus Price led a small group of pioneers into the Chickasaw Nation and settled north of the Red River by a grove of cedar trees. Others followed until the settlement included general stores, a cotton gin, wagon yards, and other accoutrements of a rural frontier village. A post office was established in 1885.

An entirely different type of town celebrated its centennial on May 4, 1985. Today, Lone Grove has a charter form of government to protect it from absorption into Ardmore. Many residents work in Ardmore, but they prefer the small-town rural atmosphere of Lone Grove. The city limits encompass forty-eight square miles. In 1985-90 it experienced thirty percent growth.

—*Wilson* - US 70—OK 76————

Another product of the oil boom, Wilson was established in 1914 on the railroad built by John Ringling and Jake Hamon. It was named for Charles Wilson, Ringling's secretary.

In 1924 the chamber of commerce boasted a population of 5,000 with an immediate trade area of 20,000. There were two cotton gins, three oil refineries, several wholesale houses, six lumberyards, and forty-eight retail stores. L. B. Mason's Free Coffee Cafe advertised that it never closed and that regular meals cost only thirty cents. The economy of Wilson is still based upon petroleum production as well as ranching in the surrounding area.

—*Ringling* - US 70—OK 89————

Ringling is another oil-camp town spawned by the Healdton field. In 1913 John Ringling and Jake L. Hamon launched plans to build a railroad from Oklahoma to the Pacific coast. They gave it a grandiose name, the Oklahoma, New Mexico and Pacific Railway Company, but most people called it the Ringling Railroad. The first spike was driven in Ardmore on August 4, 1913, the same day the discovery well for the Healdton field came in.

In actuality the railroad got only as far as twenty miles west of Ardmore. It brought about the founding of Ringling in 1914. Ringling became an oil camp; during the boom days it teemed with oil field workers and supply companies.

—*Cornish* - OK 89————

Located a mile south of Ringling, Cornish began in 1891 and took its name from John H. Cornish, a local rancher. In 1903 Moses E. Harris established an orphans' home at Cornish, a private philanthropy. The home continued to operate until 1956; however, most of the residents of Cornish moved north to Ringling in 1916 to benefit from the oil boom.

———— EXCURSION

—*Grady* - OK 32————

This community established in 1890 has not worn well, but the area is of considerable historical significance. Spanish and French activity along the Red River during the eighteenth century is well documented. Between 3,000 and 4,000 Indians lived along the river. In 1759 the Spanish lost a battle to the French here and retreated to San Antonio. The French maintained a trading post for many years.

Scattered artifacts of Spanish and French origin have turned up, fueling rumors and stories of buried treasure. As a result, archaeologists began a study of the San Bernardo site, locally referred to as the Spanish Fort. However, if the story that appeared in the *Fort Worth Gazette* on November 3, 1884, was correct, the archaeologists may have come too late.

While chasing a panther, hunters found a cave about 40 feet long and 130 feet wide. In it were an old cannon, copper kettles, packsaddles, and agricultural implements:

> But the thing which attracted our attention at once was the sight of six large boxes all of the same size and shape. They were about five and one-half feet long, two feet wide and 18 inches deep, the lids being fastened by crude copper hasps. We found little trouble in prying up the lids. We found quite a lot of old arms such as swords and blunderbusses and stilletoes, some old quilted coats of mail, many old Spanish books and a complete wardrobe for an old convent.
>
> But the contents of the third box which we opened was the one which excited us. This one had a partition which cut off about two feet from one end and in this we found two bushels of Spanish money and bullion. The gold consisted of old Spanish doubloons and was contained in five leather sacks. The silver coin was

principally in Spanish Rex dollars. There was also three silver bricks and two golden crucifixes of considerable value.

OK 102
McLoud—Wanette

—McLoud - OK 102————

When the town was established in 1895, it was named for John W. McCloud, an attorney for the Choctaw, Oklahoma and Gulf Railroad. The area was part of the Kickapoo Indian reservation. A number of Kickapoos still live northeast of town and there is a Kickapoo Tribal Office. A Society of Friends Mission established in 1893 is still active.

—Dale - OK 102————

Dale is one of the oldest towns in Pottawatomie County, a survivor of the five towns in existence when the run for homesteads was staged in 1891. Originally it was named King for John King, a Shawnee Indian allottee. In 1893 a petition was circulated to change the name to Dale for Frank Dale, a territorial judge who lived in Guthrie. For many years there were hard feelings over the name change. As one writer put it, people "felt the Indians had been robbed and gypped enough, and the little town founded by John King should remain that way for posterity."

Before the coming of the railroad, Dale was on the Tecumseh-Oklahoma City stage line. Three stages a week brought passengers and mail. The town has moved twice, first in 1893, and again in 1895 so it could be on the railroad.

—Tribbey - OK 102————

This faded agricultural trading center has seen better days. It started in 1904, a year after the Santa Fe came, and a post office was established the following year. Alpheus M. Tribbey operated the Tribbey House, a residence-type hotel. In 1910 the population was 200; it doubled by 1912, and reached 500 in 1920. During harvest time, dirt streets were crowded with farm wagons hauling bales of cotton. There was a wagon yard where people could sleep, cook meals, and feed and water their teams for $1.50 a night.

—Eason - OK 39————

This town on OK 39, west of its junction with OK 102, began when Scott Eason opened a general store shortly after he homesteaded 160 acres in the run of 1891. In 1895 James F. Quillan came to the county and opened a larger general store, and the town moved. Nate P. Willis arrived in 1892 and established the Eason Nursery. He was first in Cleveland County to irrigate a farm, with water pumped from wells with windmills.

—*Wanette* - OK 102————

Wanette's post office dates from 1894. There is stout debate over the name. A historical authority has maintained Wanette is a misspelling of the title of the once-popular song "Juanita"; local residents insist the name is of Indian origin, perhaps "Pleasant Prairie" in the Pottawatomi language.

After the railroad arrived, Wanette had three newspapers, the *Standard*, the *Times*, and the *Winner*. Prior to statehood, nine saloons lined the main street. Press Stovall's was the largest and the fanciest. During those days, Wanette was a Saturday night town. As many as 500 buggies and wagons would bring celebrants from the surrounding area.

—*Harrah* - US 62—OK 270————

This agricultural trading center began in 1894 as Pennington, changed its name to Sweeney in 1896, and finally became Harrah in 1898. Now virtually a suburb of Oklahoma City, the community's principal claim to fame is being the birthplace of Paul and Lloyd Waner, ace major league batters of the 1930s. Playing outfield for the Pittsburgh Pirates, they became known as Big Poison and Little Poison and were of sufficient annoyance to opposing batters that they were elected to the Baseball Hall of Fame.

—*Byars* - OK 59————

The present community was established in 1903 on the Oklahoma Central Railroad. Its principal crops were cotton and corn. As early as 1876 there had been a settlement called Johnson and Johnsonville just to the north, near old Camp Arbuckle. Both the California Road and the Fort Sill-Fort Smith Military Road came past. After Camp Arbuckle was abandoned by the army it was occupied by Delaware Indians under Black Beaver and known as Beaversville.

By 1908 the population of Byars exceeded a thousand. The town had two hotels, two cotton gins, two mills, and a Farmers' Union warehouse.

—*Rosedale* - OK 59————

Established in April 1908, when a townsite of ninety acres was opened to settlement, Rosedale attracted more than three hundred people during its first six months. Two gristmills, two cotton gins, and a sawmill went into operation as the town clustered about the Oklahoma Central

Railroad's depot. After the line was abandoned, the town declined rapidly.

—*Maysville* - OK 19-74————

In 1878 a post office called Beef Creek was established at this site. The name was changed to Maysville in 1902 for ranchers David and John Mayes. The principal economic resource of the community was broomcorn production until 1946, when the Golden Trend field spread petroleum production through Garvin, Grady, and McClain counties. After that Maysville called itself the "Heart of the Golden Trend."

Maysville's best-known citizen was Wiley Post, the pioneer aviator who was killed in an Alaskan plane crash in 1935 along with Will Rogers. Maysville pays tribute to Wiley Post annually in November.

—*Alex* - OK 19C————

This farming community in the fertile Washita River valley was established in 1885 and named for the first postmaster, William V. Alexander. Alexander is believed to have been the first white man to settle in this part of Grady County. Known as "Uncle Red," he was born in Gordon Springs, Alabama, in 1833. After going to California in 1857, he joined the Confederacy and fought with Gen. Stand Watie.

He came to the Alex area in 1878, settling about a half-mile west of the present townsite. In 1881 Alexander established a store in his home. Settlers began to move into the area in 1904 after arrival of the railroad.

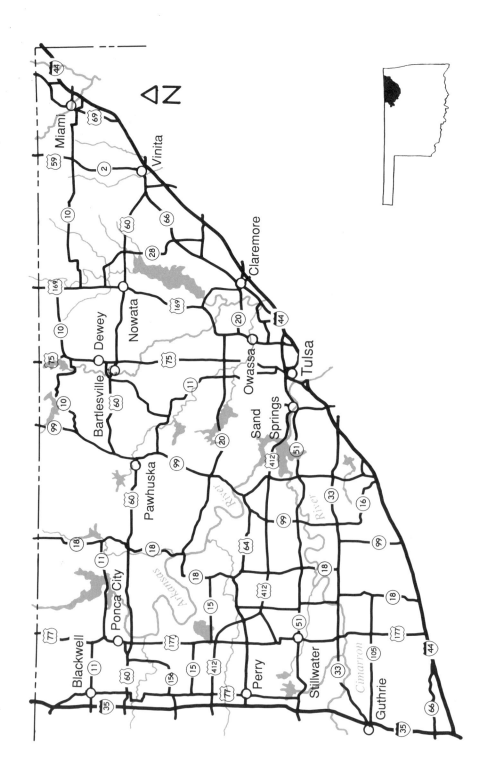

V. Land of the Osages

Prior to the Louisiana Purchase, the Osages were the largest of the southern Siouan tribes, occupying much of the area now included in Missouri and Arkansas. They obtained guns by trading peltries and furs with the French; they acquired horses from the Spaniards by way of the Kiowas. Twice a year, always during a full moon, they went out on the "Grand Prairie" in pursuit of buffalo, deer, and antelope and to trade with the Comanches, sometimes trekking as far as eight hundred miles.

As the removal of Indians from the East began, the Osages resented the encroachment of emigrant Cherokees upon their traditional hunting grounds. Alternating warfare and negotiation culminated in a treaty on January 11, 1839, at Fort Gibson. The Osages ceded their lands in Missouri, Arkansas, and Oklahoma in exchange for a greatly reduced reservation in Kansas.

Life became difficult for them. The Osages continued their semiannual hunting and trading trips; but, by 1853, white emigration through the hunting ground had driven the game so far away that they returned with few buffalo robes and skins and little buffalo tallow—articles which they bartered for food. To make matters worse, the United States government began to pay an annuity to the Comanches. This made the Comanches independent of the trade they had formerly carried on with the Osages.

The Osages decided they too should receive compensation. They collected by making raids upon passing travelers. In 1854, few emigrants and freighters were allowed through territory the Osages haunted without molestation; troops were called out to protect roads and trails.

Following the Civil War, eager settlers clamored for the Osages' land in Kansas. On September 19, 1865, the United States government came up with a treaty claiming the Osages had more land than they needed. Since payments to the Osages under former treaties had ceased, the tribe wanted to improve its condition by selling their surplus land to the United States.

After the fact, the Osages learned that money received for their reservation would go into a "civilization fund," to be spent by the secretary of the interior for the education and civilization of *all* Indian tribes in the United States. The Osages objected; they would never have signed the treaty had they known the money would not be used solely to benefit their tribe.

The Osage tribe was divided over whether they should move farther west in Kansas, where there were still buffalo herds, or take land in Indian Territory south of the Kansas border. Paw Hue Skah spoke in favor of going west. In *Wah'Kon-Tah: The Osage and the White Man's Road*, John Joseph Mathews told of Wah To An Kah's address to the council on advantages of the land to the south:

> I have been in the south. I have seen much there. There are many trees with black boles where deer sleep when sun is hot. I saw many deer there, and many other things. I said, this land will be good for my people. I said, there is much game in this country; there is much grass and much water. I said, my people will be happy in this land. White man cannot put iron thing in ground here. White man will not come to this land.

In 1872, with the proceeds from the sale of their land in Kansas, the Osages bought a reservation from the Cherokees in Oklahoma Territory, roughly a million and a half acres for 70 cents an acre. The tract is present-day Osage County. Ironically, mineral rights on their new reservation eventually made the Osages the wealthiest tribe in the United States.

The lush virgin bluestem grass that covered most of their reservation made it choice cattle country, and the Osages enriched tribal coffers by leasing grazing rights to ranchers. By 1890 they had thirty-two leases ranging from 4,800 to 80,000 acres, at 3 and a half cents an acre. In 1890, when the Department of the Interior wanted to remove cattle from Indian lands as a prelude to opening the lands to white settlement, the Osages had to remind the government that the tribe owned their reservation. In 1906 the Osage reservation was distributed by allotment. Each member of the tribe received 657 acres. Mineral rights belonged to the tribe as a whole.

Pawhuska was the capital of the Osage Nation. All Osage business was—and still is—conducted at the Osage Agency, a 104-acre tract on Agency Hill immediately north of the Pawhuska business district. Oil was discovered in the nation in 1897. In 1912, open-air auctions for the sale of oil leases began at the Osage Agency.

Bidders sat on bleachers under an elm tree to the north of the agency while an auctioneer "cried" the sales. The first sale, during which a 160-acre tract brought a bonus of $1 million or more, was held on March 2,

1922. The largest bonus ever paid for a tract was $1,990,000 on March 19, 1924. The tree under which the auctions were held became known as the "Million Dollar Elm." As more and more oil fields were opened and developed, tribal wealth continued to grow. The peak year was 1926, when each full Osage headright was worth $15,000.

Some Osages were wildly extravagant with their money. A 1927 account tells of an Osage lady who in one afternoon purchased a $12,000 fur coat, a $3,000 diamond ring, a $5,000 automobile, and $7,000 worth of furniture that she shipped to California for an additional $600. She made a $4,000 down payment on a home in California and, in the same transaction, invested $12,000 in Florida real estate.

In 1926, a newspaper reporter asked a venerable Osage who was seated in the back seat of a chauffeur-driven Packard touring car what he thought of the riches oil had brought to his tribe. The Osage replied, "I believe it is right that we be paid for the loss of our buffalo."

US 169—OK 10-88
South Coffeyville—Oologah

—South Coffeyville - US 169————

The original community at South Coffeyville dates from 1906, when it was called Polson because the townsite occupied the allotments of Martin and Earl Polson. In 1909 the name was changed to South Coffeyville. The manufacture of liquors in the Cherokee Nation was prohibited by law. So much liquor was imported from Kansas that the road by which it entered became known as the Whiskey Trail.

In the early days a few homes were scattered among a proliferation of saloons masquerading as beer halls, pool halls, and dance halls. Since both Indian Territory and Kansas were dry, bootleggers flourished. When U.S. marshals from Indian Territory arrived to raid the whiskey joints, the proprietors moved their stock out their back doors and a few yards across the border into Kansas.

—Lenapah - US 169—OK 10————

This community is named after the Delaware Indians who, in 1867, used tribal funds to purchase equal rights with the Cherokees in the Cherokee Nation. (*Lenápe* was the original name of the Delaware tribe.) During its heyday, Lenapah had two banks, several churches, and a newspaper. The town seemed to have an attraction for outlaws. In 1892, H. C. Schufeldt, proprietor of the first general store, was robbed of $300 by Henry Starr, a young outlaw. The following year Schufeldt was again victimized by Cherokee Bill and the Verdigris Kid.

Henry Starr: Champion Bank Robber

Henry Starr was nineteen at the time of the Lenapah robbery. Robbing Schufeldt may have been his first act as an outlaw. Shortly before, Starr had been working on a ranch between Bartlesville and Nowata when he was arrested for the first time.

There are two stories regarding Henry Starr's first arrest. One says he was arrested in Nowata when the owner of the horse he was riding recognized the animal. Starr maintained the horse was an unclaimed stray that had wandered onto the ranch where he was working. By the other story, he was on his way to Nowata when he agreed to carry a valise for a stranger. U.S. marshals stopped him and found whiskey in the suitcase. Starr was acquitted at his trial, but by then had already spent several months in jail awaiting due process.

Starr maintained that the time he spent in jail set him on a criminal path: "I was only a kid, and father and mother had brought me up to think it was an awful disgrace to be in jail. They chained me to a bed that time. I was innocent. I felt I might as well be dead as disgraced. I came out with blood in my eyes."

Henry Starr specialized in bank robberies. On his deathbed he maintained he had robbed more banks than any other outlaw; that

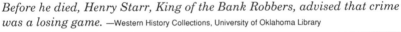

Before he died, Henry Starr, King of the Bank Robbers, advised that crime was a losing game. —Western History Collections, University of Oklahoma Library

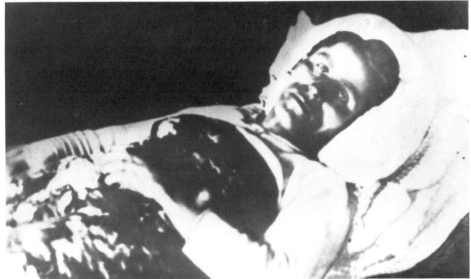

included Jesse James and the Younger brothers, definitely experts in the field. On March 15, 1915, Starr and his gang robbed two banks on the same day, a feat attempted by others but never equaled. Starr's trademark was to warn the victims as he covered them with a gun, "Hands up and hands steady."

Henry Starr was a well-educated Cherokee. He was born December 3, 1873, at Fort Gibson and attended the Cherokee mission school until the death of his father. After his mother remarried, he left home to work as a cowboy because he did not get along with his stepfather.

In 1892, after the robbery of the express office in Nowata, Deputy United States Marshal Floyd Wilson, also a special officer for the Iron Mountain Railroad, recognized Henry Starr in Lenapah and tried to arrest him. Starr killed Wilson, the only man to suffer such a fate at the hand of the outlaw.

Arrested in Colorado Springs, Colorado, and tried in Fort Smith, Arkansas, Henry Starr was sentenced to be hanged for manslaughter. During a two-year delay, prominent members of the Cherokee Nation succeeded in getting a new trial. The final sentence was five years for manslaughter and ten years for bank robbery.

After serving eight years, Starr was pardoned by President Theodore Roosevelt because he disarmed a berserk prisoner. Starr told the president he intended to go straight. He married, opened a real estate office in Little Rock, Arkansas, and named his son Roosevelt Starr. When Oklahoma became a state, Mr. and Mrs. Henry Starr were guests at the inauguration of Governor Charles N. Haskell. Then the state of Arkansas dusted off an old indictment for the robbery of a bank in Bentonville in 1893. Starr moved to Oklahoma and took up his old trade. Twice more, in Colorado and Oklahoma, he was convicted and sentenced, and twice more he was paroled.

In Stroud, Oklahoma, he went into the movie business and made a picture called *Debtor To The Law,* in which he played himself in a bank robbery. Later, someone noticed that wherever Starr went on weekends, the local bank was robbed.

On the morning of February 18, 1921, at ten o'clock, four men strolled into the Peoples' National Bank in Harrison, Arkansas: "*Hands up and hands steady!*"

As Starr stuffed money into a sack, he was shot. His companions took to the hills. During the four days before he died, Starr confessed to his crimes, bragged about his career as a bank robber, and advised that crime was a losing game.

—*Delaware* - US 169—OK 28————

The first settlement or trading post here was called Kammama. In the late 1890s the post office was formally renamed Delaware. After 1907, at the height of the oil boom, the little town became a highly congested resort of drillers, roustabouts, pipeline workers, pumpers, lease hounds, gamblers, bootleggers, and "entertainers." In one block there were fourteen saloons and gambling houses; brawls were common and killings not uncommon.

—*Coodys Bluff* - US 60————

Three miles east of Nowata, Coodys Bluff is the oldest landmark in Nowata County. Richard Coody, a Cherokee, settled at the base of the red bluff in 1853. What was generally designated as "the first church for white people" was built by L. T. Kinkead, who came in 1878. The oldest cemetery in Nowata County is on the crest of the bluff.

—*Nowata* - US 60-169————

Contrary to the oft-told story, Nowata did not get its name from a sign that said "NO WATA" on a nearby spring that had gone dry. *No-we-ata* is a Delaware word meaning "welcome." The Post Office Department spelled it "Nowata."

In 1889, as the St. Louis and Iron Mountain Railroad extended its line from Coffeyville, Kansas, it established towns every six miles. William Carey brought the first business to what became Nowata almost a year before the railroad arrived. The Carey Hotel accommodated railroad

As the faded sign proclaims, the Savoy Hotel was built to accommodate health-seekers who came to Nowata to partake of "radium water baths."

men and speculators who preceded the railroad. Other businesses followed.

In 1892 the Cherokee Nation platted the townsite—a mile square—and auctioned off lots. Municipal government conformed to tribal law of the Cherokee Nation. Early settlers had built upon lots to which they had no legal title. Subsequent litigation was avoided because public sentiment was against anyone else trying to buy one of the previously occupied lots.

A producing oil well was "brought in" in 1904, precipitating development of fields of shallow oil and natural gas wells in the county. One well struck "radium water" instead of oil, and a hotel was built to house those who came to bathe. In 1909 the hotel burned, two days before its scheduled opening. Two years later Charlie Good opened the Savoy Hotel on the same site. There were rooms for 200 guests and an orchestra for their entertainment. The hotel advertised the water as a cure for arthritis, rheumatism, skin diseases, obesity, diabetes, and kidney, stomach and bladder ailments. In the basement there were nine rooms in which guests could drink radium water, bathe, and sweat their ailments away. A faded sign on the west side of the old Savoy Hotel still proclaims "RADIUM WATER BATHS."

—*Talala* - US 169————

This present-day, small farming community does not hint of its past. It was established in 1890. Ranchers brought their cattle to the stockyard and loaded them on the Missouri Pacific as townspeople turned out to watch the cowboys work. There were two passenger trains a day.

The town was named for Captain Talala, a Cherokee officer in the Third Indian Home Guard Regiment during the Civil War. Documentation is lacking, but it is a pretty good bet that he was redheaded. *Ta-la-lah* is the Cherokee word for woodpecker. Cherokee girls and boys who had red hair were called Ta-la-la.

—*Oologah* - US 169————

This ranching and farming community began in 1887 with the coming of the railroad. Locals pronounce the name *Ou' la gah'*, with a long drawl on the "gaaaah." The word means "dark cloud" in Cherokee. Prior to statehood, Oologah became a shipping point for coal mines in the area.

Today, by virtue of an active restoration program, the downtown area has an unusually fine collection of historic buildings. The influence of Will Rogers on the town closest to his boyhood home is ever-present. The old town pump now shares its position in the center of Cooweescoowee Avenue (the main street) with a miniaturized replica of Will Rogers' birthplace.

Oologah keeps Will Rogers memory green with a miniature replica of his birthplace beside the old town pump on Cooweescoowee Avenue.

US 75
Copan—Vera

—*Copan* - US 75—OK 10————

During the 1880s a settlement grew around a trading post that served the Delawares, Osages, and Cherokees in the area. In 1898 the railroad arrived, and a post office named Lawton was established. The following year the name was changed to Weldon. In 1904 there was yet another name change when it became Copan, after a town in Honduras. The development of small oil fields in the vicinity brought mild excitement. A far greater economic boon was the construction of Copan Dam and the consequent formation of the 4,850-acre Copan Lake.

—*Hulah* - OK 10————

The faded town of Hulah owes its origin to lush bluestem grass in the surrounding area. Cattlemen fattened cattle on this grass before taking them to market. In 1918 the Santa Fe built a feeder line from its main line south of Caney, Kansas, to Pawhuska to handle the shipments.

The town grew around the stockyards and loading pens near the state line about fifteen miles north of Bartlesville. The townsite plat was filed in 1918. The name is from an Osage word meaning "eagle." The railroad built a depot in 1923 for freight and passengers. By this time, the economy was getting a boost from the Burbank oil field some forty miles southwest.

Soon the town had about fifty people, a general store, a dozen houses, a gas compressor station, and a school. In 1951 Hulah Dam was completed on the Caney River, and many of Hulah's people moved to new sites on the lake created by the dam.

This area was once the domain of the vast Cross Bell Ranch, owned and operated by three generations of the E. C. Mullendore family. Until 1972, the Cross Bell outfit ran cattle on 445,000 acres in four ranches owned and leased in Oklahoma and Kansas. The operation has shrunk to about a thousand acres near Hulah.

—Dewey - US 75————

Jacob H. "Jake" Bartles, the founder of Dewey, was frequently referred to as an empire builder. He was also a road builder and an ingenious businessman. He surveyed and constructed the grade for a projected railroad from Caney to Dewey—the Kansas, Oklahoma and Southwestern. The Santa Fe purchased the roadbed and began to lay rails on it.

Bartles then needed to move his store from the deserted town of Silver Lake to Dewey. He built a road and mounted the store on rollers; oxen could barely inch it along through the mud of the Caney River bottom. Bartles lost little trade during the five months it took to move; he kept the store open for business as usual while it was on the road.

Dewey was founded in 1898. Admiral George Dewey's victory in Manila Bay was fresh in everyone's mind. The town was named in his honor. The first building of any size was the Dewey Hotel. Bartles started construction of the elaborate Victorian structure in 1899. It was directly connected with the early economic and social history of both Dewey and Bartlesville.

The three-story building with surrounding porches and cupolas has been restored. The parlor is as it was when Jake's wife, Nannie Journeycake Bartles, entertained her friends and distinguished visitors. The gaming room in the tower drew the early oil developers like a magnet, and many lingered into the morning hours.

The Tom Mix Museum is across the street from the hotel. Tom Mix— "King of the Cowboys"—was the original good guy with the white hat. Memorabilia includes artifacts from his days as a cowboy for the 101 Ranch Wild West Show, as a member of the Rough Riders during the Spanish-American War, as town marshal of Dewey, and as an actor in more than 300 films.

Tom Mix talking over old times with Emmett Dalton, a former member of the notorious Dalton gang. —Western History Collections, University of Oklahoma Library

In 1906 the Portland Cement Company came to Dewey, attracted by cheap natural gas and plentiful limestone and shale in the area. It was the first production of cement in the state. Wages were 20 cents an hour for common labor; operators worked twelve hours a day. Both Tom Mix, the future silent-screen star, and Henry Starr, the outlaw, are reputed to have worked there.

—*Bartlesville* - US 60-75————

The first settler on the horseshoe bend of the Caney River where Bartlesville is was Joseph Hardin Bennett, who set up a trading post for Louis Chouteau's American Fur Trading Company among the buffalo-hide tepees of the Osage Indians in 1860. Nelson Carr came in 1867 and opened a gristmill. The settlement was called Silver Lake. In 1875, Carr sold his mill to Jacob H. Bartles for $1,000 and devoted his time to farming.

After the Civil War, Jake Bartles married a widow, Mrs. Nannie Journeycake Pratt, daughter of Charles Journeycake, chief of the Delawares. Like Carr before him, it was his marriage to an Indian that allowed Bartles to enter Indian Territory. In 1873, he and his wife came to Silver Lake. He enlarged the gristmill and started giving wheat seed to settlers. Soon, what is now Bartlesville was covered with wheat fields extending as far north as present-day Dewey.

On May 6, 1879, Bartlesville was officially granted a post office. As the population grew to a hundred, Bartles imported a generator to be used for electrical power.

On April 15, 1897, William Johnstone, George Keeler, and the Cudahy Oil Company brought in the Nellie Johnstone No. 1, the first commercial oil well in Indian Territory. There were no storage tanks or a railroad to carry oil to a refinery. So the Nellie Johnstone was shut down. A defective seal allowed oil to leak around the casing. People came with buckets and carried the goo away to grease farm tools, to light fires, and to smear on cows and hogs to protect them from ticks. One winter, children ice skating on the Caney River built a fire on the bank. The fire ignited the leaking oil and burned the wooden derrick. A replica of the derrick has been constructed in Johnstone Park on the original site.

The railroad came in 1899 and opened Bartlesville to oil production. Oil-related commerce and industry have controlled the city's destiny ever since. In 1901, H. V. Foster founded the Indian Territory Illuminating Oil Company (Cities Service), and in 1917 Frank and L. E. Phillips established the Phillips Petroleum Company. Both companies shaped the future of Bartlesville.

Nellie Johnstone No. 1, the first commerical oil well in Indian Territory, came in on April 15, 1897. A replica of the well is located in Johnstone Park in Bartlesville. —Bartlesville Public Library

The nineteen-story Price Tower dominates the Bartlesville skyline. It was designed by Frank Lloyd Wright. The skyscraper has been called "the tree that escaped the forest." —Bartlesville Public Library

Phillips Petroleum Company

Frank Phillips, founder and first president of the Phillips Petroleum Company, came to Bartlesville in 1903, drawn by the new oil field recently discovered in Indian Territory. The Phillips Petroleum Company was incorporated in 1917. For the first ten years the company produced crude oil, natural gas, and natural gasoline. Sales were on a wholesale basis, primarily in tank cars and through pipelines. In 1927, the company took its first step toward diversification by marketing automobile fuel.

The company needed a catchy name. "Phillips 66" was suggested early in the discussion because the number suggested a high gravity content. (Octane ratings had not yet been developed.) However, the idea was rejected because the company planned a broad marketing area and did not want to be associated with only one highway. On the day before the final conference for selection of a name, a company official made a road test of the new gasoline.

"Goes like sixty with our new gas," the official commented as the car sped down the highway.

"Sixty nothing!" said the driver. "We're going sixty-six!"

Later, the official told about the incident. He was asked where the test had been made.

"On Highway 66."

That was taken as an omen. A year later the gasoline came on the market at the company's first service station in Wichita, Kansas, displaying the Phillips 66 shield which was adapted from the markers on Route 66.

EXCURSION

—Woolaroc - OK 123———

Over the years, a bond formed between Frank Phillips and the Osage land around him. That bonding resulted in Woolaroc Lodge, a retreat where he could spend sunfilled afternoons talking with old friends of earlier days, chiefs and tribesmen of the Osages, ranchers and cowhands, and old-timers with whom he had watched dusters and gushers spread across the land. He named his lodge for the land: WOOds, LAke, ROCk. And he chose it as a final resting place for himself and his family.

The 3,500-acre spread became a wildlife refuge for the bison, deer, and elk that once roamed the land. Visitors can now see longhorn cattle, Brahmas, and Scottish highland cattle as well as Japanese deer and other exotic animals imported from afar.

The retreat became a museum with a "hangar" to house the tiny monoplane, *Woolaroc*, in which Col. Arthur Goebel had won the Dole Air Race between Oakland and Honolulu using Phillips' aviation fuel. Frank Phillips had capitalized on the flight by having Goebel write the name of the company's new automotive fuel across the sky in mile-high letters, PHILLIPS 66.

At Woolaroc, Frank Phillips entertained prominent people from around the world: future and former presidents, religious leaders, singers, actors, musicians, artists, authors, movie stars, and even former outlaws. When an important personage was being feted, a Phillips Petroleum Company official stood guard at the gate to screen visitors against a master guest list.

Woolaroc, *the plane that Arthur Goebel flew to win the Dole Air Derby in 1927, is displayed at Woolaroc.* —Oklahoma Tourism & Recreation, Fred W. Marvel

Today, Woolaroc does not maintain a guest list. It is ten miles southwest of Bartlesville on OK 123, and visitors are welcome. There are few restrictions, but animals *do* have the right of way. If the herd of ninety buffalo wants to use the road, drivers must stop and wait.

The Woolaroc Museum contains a vast array of artifacts pertaining to the development of humans in the Southwest. It displays a dazzling collection of works by Western artists.

—*Ramona*——————

This community just east of US 75 was also a product of the railroad. Its post office spent a couple of months answering to the name Bonton before it changed to Ramona, after the heroine of a novel by Helen Hunt Jackson that dealt with governmental injustices against Indians.

Three earlier trading posts—Ringo, Austin, and Hillside Mission—merged with Ramona. Nearby Hillside Mission was opened in 1884 by John Murdock, a Quaker missionary who worked with the Osages, Cherokees, and Delawares. When John Watson came to relieve Murdock, he brought a cutting from the ancient elm under which William Penn signed a treaty with the Delaware Indians in 1682. The shoot was planted in the mission garden and grew into a large tree.

—Vera————

Located east of US 75 on a county road, Vera was another railroad town established to serve area ranchers. W. C. Rogers, a principal chief of the Cherokee Nation, donated the land upon which to build the railroad station. Earlier, the Santa Fe had laid out a town two miles north. The few residents who occupied the site moved to Vera.

OK 11
Barnsdall—Sperry

—*Barnsdall* - OK 11————

Originally, the town was called Bigheart, for Chief James Bigheart of the Osage Nation who had been most instrumental in securing for his people the mineral rights that brought them wealth from oil production on their lands. The Midland Valley Railroad pushed into the Osage Reservation and built a station at Bigheart in 1905.

The area overflowed with prospective residents who settled in tents and crude homes along the right of way and west of the townsite. It was May of the following year before the townsite survey was completed and lots sold.

The first hotel was typical of hostelries hastily constructed in railroad towns and oil camps during the early days. The ground floor had an office and lobby. Meals were served family-style in a large dining room. A huge kitchen was equipped with a cast-iron range. It had fifteen rooms on the second floor, each equipped with a rope to serve as a fire escape. Furnishings consisted of a bed, a combination washstand and dresser, a wash basin, and a pitcher. Toilet facilities were under the beds. The third floor had an array of cots for less permanent guests.

Oil became the community's economic base. In 1914 a well was brought in squarely in the center of town. The pumping jack was neatly fenced and a sign erected: "America's Only Main Street Oil Well." The well is still there. In 1921, when the boom was at its peak, the name was changed to recognize the Barnsdall Oil Company.

During early days in the "oil patch," accidents were common, but Bigheart-Barnsdall has had more than its share of disaster. On April 12, 1911, a tornado wiped out a swatch of the business section and left death and injury in its wake. The following year fire destroyed most of the businesses that had been rebuilt. Bird Creek flooded the town in 1915. In 1919 a nitroglycerine truck exploded, killing four. A refinery explosion killed two and injured others in 1925. The high school caught fire in 1949.

—*Skiatook* - OK 11-20————

This area was originally an Osage Indian camp called Skiatooka's Settlement, to honor a prominent Osage resident. In 1890 its post office was officially named Ski-a-took. The hyphens proved too difficult for postal patrons; the Post Office Department removed them in 1892. Over the years, Skiatook has developed into a Tulsa suburb, but it has retained its rural ties with an annual quarter-horse show and rodeo.

—*Sperry* - OK 11————

First, in 1905, there was a townsite named Buehler, for Charles Buehler, an oil producer. In 1907 the Sperry post office was moved in, and Buehler was no more. Sperry is an adaptation of Henry Spybuck's last name.

OK 99
Pawhuska—Cleveland

—*Pawhuska* - US 60—OK 11-99————

The Osage Agency was established at present-day Pawhuska, and the Osages assembled there periodically to get their government allowances and to trade. In 1875 the *Indian Herald* reported on conditions during the preceding year:

> The Indian Population—Mixed Bloods, 280. Full Bloods, 2701. White men who have married into the tribe, 18. Families have houses, 50. Acres in cultivation, 993. . . . Children in school, 50. Number of cattle, 50. Whole number of ponies, 8,042.

The tribal governor reported that "fat buffalo are between Camp Supply and Cheyenne Agency" and twenty or more Osage families were off on a hunt.

In 1906, Charles M. Hill converted the weekly *Pawhuska Capital* to a daily newspaper and reported 500 inhabitants. Presumably, Hill's tally included only whites; the governor of the state issued a proclamation designating Pawhuska as a "city of the first class" with a population in excess of 2,500. That year the Osages held a town lot sale, and a building boom began. An active program of preservation and restoration has preserved Pawhuska's historic downtown district. A monument to the first Boy Scout troop in America, established in Pawhuska in 1909, decorates the grounds in front of the Osage County Historical Museum.

Pawhuska nurtures both its Indian and Western heritages. There is an annual steer roping contest, and the Osages hold war dances on three weekends each June. A fortunate visitor may get to attend a traditional Osage wedding. The style of the bride's dress dates from about 1803, when President Jefferson invited Indian leaders to Washington so they could see the power of the new nation. Each was presented with a medal and a dress tunic worn by army officers of that period. The Osages did not know what to do with the tunics; they took them back to their land and dressed their brides in them for wedding ceremonies.

HISTORICAL HIGHLIGHT

Chief Pah Hue Skah ("White Hair")

In 1791, a young Osage boy wandered very far from his native hunting ground on the prairies of Oklahoma. He went to St. Louis and then ventured up the Ohio River to where Little Turtle, a member of the Miami tribe, and Bluejacket, of the Shawnees, were martialing forces against the Americans.

In the summer of 1791, Maj. Gen. Arthur St. Clair went to far-western Fort Washington, on the border between modern Ohio and Indiana, with orders from President Washington to prevent Indians from harassing settlers. On the morning of November 4, 1791, the Indians attacked the force that threatened their land and administered a smashing defeat. Of the some 1,400 troops under St. Clair, less than 500 escaped without injury. The army retreated across ground littered with dead and dying, their freshly scalped heads looking like pumpkins in a cornfield. Indian losses stood at 21 killed and 40 wounded.

For General St. Clair, the battle marked the end of his career. For the Osage boy, "St. Clair's Defeat" was the beginning of a distinguished future. During the battle, he encountered a white-haired American soldier with a short braid protruding from under the back of his tri-cornered hat. The boy snatched at the hair, a potential scalp if he could stop the soldier and do him in. To the boy's amazement, the man ran away, leaving the scalp in his hand, a fluffy mass of soft white hair. Surely it was big medicine; it had saved the life of the man who wore it.

The boy fastened the wig to his own scalp lock and from that time never let it out of his reach. He took the name Pah Hue Skah ("White Hair"), and indeed the powerful medicine of the scalp served him well. He rose to become a chief, usurping Clermont, the hereditary chief of the Osage tribe.

Later, the magic continued to work for his son, young Pah Hue Skah, who inherited the white hair and who brought his presence to bear when the United States agreed to pay the Osages for the land they were leaving in Kansas. The spirits of both Pah Hue Skah and his son lived on in the name of the capital of the Osages' new land in Oklahoma—Pawhuska.

—*Wynona* - OK 99————————

Territorial maps designate the present site of Wynona as Rogers for Antwine Rogers, who established the headquarters of the Rogers Ranch about a half mile south of the townsite. As late as 1900, Wynona was open range. The Missouri-Kansas-Texas Railroad built its line through in 1902, and a Mr. Duke built a store near the depot.

Wynona was founded in early 1909 by the Osage Townsite Company, and lots went on sale. The name is Sioux for "first-born daughter." The December 28, 1911, issue of *The Wynona Enterprise* touted the advantages of the community:

> Golden opportunities await the coming of the homeseekers in the Osage Nation, the last Indian Reservation to be opened in the United States. This is the richest section of country in the world, produces more oil than Pennsylvania, has more cattle to the square mile than Texas, is rich in lead and zinc, and is inhabited by 2,200 Osage Indians, who own 657 acres of land each and are estimated to be worth from $25,000 to $40,000 per capita. Their annuity from the government for every man, woman, and child is $400 per year, paid quarterly. This brings $250,000 in cash every 90 days, which is thrown broadcast through this thinly settled section of Oklahoma. The Osage can sell their land, and it is bought on easy terms, all the way from $5 to $35 per acre. It is a fine place to live, and is centrally located in the United States.

Today, many empty brick buildings attest to what was a thriving community during oil-boom days.

—*Hominy* - OK 20-99————————

Hominy was established as a sub-agency for the Osage Indians in 1874 after their arrival from Kansas. It became a trading point for Indians who lived in the southern part of the Osage reservation.

The post office was established in 1891, and the first Missouri-Kansas-Texas train came through Hominy on July 4, 1904. The townsite was set aside by the government in 1905, and the town was incorporated on March 3, 1908.

Agriculture, cattle, and oil were the mainstays of the economy. The Osage Cotton Gin, erected in 1909, processed 5,000 bales of cotton from the surrounding area. In 1910, grazing lands fattened 500,000 head of cattle a year. The oil boom arrived and hit its peak during the 1920s.

Hominy is essentially an Indian town. Two annual events emphasize ties to Osage heritage. Ceremonial dances are held during the last week in June. The last week in September is reserved for celebration of the Osages' move from Kansas to Oklahoma.

—*Cleveland* - US 64-OK 99————

This community, located on the Arkansas River, was established shortly after the opening of the Cherokee Outlet in 1893. It became a shopping center for Indians living on the Osage reservation just across the river.

For a time, the bridge at Cleveland was the only way to get across the Arkansas River between Tulsa to the east and the Kansas border. Cleveland became known as Gate City. After development of the 1904 oil discovery in the Cleveland Sand, some 1,200 producing wells inspired Cleveland to dub itself the "Pioneer Oil City of Oklahoma."

OK 11-18
Grainola—Ralston

—*Grainola* - OK 18————

This small community in the Osage ranching country began as Salt Creek in 1906. The name was changed to Grainola in 1910, and it became a thriving trade center. Grainola's peak came in 1920, when the population neared 500 and a chautauqua came to town. Since then, the town has dwindled. There are still ranches in the area, and the Phillips Agricultural Demonstration Project is east of town, but improved roads and transportation facilities have made it too easy for residents to get to larger towns for shopping.

DeNoya, about 1924. Three miles southwest of Shidler, DeNoya was known locally as Whizbang. —Western History Collections, University of Oklahoma Library

—Foraker————

Established on the Midland Valley Railroad in 1903, Foraker had high hopes. It was a "government town," platted in 1905 under the supervision of the Department of the Interior. When only four years old, concrete sidewalks lined the business district.

When the railroad was extended into the oil producing area, the population increased to more than 2,000; Foraker built a $20,000 schoolhouse and the residents voted a $30,000 bond issue for a light and water system. But oil production decreased during the 1930s. The railroad was abandoned in 1963, and Foraker gradually lapsed into near ghost-town status.

—Webb City—Shidler—Apperson - OK 11-18————

These three communities were established as oil camps in the early 1920s during the Osage oil boom. More than 10,000 people received mail at the Shidler post office when the town was touted as the "Oil Capital of the Osage." Only a few workers are required to service the wells today.

—Burbank - US 60————

In 1902 the Eastern Oklahoma Railway ran across the western edge of the Osage Nation. Near the right of way along Salt Creek cockleburs grew on a rocky bluff. Railroad men called it Burbank, and that became the name of the community when a post office was established in 1907. The town was primarily an Osage settlement until the discovery of oil in the 18,000-acre Burbank field.

At the beginning of development of the Burbank field, leases brought less than $10 an acre. As production got under way, the price went as high as $10,000 an acre. In 1922, two 160-acre leases sold for $1,335,000 and $1,160,000 respectively.

—Fairfax - OK 18————

In the winter of 1902-03, the Santa Fe Railway extended its line from Pawnee to Newkirk, bypassing a small Indian trading post called Gray Horse. Several residents of Gray Horse decided to move to the railroad. A representative went to Washington to negotiate for forty acres to be surveyed into a townsite. A lease was consummated. Businessmen could build on the land, but they were not allowed to buy. To do business in Indian Territory, each businessman had to post $10,000 bond.

Early residents of Fairfax got used to seeing an Indian named Hun-Kah-Hop-Py walk to the top of a hill every morning. Hun-Kah-Hop-Py was the chief mourner for the Osage tribe. The grave and a statue of the Osage Chief Ne-Ka-Wa-She-Tun-Ka is located just southwest of Fairfax. He was the last chief accorded the traditional Osage burial. This involved killing his favorite horse and placing a human scalp on his grave.

The scalp was lifted from the head of a Wichita chief. The Osages settled the resulting intertribal conflict by making large payments of money and goods to the Wichitas. Because of this incident, the United States government forbid future scalp-taking.

—*Ralston* - OK 18-20————————

This small farming community was originally called Riverside because of its location on the Arkansas River. It was renamed in 1894 for the townsite developer. During the early 1900s, a steamboat made several trips between Tulsa and Ralston. The craft was powered by a threshing machine engine.

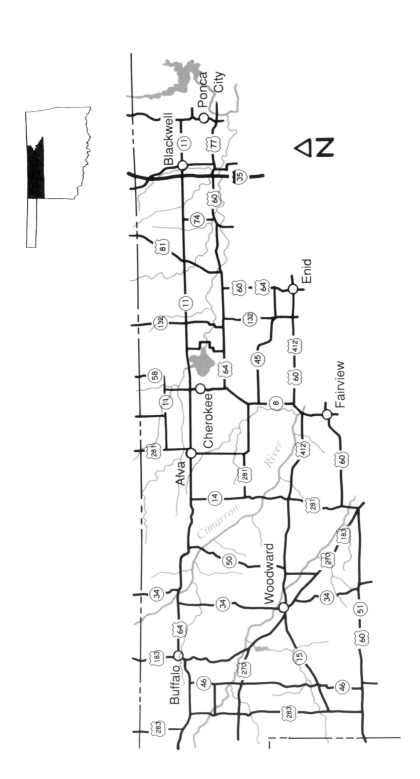

VI. The Cherokee Outlet

As early as 1804 attempts were made to induce the Cherokees to move from their homelands in Georgia to new lands somewhere in the Louisiana Purchase. The Indians refused, but in the spring of 1808 a delegation of Cherokee chiefs visited President Thomas Jefferson in Washington.

On July 8, 1817, a treaty was concluded. About one-third of the Cherokees surrendered their lands in the East and moved to a new territory set aside for them in what is now Arkansas, between the Arkansas and White rivers. They soon discovered that they had not moved far enough west if the expected to get away from the whites and continue to live the old Indian life of hunter and fisherman.

A new treaty was concluded in 1828. This time the Cherokees gave up their land in Arkansas in exchange for seven million acres in what is now Oklahoma. The land became known as the Cherokee Outlet. This strip of land reached west to the 100th meridian, 58 miles deep and extending 220 miles along the northern border of present-day Oklahoma.

The area has erroneously been called the "Cherokee Strip." The true Cherokee Strip was a long, thin band of land two and a half miles wide extending north of the 37th parallel into Kansas. It was ceded to the United States in 1866 and eventually was sold to settlers; the Cherokees received the proceeds.

Also in 1866, a treaty was consummated providing that friendly Indian tribes might be settled on the Cherokee Outlet at a price agreed upon between the Cherokees and the purchasers. The Osage, Kaw, Otoe-Missouri, Tonkawa, Ponca, and Pawnee tribes were settled on reservations. In 1878 a band of Nez Perces came, but they became so unhappy that they moved back to their earlier home in Idaho in 1885.

For about fifteen years following the Civil War, cattlemen slowly grazed and fattened their herds on Cherokee land without charge during their treks to northern markets. In 1880, the Cherokees voted to levy a dollar-a-head tax on all cattle in the outlet. The cattlemen protested, and

Cowboys around the chuck wagon at mealtime during a roundup in the Cherokee Outlet. —Western History Collections, Univeristy of Oklahoma Library

the tax was lowered to 40 cents for cattle two years and up, 25 cents for younger cattle, and no tax on calves under six months. In 1881 the tax collector garnered some $20,000; the following year he got more than $40,000.

Early in 1883 cattlemen founded the Cherokee Strip Livestock Association. On October 1, 1883, the organization leased the entire unoccupied portion of the Cherokee Outlet for five years at $100,000 a year.

They divided the region into pastures, leaving a wide unfenced strip along each of the cattle trails so that Texas drovers could pass through on their way to Dodge City, Wichita, or Abilene. Brands were recorded and printed in books. Small cabins and dugouts were built as line camps for cowboys who rode fence and tended the cattle.

In 1889 the Cherokee Strip Livestock Association renewed its lease for $200,000 a year. But trouble was on the horizon for the thriving cattlemen. Unassigned lands just to the south were opened to settlement on April 22 of that year, and Boomers and speculators were clamoring in the halls of Congress for more land. Congress appointed a commission to purchase the Cherokees' land.

At first the Indians refused to sell, but on January 4, 1892, the Cherokees gave in to pressure. The Cherokee Council agreed to sell at $1.25 per acre—$8.3 million—and President Grover Cleveland ordered all cattlemen out of the Cherokee Outlet. He sent troops from Camp Supply to see that they obeyed.

On March 3, 1893, Congress enacted legislation opening the Cherokee Outlet to homestead settlement. The government was determined to avoid past mistakes and, particularly, to deter the activities of Sooners. Participants were required to preregister. Booths were set up at nine locations in a 100-foot strip of neutral ground outside the outlet. For five days prior to the run, prospective settlers could enter this area to register. The registration fee was $4.00.

Surveyors laid out seven alphabetically labeled counties, complete with townships, sections, and 160-acre quarter-sections available to claimants. Each claimant had to be twenty-one years of age and not have previously used his homestead right. Those owning more than 160 acres elsewhere were not entitled to a homestead.

The Cherokee Outlet was divided into three zones. The eastern part cost $2.50 per acre; the central section, $1.50; and the western portion, $1.00. Homesteaders were later relieved of this payment by the "free homes act"; in consequence, most settlers received their land as an outright gift except for land-office fees.

Registration turned into a fiasco. People began gathering weeks in advance of what would be headlined as "The Greatest Horse Race That Ever Occurred on Earth." Estimates vary between 100,000 and 500,000 participants. Towns were crowded beyond their capacities to handle housing, water, sanitary facilities, and food for humans and animals. Endless lines at registration booths led to flared tempers. The average law-abiding citizen stood in line for hours or even days.

The military moved in: eight troops of cavalry and four companies of infantry from Ft. Reno and Camp Supply in Oklahoma, and Ft. Riley in Kansas. Homeseekers watched as the troops burned farmers' haystacks and set prairie fires to flush out Sooners. The final day was spent inspecting and grooming horses, examining bits and harnesses, filling canteens and checking equipment.

At dawn on September 16, 1893, the weather was stifling. The crowd tensed as noon approached. Vehicles were jammed hub-to-hub as soldiers on horseback in the neutral zone patrolled the line. All watched the horseman assigned to fire the starting signal. A spirited horse ridden by a gray-haired man from New Jersey bolted. A soldier, unable to catch him, shot the rider through the head minutes before the signal. South of Arkansas City a stray shot sent the line surging forward at four minutes before twelve. Nothing could stop the flow of humanity across the burned and blackened prairie.

Wagons overturned, scattering contents and people. Horsemen took the lead, with light carts and buggies close behind. A few rode bicycles; others ran on foot, hoping to secure close claims. One man hitched a horse to a plow and at the signal he claimed the nearest ground, "proving it up" as he went.

Start of the run for land in the Cherokee Outlet. This photgraph was taken a few seconds after high noon on September 16, 1893. —Western History Collections, University of Oklahoma Library

Railroads prepared for their part in the race. Cattle cars were jammed with people inside, on top, hanging on sides; some even rode the coal tenders. The trains were limited to fifteen miles per hour to remain competitve with the horses; passengers jumped off at intervals to vie for homesteads and town lots.

When a settler found a vacant site to his liking, he drove a stake with his name on it in the center, searched for the corner markers, and then stood ready to guard his land against claim jumpers. A claim occupied by a man with no sign of sweat on a fresh horse signaled a Sooner.

By nightfall, the "government towns," where surveyors had platted townsites, were teeming tent cities swarming with humanity. Eating houses, grocery stores, and places of amusement sprang up. In Alva a circus tent was erected as a hotel, but most families slept in or under their wagons.

The homesteaders did not have it easy that winter. Many who did not have a financial backing had to go to Kansas to earn a grubstake. One found a job shucking corn. He returned in eight weeks with $25, a sack of dried apples, and a side of meat to last his family through the winter. Many gave up and returned to their former homes.

Today the former Cherokee Outlet is prime farming and ranching country, studded with towns that came to life during the run of '93. Many ranches trace their heritages back to when the land was leased from the Cherokees and stocked with longhorns driven over the cattle trails from Texas.

—*Kaw City* - OK 11————

The original town was established in 1902 when the Santa Fe Railway built through the Osage country. In 1919 an oil derrick sprouted eight miles east of Kaw City. The population doubled as the oil field grew around the town. Old Kaw City is no more; it is under Kaw Lake. "New" Kaw City, on the shore of Kaw Lake, has found new life servicing vacationers.

—*Kildare* - US 77—OK 11————

In September 1893, the dust had hardly settled on emigrants from Kansas before Kildare sprang to life. For almost five years it was the nearest point on a railroad to Blackwell, making Kildare a distribution point for mail and commodities needed on the frontier.

Business establishments and saloons proliferated. The prosperity attracted horse thieves, who stole from private residences and livery stables and escaped into dense timber across the Arkansas River.

The Kildare schools had an early version of "school buses." Children were brought from surrounding farms in orange and black "kidwagons." These were wooden wagons encased in glass and drawn by horses or mules. Five kidwagons were required to transport the children.

—*Blackwell* - US 177—OK 11————

The town of Blackwell was conceived immediately after the proclamation calling for the opening of the Cherokee Outlet. A group of Winfield, Kansas, businessmen organized the Cherokee Strip Business Exchange and Protective Association. The association selected a site near the center of "K" County, as it was then known, to establish a town that later became the county seat.

Through Andrew J. Blackwell, an intermarried white among the Cherokees, the association managed to have the allotments of three Cherokee children near the site sold to the association. Blackwell went to southern Kansas selling certificates for lots in the town that was to be established on the bank of the Chikaskia River.

A townsite plat was prepared in advance, and on the afternoon of the opening the certificate holders held a drawing for lots and elected Andrew J. Blackwell president of the town council. Blackwell's rule was despotic. He was a self-ordained Baptist preacher and a hot-headed frontiersman. He was twice indicted for murder but never convicted.

Initially Blackwell was called Blackwell Rock; then, for a short time, Parker, as result of consolidation with a rival town across the river. Blackwell had a population of 600 to 800. Substantial improvements did not begin until about 1900. By 1910, Blackwell was one of the largest grain centers in the area. During 1909, 1.25 million bushels of grain were shipped. The town had five grain elevators and one of the largest flour mills in the state. Two poultry houses and a creamery provided a cash market for area farmers.

By 1910 natural gas had been discovered near Blackwell. Eighteen wells operated within a mile of the center of town, and gas was piped through town for heating, lighting, and the operation of mills, grain elevators, and factories. Within a few years the Blackwell field supplied gas to a large part of southern Kansas. As oil and gas fields became depleted, Blackwell's economy returned to dependence on farming and ranching.

—*Deer Creek* - OK 11————

This community was established as Orie in 1894, the year after opening of the Cherokee Outlet. It was formed by a group of German Mennonite farmers who homesteaded in the area and planted wheat. The name was changed to Deer Creek in 1899. The Deer Creek *Echo* began publication that year, noting that the population of the town was 200. Wheat is still the principal crop in the area.

HISTORICAL HIGHLIGHT

Kay County: "The Banner Wheat County"

The first winter after the Outlet opened was severe, followed by a summer of intense heat and drought. In 1894 Kay County encompassed 730 square miles of raw prairie. Most homesteaders managed to do little more than build sod houses and plant gardens.

In 1896, a generous estimate of Kay County's wheat crop was one million bushels. The first really good year was 1897, when four million bushels were harvested and homesteaders were able to think about moving out of their "soddies" into frame houses. Kay County soon became "The Banner Wheat County."

Homesteaders farmed with a team and a walking plow, harrow, and drill or, more rare, a riding plow pulled by horses. Binders required about five horses. The land was plowed as soon as wheat was cut, then harrowed with a drag harrow, and drilled. Wheat was cut as soon as it showed a touch of yellow; it finished ripening in bundles. Harvesting ten acres was a good day's work.

When it was time to stack the crop, one or two bundle wagons were used to gather the bundles. One person drove the wagon and loaded the bundles as they were pitched on. Another person walked beside, pitching bundles onto the wagon. The bundles were pitched off at the stack.

A good stacker was the most important member of the crew. A stack started about twelve feet in diameter and grew to eighteen or twenty feet and as high as bundles could be pitched from the wagon. The last three bundles on top were staked down with willow saplings about six feet long, sharpened on the ends and peeled to make them slick for easy driving. A good stack had no bulges, did not leak, would not lean, and never lost bundles blown off by the high winds that plague the region. After the wheat was stacked it went through a "sweat," which took about a month.

Threshing took place in the early fall, usually September. The crew consisted of an engineer, a separator tender, a water hauler, and two pitchers. The farmer caught the grain from the separator in his wagon and either stored it in bins or took it to a mill or a grain elevator. In 1900, the Nardin *Star* reflected the rejoicing of homesteaders as they received 99 cents a bushel for a bumper crop.

Cutting, hauling, and stacking wheat. —Western History Collections, University of Oklahoma Library

—*Wakita* - OK 11A———

This isolated rural community on a railroad branch line dates back to the opening of the Cherokee Outlet. Its name is a Cherokee word indicating a pond or a buffalo wallow. The Wakita *Herald*, a Republican weekly, began publication in 1897, and in 1902, Editor P. H. Loomis demanded "immediate statehood and free school books." More recently, the University of Oklahoma Medical School established the Wakita Clinic, a pilot project for delivering medical services to a large sparsely populated farming and ranching area.

—*Ingersoll* - US 64———

The Choctaw, Oklahoma and Gulf Railroad reached Ingersoll during the summer of 1901. For a time, Ingersoll bustled as a railroad center. Within a month the population reached 1,000, and both the Ingersoll *Review* and the *Ingersoll Times* expressed a vain hope that the community would eclipse Cherokee and become the county seat of Alfalfa County. The Tuscan Masonic Lodge Number 193 is the oldest Masonic lodge in the county.

———— EXCURSION

—*Driftwood* - OK 8————

Before the Cherokee Outlet opened to settlement, this area was in the heart of ranching activity on Cherokee land. Squatters began arriving from Texas with their cattle during the 1870s. The headquarters of Andrew Drumm's U Ranch was three miles southeast of present Driftwood. The 150,000-acre spread extended from the Kansas line to a mile south of Cherokee and east to the Salt Plains. Only a granite monument now remains to mark the location of the headquarters of the U Ranch.

The Short Ranch was west of the U Ranch. Others in the area included the Spade Ranch, the Cragin Ranch, and the T 5 Ranch owned by the Texas Land and Cattle Company, Ltd., a British company based in Texas. Gus Johnson, the ranch manager, brought an English accent to the Cherokee Outlet. The era of big ranches ended when cattlemen were ordered to make way for homesteaders.

Like many towns in Oklahoma, Driftwood moved a couple of times in the process of keeping up with the railroad. The present townsite was laid out in 1901 by the Choctaw Railroad's townsite company. It took its name from Driftwood Creek, a stream noted for the "drifts" it accumulated during heavy rains.

—*Byron* - OK 11-58————

This is one of the oldest communities in Alfalfa County. It was settled in 1894 a half mile northeast of the present site. According to the *Cherokee Republican* for June 18, 1909, the town's name was suggested by an old-timer who was an admirer of Lord Byron's poetry; however, the operator of the first store in Byron, the owner of the first house constructed in the community, and the first postmaster was named Byron J. Spurrier. The town moved to its present location in 1902 to be on the railroad.

—*Amorita* - OK 58————

In 1901 the Amorita Choctaw Northern Townsite Company laid out the town in preparation for arrival of the Choctaw, Oklahoma and Gulf Railroad. The railroad reached the site of Amorita in 1902, and the nucleus of this small rural trade center began to gather around the siding. The community was named for Amorita Ingersoll, wife of the president of the railroad. The Bank of Amorita was established that year, and the Cumberland Presbyterian Church, the oldest church in town, was constructed.

—*Burlington* - OK 11————

The initial name of the community was Drumm, for Maj. Andrew Drumm. Andrew Drumm was one of the first cattlemen to graze herds in the Cherokee Outlet. During 1906, the Denver, Enid, and Gulf Railroad (the D.E.&G., popularly known as "Dirty, Easy, and Greasy") arrived. The railroad named the station Wheaton, but the following year they changed the designation to Burlington, after a short-lived, nearby settlement.

—*Capron* - OK 11————

This small trading center began as Sterling in 1894, just after the opening of the Cherokee Outlet. The following year the name was changed to Virgel. It became Capron in 1899, named for Capt. Allyn K. Capron, commander of the territorial troops in the Spanish-American War.

—*Alva* - US 64————

Designated as one of the four land-office towns at the opening of the Cherokee Outlet in 1893, this incipient community was named for Alva B. Adams, attorney for the Santa Fe Railway. (Adams later became governor of Colorado.) Government surveyors had platted the townsite around the "government acre," which was reserved for the land office.

The Northwestern Normal School in Alva, founded in 1897, became Northwestern Oklahoma State University. —Western History Collections, University of Oklahoma Library

Al Galbraith of Hazelton, Kansas, was the first to arrive. He came by horseback and claimed a choice lot on the corner of the courthouse square. Two men in a double rig arrived next, covering the distance of fourteen miles from the Kansas line in fifty minutes. They beat the train by twenty minutes. Passengers on the train complained at the slow speed, saying they felt as if they had been on a sight-seeing excursion. By evening Alva had a population of 2,200. Small tents were scattered around the square, and a circus tent served as a hotel.

Alva became an agricultural trading center. The Alva Commercial Club, forerunner of the chamber of commerce, was established in 1896. Known as the "Alva Push Club," the organization was successful in obtaining community backing for the state's second oldest normal school. Today known as Northwestern Oklahoma State University, it sits on a rise overlooking the town. Ranching buffs will be interested in the Cherokee Strip Livestock Association's brand book for 1886. The university library has a copy. It contains about 600 listings for the 300 ranches registered with the association.

—*Freedom* - OK 50————

This community has to be described as "a going western town." It was established in 1901, five miles north of its present location. In 1919 it moved to the north bank of the Cimarron River with the construction of the Buffalo and Northwestern Railway. Throughout its history, Freedom has been dedicated to the old cowhands who helped settle the Cherokee Outlet.

A 15-foot-long, 9,000-pound granite monument in the municipal park commemorates "The Cimarron Cowboy." One side displays the region's history from 1883 to 1890—the big ranches, the coming of the railroad in 1886, and the killer blizzard of that year. The other side details events from 1890 to the opening of the Cherokee Outlet in 1893—the names of cattlemen and their brands and a tribute to rodeo, the sport that evolved from the cattle industry. For more than half a century, Freedom's annual rodeo has attracted spectators and contestants from across the nation.

In 1973 Freedom began restoring and refurbishing its downtown section. Fronts of buildings have been finished in rough-hewn cedar in designs typical of early days in the community. The Freedom Museum on "Cowtown Main Street" displays artifacts pertaining to history of the area including furniture, clothing, quilts, musical instruments, documents, barbed wire, and early-day tools.

In 1986, a bulldozer operator working on a farm pond near Freedom turned up prehistoric bison bones. The National Geographic Society provided the Oklahoma Archaeological Society with funding for excavation of the Burnham site in 1988. Radiocarbon tests on animal bones, seeds, flecks of charcoal, snail shells, and rare flakes from resharpening chipped wood tools indicate that ancient peoples

"Cowtown Main Street": The architecture along Freedom's main street leaves no doubt of the town's Western heritage.

inhabited the area between 26,000 and 40,000 years ago. Previous estimates put earliest human arrival at no more than 20,000 years ago.

The Edith Salt Plain lies a few miles west, stretching about three miles wide for twelve miles along the Cimarron River. It has long supplied salt for ranchers in the area. A salt plant still produces salt for commercial usage.

—Buffalo - US 64————

When the post office opened in 1899, the community that later became the county seat of Harper County was called Brulé, after a subtribe of the Sioux. The area was spotted with buffalo wallows and littered with horns, bones, and flint arrowheads, testifying that it had once been a hunting ground of the Plains Indians.

Initially, the town was called Stone City because only fireproof buildings were allowed in the business district. After statehood in 1907, it was renamed Buffalo after Buffalo Creek. In 1917, nearby Doby Springs was tapped to provide a municipal water supply through a leaky wooden pipe that froze in the winter. During the 1930s, WPA labor replaced it with cast iron.

When the Santa Fe Railway did not build a spur line to Buffalo, the citizens voted a bond issue to construct the Buffalo Northwestern themselves. The first train finally arrived in 1920 and everyone was happy until they discovered a four hundred percent increase in property taxes. Buffalo has now overcome its growing pains.

—Selman————

This tiny rural trading center on a county road off US 64 southeast of Buffalo began in 1901 as Charleston, a store and post office operated by Charles Eilerts. Saturday horseracing was the principal entertainment. One memorable Saturday a young man called Johnny Fewclothes showed up from a small ranch to the south with a horse that "looked like crow's bait" and took all the money home with him. Johnny Fewclothes showed up some years later as J. O. Selman, and the town was renamed in his honor in 1923.

—Rosston - US 64————

This railroad-siding town grew from a store owned by R. H. Ross of West Virginia. Ross came to what is now Harper County in 1901 and opened a lumberyard at the former town of Readout. In 1907, a storekeeper who operated a general store in the vicinity closed his business and sold part of the building to Ross. The building was sawed in half by hand, and

Ross's part moved to the site of present-day Rosston. In 1912, the railroad arrived. The track was about a half mile from the Ross store. The town was surveyed and platted in May, and Ross built a new store near the railroad depot.

US 281—OK 45
Goltry—Waynoka

—*Goltry* - OK 45————

The town of Goltry was platted on a branch line of the Frisco railroad in 1903 by the Goltry brothers of Enid. With the coming of the railroad the residents of two nearby inland towns, Alvaretta and Karoma, moved to Goltry. Both Alvaretta and Karoma had been products of the opening of the Cherokee Outlet.

—*Helena* - OK 45-58————

Helena has been a small trading center since the opening of the Cherokee Outlet. When the route of the Frisco railroad was staked out in the summer of 1903, residents raised $5,000 by public subscription and purchased a quarter-section of land, which they gave to the railroad. The railroad laid out the townsite and donated lots to the businessmen of Carwile, a town two and a half miles to the southwest, if they would move to the new location.

Helena continues as a rural community serving farms and ranches in the area.

—*Carmen* - OK 45————

In 1894 there was a post office called Eagle Chief in a store owned by J. C. Duncan about two miles west of Carmen. In 1895 the store and post office moved to about a mile and a half west of Carmen. The post office was renamed Augusta, and a town of about 1,000 grew around the post office.

In November 1900, the grading crew for the Kansas City, Mexico and Orient Railway reached the site of Carmen. On December 18, 1890, lots were sold in New Augusta—125 lots for $50,000—and Old Augusta moved to New Augusta, buildings and all. The president of the railroad was a friend of Porfirio Díaz, the president of Mexico. New Augusta was renamed Carmen for Díaz's wife.

The Carmen *Headlight* of April 24, 1903, told about the celebration in honor of the arrival of the Orient. It was the greatest crowd ever assembled in the county, "at least ten thousand people" took part in the festivities. Celebrants consumed 1,800 pounds of beef, 1,500 loaves of bread, and 300 gallons of coffee. Today, the small rural trade center by the railroad track reveals no hint of the excitement it has witnessed.

—*Waynoka* - US 281-OK 14————

This town grew from a railroad siding called Keystone, established in 1886, to become a division point on the Santa Fe. In 1889 the name was changed to Waynoka (from Cheyenne *winneoka*, "sweet water").

During its days as a railroad terminal, Waynoka had extensive maintenance and repair shops and the state's largest ice plant for servicing refrigerator cars. Waynoka's Santa Fe depot, with its Harvey House, is listed in the National Register of Historic Places.

In 1929, Waynoka gained brief fame as the location of Oklahoma's first transcontinental airport, owned by Trans-continental Air Transport (TAT), forerunner of TWA. Passengers arrived by air in Ford trimotor planes from the east and by rail from the west, dined in luxury at the Harvey House, and continued their journeys by air or rail. Charles Lindbergh and Amelia Earhart, officers in the company, were familiar faces in Waynoka. Amelia Earhart's memory is kept green in Waynoka by a play entitled *Amelia Lives*.

Agriculture is the mainstay of the local economy. The main crops are wheat and alfalfa. Farming methods include both dryland and irrigated. Cattle dominate local livestock production with some hogs, sheep, and horses raised as well.

Waynoka bills itself as "The City by the Sea of Sand" because of the nearby Little Sahara State Park, a 1,520-acre area known by early explorers as "walking hills." The sand dunes were deposited by the Cimarron River thousands of years ago. The dunes range from twenty-five to seventy-five feet high. For a time camels were maintained in the park, but they have been replaced by dune buggies and other off-road vehicles. The park is off US 281, four miles south of Waynoka.

US 412
Lahoma—Mooreland

—*Lahoma* - US 412————

The single grain elevator remaining at Lahoma does not reflect the bustling agricultural center that developed after the town was established in 1894. The original townsite was about a mile northwest of the present town. In 1901 the community moved to the Enid and Anadarko Railway, a division of the Rock Island. The landowner sold the right of way to the railroad for a dollar, creating a ready market for the remaining town lots in his block of property.

The Lahoma *Sun* began publication in 1898 with a circulation of 50 in a town of "about 100" people. The newspaper's circulation grew as it began to publish from 35 to 50 notices a week for the U. S. General Land Office as well as the brands of stockmen in the area. Ranchmen paid $12 a year to have their brands published; seventeen could be printed in a single column, so the newspaper prospered. By 1907 it had a circulation of 650.

—*Meno* - US 412————

This town is the trade and cultural center for the largest Mennonite community in the state. The area was settled by Mennonite farmers when the Cherokee Outlet was opened in 1893. Presumably, the town was named for Menno Simons (1492-1559), a Dutch Roman Catholic priest who left the Catholic church and founded a new religious sect.

—*Ringwood* - US 412—OK 58————

This area was homesteaded in 1895. In 1901 the townsite was platted and lots were sold at auction. The community took its name from the circle of trees about the town. As an agricultural community, Ringwood is best known for watermelons. A Watermelon Queen is crowned at the Watermelon Festival every September, and all comers get free watermelon. Oil and gas have aided the economy of Ringwood.

—*Orienta* - US 412————

The grain elevators testify to this small community as an agricultural shipping point. Established in 1901, the town took its name from the Kansas City, Mexico and Orient Railway, now part of the Santa Fe.

The Glass Mountains are visible in the distance to the west. They were so named because of the sparkling, glassy-like selenite crystals covering the buttes. The name has appeared as "Gloss" on some maps. A popular legend has the mountains named by a British engineer who said they looked like glass, pronouncing the word "glaws." Actually, a cartographer once misread an "a" for an "o" and the error remains on a number of maps.

—Mooreland - US 412—OK 50————

This community was founded as Dail City in 1901, named for J. H. Dail, the townsite owner. The name was changed in 1902. According to George H. Shirk, Oklahoma's authority on place names, the intent was to call it Moorland because the surrounding terrain was suggestive of moors; however, the Post Office Department added an "e" and the town has been Mooreland ever since.

Mooreland's economy is primarily agricultural, but it is boosted by petroleum.

US 283—OK 15
Tangier—Laverne

—Tangier - OK 15————

This community began as a railroad siding called Orlando; the name was changed to Tangier in 1901 to distinguish it from another town named Orlando near Stillwater. At that time residents could have had no idea of what the oil boom would bring. Today a tight cluster of suppliers to the petroleum industry huddles by the railroad track while behemoth vehicles snort up and down the street under burdens of oil field supplies.

—Fargo - OK 15————

First it was Whitehead, then Oleta, and finally Fargo. According to local tradition, when the Pecos Valley Northwestern Railroad (now Santa Fe) built across the Cherokee Outlet in 1886, a station was manned by a snowy-haired old man. As a train approached, the station agent came out and trainmen could see his head bobbing about. They called the place Whitehead and the name stuck when the post office came in 1893.

In 1901 Ooley renamed the town Oleta for one of his daughters. In 1905, the Post Office Department, took exception to Oleta as a personal first name and renamed the town Fargo for the ubiquitous Wells Fargo express company.

—*Gage* - OK 15-46————

In July 1887, the Santa Fe Railway established a sidetrack and a station near the confluence of the Wolf and Little Wolf creeks. Cattle pens were built and the station became a shipping point for ranchers from miles around. It wasn't until March 1894 that homesteaders began to arrive. A post office opened the following year. During the fall of 1900 and the spring of 1901 settlers attracted by the rumored opening of the Kiowa-Comanche country appeared. Many decided to settle around Gage rather than participate in the opening.

Early-day Gage was a typical frontier cowtown with the usual complement of saloons. During 1905, Carrie A. Nation, the militant temperance advocate who gained her reputation by wielding a hatchet in saloons, lived in Oklahoma. In December 1905 she came to Gage. In reporting her visit to the Gold Front Saloon, the *Gage Record* showed little sympathy to her cause:

> She promised to read the names of the signers of the saloon petition Monday night but lost the list Monday. She thinks it was swiped out of her Bible. One remarkable statement made by her was that there were two prostitutes on the petition. She went into the Saloon Monday morning and asked for their best drink, and was given a cup of cold water. She went in again Monday afternoon and was hooted out. When she was on her way to the train she was greeted with a few eggs from an unknown hand. Her trunk was also stolen from her.

In the following issue, the *Record* reported that Mrs. Nation's valise had been found in Wolf Creek. The editor recovered sufficient grace to remark: "The person who stole that grip did the town more dishonor than he did to Carrie."

As the oil boom came to Oklahoma, a farmer named C. J. Minton became convinced there was oil under his property. He organized a drilling company and sold shares at $10 each. Drilling of "Minton No. 1" began on June 12, 1918. By August 15, the well was down to 507 feet and the drillers encountered a "slow flow of water over the casing."

Spectators gathered, and on the morning of August 16 the drill bit punched through eight feet of shale and dropped into a cavity. There was a rumbling deep within the earth. The ground trembled and the well erupted, hurling a liquid stream mixed with sandstone boulders against the top of the derrick.

Onlookers sailed their hats into the air, but cries of joy turned to dismay as the spectators and workers tasted the discharge from the well. It wasn't oil; it was water—water that wasn't even fit to drink. The farmers left and the shareholders demanded their money back as artesian water flooded the Minton pasture.

Minton dammed the water around the well and dug a sandy-bottomed swimming pool. He invited the public to luxuriate in "the greatest

251

mineral water in Oklahoma," good for "kidney troubles, rheumatism, eczema, and all stomach trouble." People came from Kansas, Oklahoma, and Texas to bathe in icy water so full of minerals one could float with ease. Eventually the city of Gage acquired the property and during the 1940s and 1950s Gage Artesian Beach reigned as a recreation center for northwestern Oklahoma.

—*Shattuck* - US 283—OK 15————

When the Santa Fe Railway built across this part of the Cherokee Outlet in 1886, the water tank at present-day Shattuck was called Norice. A substantial number of descendants of German-Russian emigrants who had come to the United States during the 1870s were among the settlers in the area. The post office was named Shattuck for George O. Shattuck, a Santa Fe railroad official.

Until statehood, in 1907, the nearby town of Grand had been the county seat of Day County. Statehood brought a reorganization of county lines. Ellis County was formed from parts of Day and Woodward counties. Grand lost out. Almost overnight, it became a ghost town as a substantial number of its residents relocated in Shattuck. Dr. O. C. Newman was among those who moved.

Dr. Newman formed the Newman Hospital and Clinic (now Newman Memorial Hospital and Clinic). Serving a three-state area, it grew to become one of northwestern Oklahoma's most respected medical institutions. Today Shattuck continues as a prosperous agricultural community.

—*Laverne* - US 283————

The first principal crops on this treeless short-grass plain were wheat, alfalfa, native hay, broomcorn, and sorghum. There has been a post office named Laverne since 1898, but the town did not really begin to blossom until 1911 with arrival of the Missouri-Kansas-Texas Railroad. A general store opened, doing business in a tent until more substantial quarters could be built. During the 1950s Laverne became a participant in the oil boom that spread across the area. More than 200 mobile homes came to town to alleviate the housing shortage.

Laverne has had a day in the sun. In 1967, hardly a soul in Laverne stayed home on the day Jane Jayroe returned to town as Miss America.

US 270—OK 3
Woodward—May

—*Woodward* - US 270—OK 3-15-34————

In 1887 Woodward was one of a succession of sidings strung along the "Pan-Handle Extension" of the Southern Kansas Railway between Kiowa, Kansas, and Texas: Warren, Alva, Noel, Eagle Chief, Keystone, Nimrod, Sutton, Griffin, Warwich, Woodward, Orlando, Norris, Gage, Stockton, and Goodwin. At Woodward the railroad intersected the Camp Supply to Fort Reno military road, allowing supplies to travel the last few miles to Camp Supply. A sixty-car siding was built, along with a freight and passenger depot, a five-stall roundhouse, a two-story restaurant and hotel, a coal chute, and a water tank.

In preparation for the September 1893 run, Woodward received a post office the previous February, six months before other towns in the Cherokee Outlet. By nightfall Saturday, September 16, the first day of the run, there were two adjacent tent cities—Woodward, clustered about the government land office tract, and East Woodward, or Denver, south of the railroad depot. The latter was occupied by a colony of settlers from Denver, Colorado. Eventually the two communities blended.

Over the years, Woodward has had many farsighted businessmen, but perhaps J. O. Selman (also known as Johnny Fewclothes) was the most gifted of all. In 1929, during the height of the motion-picture boom, Selman financed construction of the Woodward Theater; however, he did not believe motion pictures would last. He insisted the theater include dressing rooms and an orchestra pit for the return of vaudeville shows. In 1981 the Woodward Arts Theatre began using the renovated vaudeville accommodations.

On the evening of April 9, 1947, one of the most destructive tornadoes ever analyzed by the U. S. Weather Bureau slashed across Woodward. Its core was 1.8 miles in diameter. It destroyed 200 city blocks, killed 107 people and injured 700 more. The devastated city rebuilt. Today, few physical scars remain; a plaque in the reception room of the Woodward Memorial Hospital commemorates the tragedy.

HISTORICAL HIGHLIGHT

Temple Houston: Woodward Lawyer

Temple Houston, the youngest son of General Sam Houston, hero of San Jacinto, was on the crest of a successful legal and political career in Texas when he heard the call of the frontier and came to participate in the opening of the Cherokee Outlet. After the run he moved to the

Woodward lawyer Temple Houston was the model for Edna Ferber's principal character in her novel Cimarron. —Western History Collections, University of Oklahoma Library

growing town of Woodward with his wife Laura and opened a law practice. He became legendary in his defense of "hopeless" clients.

On one occasion a friendless cowboy was accused of murder. He had killed a notorious gunslinger but he did so by drawing first, thus violating the unwritten Code of the West. The prosecution demanded hanging. Six-foot-two Temple Houston appeared in court, graceful and slender with jet-black hair reaching his shoulders. He wore Spanish-style trousers, a long-skirted coat, an embroidered vest, and high-heeled boots. The outfit was topped by two six-shooters strapped about his waist.

After the prosecuting attorney had presented a damning case, Houston approached the jury box. He spoke in a conversational tone:

"This man before you, this harmless cowpoke, knew that he didn't stand a chance when he incurred the enmity of the man he killed; and I maintain, gentlemen of the jury, that he killed in self-defense. The decedent had a reputation as a fast gun. All of you know that. So when my client saw this gunman coming at him with malice in his eyes, he knew that his life was at stake. Not one of you worthy gentlemen of the jury would have had a chance against such a character, that is, unless you had drawn first! Now would you—?"

In a split second Houston drew his guns and began firing at the jury. The judge headed for the back door of the courtroom; jurymen scrambled over the rail of the jury box and mingled with spectators in a wild dash for cover. When order was restored, Houston explained:

"Gentlemen, you need not have been afraid. My guns were loaded with blanks. I felt that I must show you what little chance an ordinary peaceful citizen, such as my client, would have had against the fast weapon of the deceased."

Perhaps because they felt they had been victims of trickery, the jury returned a guilty verdict, but Houston won a retrial. In their scramble to get away from Houston's blazing guns, the members of the jury had separated during the trial, a gross violation of the law. Houston won acquittal for the cowboy in the new trial.

Temple Houston's most celebrated case was his defense of Minnie Stacy, a penniless prostitute. The judge asked Minnie if she had an attorney. She didn't. The judge looked about the courtroom, spotted Houston, and appointed him to represent the defendant. After a ten-minute conference with Minnie, Temple Houston delivered an extemporaneous defense to the jury:

> "Gentlemen, you have heard with what cold cruelty the prosecution referred to the sins of this woman, as if her condition was her own preference. The evidence has painted you a picture of her life and surroundings. Do you think they were of her own choosing? Do you think she willingly embraced a life so revolting and horrible? Ah, no, gentlemen, one of our own sex was the author of her ruin, more to blame than she; then let us judge her gently. . . .
>
> "If any of us can say unto her, 'I am holier than thou,' in the respect which she is charged, who is he?
>
> "No, gentlemen, do as your Master did twice under the same circumstances that surround you. Tell her to 'go in peace'."

Minnie Stacey was acquitted. She left Woodward for a new life. She married and became an "angel of mercy" in nursing wards.

Temple Houston died April 14, 1905, at the age of forty-five of a cerebral hemorrhage. A wreath appeared at his funeral bearing the name and condolences of Minnie Stacey and her family. Temple Houston was gone but not forgotten. Edna Ferber resurrected him as Yancey Cravat, the hero of her novel, *Cimarron*.

—*Fort Supply* - US 183-270—OK 3————

This small community on the highway developed from the nearby military installation called Camp Supply. Camp Supply came to life in 1868 as an advance base for Gen. Philip H. Sheridan's winter campaign against the Cheyennes and Arapahos. It was from here that Lt. Col. George Custer embarked during a snowstorm for the attack upon Black Kettle's village, called a massacre by some and the Battle of the Washita

A cavalry inspection at Fort Supply. —Western History Collections,
University of Oklahoma Library

by others. As he returned with the band playing "Garry Owen," long lines of Indian women and children watched in silence. When asked if it had been much of a fight, Scout California Joe reflected an attitude common among the military at that time: "You may call it fightin' but I calls it wipin' out the varmints."

The troops stationed at Camp Supply cut timber to build a stockade. The post never experienced a direct attack to necessitate the use of the stockade's loopholes, but there were more than 1,100 Arapahos and 1,500 Cheyennes not yet on reservations. Kiowas and Apaches were on the prowl. Ambushes and killings were common in the area; in 1870 Indians captured a supply train of fourteen wagons.

In 1872, Frances M. Roe, a second lieutenant's wife, wrote that Indians were "skulking about the post all the time." Fifty Indians rode into the post, past the officers' quarters, and trampled the vegetable gardens with their ponies. Mrs. Roe explained that the Indians could act with impunity because they knew that when troops were sent in pursuit the soldiers were restricted to pushing Indian ponies away with bayonets rather than using their rifles for fear of precipitating an Indian uprising.

As Indian troubles subsided, various tribes came to Camp Supply to hold powwows.

Amos Chapman, a retired army scout who had lost a leg in the Buffalo Wallow fight, returned to the post where he had once served to attend a Cheyenne powwow. He approached a group of young Cheyennes sitting around a pot of dog stew. The Indians did not know Chapman or that he had a wooden leg; it was obvious that they did not want his company. He walked up to the bubbling kettle, stuck his wooden leg into the stew, and gave it a vigorous stirring. Then he sat down in the circle of warriors. They looked at each other.

"Big medicine," one grunted, "no burn leg."

The post office at Camp Supply was finally dubbed Fort Supply in 1889. In 1893 the post was abandoned and turned over to the territory of Oklahoma. In 1903 the territory authorized the establishment of the Western State Hospital for the mentally ill.

—May - US 270—OK 3————

In 1896 the first store and post office was built in May. The railroad came during 1911-12, and four elevators were constructed to process and store grain grown in the area.

During early days, the Beaver River on the north edge of town overflowed its banks when there was heavy rain upstream. Sometimes water ran deep enough to use boats in the streets. On one occasion the owner of a produce house built a raft and attempted to float downriver to Dunlap. Unfortunately, he drowned and rafting on Beaver River got a bad name.

US 60—OK 51
Seiling—Arnett

—Seiling - US 60————

This agricultural community was established in 1894 and named for the townsite owner, Louis A. Seiling. With wheat as the principal crop in the area, Seiling prospered as a farming and ranching community. For a time during the early 1900s, it was the home of Carrie A. Nation, the hatchet-wielding prohibitionist.

Carrie Nation married a drunkard in 1867. A brief unhappy life with her husband prompted her later career as a saloon-smashing temperance advocate. With a few hymn-singing women, or alone, she would march into a saloon, sing, pray, hurl vituperations at all "rummies" on the premises, and smash fixtures and the stock with a hatchet.

The fact that her husband had been a Mason as well as a drunkard led her to fight fraternal orders along with saloons. Her destruction list included tobacco, foreign foods, corsets, skirts of improper length, and the paintings of nudes usually found in saloons. She launched many of her tours from Seiling. Her second husband, David Nation, divorced her in 1901 on grounds of desertion, presumably because of her frequent absences for what she called "hatchetation" of "joints." From Seiling she moved to Guthrie, where she published a newspaper called *The Hatchet*.

—*Vici* - US 60—OK 34————

This community is believed to have gotten its name as a joke by a settler who was familiar with Julius Caesar's *Veni, vidi, vici* ("I came, I saw, I conquered"). Vici has long been a center for the production of bentonite, a white clay used in the manufacture of cosmetics and in refining crude oil.

—*Harmon* - US 60—OK 51————

In 1906 Charles Castiller built a tiny 10- by 12-foot frame building in the corner of his homestead and stocked a few necessities. The Post Office Department assigned Castiller's place the name Harmon, for Judson C. Harmon, governor of Ohio and later United States secretary of state.

Lumber for buildings had to be hauled twenty-two miles from Gage, the nearest railroad town. In 1927, the buildings in Harmon were jacked up and moved, one by one, a mile south and a mile east to the present location to be on the highway between Arnett and Vici.

—*Arnett* - US 60-283—OK 51————

The county seat of Ellis County began in 1900 when a man named Sweezey from Arkansas opened a crossroads store and post office and named it for himself. In 1902, Victoria Dawson, commonly known as Grandma Dawson, came with her sons and opened a store across the road from Sweezey. She acquired the Sweezey store and renamed the post office Arnett to honor her minister back in Fayetteville, West Virginia.

In 1907, with the coming of statehood, Arnett won out over Gage and Shattuck to become the county seat, and then discovered it had no building to house county records. The town had to get busy and build a courthouse on the square.

By 1932 the oil boom had come to Oklahoma, but Arnett was still a quiet rural community. Then W. D. Gladwell came to town: "If any place in the world has oil beneath the surface," said Gladwell, "it's right here in Ellis County."

Gladwell and his son began to bring hope to Ellis County by paying a dollar an acre for oil leases. After running out of money and soliciting donations "to try to get something started," Gladwell left town. Eventually, he returned with an oilman from Oklahoma City and a truck loaded with equipment.

The derrick was started on the nearby Roper place. More trucks came with a storage tank and steam boilers to power the drilling equipment. Farmers were hired to dig a slush pit. After a month, things were almost ready for "spudding in" (initial drilling) but the well would cost somewhere between $10,000 and $60,000.

An idea evolved to publicize the stock in Roper No. 1 by inviting the public to the spudding in. Word spread across the county: bring your dinner and spend the day. A welcome sign pointed to the drilling site. Wiley Post, back from his around-the-world flight in the *Winnie Mae*, promised to be on hand to give sight-seeing rides. LaVeta Howlett, a daring young lady from Shattuck, would climb the 122-foot derrick and raise a flag to cap the festivities.

Sunday, July 18, 1932, dawned bright and clear. Wiley Post and another pilot set planes down in a nearby pasture to offer rides at $2 each. Beef cooked on the barbeque rack. Women spread picnic baskets under a makeshift awning. Gladwell and his partner joined the crowd, ready to sell stock. Miss Howlett, clad in a red dress with petticoat and black bloomers, climbed the tower and placed an American flag to a burst of applause. Gladwell lowered his arm in a signal to start drilling.

Machinery rumbled as the block and tackle with its massive drill stem assembly rose toward the crown block. The crowd pushed forward. Then a cable snapped. The drill stem hurtled downward, smashed through the drilling platform and into the earth below. Dust billowed as men hollered and the rumbling machinery screeched to a halt. Gladwell hurried through the departing crowd vainly trying to sell stock. Oil interest did not resume in Ellis County until the late 1940s. The derrick for Roper No. 1 stood until World War II, when it was dismantled and sold for scrap metal.

Today, agriculture is Arnett's principal economic resource.

US 60-64
Pawnee—Jet

—*Pawnee* - US 64———

In 1876 the Pawnee Agency was established at the site of Pawnee when the tribe moved from its Nebraska home to new lands in present-day Oklahoma. George A. Custer recruited Indian scouts from this agency for his campaign against the Plains tribes.

On June 10, 1876, a group of these scouts was sent north to Wyoming. A few of the men who had been away on a hunting trip were sent along after their return. They returned in a few days and explained that there

Blue Hawks Peak, Pawnee Bill's home. —Western History Collections, University of Oklahoma Library

was no use going. Smoke signals had told them Custer was dead. The Indian agent did not receive official word of Custer's death at the Battle of Little Big Horn until ten days later.

In 1893, when the Pawnees accepted allotments, the remainder of their land was opened to settlement and the present-day town developed. Pawnee has always been an "Indian town." In 1946, a group of older Indians decided to welcome their sons and daughters who had served in World War II with a powwow. The event has since expanded to become the "world's largest free Indian powwow." The Pawnee Indian Homecoming takes place the first weekend in July.

The Pawnee Bill Museum is located in the vintage 1910 home of the former Indian interpreter and frontier scout. Major Gordon W. Lillie came to Indian Territory in 1882 and went into the cattle business. He organized Pawnee Bill's Historical Wild West Circus and toured the United States and Europe. In 1909, Pawnee Bill and Buffalo Bill combined their shows to present "an unrivaled spectacle" of Western-style entertainment.

As time passed, Pawnee Bill viewed the early flickering movie screens of the day as presaging disaster for the wild west shows. He closed his show in 1913 and retired to his sprawling ranch near Pawnee, where he developed and maintained the world's largest privately owned buffalo herd.

Most of the early settlers in the vicinity of Jet made the run into the Cherokee Outlet from Manchester on the south line of Kansas. They were people who had moved to Kansas from Missouri, Iowa, Kentucky, Tennessee, and other states to await the opening. The Drumm Cattle Company had a ranch near the present town of Jet before the opening. This company had sunk a barrel in a spring to provide water for camp use.

Newton Jett found the barrel and staked his claim there. People came from miles around to get water, and the place became known as Barrel Springs. In 1894 the Jett brothers applied for a post office. A "t" was dropped from their name in the petition, so the town became Jet.

Jet profits from being on the south edge of the Great Salt Plains, which was established as a national wildlife refuge in 1930. When the U.S. Army Corps of Engineers built the Salt Plains Dam and Reservoir in 1941, the area was enlarged to 32,400 acres. About 400 acres were subsequently transferred to the state of Oklahoma to become part of the Great Salt Plains State Park. Visitors to the Great Salt Plains are allowed to dig for selenite crystals in the gypsum flats. Each person is permitted to take away up to ten pounds for personal use.

Digging for selenite crystals at the Great Salt Plains National Wildlife Refuge. —Oklahoma Tourism & Recreation, Fred W. Marvel

The Treasure of Great Salt Plains Lake

Local legend has it that some 1,400 pounds of gold bullion was buried near the site of the dam that forms Great Salt Plains Lake. In 1854, miners returning from California were attacked by Indians. After crossing the Salt Fork River they decided to bury their treasure, 1,400 pounds of gold wrapped in buffalo hide.

The red bluffs by the river crossing identified the area. Only one man survived the Indian attack. He drew a map and returned to civilization. Carl Joseph Sheldon, a homesteader and piano tuner from Fort Cobb, got a map of the buried treasure, made his way to the Cherokee Outlet, and found the area.

Sheldon and a partner found a rod driven into the ground to mark the treasure. Their drill ran into water and quicksand. Analysis of the core revealed buffalo hide and gold; but, by the time Sheldon returned with the analysis, his partner had pulled the drill and left no marker.

Sheldon purchased twenty acres of land and spent the next thirty-five years in a futile search for the buried gold. In 1940, when construction of the dam was imminent, the Oklahoma Planning and Resources Board bought his land for $350, fifty dollars less than he had paid for it.

US 77-177
Tonkawa—Perry

—Tonkawa - US 60-77————

The mainstay of Tonkawa's economy is inscribed on its water tower: "Tonkawa Wheatheart of Oklahoma." The town was founded in 1894, taking its name from the tribe of Indians who had occupied a nearby reservation. The word is a Waco term meaning "they all stay together."

In 1901 the territorial legislature made Tonkawa the site of the University Preparatory School, now greatly expanded and modernized to become Northern Oklahoma Junior College. In 1921, following the discovery of an oil field to the south, the population exploded. Within a two-year period Tonkawa grew to 15,000. Tonkawa emerged from the Three Sands oil boom with a number of manufacturing enterprises added to the agricultural economy upon which the town had thrived before the discovery of oil.

—*Three Sands* - US 77————

Now virtually a ghost town, this wide spot on the highway awakens memories of when it was called the "billion dollar spot." The oil strike came in June 1921. Almost overnight the town became a jumble of derricks and jerry-built shanties. In 1923, when the boom was at its height, the population was estimated at 6,000. More than five hundred wells gushed at the rate of 100,000 barrels a day. The town's name comes from the fact that the wells pumped oil from three distinct sand formations.

EXCURSION ————

—*Marland* - OK 156————

OK 156, east of US 77, leads to Marland, a sleepy ranching town. But it has not always been that way. The community came to life in 1898 as Bliss, named for Secretary of the Interior Cornelius N. Bliss. It was in the homeland of the 101 Ranch, operated by George, Joe, and Zack Miller.

In 1905 the 101 Ranch presented an exhibition of riding, roping, and other ranch-related skills to members of the National Editorial Association, which met in Tulsa. An estimated crowd of 65,000 newspapermen and visitors came to the ranch in thirty special trains. As a result of the publicity, President Theodore Roosevelt invited the Miller brothers to take their exhibition to the 1907 Jamestown

Billboard for Miller Brothers 101 Ranch Wild West Show. —Western History Collection, University of Oklahoma Library

Although the 101 Ranch might be thought of primarily in terms of cattle and cowboys, hogs were a primary crop. They foraged in clover fields. —Western History Collections, University of Oklahoma Library

Exposition in Norfolk, Virginia. Thus was born the Miller Brothers' 101 Ranch Wild West Show, which toured the United States and Europe until 1931.

By the early 1920s E. W. Marland was on the scene, a highly successful wildcatter reputed to have a "nose for oil and the luck of the devil." His oil leases covered the site of Bliss, and most of them produced. In 1922 the name of the town was changed to Marland.

With George L. Miller, E. W. Marland organized the 101 Ranch Oil Company to drill the first well on ranch land just north of the "White House," headquarters of the ranch. In 1923, oil income of more than $1.3 million bailed the 101 Ranch out of debt. The company later became the Marland Refining Company, then the Marland Oil Company. Finally, Marland's luck ran out and his organization was absorbed by the Continental Oil Company. During the 1930s he went into politics and was elected governor of Oklahoma.

HISTORICAL HIGHLIGHT
Bill Pickett: The First Bulldogger

Bill Pickett, who spent almost thirty years as a cowhand and star of the Miller Brothers' 101 Ranch Wild West Show, was born of slave parents about 1850 in Travis County, Texas. Pickett had seen early-day cowhands send in bulldogs when cattle were too deep in brush to be worked with horses and ropes.

One day Zack Miller saw Pickett leap from his horse, sink his teeth into a steer's lip, and subdue the animal to be roped and tied. Miller promptly promoted Pickett to star status. He performed the stunt in Madison Square Garden in 1907 and was acclaimed world champion bulldogger. Pickett took to the tamer method of wrestling a steer down by its horns after one particularly tough critter ripped away four of his front teeth.

Dubbed the "Dusky Demon," Pickett appeared in Canada and South America. He gave command performances before European royalty. Zack Miller described him as "the best cowboy the ranch ever had." Pickett was still working at age 72 when he was fatally injured while breaking a vicious horse at the 101 Ranch.

During his funeral at the 101 Ranch, a friend summed up his character: "A man who would do to ride with." In 1968 Bill Pickett was accorded a place in the Cowboy Hall of Fame.

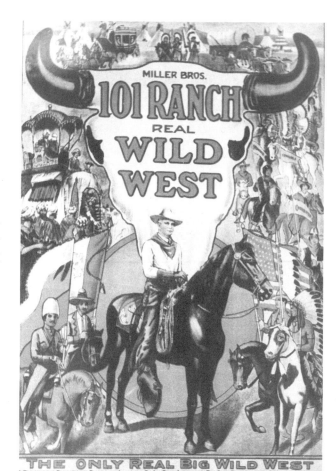

Poster for the 101 Ranch Wild West Show. —Western History Collections, University of Oklahoma Library

—*Billings* - OK 15————

This agricultural community on OK 15 west of US 77 was founded in 1899 on a branch line of the Rock Island railroad. The railroad's townsite agent gave the town his wife's family name. It was the home of Henry Bellmon, a politician who became United States senator and twice governor of Oklahoma. Mrs. Bellmon operated a dress manufacturing establishment on the main street of Billings.

—*Perry* - US 64-77————

Having been designated a land-office town by the Department of the Interior, Perry was a favorite destination during the run that heralded the opening of the Cherokee Outlet. The Santa Fe Railway had sold some 12,000 tickets to Wharton, the station a mile south of the townsite. By nightfall on September 16, 1893, the crowd was estimated at 40,000.

Tents and crude shelters were being erected by the light of flaming torches. The Blue Bell Saloon was in operation, selling beer at a dollar a bottle. Daylight revealed a sea of tents, shacks, wagon covers, and dugouts. Some lots were held down by as many as half a dozen claimants. There was Perry, North Perry, West Perry, and South Perry or Wharton. Each covered 320 acres and each elected its own set of officials.

Saloons and gambling houses were concentrated east of the town square, an area known as "Hell's Half Acre." The government brought in three U.S. marshals to keep order, including Bill Tilghman from Guthrie. Tilghman's reputation as a law enforcer was already legendary. Fred E. Sutton told a reporter from the *Dallas News* how Tilghman worked:

October 3, 1893, view of Perry. The Short Order House and law office of Thompson & Logan are in the foreground. —Western History Collections, University of Oklahoma Library

About six o'clock Tilghman and I were walking over the town site when we met a man known as Crescent Sam, . . . Mr. Tilghman said: "Hello, Crescent, when did you leave the Horseshoe outfit, and when are you going back?" He replied, "I left this morning and will go back when I feel like it and not before." Mr. Tilghman said: "I have been sent here to keep such as you away from here and I will not allow you to stay after the sun goes down," to which Crescent replied: "I'll be here after the sun goes down." Mr. Tilghman's quiet response was: "If you are I shall have to kill you," and we walked on.

An hour after sundown Crescent lifted the flap of the tent that housed the Buck Horn saloon and walked out. He raised a gun, took aim at the moon, fired twice, and announced that "he was a wolf and it was his night to howl and he was waiting for some Hombre to send him home." Tilghman stood watching him.

Crescent reached for his other gun, at the same time firing the one in his right hand. Tilghman's silver-mounted Colt responded, and Crescent crumpled to the ground. Tilghman blew smoke from his gun, inserted another cartridge, inspected a bullet hole under his left arm through his coat and shirt, and then walked up to Crescent.

"Poor devil," he said as he took him by the collar and dragged his body into the Buck Horn. Tilghman straightened him out near the wall of the tent, and crossed his hands on his breast. Crescent's body lay there for two nights and a day while dancers danced and gamblers played their games without so much as a glance in his direction.

Perry outlived its growing pains to become a city with a solid economy based upon a blend of agricultural and business activity. It keeps its Western heritage green with an annual Cherokee Strip Celebration.

HISTORICAL HIGHLIGHT
Bethsheba: A Woman's Domain

If the word of a Kansas newspaper reporter can be believed, in September 1893 there was—briefly—a town about halfway between Perry and Enid populated entirely by females, even to the extent of a ban on male chickens, horses, and hogs.

With the opening of the Cherokee Outlet on September 16, 1893, the tent village was formed by disgruntled women who came to the new country to get away from men. The Kansas reporter wrote: "The village originally consisted of 33 members, but 12 of them deserted after the first week, and one was expelled when it was learned she had a razor in her possession. The local court held that masculine implements were subversive to the vital principles of the community."

The community had a mayor, a town council, and a chief of police whose principal duty was keeping men beyond shotgun range of the village. The editor sent the reporter back for more information. Using field glasses from a distance, the reporter recognized the mayor as a Kansas woman who had married a traveling salesman only to learn that he had a wife and seven children in another state.

As I moved closer the woman raised the gun once more, while the remainder of the population held their hands over their ears. Some averted their faces, presumably dreading to see the death throes of another human being, even though he happened to be a man.

I heard a loud report, and a cloud of black smoke billowed out of the gun barrel. Since the gun was pointed in my general direction, obviously the shot was for me. I felt no pain, and saw no blood darkening my once white shirt. My presumption, nurtured by hope, was right. Annie Oakley did not live in the village.

The woman dropped the gun as soon as she discharged it, and all raced toward their tents and disappeared. The chief, gathering her long skirt up around her hips, outran all the rest. . . .

Some miles further on I met a farmer. He told me the village was made up entirely of women, who abjured the masculine sex completely. In proof of this he said that some of his chickens strayed into the settlement, and among the chickens was a rooster. The women killed this unlucky fowl with druidistic rites.

Again, the editor sent the reporter back to make a census of the town and interview residents; but, alas, not a trace was left of the gynecæum. The women had told a neighbor's wife they were going back to the land of men because they were lonely and afraid.

This curious remnant of Oklahoma history was reported by Robert E. Cunningham in *Oklahoma's Orbit*, February 19, 1961. Neither the Kansas newspaper nor the reporter has been identified. No physical or historical trace of the town has been located.

US 77
Chilocco—Ponca City

—*Chilocco* - US 77 ————

In 1882, a non-reservation boarding school was established here by act of Congress for Plains Indians in the western part of Indian Territory. It grew to be a highly respected institution, stressing vocational as well as academic training. Starting about the beginning of the century, the school published the *Chilocco-Farmer and Stock-Grower*, "devoted to the interest of Indian education." It was a monthly magazine that treated such diverse subjects as the St. Louis World's Fair and the proper time to plant wheat.

—*Newkirk* - US 77————————

With the opening of the Cherokee Outlet, Newkirk became a town in a matter of hours. Most of those who came here were among the 30,000 who registered in Arkansas City, Kansas, twelve miles north of the government townsite previously platted as the county seat of "K" County.

Each eligible claimant was allowed two town lots, one for residence and one for business, or two combined. The original townsite was called Lamoreaux, for the commissioner of the General Land Office of the United States, but people did not take kindly to the name. Only one issue of the *Lamoreaux Democrat* was published.

At a mass meeting the town's name was changed to Santa Fe, in the hope of currying favor with the railroad. The newspaper became the *Santa Fe Democrat*. However, officials of the Santa Fe Railway refused to call their railroad station Santa Fe. At another mass meeting the name was changed to Newkirk, the "New" distinguishing the town from an abandoned railroad depot to the north.

Newkirk has prospered from the rich surrounding farmlands and profited since 1919 from oil development. Because of its location near the Kansas border the community has assumed the title "The Gate City of Oklahoma."

HISTORICAL HIGHLIGHT

Ferdinandina: First White Settlement in Oklahoma

The designation was found on old English maps—Ferdinandina. The site was found by archaeologists six miles east of Newkirk at the mouth of Deer Creek on the west bank of the Arkansas River. Excavation unearthed flint spear points and scrapers, stone hoes, and redstone pipes, revealing that it had been the site of an Indian village. However, there was more: crudely fashioned iron implements—axes, hatchets, hoes, and knives; pieces of French guns; and brass with the fleur-de-lis emblem.

A diligent search of the literature revealed that Lt. Charles Claude du Tisné, an explorer acting for the French Colony of Louisiana, came to an Indian village beside the river open to trade and, hopefully to extend his contacts to trade with the Spaniards to the west.

Du Tisné's description fits the site on the bank of the Arkansas, and artifacts offer mute testimony to French presence. Moreover, the imprint of a stockade some 250 feet in diameter has been found. Indications are that it was named Ferdinandina shortly before the middle of the eighteenth century. The United States Army Corps of Engineers and the Department of the Interior have designated the area as a historic site.

—Peckham———

This small rural trading center seven miles west of Newkirk was established in 1899 and named for Ed L. Peckham of Blackwell, who promoted the Frisco railroad southwest of Arkansas City, Kansas, to Enid. During the oil boom the town had four lumberyards dealing in oil field equipment and rig timbers. Occupants of the cluster of neat homes have long since returned to a quiet life in the midst of rich wheat land and dairy and cattle farms.

—Ponca City - US 60-77———

The people of Ponca City used to have a saying: "Built on oil, soil, and toil." For one interested in the history of the Cherokee Outlet, Ponca City calls for more than a passing visit. Like so many communities in the Cherokee Outlet, Ponca City was born out of the raw prairie on that afternoon of September 16, 1893, but its genesis did not not follow the usual pattern.

The post office at the Ponca Indian agency was called White Eagle. The Santa Fe Railway had a station there, which they called Ponca. In preparing for the opening, government surveyors had laid out a townsite named Cross; by the end of the day some 3,000 homeseekers were camped on the site. But B. S. Barnes had other plans.

A year before, Barnes had sold his furniture manufacturing plant in Adrian, Michigan, and headed west. He traveled the country around the old Ponca Indian agency and found a spring on the main road to the Osage country where travelers stopped to refresh themselves. Barnes was convinced that there must be underground water in the area. It was a mile south of Cross, the government-designated townsite.

Barnes went back to Arkansas City and organized the Ponca Townsite Company. He sold two-dollar certificates that guaranteed each purchaser a lot; who owned which lot was decided by a drawing. Surveyors came along with participants in the run. While the site was being surveyed, teamsters hauled in tents, lumber, food, and supplies. One teamster distributed water from the spring at 15 cents a barrel to those who had sufficient foresight to bring an empty barrel.

A platform was erected. On Thursday, September 21, the drawing began. Certificate numbers were written on cards and placed in a cardboard box. Lot numbers were in another box. A little girl was hoisted to the platform to draw a card from each box. A recorder entered the names of the certificate owners and the descriptions of their lots in a bound ledger. More than 2,300 certificates had been sold; the drawing took two days. That was the birth of New Ponca.

Barnes and his associates immediately launched a campaign to "wipe Cross off the map." At first, the Santa Fe Railway refused to cooperate.

Trains would not stop at New Ponca. Finally, New Ponca prevailed. Elated citizens went to Cross to catch the first train scheduled to stop in New Ponca. They distributed cigars to male passengers, flowers to the women, and cards that read, "The train stops at New Ponca the same as Chicago." Ponca City grew northward until it absorbed Cross, making Barnes' victory complete.

E. W. Marland, the wildcat promoter from Pennsylvania, contributed to Ponca City's growth as he precipitated development of the Ponca Pool. Before his luck ran out, he built an Italian Renaissance "Palace on the Prairie" and commissioned the Pioneer Woman, a memorial to the courage of thousands of women who suffered hardships to create homes in new and untried lands.

Ponca City renews its Western heritage every August as the 101 Ranch Rodeo roars into action at the rodeo grounds north of town. Also during August, the Ponca Indians stage a powwow at White Eagle south of Ponca City.

A 17-foot, 6-ton bronze of a pioneer woman and her child has become one of Oklahoma's best-known symbols. Bryant Baker's design was selected from twelve models. The statue was dedicated in 1930. The park is in the southwest corner of the former estate of E. W. Marland.
—Western History Collections, University of Oklahoma Library

—*Garber* - OK 74————

For slightly more than a month in 1894, the post office was called McCardie. The post office, a mile southeast of the present townsite, was in a store operated by the Garber family. In 1899, when the Enid and Tonkawa Railway (now the Rock Island) came through, Milton Garber bought the site and moved "Old Garber" to the railroad.

The town pump was the social center of the community. Both town and country people used the troughs to water their horses. On the evening before wash day, women set wash boilers on little red wagons and came to the pump to get water. There was a laid-back atmosphere to life in Garber. On occasion a Rock Island crew would stop their train out on the prairie to hunt quail.

Agriculture was the basis of the local economy until 1919, when the Hoy well was brought in. The well was a precursor to development of the Garber field, one of Oklahoma's most productive shallow-well oil fields.

—*Fairmont*————

The Denver, Enid and Gulf and the Frisco railroads put Fairmont on the map in 1902. The Enid Right of Way and Townsite Company laid out the plat. Lots were described, advertised, and a goodly number sold by mail for $5 each. On October 10 a public sale was held; a beer wagon was on hand to cater to those who attended. The remainder of the lots in the still-nameless town were sold in one day.

Lou Burnes moved a saloon from North Enid, the first building on Main Street, and there was a meeting to decide on a town name. Junction City was suggested first, because there was a railroad junction south of town; then Wheathoma was suggested because wheat was the most important crop. But someone said the name should be "more aesthetic—like Fairmont." A vote was called for and the name was adopted.

—*Douglas*————

In 1902 six Frantz brothers of Enid planned and organized the Denver, Enid and Gulf Railroad to be built southeast out of Enid. The line was locally known as the Frantz Road until it sold to the Santa Fe. The first station was twenty miles from Enid. A post office named Onyx had been operating in a farm house a mile and a half east of the station since 1894. The post office was moved to the developing town and renamed Douglas as a memorial to Edmund Frantz's son.

When the Santa Fe acquired the railroad line officials changed the name of the station back to Onyx because there was already a Douglas on the Santa Fe. The Douglas *News* reflected the community's displeasure. The elected representative from the district got the territorial legislature to pass a bill requiring a railroad to use the name of the local town as the name of the station in the town. The plaque bearing the word Onyx was replaced with Douglas.

—*Covington* - OK 74-164————

Grain elevators testify to the bumper wheat crops harvested in the area. The community began as Tripp in 1902 when the railroad came, but John H. Covington, a prominent resident, had no sons and he wanted his family name perpetuated. He persuaded the Arkansas Valley and Western Railroad to rename the station at Tripp in his honor.

Oil production from development of the Garber field between Covington and Garber bolstered the town's economic strength sufficiently to bring the community through the Depression. A visitor can rub elbows with history by lunching in the diner that once served as the officers' and advance publicity car for the famed 101 Ranch Wild West Show.

OK 132
Nash—Barr

—*Nash* - US 64—OK 132————

In 1894, a year after the run, the little town of Nashville grew around the grain elevator by the railroad track. The Nashville *News* started publication in 1905 and had a circulation of 336 the following year. In 1911 the town's name was changed to Nash. The name derived not from the town in Tennessee but from Clark L. Nash, the first postmaster.

—*Drummond* - OK 132————

During the late 1800s, the site of Drummond was called Wild Horse Flats. The easily flooded plain grew rich stands of grass, which attracted wild horses from the blackjack oaks to the west. During the bird migration season there were a profusion of herons, sandpipers, yellowlegs, and ducks. Residents cut the blackjack trees for firewood, and merchants ricked the wood behind their stores.

Drummond was established on the Blackwell, Enid and Southwestern Railroad and took its name from Harry Drummond, a railroad official. In 1901 the railroad acquired a hundred acres and sold lots to residents and businessmen. Although the flooding that plagued early residents and homesteaders has been controlled, the flatlands west of town still provide excellent duck hunting.

—*Barr* - OK 132————

This tiny settlement was built on the claim of James Ryan. It was established in 1899 and named for Fred Barr, the postmaster. During its peak, besides the post office and store, Ryan's house served as a schoolhouse, a church with a parsonage, and a telephone switchboard. Folks brought their milk to a creamery where the separator was powered by a horse on a treadmill.

In 1906 the post office was discontinued and residents were put on a rural route. The store passed from hand to hand until the last storekeeper left in 1916, when the building was moved to a farm and converted into a barn.

OK 8
Cherokee—Fairview

—*Cherokee* - OK 8————

The county seat of Alfalfa County was platted on February 9, 1901, on the line of the proposed Orient Railroad. During the formation of Cherokee, four post offices were moved to the townsite: Friends, Erwin, Alger, and Cherokee. For two weeks all four post offices were within the same block in the new townsite, continuing to distribute mail.

Erwin was the only one of the post offices that showed promise as a community; however, in 1901 twenty-two businesses moved from Erwin to Cherokee. "Cherokee" won out as a name over the other three designations; a rival town called New Erwin, a mile south of Cherokee, died aborning. The first passenger train on the Orient reached Cherokee on February 10, 1903. The Denver, Enid, and Gulf Railroad arrived in the fall of 1903.

Alfalfa County was carved out of the original Woods County. After lengthy litigation over dividing Woods County into three counties, Cherokee won out as county seat over Carmen, Ingersoll, and Jet. At 9:20 A.M., November 16, 1907, news was received that President Theodore Roosevelt made the division and boundaries legal. Guns were fired, bells rung, and 3,000 people turned out for a parade.

Since the opening of the Cherokee Outlet to settlement, wheat, alfalfa, and livestock—with a contribution from oil and gas—have formed Cherokee's economic base. More recently, development of the

Great Salt Plains as a recreational area has made a substantial contribution. Cherokee advertises itself as "Gateway to the Great Salt Plains, Home of the Nation's Only Selenite Diggings."

—Yewed—Lambert - OK 8———

Yewed was founded in 1898, the year of the Spanish-American War victory. In keeping with the spirit of the time, the citizens wanted to honor Admiral George Dewey, the hero of Manila Bay, but there were already two Deweys in Oklahoma. The Post Office Department turned the name backwards.

Lambert came about in 1901 when a group of farmers and the Choctaw Townsite Company acquired land and platted the town on the Choctaw Railroad, now the Rock Island. The Choctaw was in operation eighteen months before the Orient Railroad reached Yewed. The Orient turned thumbs-down on the proposition to unite the two towns.

—Aline - OK 8B———

A post office was established and the community began to grow in 1894, a year after the opening of the Cherokee Outlet. The town was named Aline for the baby daughter of Mr. and Mrs. E. E. Hartshorn. A five-block townsite was laid out just south of the present town in 1901 by an engineer of the Choctaw Railroad. By 1907 the population was 300.

Many museums in Oklahoma display farming implements used by homesteaders. This exhibit is maintained by the Oklahoma Historical Society at the "old sod house" between Aline and Cleo Springs.

Sod Houses

"Soddies" were the humble, cheap homes occupied by a majority of rural homesteaders during their first year in the Cherokee Outlet. The homesteader used a sod plow, a wooden plow with a horizontal shearer in front to slice through the earth at a depth of eight inches. Vertical blades on each side cut the sod out in foot-wide strips. The going price for a sod plow was $10.

The homesteader found the grassiest, or grass-rootiest, piece of land on his claim and proceeded to collect his building material. He used a spade to chop the strips of sod into 18-inch or 2-foot lengths, loaded them onto a homemade sled, and dragged them to the site chosen for his future home.

The house's walls were constructed much as a mason lays bricks. One or two windows were usually framed into the walls, as well as a doorway. Some houses were windowless, and some had only flaps of canvas to serve as doors. A typical sod house was a one-room structure about 18 by 20 feet.

A slanting roof was made of stout poles laid close together, or boards if they were available, and the roof was covered with pieces of sod. The exterior of the house, roof and all, was plastered with mud which dried hard and would shed water. A sod house usually lasted a year or two, by which time the homesteader hoped to make a crop and build a frame house in front of his soddie.

Three women and two children in front of a sod home typical of the 1890s in Oklahoma Territory. —Western History Collections, University of Oklahoma Library

The interior was also plastered with mud, preferably sand mixed with white clay—"white gyp," it was called. A cloth stretched across the ceiling was almost essential to keep bugs, centipedes, and snakes from dropping down into the living quarters. Sod houses had dirt floors. No rugs or floor coverings were used, and the dirt became hard-packed and could be swept like a regular floor.

In some cases, homesteaders constructed half-dugouts by digging into a hillside and using sod to build up to a liveable height. In the case of a half-dugout, a sod roof could be disastrous. The grass sometimes continued to grow, and there were cases of the family milk cow grazing onto the top of the dugout and falling through. A trap-doored storm cave was usually dug thirty feet or so from the sod house.

An original sod house is located on OK 8 between Aline and Cleo Springs. It is a two-roomed soddie built in 1894 by a homesteader named Marshall McCully. Owned by the Oklahoma Historical Society, it has been enclosed by a building to protect it from the elements.

—*Cleo Springs* - OK 8————

This agricultural community dates from 1894. It was known simply as Cleo until 1917, when "Springs" was added. The name comes from nearby Cleo Springs, which, according to local folklore, was named for an Indian maiden who was called Cle-oh-i-to-mo. According to the January 17, 1895, *Hennessey Clipper*, a farmer named Alfred Abrams was digging a well near Cleo Springs when his shovel struck metal. It turned out to be a cache of gold coins dating from the early 1850s. The find totaled more than $2,000.

—*Fairview* - US 60—OK 8————

This prosperous agricultural and industrial community was established in 1894, taking its name from its outlook on the Glass Mountains to the northwest. It is the county seat of Major County. At the opening of the Cherokee Outlet, the flat fertile land attracted a large number of Mennonite farmers from Kansas, and their influence is still strong in the community.

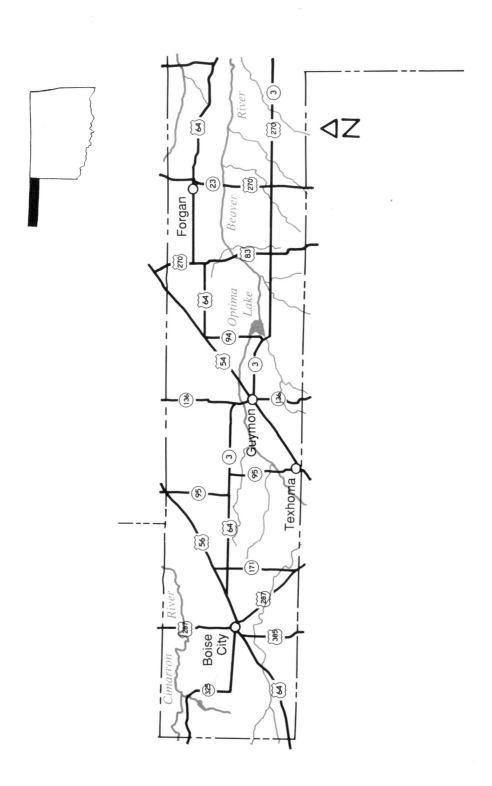

VII. No Man's Land

The Oklahoma Panhandle, the far western extension comprising present-day Beaver, Texas, and Cimarron counties, has had a variety of names: Cimarron Territory, Neutral Strip, Robber's Roost, Public Land Strip, Unassigned Lands, Beaver County, and No Man's Land. Historically, the latter designation is most descriptive.

Archaeological discoveries reveal that the land has a venerable history. Paleolithic flint artifacts and gigantic bones tell of mammoth hunts. The mummified corpse of a child testifies that Indians from the Basketmaker period inhabited the area some 2,500 years ago. Later, Plains Indians hunted buffalo and left mementoes of their passing in trash heaps beside their camps along streams. Then came the white man.

Sometime in 1542, Francisco Vásquez de Coronado and a few Spanish conquistadors traced an uncertain path across the strip of land in their futile search for gold. There were no borders, no boundaries, and no landmarks, only limitless sky and false directions from an undependable Indian guide. A few more conquistadors came later, but for the most part the Spaniards left the land to the Indians.

In 1821, just after Mexico won its freedom from Spain, Missouri traders forged a trade route from Franklin, Missouri, to Santa Fe. The Santa Fe Trail led across what later became the Oklahoma Panhandle; during sixty years of use, the Santa Fe Trail was traveled by so many wagons that their ruts have lasted for more than a century.

Despite traffic on the trail and subsequent use of the land by ranchers, cowboys, outlaws, and settlers, a strip of land 34 miles wide by 167 miles long remained an unorganized public domain beyond the pale of any state or territory. One historian dubbed the land a "governmental orphan."

Devoid of law enforcement and beyond the jurisdiction of any state or territory, following the Civil War the strip of land became a haven for outlaws, gamblers, cattle rustlers, and murderers. Thus, it earned the name Robber's Roost. But the land was too good to lie fallow.

First came sheepmen from New Mexico. Then cattlemen brought herds from Texas ranches, from the ZH, the OX, the Prairie Cattle Company, the CCC Ranch, the 101 Ranch, the Anchor D, and others. Settlers came looking for homes. Ranchers called them "pumpkin rollers."

Communities grew, towns like Beaver City and Hardesty; but there was still no government, no legal authority. The citizens formed vigilante groups to rid the area of renegades. On March 4, 1887, a meeting was held in Beaver to begin a movement to organize No Man's Land into a formal territory of the United States. Without legal authority or legal precedent, the citizens held an election. In November 1887, some 6,000 residents of No Man's Land elected nine senators and fourteen delegates to a territorial council which met at Beaver. The convention organized Cimarron Territory, complete with five counties, a governor, and a provisional legislature. They adopted the laws of Colorado for their government and elected delegates to Washington.

The delegates introduced bills petitioning Congress for aid in establishing their own government for the area or attachment to an adjoining state. The bills failed, but Congress included the so-called Territory of Cimarron or No Man's Land within the jurisdiction of the United States Court established at Muskogee on March 1, 1889.

This act established the area as part of Indian Territory. By the Oklahoma Organic Act of 1890, No Man's Land was absorbed by Oklahoma Territory. At first it was all one county; however, as Oklahoma became a state in 1907, Beaver County was divided into Beaver, Texas, and Cimarron counties.

During its early days, 173 post offices in small country stores dotted the Panhandle area. Some were "half dugouts"; others were frame houses. They became community centers. Gradually these country stores disappeared as improved roads and automobiles extended the shopping range of farmers and ranchers. Also, rural free mail delivery made many of the post offices unnecessary. When a post office was discontinued there was no longer need for the store. Today, communities such as Abe, Coin, Dombey, Esther, Sixmile, Pronto, and Venus are memories.

No Man's Land survived the devastation and catastrophe of the Dust Bowl era to become prime agricultural and ranching land. Its economy is enriched by a sprinkling of oil and gas wells, and its chambers of commerce point visitors toward vestiges of the historical past, even those with names like Robber's Roost.

—*Gate* - US 64————

This small agricultural community dates from the 1880s, when a sod house served as a post office. On their way to make formal application for a post office, the residents in this patch of No Man's Land had to ride many miles along a drift fence before they found a gate. When asked what name they wanted for the new town, they said Gate City.

After the railroad came, in 1912, buildings in the town were moved to the track. It took two days to drag the post office to its new location, and during that time postal patrons drove their buggies and wagons up beside the slow-moving building to get mail.

Joe Woten, a local blacksmith, used a crooked stick to witch a site for an oil well a mile east of Gate, firmly convinced that he had found oil. In 1918, local citizens formed the Gate Valley Drilling Corporation to pursue Joe's belief. Alas, at 3,400 feet, funds ran out. The project lay dormant, but, after a time, they hired a professional to shoot the well with nitroglycerine. People turned out en masse, hoping to see a gusher. Again, disappointment. Finally, in 1969 a gas well was brought into production in the same section, but at a depth of 6,800 feet. Joe had always known it was there.

North of town there are remains of an ancient irrigation system believed to have been used by prehistoric Indians. Portions of the system are still in use by local farmers.

—*Knowles* - US 64————

This minuscule agricultural community was incorporated December 27, 1906, as Sands City, named for the only doctor in the vicinity. There was a grocery store, a hardware store, a livery stable, and the White House Hotel. In 1912 the railroad came and buildings were relocated along the Missouri-Kansas-Texas track. Sands City faded into the past after the name of the town was changed to Knowles in honor of Alice Knowles Lundy, the postmistress.

—*Mocane* - US 64————

There were settlers in the area of this tiny unincorporated community from 1906. The winter of 1911-12, when the railroad was being built, was exceptionally cold. Farmers working on construction of the roadbed had no overshoes; they wrapped their shoes in gunny sacks.

After the coming of the railroad, the post office moved closer to the tracks, and the town flourished for a while. During the 1920s trains ceased stopping at Mocane for mail. Outgoing sacks were picked up on the run from a metal arm on a pole by the track; incoming mail sacks were thrown on the ground from the passing train. With the advent of a rural delivery route from Woodward, the Mocane post office was discontinued on April 30, 1948. Since that time, the town has gradually withered away.

EXCURSION

—*Beaver* - US 270—OK 23———

Beaver City, which the Post Office Department abbreviated to Beaver, started as a watering and feeding place for Texas cattlemen on the Jones-Plummer Trail between Tascosa, Texas, and Dodge City, Kansas. Supplies were hauled south over the trail to fuel campaigns against the Plains Indians and to build Fort Elliott in northwest Wheeler County, Texas. During the slaughter of buffalo on the plains, hides were hauled north over the trail to provide robes for Easterners.

About 1880 Nels Cary and James Lane came from Dodge City and built two sod houses. A room in one was used as a store. The stock consisted of underclothes, boots, pants, shirts, playing cards, beer, cheap whiskey, and tobacco. Another room served as a public sleeping room. The traveler got one or two pairs of blankets and some buffalo robes to make a bed. Buffalo robes were worth about two dollars each at that time.

The rutted Jones-Plummer Trail became Beaver's main street. The usual accumulation of frontier riffraff gathered the saloon and dance hall at the freighters' camp north of the town, characters with such names as "Slough Foot Nell," "Six Gun Pete," "Red Licker Sam," and "Dare Devil Dick." The south end of town contained a church, the newspaper, and a scattering of homes belonging to business people.

Main Street of Beaver in 1893. —Western History Collections, University of Oklahoma Library

Pioneer woman gathering buffalo chips. —Western History Collections, University of Oklahoma Library

No Man's Land was absorbed into Oklahoma Territory in 1890 as Beaver County with Beaver as the county seat. Upon achieving statehood in 1907, the area was divided into three counties; and Beaver became the county seat of Beaver County, the eastern county in the Panhandle.

In 1911, when the Missouri-Kansas-Texas bypassed Beaver by routing through Forgan, local business and professional men dug into their pockets to finance the construction of the Beaver, Meade and Englewood Railroad between Beaver and Forgan. Farmers contributed teams and labor to build the roadbed. At first, Beaver tried to give its railroad to the Katy; the offer was refused. Eventually, the Santa Fe paid more than two million dollars for the line. In 1973 both lines were abandoned.

Beaver advertises itself as the "Cow Chip Capital of the World." Buffalo hunters found a substitute for firewood in the form of dried buffalo "chips." In the autumn, pioneers laid in a supply of cow chips for the coming winter. If money was short, a wagonload could be taken to town and traded for food or supplies.

As homesteaders gathered chips, they engaged in informal contests to see who could hit the wagon from the farthest distance, but until 1970 no one considered making a sport out of throwing cow chips. Now, every April 22—the anniversary of Oklahoma's opening to settlement, Beaver stages the World Championship Cow Chip Throwing Contest.

—*Forgan* - US 64—OK 23————

During the summer of 1911, J. N. Cook purchased 1,600 acres in the North Flats of Beaver County. When asked why he was purchasing the land, Cook replied, "Just say that a colonization of little white bonnet people may be coming in for settlement."

The town began in 1911-12 with the arrival of the Wichita Falls and Northwestern Railway, the first railroad to enter Beaver County. It was named for James B. Forgan, a Chicago banker who arranged financing for the railroad. On January 3, 1912, the townsite was surveyed. On February 15, the sale of lots was opened; the first day's sale totaled $62,000. "The little white bonnet people" had arrived.

Broomcorn thrived in the rich sandy loam between the Cimarron River on the north and the Beaver River on the south. The Missouri-Kansas-Texas Railroad arrived, and the community became something of a rail center. However, the Katy abandoned the line from Altus in 1973, and Forgan began to fade. The depot now serves as a museum. The community is still surrounded by farms and ranches.

US 270—OK 3
Slapout—Hardesty

—*Slapout* - US 270—OK 3————

In 1932 two frame buildings were moved to a plowed field beside a dusty road. Shortly thereafter, Nye, the town that would soon be called Slapout, came into being.

Thomas L. Lemmons founded the town. He rented land and opened a store. He sold groceries and gasoline in five-gallon cans. He also bought cream. The state Highway Department let a contract for construction of a road past the store. Tom Lemmons' sister Artie helped in the store. Tradition has that it she was responsible for the unusual name of the town.

When a member of the highway crew would ask for an item that was out of stock, she would usually say, "We're slapout of that." Soon, members of the road crew started calling the community Slapout.

Then, Joe Johnston arrived in town and opened a store across the road from Tom Lemmons' store. Joe followed the lead of the highway crew and called the town Slapout, but Tom Lemmons did not take to the name. Tom put a sign over his store's entrance: NYE MERCANTILE. When someone stopped on his side of the road and asked for Slapout, he would point across the road and say:

"There's Slapout over there. This is Nye. Can I do something for you."

Rural Free Delivery signaled the end for many post early-day offices, the general stores from which they operated, and ultimately many of the towns to which people came to get their mail and shop. —Western History Collections, University of Oklahoma Library

—*Logan* - US 270—OK 3————

The remains of this small community do not show on the official state highway map; however, there is a post office and a church on the ground. There has been a post office since 1888, but it has moved about, depending upon who was postmaster. It was in the back of the Harlan hardware store until 1914, when the store was destroyed by a tornado. Four mail routes operated out of Logan when the cabs were pulled by horses; the routes were reduced to two when automobiles took over.

—*Elmwood* - US 270—OK 3————

Postal service began in this tiny crossroads community in 1888, almost twenty years before Oklahoma became a state. William James Plain was the first rural carrier between Beaver and Elmwood. He made the 28-mile roundtrip in a horse and buggy every week and was paid 50 cents. There was enough going on in Elmwood to warrant a column in the *Beaver City Tribune* entitled: "Elmwood Squibs."

—*Hardesty* - OK 3——————

The present town of Hardesty is a comparatively new community that bears little resemblance to its predecessor. In 1887, Hardesty was located near the North Canadian River some four miles to the north. The first Hardesty, now under Optima Lake, was a mecca for thirsty cowboys from the surrounding countryside.

One issue of the *Hardesty Herald*, established in 1891, was destined to become a collector's item. Editor Richard B. Quinn had been summoned to the county seat to answer a charge of libel filed by an irate citizen. He left the paper in charge of a tramp printer. The printer amused himself by setting vulgar stories into type; then he got drunk and deserted the shop.

Hardesty was visited by two of Quinn's friends. They noted that no paper had been printed for that week; the *Hardesty Herald* was in danger of losing its status as a legal publication. Acting as good Samaritans, they filled the forms with type left by the tramp printer, old illustrations, and standing ads.

Without reading the contents, they ran the issue off on a hand press and put it in the mail. The following week, Editor Quinn had a lot of explaining to do about some of the stories he had published.

US 54-64
Tyrone—Texoma

—*Tyrone* - US 54——————

This agricultural community on the Chicago, Rock Island and Pacific Railway was established in 1902. However, prior to that, as early as 1888, Shade's Well in the area served to water thousands of head of cattle driven out of Texas over the Tascosa Trail to railheads in Kansas. The well was originally owned by J. U. Shade and H. B. Fore. It was managed by Zachariah Cain until 1901, when traffic on the cattle trail petered out. Gas and oil development has helped save Tyrone from economic extinction.

Hooker - US 54-64

With the coming of the Rock Island railroad in 1901, this community started as a modest trading center for surrounding farms and ranches. In 1923, with the beginning of development of the Hugoton gas field, which lies beneath the wheat fields, Hooker's population began to increase. The gas field extends from about seven miles east of Hooker to fifty miles west.

An archeological dig near Optima. —Western History Collections, University of Oklahoma Library

—*Optima* - US 54————

This village made a brave start in 1886 with its postmark proclaiming in Latin that it was the "best" or "greatest." Today it is a shrinking agricultural community. Nearby is the site of a prehistoric village that contained at least six slab-lined pit houses. A number of significant archaeological discoveries have been made in the area.

—*Guymon* - US 54-64—OK 3-136————

E. T. Guymon was one of the founders of this townsite that grew with the coming of the Rock Island in 1900. The fledgling community was called Sanford, but there was a problem; freight destined for Sanford was confused with freight for a railroad town in Texas named Stratford. One day the freight agent said, "Mr. Guymon is the only one who ever gets any freight anyway so why don't you call this town Guymon."

Guymon became county seat of Texas County because of a political deal. There was an understanding between Guymon and Goodwell to the southwest. The political powers in Guymon agreed that if Goodwell would support Guymon for county seat, Guymon would support Goodwell in its bid for a district agricultural school.

Guymon reaped its greatest economic benefit from gas and oil development, which began in 1923, particularly the Hugoton gas field.

—Goodwell - US 54————

The name of this town derives from the quality of water in a well drilled by the Rock Island railroad in 1902. In 1909, Panhandle State University was established as an agricultural school on a high-school level. It is now a four-year institution with more than 2,000 acres of experimental farm land in the area. No Man's Land Historical Museum is on the campus. In addition to historical exhibits pertaining to the area and the Dust Bowl era, there are archaeological and geological collections.

—Texhoma - US 64—OK 95————

From both the community's name and its location, residents have had trouble telling if they were in Oklahoma or Texas. A grain elevator straddled the state line with a door opening to each state. Before the state line was adjusted in 1934, passengers stood in Texas to buy tickets from the Rock Island railroad agent standing in Oklahoma.

The town owes its birth to the Rock Island, which was completed through town in 1902. Grain elevators, feedlots, and implement dealers testify to the agricultural economy that provides lifeblood to the community. There is a weekly livestock auction.

US 56-64
Keyes—Felt

—Keyes - US 56————

The first settlement here was named Willowbar for the Willow Bar Crossing on the Cimarron River. It was awarded a post office in 1906. The community was so small that it was no trouble for it to move from one location to another, depending upon where the store containing the post office was located. That changed when the Santa Fe Railway came past in 1925. The town was forthwith renamed Keyes for Henry Keyes, president of the railroad.

Keyes blossomed as a farming and ranching center, and grain elevators sprouted. Further economic development came in 1959 with the completion of the Keyes Helium Plant, a $12 million facility for reclaiming helium from natural gas produced in the Keyes field. The plant was operated by the U.S. Bureau of Mines, processing almost 300 million cubic feet of helium a year until it closed in 1982.

—*Boise City* - US 56-64————

This community was established in 1908 by the Southwestern Immigration and Development Company of Guthrie. The company circulated enticing brochures in Illinois, Indiana, Missouri, and other states; illustrations showed paved streets, sidewalks, numerous shade trees, dwellings, and flourishing businesses. According to the brochures, "King Corn and King Cotton grow side by side, yielding in excess of 45 bushels of corn and a bale of cotton per acre"; three railroads were scheduled to come through the flourishing town.

Some 3,000 lots were sold at $45 each. Upon arrival in Boise City (the name rhymes with "voice"), not only did the buyers learn that there were no paved streets, no corn, no cotton, and few trees, they found that the promoters did not have clear title to the lots they sold.

The Post Office Department arrested the three promoters in September 1909 on a mail fraud charge. They had "grossly misrepresented the natural resources of Boise City and Cimarron County." Two of the promoters spent time in a federal penitentiary and the third died of tuberculosis before beginning his term. A Panhandle newspaper reacted to the verdict: "There are not many people living in this strip who would believe that Cimarron county is a desert, even though the jury by its verdict has said it is."

Boise City survived and won out in an election against six other small communities to become the county seat of Cimarron County. The Santa Fe Railway finally arrived in 1925, at which time Boise City had about 350 inhabitants. Today Boise City draws its sustenance from farming and ranching, the principal industries in the area. It is a gateway to numerous tourist attractions to the north.

Boise City enjoys the dubious distinction of being one of the few towns in the continental United States that was bombed during World War II. On the night of July 5, 1943, a flight of B-17 bombers took off from Dalhart Army Air Base on a practice mission. They were supposed to drop their bombs on a range about thirty miles from Boise City, but the navigator got lost and mistook four street lights around the Cimarron County courthouse for the target.

Six practice bombs, each containing a hundred pounds of sand and four pounds of explosive, peppered Boise City. Fortunately, there were no casualties and minimal property damage. Fred Kreiger, writing in *The Boise City News*, was prompted to remark: "There are many things Boise City needs, among which I could suggest some searchlights and anti-aircraft guns." Contrite Air Force officers visited to admit the bombing was a mistake, and a notice appeared on the bulletin board at Dalhart Army Air Base: *"Remember the Alamo, remember Pearl Harbor, and for God's sake—remember Boise City!"*

Townsite Land Swindles

The rich profits to be reaped from developing a townsite led to many fictitious and fraudulent claims. Speculators could buy a section of land for $800; then they would have it surveyed into blocks and lots to form a town plat. With eight lots to the acre, promoters would have 5,120 lots for sale.

The next step was to advertise that this town, located in the midst of a rich farming area, was a cinch to be named a county seat; it was sure to be on one or more railroad lines. Brochures with illustrations portraying blossoming towns were printed for circulation among land-hungry people in the East and Midwest. "For only $100 you can own a share of this Eden in the West!"

Promoters stood to clear half a million dollars from the sale of lots at $100 each. When gullible purchasers visited this Eden in the West, they found their lots on a barren, treeless prairie or in a sparsely settled town destined to dry up and blow away.

After the promoters of Boise City were sentenced to prison, land developers for spurious townsites generally refrained from circulating advertising matter by mail.

—Felt - US 56-64————

This isolated farming and ranching community owes its existence to the Santa Fe Railway, which built southwest from Boise City in 1925. It was named for C. F. W. Felt, chief engineer during construction of the railroad. The oldest home in the area was the headquarters of a sheep ranch established northwest of the site of Felt by Juan Cruz Lujan in 1879. Lujan acquired the land by exercising "squatter's rights." In 1907, when statehood became a fact, he went to Beaver to pay taxes.

OK 325
Boise City—Kenton

Santa Fe Trail

About fifteen miles from Boise City, OK 325 crosses the route of the Cimarron Cutoff of the Santa Fe Trail. The Santa Fe Trail between Franklin, Missouri, and Santa Fe, New Mexico, was established in 1821 by William Becknell. On his second trip, Becknell tested a shortcut through the Cimarron desert between the Arkansas River in Kansas and the Cimarron River in Oklahoma, waterless except during the rainy season.

On the Santa Fe Trail wagons traveled in four parallel columns to facilitate forming a square for defense in the event of Indian attack. —Josiah Gregg, 1844

After more than a century, ruts of the Santa Fe Trail are still visible in undisturbed prairie land. —New Mexico archives

The party ran out of water after leaving the Arkansas River; men and animals suffered from thirst. Becknell shot a buffalo and found water in its stomach, indicating the animal had drunk recently. After an hour's ride his party reached the Cimarron River and filled their water kegs. After that the Cimarron Cutoff was used regularly until 1880, when the Santa Fe Railway completed its line running parallel to the trail between Kansas and Santa Fe.

Wagons carried about 5,000 pounds; each required ten or twelve mules or oxen. Caravans of more than a hundred were commonplace. They traveled in four parallel columns to facilitate forming a square in the event of Indian attack. The wagons wore twenty-foot paths in the prairie in places up to ten feet deep. The ruts can still be seen southwest of the historical marker on OK 325.

—Fort Nichols————

Along the Santa Fe Trail some two miles north of the ghost town of Wheeless, Fort Nichols was established in May 1865 by Kit Carson "to give protection to trains passing to and from the States."

Colonel Carson chose a site on the rocky bluff of South Carrizo Creek, which feeds the Cimarron River. Actually, Carson thought he was in New Mexico. His dispatches from the new post bore the heading, "Fort Nichols, New Mexico." It was a sturdy fort with a good view of the surrounding country. It was built of stone and had a cobblestone parade ground.

The first escort left Fort Nichols June 19, 1865, guarding a seventy-wagon caravan. A fifty-man escort was usually provided for mail and stage coaches as well as caravans. Civilian wagon trains could proceed without escort, but only if there were at least a hundred armed men in the party.

Fort Nichols was abandoned in September, less than a year after it began. With the Civil War over, the army's budget was cut, and Fort Nichols fell prey to a shortage of funds. By the following summer Indians virtually destroyed the fort by caving in walls, scattering stones, and breaking and burning roof poles. Today only a few stone footings are visible.

—Black Mesa State Park - OK 325————

The road to Black Mesa State Park and Lake Carl G. Etling leaves OK 325 toward the west about twenty-five miles from Boise City. There are camping, picnicking, fishing, and boating facilities at the park. The lake is a winter goose refuge, and it is closed to all activities except bank fishing from November 1 to February 1.

Fishing in Lake Carl Etling, Black Mesa State Park.
—Oklahoma Tourism & Development, Fred W. Marvel

The mesa from which the park takes its name is eight miles north of the park. This lava-tipped mesa is 4,972.97 feet above sea level, the highest point in Oklahoma, a fact noted by a granite monument atop the mesa.

Dinosaur Quarry

The first piece of fossilized dinosaur bone was discovered here by accident—kicked up by a road grader working on the highway east of Kenton. It was obviously not from a steer that had run afoul of a wolf. The late Dr. J. Willis Stovall, a paleontologist at the University of Oklahoma, was notified. He visited the site and unearthed a six-foot femur of a *Brontosaurus*.

Under the supervision of Dr. Stovall, a WPA project excavated more than 18 tons of fossilized prehistoric animal bones from the Cimarron quarries. A *Brontosaurus* skeleton measuring 65 feet in length was taken from the quarry, 85 percent complete. It has been reassembled and is on display in the Stovall Museum on the campus of the University of Oklahoma.

A concrete replica of the femur of the *Brontosaurus* marks the quarry from which the skeleton was taken. It is six feet long, 24 inches across the base and 21 inches across the opposite end. The fossil weighed 425 pounds. Five distinct species of dinosaurs were found in the same quarry.

When the beasts roamed the land, the plains of present-day Oklahoma were a vast tropical swamp, mud flats over which the dinosaurs

A concrete replica of a femur of the Brontosaurus *marks the quarry from which the skelton was taken.* —Oklahoma Tourism & Development, Fred W. Marvel

Main Street, Kenton, July 20, 1916. —Western History Collections, University of Oklahoma Library

fought, hunted, and died. Their bodies sank into the almost bottomless mire. In time, heavily mineralized water replaced the natural elements in the bones. The mud around them hardened into shale. Then sandstone stratas formed on top from sediments laid down over eons by the great inland sea that later flooded the plains.

—*Kenton* - OK 325————

At first there was Carrizo in the northwest corner of Cimarron County, or maybe it was in New Mexico Territory. It was little more than a place where cowboys and ranchers came to sort through mail sacks to see if they had letters. It was west of present-day Kenton; the post office was officially established September 9, 1886.

A village grew: the inevitable saloons, a blacksmith shop, a boarding-house, and a store. In 1890 the name was changed to Florence for the daughter of George W. Hubbard, the first postmaster. Then Fairchild B. Drew, a nephew of P. T. Barnum, arrived. He became postmaster and changed the name to Kenton. Some say it was a misspelling of Canton, Ohio; others say it was in memory of a Civil War officer named Captain Kent.

Drew filed on a homestead to the east, moved his store and the post office, and platted the south forty acres into lots. He was apparently trying to get away from the saloons in Florence, but the saloon keepers followed and carousing cowmen soon earned the title "Cowboy Capital" for the new town.

As the only established community in the county when Oklahoma became a state, Kenton was named the county seat. A 1908 election awarded the distinction to Boise City, and a delegation of Boise City citizens went to Kenton to get the county records ahead of the legal date when they should have been transferred. For years there was discussion of "how Boise City stole the courthouse."

HISTORICAL HIGHLIGHT

Robber's Roost

Details of the end of the story are hazy, but there is no doubt that there was a Capt. William Coe who headed a band of outlaws that preyed on stockmen in the area during the late 1860s. Their hideout was in No Man's Land, east of Black Mesa.

The bastion was a 16- by 30-foot rock building. There were no windows, but twenty-seven gunports commanded approaches. Coe's gang of several dozen men raided ranches and nearby military installations, selling cattle, sheep, and horses with botched brands to settlers in Kansas and Missouri at bargain prices. Coe provided entertainment for his men when they were not out marauding. In Robber's Roost he maintained a bar complete with a piano and girls.

There are numerous stories but no definitive information regarding Coe's origin. His end is also somewhat clouded. The most prevalent story is that after his men raided a sheep camp in New Mexico Territory in 1867, killing two herders and driving off 3,400 head of sheep, a delegation visited Fort Lyons, Colorado, and prevailed upon Col. William H. Penrose to help eradicate the scourge.

A detachment of soldiers under Penrose is supposed to have used a howitzer against the stone fortress, battering in one end and causing the outlaw gang to scatter. Coe was eventually captured, and taken to Pueblo, Colorado, for trial. One night he was taken from the flimsy jail and hanged from a cottonwood tree.

But no military records have been found to verify the expedition. At the time, Penrose and his troops were supposed to be chasing renegade Indians. However, years later workers excavating in the area where Coe was supposed to have been hanged on that night of July 21, 1868, unearthed a skeleton. Its wrists were handcuffed and the legs were manacled.

Ruins of the stone house are still visible at Robber's Roost Mesa. The land around has been pockmarked by treasure hunters searching for loot buried by the Coe gang. The owner took a dim view of trespassers, particularly after one of his cows broke a leg stepping in an unfilled hole. At first he banned digging and charged 50 cents per person to go on the property to search; then he mounted guard with a rifle to ward off those who returned after dark with shovels.

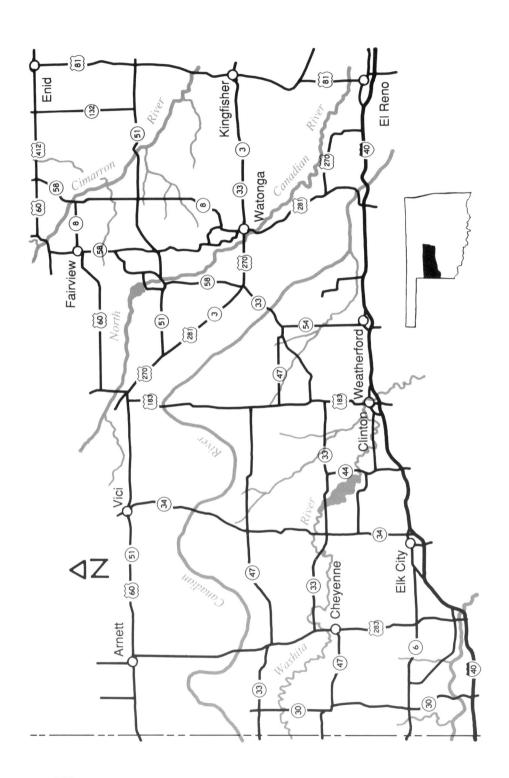

VIII. The Short Grass Country

Until it was disturbed by settlers' plows, a virtually unbroken expanse of grass stretched from the Saskatchewan River in Canada almost to the Mexican border, a strip of land some 1,500 miles long and 500 miles wide. It was covered by a mat of buffalo grass, grama, and mesquite (the genus *Muhlenbergia*, a short grass not to be confused with *Prosopis*, the mesquite shrub or tree). These are all short grasses, scarcely six inches high. Buffalo grass was the most abundant, spreading over the ground with runners like a vine, curling back upon the earth and looking rather like oversized moss.

The western half of Oklahoma, from El Reno, was in a portion of the short grass country known as the high plains, a tableland about 1,500 feet above sea level and 400 feet higher than the bordering plains. The prevailing type of soil is a dark red loam. Infrequent rain comes in scouring torrents. During hot summers, incessant wind blows warm and dry, hour after hour, day after day, month after month. Newcomers and strangers tend to become irritable, but long-time residents are so inured to the constant parching current that they notice the wind only when it stops blowing.

Oklahoma's short grass country has had a succession of occupants and transients: Indians, conquistadors, traders, buffalo hunters, sheepherders, cattlemen, Pony Express riders, railroad builders, farmers, rustlers, outlaws, vigilantes, oilmen, and business entrepreneurs. It has been scarred by prairie schooners, bull trains, pack mules, cattle drives, plows, tractors, paved highways, railroads, and pipelines. It is subject to prairie fires, tornadoes, cloudbursts, droughts, northers, and dust storms. For all comers, the land has dictated their way of life. When the land was violated, it retaliated by turning into a dust bowl.

The short grass country could also be a provider. The thick virgin sod provided building blocks from which to construct homes. When grass gave out, cattlemen burned the spines from prickly pear to provide feed for their cattle. During hard times following the first settlement, the pioneers turned to gathering the bleached and crumbling bones of millions of prairie grazers by the wagonload and hauled them to the railroad where they were piled in heaps stretching hundreds of yards along the tracks. They sold by the pound.

The history of Oklahoma's short grass country has been written by a melange of prosperous agricultural communities and withering villages, of ghost towns and boom towns, of industrial cities and rusting oil camps, of struggling municipalities and successful business centers. Each provides in one way or another a story of human confrontation with the environment.

US 270-281—OK 8
Okeene—Geary

—Okeene - OK 8-51————

When its post office was established in 1893, the name of this prosperous farming community was coined from the words Oklahoma, CheroKEE, and CheyenNE. Massive grain elevators and a flour mill testify to the importance of the surrounding wheat fields to the economy. Early settlers were predominately German, and read the locally published *Deutscher Anzeiger.*

—Hitchcock - OK 8————

This town was established in 1901 on the Rock Island railroad and named for Interior Secretary Ethan A. Hitchcock. A headline in the February 22, 1906, issue of the *Hitchcock Vanguard* said: "Hitchcock in Ashes." Twenty-three buildings were destroyed, but six hours after the disaster people from neighboring towns arrived with donations of money and food. Hitchcock recovered from the fire, but more recently it has suffered from attrition and desertion.

—Watonga - US 270—OK 8-33————

This town was established in 1892 with the opening of the Cheyenne-Arapaho reservation to settlement. It was named for an Arapaho chief. During its early days, Watonga had a decidedly Indian flavor. In 1907, "Watonga Items" in the *Indian Outlook,* published at Darlington, noted that Man-on-Cloud had built himself a good house and barn; Raymond Buffalo Meat had charge of the blacksmith shop at the Watonga station and a number of Sioux Indians were visiting there; Carry Short Teeth was born on January 10, but she died fourteen days later.

The *Watonga Rustler* was Watonga's first newspaper. Its editor, Thompson B. Ferguson, was appointed by President Theodore Roosevelt as governor of Oklahoma Territory in 1901. The Ferguson home has been restored and is open to visitors as a museum. Both Ferguson and his wife Elva were writers, and Edna Ferber began writing her novel *Cimarron* while visiting them.

—*Omega* - OK 33————

According to the story, this small rural community was inadvertently named by an Eastern college professor while visiting the West to gather information about the cattle industry. His covered wagon broke down. Before abandoning the wagon, he used axle grease to write "Omega" on the side, the last letter of the Greek alphabet, signifying the end of his project.

The wrecked wagon remained to become a reference point: "North to Omega, then west." When the town was established in 1892, the name was adopted. For a time Omega was plagued by outlaw bands who hid out in the nearby hills and raided caravan routes in the area.

—*Loyal*————

In 1894, homesteaders of German descent founded a farming settlement northeast of Omega. They called it Kiel, for a city in their native country. The community managed to survive hard times and the promise of a railroad branch line that never materialized. During World War I it became politic to avoid anything that gave the appearance of sympathy with the German cause. The name of the town was changed to Loyal on October 1, 1918.

—*Geary* - US 281————

This settlement was established in 1892 and named for Edmund Charles F. C. Guerrier, a French-Canadian Indian scout. With the arrival of the Rock Island railroad in 1898, the community moved several miles southeast and became a busy railroad junction in the midst of wheat fields.

Jesse Chisholm, for whom the Chisholm Trail was named, died on March 4, 1868, at Raven Spring, about eight miles northeast of Geary, while visiting an Arapaho chief named Left Hand. Left Hand later took the spring as his allotment and it became known as Left Hand Spring. The exact location of Jesse Chisholm's grave is unknown, but a marker had been placed at the approximate spot near Left Hand Spring, and the spring and the gravesite are maintained by the Oklahoma Historical Society.

OK 51A
Southard—Roman Nose State Park

—Southard - OK 51-8A————

Established as Cherryvale in 1896, the name of this town was changed to Southard in 1905, honoring George A. Southard, developer of a local gypsum mill. Since 1905 Southard has been a company town that produces wallboard, lath, sheeting, and other products for the construction industry.

—Roman Nose State Park - OK 8A————

Henry Roman Nose was the last warrior-chief of the Cheyennes. He used the site of present-day Roman Nose State Park as a winter campground for his braves. When the land was opened to settlement, he took the area as his allotment. He lived there until his death in 1917. The Spring of Everlasting Waters, near where Roman Nose had his dugout, flows at 600 gallons per minute to fill the park's swimming pool.

OK 33-58-58A
Longdale—Custer City

—Longdale - OK 58————

The first post office here was established in 1900, and the settlement was named Cainville for its first postmaster, William Cain. In 1903 the name was changed to Longdale for L. W. Long, the townsite owner. The land had been homesteaded by Long's wife prior to their marriage. Formerly an agricultural trading center, the town now exists primarily to serve visitors to nearby Canton Lake.

—Canton - OK 51-58————

This agricultural trading center was established in 1905, taking its name from the old military post about three miles to the northeast known as Cantonment. Today Canton is a trading center for vacationers at nearby Canton Lake.

Cantonment was established on March 6, 1879, when Col. Richard I. Dodge and six companies of the Twenty-third Infantry pitched camp on the North Canadian River to protect Kansas from invasion by Indians and to protect Indian Territory from invasion by whites.

Cantonment was on one of the cattle trails between Texas and Dodge City. Indians demanded toll from every herd that went through. Efforts were made to protect cattlemen, but the military ended up advising the drovers to give the Indians two or three head from each herd. After the post was abandoned, the May 9, 1884, issue of the *Cheyenne Transporter* reported the harrowing experience of a drover named Horton. Horton was driving a herd of three hundred horses and colts. Indians demanded their usual toll; Horton refused. In the subsequent altercation, an Indian was killed. The Cheyennes attacked, and Horton and his men barricaded themselves in one of the old stone buildings of Cantonment. They held the Indians at bay until troops came from Fort Reno. The troops had difficulty saving Horton. He finally had to sacrifice half his herd before the Indians would permit him to depart.

The post was abandoned in 1882 and taken over as an Indian agency. Mennonite missionaries operated an Indian school that made brooms. The post office closed in 1917.

—*Fay* - OK 33————

This tiny rural community was established in 1894, two years after the opening of the Cheyenne-Arapaho reservation to settlement. It has stood the test of time somewhat better than other towns along the railroad. In 1905, the editor of the *Fay Observer* lamented the absence of a doctor in town and noted that Mrs. Fiscos, the wife of the postmaster, was willing to loan her copy of *Dr. A. W. Chase's Receipt Book and Household Physician* to anyone who needed it.

HISTORICAL HIGHLIGHT
Home Remedies on the Frontier

Homesteaders found the shortage of doctors a constant problem in Oklahoma, and most had a book of home remedies upon which they depended. Many adopted nostrums from the Indians. Herbs were used for a multiplicity of ailments.

Jimson leaves served as a sedative for pain or were made into an ointment for burns. But the Indians knew that too much jimson weed would cause a man "to act a fool," so they advised moderation. A tobacco poultice was applied to insect stings; a slice of salt pork was used on boils. A brew made from poke root was put in bath water for itch; a mixture of poke root and whiskey was prescribed for rheumatism. Stoneseed, dogbane, Indian turnips, wild ginger, milkweed, Indian paintbrush, deer's tongue, squaw root, and mistletoe were used for various ailments.

Mustard plasters on the chest were in common usage for colds. Mixtures of goose grease, turpentine, kerosene, camphor or menthol were also applied. Children wore asafetida bags on strings about their necks to ward off disease. The ploy probably worked because the highly malororous asafetida bag was guaranteed to keep nonwearers at a

In early-day Oklahoma doctors made calls by horse and buggy over muddy roads and streets. —Western History Collections, University of Oklahoma Library

distance. The efficacy of a remedy was judged by how bad it tasted or smelled. For a sore throat the author of an 1890 book of home remedies suggested with an apparent straight face:

> Tie a sock you have worn inside your boot for almost a week, so that it has a bad odor, around your neck, leave until the soreness leaves.

James W. Murdock, one of twin boys born on November 15, 1888, in Cordell became deathly ill. A group of Cheyenne and Arapaho women watched as his father carried the almost lifeless baby out of the family's sod house. The Indian women said they could save the child. His mother agreed to let them try since James "was dying anyway."

The women wrapped the baby in layers of blankets and took him to their beehive-shaped oven. Much to the mother's horror, they put little James on a paddle used to retrieve hot loaves of bread from the oven and slid him deep inside. After a while, they took the child out, bathed him, and then repeated the procedure. Over and over, they continued for ten days, day and night, taking turns at wet-nursing the child between periods in the oven. Finally, James recovered. He grew to become a healthy man, but always walked with a limp. He was later diagnosed as having had spinal meningitis, usually fatal at that time. The Indian's treatment was strikingly similar to that developed by the Australian nurse Sister Elizabeth Kenny to treat poliomyelitis almost half a century later.

—*Thomas* - OK 33-47————

The post office of this prosperous agricultural community was established in 1894. The town was platted in 1902 on land homesteaded by Joseph W. Morris during the opening of the territory. Thomas is perhaps the only town in Oklahoma that started with a daily newspaper. In August 1902, Edgar S. Bronson and Norris Alois Nichols, newspapermen from Trenton, Missouri, began publication of a daily newspaper, the *Thomas Tribune*, in a tent in a wheat field. By 1907 it claimed a circulation of 1,275.

The rich farm land to the south of Thomas was settled by four religious groups: Amish, Mennonites, Dunkards, and the so-called River Brethern. All were pacifistic in their beliefs and abhorred ostentation. In addition to wheat, there was extensive sweet potato production in the area.

—*Custer City* - OK 33————

The first trace of this a town came in 1892, when Phillip Graves opened a post office in his dugout home. In 1902, the Frisco railroad's townsite company purchased land for a town, including forty acres from Graves. Graves found himself on the north edge of town and moved his post office closer to the depot. The official name was changed from Graves to Custer, but the railroad called it Custer City on the depot and it still appears that way on some maps.

Old-timers told about the arrival of the first train when Custer was only a depot in a cornfield. A flourishing little town called Independence was six or seven miles to the northwest. Three businessmen from Independence cut a swath through the cornfield, creating Custer's future main street. Businesses began moving from Independence to form the new town on the railroad. Between 1904 and 1910 the population climbed to more than a thousand. The Depression coupled with improved roads and automobiles caused the population to decline to about half its peak.

US 183
Taloga—Putnam

—*Taloga* - US 183————

Taloga was surveyed and designated the county seat of "D" County (now Dewey County) prior to the opening of the Cheyenne-Arapaho reservation to settlement. Its post office was established in 1892. Its destiny has been tied to farming and stock raising. As was the case with all towns where cowboys gathered on Saturday nights, there were saloons; and Carrie Nation came to Taloga.

She wore her customary long black silk dress and small black hat, and carried her Bible. As she entered Captain McFaddin's saloon, the barflies left by the back door. She asked McFaddin if she could pray. He agreed, and she knelt on the floor for a lengthy address to the Lord. The proprietor placed his elbows on the bar and bowed his head. Finally, she pointed to the pictures on the wall and asked Captain McFaddin if he would like for his daughters to see those lewd, undraped pictures. Later, Captain McFaddin removed the pictures, but he did not shut down his watering place until the arrival of statehood made it mandatory.

—*Putnam* - US 183————

This small trading community on the backbone between the South Canadian and the Washita rivers began a quarter of a mile north of its present location. Dugouts housed the post office and such other businesses as there were when the community was officially dubbed Putnam in 1895.

In 1905 the town was surveyed in its present location. A well was drilled in the center of the street and watering troughs were built around it. Buildings sprang up along boardwalks and hitching racks lined the street. Putnam suffered because the railroad that was supposed to come went past Oakwood instead. Frequently high water made it impossible for people to get across the Canadian River with loads destined for the railroad.

OK 34
Camargo—Hammon

—*Camargo* - OK 34————

The first post office for Camargo was established in 1892 in a farm house. The post office floated from one country store to another until the railroad came through in 1911 and the town was established in its present location. But for the "free ferry," Camargo would have been little different from other rural trade centers in the short grass country.

The South Canadian River near Camargo was unpredictable—one day dry sand, the next day angry roiling water from bank to bank. Even when the water was low, quicksand and holes were a hazard. With the coming of automobiles, an enterprising farmer built a shack and a barn to house a team. He hired a driver and pulled cars across the river for a dollar each.

When OK 34 was extended across the river, the crossing was made a "free ferry." The state provided equipment on the Camargo side. It

Interior of the Secrest Hardware, Camargo. —Western History Collections, University of Oklahoma Library

consisted of a tractor, a two-wheeled trailer with a bed large enough to hold a car, a water tank, a team, and a cart. The ferry operated on three eight-hour shifts. After the river was at flood stage, the team and cart were used to map a safe crossing. A crossing was marked with willow sticks so the tractor, wagons, and buggies would not stray into deep water. During summer, when the river was dry, sand became so loose in the crossing that automobiles would bog down. It was the ferry operator's job to haul water to the river to wet down the sand so cars could get across.

Fording swollen streams was a common experience for motorists before the construction of bridges.

—Trail - OK 34————

This railroad flag stop took its name from the Trail Store, a stopping place on the Western or Dodge City Cattle Trail. The post office was in service from 1898 until 1929.

—Leedey - OK 34————

This small agricultural community came into being in 1900 with a post office named for Amos Leedey, the first postmaster. Disaster struck the town on May 31, 1947, when it was virtually destroyed by a tornado. The Boswell Museum in Leedey features examples of pioneer transportation, photographs, documents, and numerous artifacts representing early-day life in the short grass country.

—Hammon - OK 33-34————

Shortly after the opening of the Cheyenne-Arapaho territory in 1882, James H. Hammon was sent west to establish an Indian agency and school. He called the agency Red Moon, for an aging Cheyenne chief. It was in present-day Custer County not far from the Washita River. Hammon's wife Ida served as postmistress, and the post office was named Hammon.

By 1900 most of the land in the Cheyenne-Arapaho reservation had been homesteaded, and the rich river land had been leased from the Indians. Hammon moved the town and it began to grow, but it was hampered by lack of transportation. In 1910, with the coming of the Missouri-Kansas-Texas Railroad, Hammon moved again and soon the town's principal attraction was a new railroad station west of the main street. The Red Moon Indian School operated until 1925.

———— EXCURSION

—Butler - OK 33-44————

Originally known as Hatcher's Store, southwest of the present site, Butler was established in 1898 and named for Maj. Gen. Matthew C. Butler, U.S. senator from South Carolina and an officer in both the Civil and Spanish-American wars. A business section was made up of substantial brick buildings on the promise of the Clinton and Oklahoma Western Railroad, but the railroad faded and so did the town.

In 1911 a tornado dealt an almost fatal blow. However, the community has revived somewhat because of visitors to nearby Foss State Park.

US 283—OK 33
Roll—Cheyenne

—*Roll* - US 283-OK 33-47————

This crossroads community, established in 1903, serves not only ranchers and farmers in the area, but travelers to Dead Indian Lake, off US 283 to the north. The lake is part of the Black Kettle National Grasslands, maintained by the U.S. Forest Service. The dam that forms the long, narrow lake was built in 1958 as a flood control project.

The California Road crosses US 283 about a mile to the north. This route to California was first traveled by gold-seekers in 1849 under a military escort commanded by Capt. Randolph B. Marcy. It was a well-traveled thoroughfare to the west for more than fifty years, a major route across the Great Plains.

—*Strong City* - OK 33————

This town was started by J. H. Kendall, a young Texan, and named for a railroad developer. In June 1912, a newspaper put out by the townsite division of the Clinton and Oklahoma Western Railroad (popularly known as the COW line) advertised: STRONG CITY WANTS YOU—NEEDS YOU. Strong City was the last stop on the railroad line for a year.

Business boomed and Strong City contended to become the county seat. It looked as if the upstart village might even absorb Cheyenne, the older town to the west. Cheyenne businessmen took a dim view of this. They set out to bring the railroad to Cheyenne. They voted water bonds and built their own line.

In spite of being a thriving broomcorn center with three lumberyards and two hotels, Strong City was not strong enough to withstand the drought that precipitated the Dust Bowl era. The community dwindled as families moved away.

—*Cheyenne* - US 283—OK 47————

This settlement came into existence in 1891 when the government established a Cheyenne Indian agency. This was a year before the 3-million-acre Cheyenne-Arapaho reservation was opened to homesteaders. The area was opened for settlement on April 19, 1892. However, because the region was far from railroads and generally considered virtually too arid for agriculture, the opening did not attract as many homesteaders as earlier runs in the east.

When the oil boom came to western Oklahoma, Cheyenne was the county seat of Roger Mills County. The community had a population of about 1,500. It was also reputed to have at least fifty millionaires, the highest per capita of any agricultural community in the state.

Cheyenne's proximity to the Washita Battlefield, where in 1868 George A. Custer attacked Black Kettle's encampment on the Washita, provides the community with a steady supply of visitors.

HISTORICAL HIGHLIGHT
Battle of the Washita

The majority of the site of the Battle of the Washita is on private land, but OK 47A leads to a monument within the battlefield. There are conflicting opinions regarding the battle. Regardless of who is right, November 27, 1868, was not a bright day in United States history.

Soon after the Plains Indians agreed to the Treaty of Medicine Lodge, they began complaining that the government had not supplied the guns and ammunition promised for their spring buffalo hunt. Restless young warriors launched a series of bloody raids against settlers in Kansas. During the summer of 1868, Maj. Gen. Philip Sheridan was assigned to mount a campaign during the coming winter to force the Cheyennes and Arapahos to move onto reservations in the land assigned to them in future Oklahoma. This was alien to Indian custom; winter had always been a time for truce.

Gen. W. B. Hazen was sent to Fort Cobb under instructions from Gen. W. T. Sherman to "make provision for all the Indians who come there to keep out of the war."

While General Hazen was at Fort Cobb attempting to feed the Indians who were arriving in the vicinity, General Sheridan was constructing an advance supply base known as Camp Supply, northwest of present-day Woodward, in preparation for the winter campaign. Sheridan selected Lt. Col. George Armstrong Custer to carry out the mission.

On November 20, 1868, Black Kettle, a Cheyenne chief, arrived at Fort Cobb for a parley with Hazen. He had a camp of about 180 lodges on the Washita: "I have always done my best to keep my young men quiet, but some will not listen, and, since the fighting began, I have not been able to keep them all at home. But we all want peace, and I would be glad to move my people down this way. I could then keep them all quietly near camp."

General Hazen replied, "I cannot stop the war, but will send your talk to the Great Father, and if he gives me orders to treat you like the friendly Indians I will send out to you to come in."

Black Kettle headed back to his camp on the Washita. Meanwhile, on November 23, Lieutenant Colonel Custer with the Seventh Cavalry set out through a blizzard from Camp Supply. Indians in Black Kettle's camp disregarded warning of the troops' approach: Maybe because Black Kettle thought he had immunity as a result of his talk with General Hazen, or maybe because the Indians thought nobody—not even the white eyes—would be so foolish as to fight a battle during the winter.

At dawn on the morning of November 27, with the regimental band striking up "Garry Owen," Custer's favorite fighting air, he charged the sleeping Cheyenne village on the bank of the Washita. Within ten minutes the troops captured the thoroughly surprised village. The number of Indians killed is controversial. The dead included Black Kettle and his wife. A herd of some 300 ponies was slaughtered; every lodge in the village was burned; the troops took hundreds of saddles and buffalo robes, arms and ammunition; and the winter's supply of meat was captured. More than 50 women and children were taken prisoner.

As the day lengthened, Custer saw warriors approaching from other villages along the Washita, and he elected to withdraw. In the meantime, Maj. Joel H. Elliott and eighteen men had ridden out to engage the Indians. Custer did not search for them before leaving the field of battle, and Elliott's detachment was annihilated. Custer maintained his reputation for leading victorious engagements, but he earned the contempt of many officers in the Seventh Cavalry for his abandonment of Elliott.

Military historians have pointed out a similarity between Custer's tactics during the Battle of the Washita and his tactics eight years later at the Little Big Horn: Custer disregarded warnings from his scouts; he took an unnecessary risk by attacking a vastly superior force. Some have called the Battle of the Washita a "dress rehearsal for disaster."

As the Custer controversy rages on, Custer has champions as well as detractors. Some of his vindicators maintain that Black Kettle's camp contained a band that had recently participated in the butchery of three of Sheridan's dispatch riders. Scalps, mail pouches, and dispatches were found in the village after the battle. Some of the squaws killed are said to have died with rifles in their hands. The true facts will never be known. The only remaining witness is the silent red earth along the bank of the Washita.

OK 30
Durham—Sweetwater

—Durham - OK 30————

This area was speckled with homesteaders soon after the opening of the Cheyenne-Arapaho reservation to settlement in 1892, but the post office was not established until May 1902. The community was dubbed Durham for cattle owned by early-day ranchers Fred Churchill, Bert Fay, and Bill Hardige.

About 1911 a rural telephone system was established, and visiting and eavesdropping became a way of life. Its replacement by a dial system was lamented, "No longer do we know who is ill or in trouble and need," a common complaint against telephone modernization in the short grass country.

—Rankin - OK 30————

Uncle John T. Rankin started this community in 1901, became postmaster, and named the town to perpetuate his name. Rankin was a typical farming community with rural mail routes from 24 to 30 miles long. It took the mail carrier two or three days to cover a route by horse and buggy for $75 a month. When automobile transportation came along two routes were combined to make one fifty-four miles long. The carrier had a Model T Ford which he had driven for a year and a half; he was to receive $150 a month. He worked for a week, quit, and went into the mercantile business.

Rankin had the distinction of electing the first woman representative in Oklahoma. The first year women voted, 1920, Bessie S. McColgin's name was put on the ballot for county representative. She was out of the state at the time. When she returned after the November election, she discovered she was the first female representative in Oklahoma.

—Dempsey————

This small rural community on a county road east of OK 30 began as a store and a post office in a half-dugout in 1902. Anthony Frankford and his wife came from Illinois in 1902. They named their post office Dempsey for a relative back home. The post office was closed in 1913, but the Dempsey Store continued until 1950. Mrs. Frankford operated the switchboard for the McColgins' Telephone Company until 1918, when the phone company raised its rates from a dollar per month and the people disconnected their telephones.

—*Sweetwater* - OK 30-6————

This crossroads village on the line between Roger Mills and Beckham counties is almost a century old. It served farmers and ranchers; the principal crop was cotton. The first post office was opened September 27, 1894, in a rock farmhouse belonging to George Coburn, the postmaster. The second post office opened in a building salvaged from a tornado that struck Mobeetie, Texas.

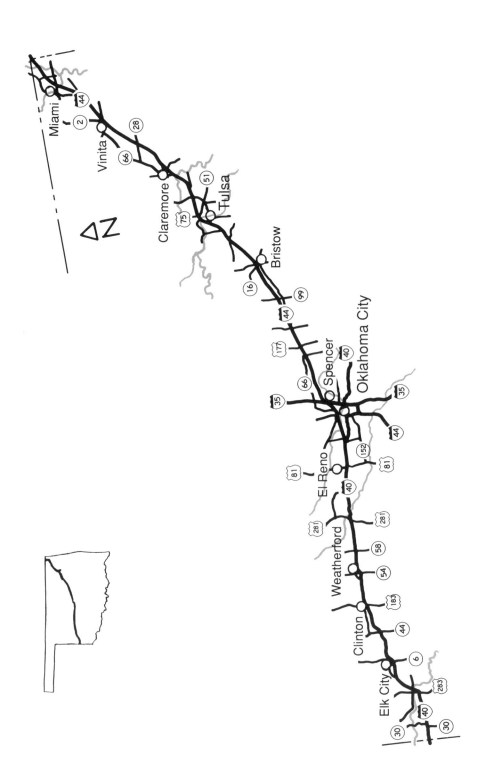

IX. Route 66:
"The Main Street of America"

Highway US 66 sliced diagonally across the nation's heartland from the corner of Michigan Avenue and Jackson Boulevard in Chicago to Santa Monica Pier in California. In the beginning there were no service stations. Motorists pulled up to curbs on the main streets of towns along the way to have their gas tanks filled from pumps in front of grocery stores.

By 1925 it was obvious the horseless carriage had come to stay, and the United States adopted a national highway system. Oklahoman Cyrus Stevens Avery was a leader in development of the plan. He became the godfather of US 66, designating the route and getting it paved. The highway went through Tulsa because it was Avery's hometown and he wanted a road connecting Tulsa to the capital. On August 11, 1926, the route was approved; its number was selected in November. By 1937 the road was completely paved through Oklahoma.

During the 1920s cars either raised clouds of dust or slithered through mud. Standard equipment for motorists included tire tools, a lug wrench, inner tube patching equipment, and a tire pump. Camping gear was *de rigueur* for long trips. Gradually, tourist courts began to appear. At first, operators expected motorists to furnish their own food and cooking utensils as well as linens.

Where paved, US 66 consisted of two nine-foot-wide lanes—slabs of concrete six to ten inches thick. State funds were matched by federal dollars. After 1930 construction got its impetus from the use of Federal Works Projects to abate unemployment. Route 66 has been most highly advertised for carrying destitute farmers from Oklahoma to California, but it also gave jobs to many, enabling them to remain in Oklahoma through the hard times.

Venturous entrepreneurs pursued ways to make money from increasing traffic. Gas stations, garages, tourist courts, cafes, souvenir shops, and Western wear stores sprang up. Short-haul truckers launched the nation's trucking industry by providing door-to-door service in competition with railroads. Hamburger stands, such as White Castle, began the "fast-food" industry.

Politics and local boosterism had much to do with selection of the route through Oklahoma. As the route shifted, some businesses went broke. Luckier or more enterprising owners picked up and moved with the highway.

The route was virtually a straight line for 130 miles west of Oklahoma City, attributable to Lew Wentz, Ponca City oil entrepreneur who sold out to Conoco and got on the state highway commission. The millionaire-philanthropist was immune to political pressure.

"I may not have learned much in school," said Wentz, "but I do know that a straight line is the shortest distance between two points." He laid a ruler on a map and drew the route between Oklahoma City and Sayre.

On May 10 and 11, 1934, howling wind foretold the scourge that would become known as the Dust Bowl. From 1934 through 1938 more than 260 dust storms blew an estimated 300 million acres of topsoil from Texas, Oklahoma, and Kansas. The worst day was April 14, 1935—"Black Sunday." The morning was calm and sunny. In mid-afternoon a "black roller" swept through the Oklahoma Panhandle on an advancing

On April 14 , 1935 —"Black Sunday"—a "black roller" swept through the Oklahoma Panhandle. —Western History Collections, University of Oklahoma Library

cold front. The daily Santa Fe mail train making the run between Waynoka and Buffalo passed Selman without stopping because the engineer could not see the town.

During those years, powdered farm land flavored food on the table before it could be eaten. People filtered the air by hanging wet towels in windows to catch the permeating dust, and mothers laid damp dish towels and flour sacks over their children's faces at night. By morning they were stained red.

On top of widespread economic depression, this was the final blow for many. Discouraged residents abandoned homesteads won by their parents' toil in the promised land of the 1890s, often leaving most of their belongings behind. A stream of "Okies" and "Arkies" flowed westward over Route 66 to another promised land in California. John Steinbeck chronicled the exodus in his Pulitzer Prize-winning novel *The Grapes of Wrath* as the Joads set out on their trek:

> 66 is the path of people in flight, refugees from dust and shrinking land, from the thunder of tractors and shrinking ownership, from the desert's slow northward invasion, from the twisting winds that howl up out of Texas, from the floods that bring no richness to the land and steal what little richness is there. From all of these the people are in flight, and they come into 66 from the tributary side roads, from the wagon tracks and the rutted country roads. 66 is the mother road, the road of flight.

On Route 66, headed for the "Promised Land" in California. —Western History Collections, University of Oklahoma Library

Oklahomans did not take kindly to *The Grapes of Wrath*. They felt it branded them as shiftless, and many libraries banned the book. Nevertheless, it presented an indelible picture of the cars that streamed along Route 66 with mattresses tied to their tops and household goods bulging from their running boards.

Businesses along Route 66 were barely on the way to recovery from the Depression when World War II brought another catastrophe—gasoline rationing. Except for military convoys and heavy equipment, traffic slowed to a trickle. A few were lucky enough to find themselves in the vicinity of military installations and war-time construction sites.

The end of the war brought a boom, and Route 66 became the mother road of the tourist industry as returning servicemen streamed across the country. Freed from gasoline rationing, families took to the roads to catch up on vacationing. Glitzy art-deco service stations, tourist courts, and cafes burgeoned; proprietors vied with each other to lure travelers from the highway with bright lights and signs, free ice water, and roadside zoos. Route 66 became a friendly road. Mom-and-pop operators extended welcoming hands; they would *give* you a map if you were lost.

In 1946 Bobby Troup wrote "Get Your Kicks on Route 66." The King Cole Trio recorded it first, and the song's popularity lasted forty years: "If you ever plan to motor west, / Try takin' my way, / It's the highway that's the best, / Get your kicks on Route 66. . . . Oklahoma City looks mighty pretty." In the early 1960s the television series *Route 66* started, creating a wave of nostalgia. Those who had been there nudged each other and pointed: "Do you remember—"

There was a push to make US 66 a four-lane road across the country, but that came to naught. Old Route 66 had been doomed back in 1934, four years before it was paved all the way to Santa Monica Pier. That was the year Congress passed the Hayden-Cartwright Act, designating funds for highway-use surveys and long-range planning.

The nation's interstate highway system was designed in 1947. In 1954, President Dwight D. Eisenhower established a president's advisory committee on a national highway program. Its report led to the Federal Highway Act of 1956. Neither song nor the lamentations of frustrated merchants along the way could save "The Main Street of America."

Highway planners knew the difficulties wartime military traffic had faced winding through villages on narrow roads. Those villages became victims of "improving the flow of high-volume traffic." Route 66 was widened, straightened, and repaved; the old road was replaced by freeways, purposefully routed around towns. It took twelve years to pave US 66 the first time; it took more than twice as long to replace it.

Turner Turnpike, between Tulsa and Oklahoma City, and Will Rogers Turnpike, between Joplin and Tulsa, made the first inroads in 1953 and 1957. These limited access toll roads encouraged speed rather than enjoyment of scenery. The death knell sounded in 1985. Highway 66 shields were taken down. The Main Street of America was gone; the

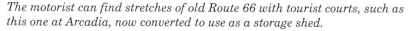

The motorist can find stretches of old Route 66 with tourist courts, such as this one at Arcadia, now converted to use as a storage shed.

mother road was replaced by I-40 and I-44, sterile freeways that avoided the retarding influence of civilization.

Today's determined travelers can span Oklahoma from border to border in six hours on I-40 and I-44, but they miss a lot. The only way modern travelers can recapture the history, the charm, and the heritage of Oklahoma that used to be visible along old Route 66 is to leave the freeways and prowl about the bypassed towns.

In recognition of a growing coterie of "shun-pikers"—motorists who seek alternate routes to freeways—in 1988, the Oklahoma legislature designated Oklahoma's old Route 66 as a historic highway. Vestigial remains are marked with brown replicas of the familiar shield.

During the summer of 1990, old Route 66 got a boost, spurred by the release of Michael Wallis's book *Route 66: The Mother Road.* The Oklahoma Route 66 Association sponsored a motorcade over the old road from Claremore to El Reno. People came from as far away as Ohio to make the nostalgic run in vintage cars that ranged from 1920 Model T Fords to 1965 Mustangs.

During the 1990 motorcade on Route 66, the check point at Arcadia featured barbecue.

Participants stopped frequently along the way to buy T-shirts commemorating the event and to patronize merchants who stocked merchandise typical of the heyday on Route 66. The Greasy Hamburger Festival at the Old Rock Cafe in Stroud was a popular stop, but trading reminiscences was the principal attraction. Most agreed with Michael Wallis: "To me Route 66 is not concrete and asphalt but people."

OK 66
Kansas Border—El Reno

From Quapaw through Vinita, Route 66 followed the route of the historic Texas Road. For information regarding Quapaw, Commerce, North Miami, Miami, Narcissa, Afton, and Vinita, see Chapter I.

—White Oak - OK 66————

This crossroads hamlet began with the coming of the Frisco railroad in 1898. Even during prime times on Route 66, it did not take advantage of its location on the highway to develop facilities for motorists. White Oak was a major shipping point for cattle for more than fifty years. The Frisco railroad owned stock pens and leased a nearby 160-acre holding pasture.

—Chelsea - OK 28-66————

The town dates from 1882. It was named by Charles Peach, a railroad official, for his home in England. One of the earliest oil wells in Indian Territory was drilled west of Chelsea by Edward Byrd, a Missourian who married a Cherokee woman and leased 94,000 acres from the Cherokee Nation.

Drilled with a wooden derrick, a spring pole, and a horse-powered winch, the well was brought in on August 15, 1889, at thirty-nine feet; it yielded a barrel and a half a day. However, the lease had not been approved by the Department of the Interior and further activity was delayed until 1904 when official approval was finally granted. Southwest of town stands a replica of the old well billed as "Oklahoma's first non-commercial oil well."

Shallow-well oil production spread northward to the Alluwe, Coodys Bluff, and Nowata-Claggett fields where wells became steady producers at less than five hundred feet. Development reached a peak in 1906-07. Strip coal mining also became important to the local economy.

—*Bushyhead* - OK 66————

A railroad siding helped start this community in 1898. It was named for Dennis W. Bushyhead, principal chief of the Cherokee Nation, 1879-87. A guide book to Route 66 published in 1946 sent travelers searching for "an old Indian lookout" west of town.

—*Foyil* - OK 66-28A————

Established about 1890, Foyil served farmers and ranchers in the area. It was named for Alfred Foyil, who established a store in 1889 and later built a hotel, a drugstore, and a substantial residence. For a while the drugstore was used as a schoolhouse and a meeting place for residents. Later, Foyil built a depot for the Frisco railroad and a corn mill for the convenience of area farmers.

Today the predominating feature of Foyil is "the world's largest totem pole." N. E. Galloway, a retired manual training teacher, built the 90-foot concrete and steel structure to house his workshop. The pyramid-like arrangement is decorated with more than 200 Indian symbols, animals,

"The world's largest totem pole" at Foyil.
—Oklahoma Tourism &
Recreation, Fred W. Marvel

322

birds, and other designs that defy classification. It is capped with four 9-foot statues of Indian chiefs. In response to the resurgence of interest in Route 66, concerned citizens of Foyil restored the old landmark.

—*Sequoyah* - OK 66————

Established in 1871 as Sequoyah, the name of this community was changed to Beulah in 1909 after the postmaster's daughter. After 1913 it reappeared on maps as Sequoyah. The 1946 guide to US 66 noted: "Listed on the maps as a 'town,' but actually consisting of a coal loader, a dozen homes, and one gas station and store."

—*Claremore* - OK 20-66-88————

In 1802, a band of Osage Indians traveled from Missouri to Indian Territory and settled near a mound adjacent the Verdigris River to establish a fur-trading outpost. Their chief has been variously called Clah-Mo, Clermos, and Clermont. Cherokees began to settle in the area. The Osages, a roving warlike tribe, resented the encroachment.

The Cherokees tracked missing lost cattle and horses to Osage camps, and Chief Too-an-tuh (Spring Frog) organized an attack. The Cherokees were armed with rifles; the Osages had only bows and arrows and a few smoothbore muskets. The Osages took refuge on Claremore Mound, northwest of present-day Claremore, and were soundly defeated. Because of enmity between the two tribes, the government moved the Osages to a reservation in Kansas.

Elijah Hicks established a trading post on the site of the old Osage village in 1842. The settlement of Clermont gradually moved east until it met up with the Frisco railroad in 1874. That year a clerical error recorded the name of the local post office as Claremore, and the present town was born. Growth was gradual. As late as 1890 the village had less than 200 inhabitants.

In 1903, a well was drilled within the town limits in the hope of finding oil or gas. At about 1,100 feet the drillers struck an artesian flow. The water was malodorous; it blackened any metal with which it came in contact. Though the water contained no radium, it was dubbed "radium water" and touted as a cure for rheumatism, eczema, and assorted other complaints. For a time, Claremore flourished as a health spa.

In 1923 Will Rogers, Claremore's favorite son, wrote a spoof of testimonials for Claremore's medicinal water in his inimitable style:

> Now it has been discovered that you can carry a thing too far and over do it, so we don't want you there too long. A man come there once entirely legless and stayed a week too long and went away a centipede.

Over the years, Claremore has attracted a number of small manufacturing enterprises, but it continues to nurture its Western heritage. Each November the city throws a four-day birthday party for Will Rogers, featuring a parade, hot-air balloon race, Indian powwow, auction, craft fair, and other events. In June the Will Rogers Stampede Rodeo is a three-day event. Will Rogers Downs features pari-mutuel racing; the 210-acre site is also home of the annual Rogers County Fair.

Claremore was also the home of Lynn Riggs, author of *Green Grow the Lilacs*, the play that inspired the long-running Rodgers and Hammerstein musical *Oklahoma!* The Lynn Riggs Memorial on the campus of Rogers State College displays a large collection of memorabilia from Riggs' professional life including photographs, manuscripts, and the famous "surrey with the fringe on top" used in the original production of *Oklahoma!*

In 1907 Claremore had one of the few "prep" schools in the area. It was taken over in 1920 by the state as the Oklahoma Military Academy. It now operates as a junior college. The Oklahoma Military Academy Memorial on the campus houses memorabilia of the Corps of Cadets. The school library has a large collection of books and other material pertaining to Gen. Dwight D. Eisenhower.

HISTORICAL HIGHLIGHT
Will Rogers, the Cherokee Kid

On November 4, 1879, William Penn Adair Rogers was born on a ranch northeast of present-day Oologah. Later, Will Rogers was fond of saying he was born "half-way between Claremore and Oologah before there was a town at either place." Will Rogers was a quarter-blood Cherokee, officially recorded on the tribal roll as Cherokee No. 11,384. He frequently told people "My ancestors didn't come over on the Mayflower, but they met 'em at the boat!"

Will's formal schooling was sketchy. He was more interested in learning to do tricks with a lariat than in academic subjects. His father entered him in Kemper Military Academy at Boonville, Missouri, in 1896. The 17-year-old boy arrived wearing a ten-gallon hat with a braided horsehair cord, flannel shirt with a red bandanna, colored vest, and cowboy boots and spurs. Without telling his father of his plans, Will left Kemper to work on a ranch in Texas.

In the winter of 1899, Will Rogers met and fell in love with Betty Blake, who was visiting in Oologah; theirs was destined to be a long romance. Will went to South America, then to Africa, where he joined Texas Jack's Circus. He was billed as "The Cherokee Kid, The World's Champion Lassoer." His romance with Betty was carried on by mail and

At the Will Rogers Memorial in Claremore, a statue of Will Rogers on his favorite horse overlooks the land that he purchased with the intention of making it a future home.

by telegraph while he rose to the top as a vaudeville performer. They were finally married in 1908 and subsequently had four children.

From the Ziegfeld Follies on Broadway Will Rogers went to Hollywood, where he made forty-nine silent films before he appeared in his first "talkie," *They Had to See Paris,* in 1929. Between 1929 and 1935, he made twenty-one films, each more successful than the one before. His last was *Steamboat Round the Bend.*

In the meantime, he wrote a newspaper column syndicated in more than 350 papers. He tweaked the consciences of both rich and poor as he covered subjects ranging from John D. Rockefeller to Henry Ford, from chinch bugs in the cotton patch to bootlegging: "A diplomat's job is to make something appear what it ain't." . . . "Our foreign dealings are an open book, generally a checkbook." . . . "The income tax has made more liars out of the American people than golf has." . . . "Everybody is ignorant only on different subjects." . . . "You have to have a serious streak in you or you can't see the funny side of the other fellow."

His service to aviation earned Will Rogers induction into the Aviation Hall of Fame in Dayton, Ohio; it also resulted in his death. In 1935, after completing his last movie, he left for Alaska with Wiley Post in an experimental plane. On August 15, the plane crashed near Point Barrow and both were killed. Will was working on a newspaper article at the time of the crash. Ironically, the last word he typed was "death."

The house in which Will Rogers was born began as a two-room log cabin and grew to a two-story ranch house.

Will Rogers' grave is on the grounds of the Will Rogers Memorial in Claremore, a 20-acre hilltop he and Betty purchased in 1911 with the intention of settling there. True to his wish, the inscription reads, "I never met a man I didn't like."

The ranch house in which Will Rogers was born is northeast of Oologah, twelve miles north of Claremore via OK 88. The house started as a two-room log cabin and grew to a two-story white house widely regarded as one of the finest in the territory.

EXCURSION

—*Tiawah* - OK 88———

When the Indians received their allotments, Joseph H. Chambers selected thirty-five acres at the base of a mound that reminded him of his home in Georgia. He paced off lots for sale in a town he called Tiawah, taking the name from the old Indian mound in Georgia. The post office was approved in 1903.

There wasn't too much excitement in town. It was part of Belle Starr's stomping ground; she hid out there from time to time without attracting undue attention. Her son, James Edward Reed, was buried in Tiawah. Occasionally train robbers watched from a nearby hill until the train left Inola, then robbed it before it got to Tiawah. And there was brief excitement over the possibility of gold in the area. Other than that, the little town has quietly pursued its rural ways.

—*Inola* - US 412—OK 88—————

This prosperous farming community at the junction of OK 88 with US 412 was founded in 1890. Its name (pronounced E-no-lah) comes from a Cherokee word meaning "black fox." The area supports a number of Mennonite farmers whose wagons and buggies can still be seen in Inola.

—*Verdigris* - OK 66—————

Founded in 1890, this rural community was named for the nearby Verdigris River. The name comes from French *vert* (green) and *gris* (gray). The river was important to the early economy of the community. In 1905 the *Catoosan*, published in nearby Catoosa, reported under "Verdigris Varieties" that "the river is on the boom." A 1946 travelers' handbook for Route 66 noted that the population was 64. You could get gas and groceries, but there were "no tourist accomodations or cafe."

—*Catoosa* - OK 66—————

Founded in 1882, Catoosa was named for a rounded hill west of town known as "Old Catoos." *Ka-too-see* is a generic Cherokee term for hill. For a while Catoosa was a stockyards town at the terminus of the Frisco railroad, a Saturday-night gathering place for cowboys who had brought cattle for shipment. In 1946 the Route 66 handbook described it as "a hamlet" a half-mile west of the highway.

However, the area has now assumed economic importance as the Port of Catoosa at the head of the 448-mile McClellan-Kerr Arkansas River Navigation System. Only a few miles north of town, the multimillion-dollar port links Tulsa with 25,000 miles of inland waterways stretching from the Gulf of Mexico and the Mississippi River to the Great Lakes and St. Lawrence Seaway.

—*Tulsa* - I-44—OK 66—————

The story of Tulsa began in 1832, when a treaty was signed in Washington by a Creek Indian delegation ceding all tribal land east of the Mississippi to the United States. In 1836 Achee Yahola, a Creek chief, led the first permanent settlers to the territory now included in the corporate limits of Tulsa.

An early photograph of Tulsa at Second and Boston, looking south. —Western
History Collections, University of Oklahoma Library

The group gathered under an oak tree, scattered ashes brought from
their council fire in Alabama, and lighted a new council fire. (The Creek
Council Oak still stands at the corner of 18th and Cheyenne.) They
named their new home Tulsey Town, from *tallasi,* the Creek word
meaning "town."

Although Tulsey Town was not of military importance during the
Civil War, its residents suffered. Cattle thieves from Kansas stripped
the area of livestock, public buildings were destroyed, weed-grown fields
lay untended, and slaves joined those who sided with the Union and fled.

Whites began to infiltrate the area. By 1879 "Tulsa" was designated
as a post office on the horseback mail route from Vinita to Las Vegas,

Main Street, Tulsa, during horse-and-buggy days. —Western History Collections, University
of Oklahoma Library

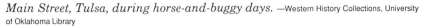

New Mexico. But Tulsa was not a town in the white man's sense of the word. People lived in scattered cabins, each with a nearby patch of corn enclosed by a fence. Their ponies, cattle, and hogs ranged in the woods. For ceremonials, public business, and recreation they came and camped near a hard-packed stretch of earth that was swept clean. It was surrounded by brush arbors. Whites called it the "stomp ground."

The most important ceremonial was the green corn festival. It celebrated the beginning of the corn harvest, and people were forbidden to eat roasting ears until this rite had been observed. The date was fixed by town officials, and each citizen was notified by a bundle of sticks from which he removed one each day until they were all gone. The celebration lasted four days.

Cattle trails from Texas invaded Creek lands, and conservative Creeks regarded this as encouragement to white immigration. Indeed, it was. And so was the Frisco railroad which came to Tulsa in 1882. Because Tulsa had an inadequate water supply, the railroad shifted its terminal to Sapulpa, and the 1900 census tallied only 1,390 people. That was shortly due to change.

On June 25, 1901, the state's first commercially important oil well was brought in at Red Fork just across the Arkansas River. Both Red Fork and Tulsa grew rapidly, but Red Fork had the edge. Cut off from oil development by the river, Tulsa was in danger of becoming a suburb of Red Fork. A bond issue to build a wagon bridge failed; the situation was desperate.

Three Tulsans invested their own capital in a toll bridge. Then Tulsa invited the ever-increasing horde of oilmen to "come and make your homes in a beautiful little city that is high and dry, peaceful and orderly."

The oilmen took Tulsa at its word. By 1910, a building boom was in full swing and brick plants worked at capacity to meet the demand. More oil was discovered at Glenpool, and petroleum became the dominant economic force as Tulsa styled itself the "Oil Capital of the World."

Oil has not only supplied Tulsa's residents with a source of income, it has endowed philanthropic citizens with the funds to provide an enviable array of museums and galleries: Tulsa County Historical Society Museum, Philbrook Museum of Art, Alexandre Hogue Gallery of Art, Harwelden Mansion, Fenster Museum of Jewish Art, World Museum-Art Centre, and the Gilcrease Museum.

—*Broken Arrow* - OK 51————

This suburb on the southeastern fringe of metropolitan Tulsa began in 1881 as a townsite developed by the Arkansas Valley Townsite Company on the Katy railroad. It was a common practice for a railroad company to sell the "townsite privilege" of its line to another company. This privilege conveyed the right to build stations along the proposed railroad. The townsite companies endeavored to establish themselves on land that could be acquired without difficulty and often belonged to a freedman or an intermarried white.

Broken Arrow is now a suburb of Tulsa; most of its residents are employed in small industries that form the community's economic base or commute to work in Tulsa.

—Glenpool—Jenks—Bixby—Kiefer————

The boom at Glenpool began when oil was discovered on land belonging to Ida E. Glenn, a Creek Indian. Today that community consists of a scattering of houses owned mostly by residents who work and shop in Tulsa. Jenks got started in 1905 as a result of development of the Glenpool discovery, gaining its name from Elmer E. Jenks, a long-time resident.

Bixby is a pleasant rural suburb to the south of Tulsa on the bank of the Arkansas River. Surrounded by truck farms, it calls itself the "Garden Spot of Oklahoma," but most of its residents work in Tulsa. Kiefer, named for Smith Kiefer, is an oil-boom town left moldering as development of the field moved on.

———— EXCURSION

—Owasso - US 169————

Founded in 1900, Owasso's name is said to be an Osage word meaning "the end." It was indeed an end, the terminus of a branch line of the Santa Fe Railway reaching into Indian Territory from Kansas. It became a busy agricultural trading center, but today it is primarily a residential suburb of Tulsa.

—Collinsville - US 169————

In 1897 a town was established about a mile east of present-day Collinsville by Dr. H. H. Collins in anticipation of the Santa Fe building a line through the site. The post office was named Collins. When the railroad came past a mile to the west the town picked up and moved. The name was changed to Collinsville in 1898.

—Sapulpa - OK 66-97————

About 1850, Jim Sapulpa, a Creek Indian, came to the area from Alabama and began farming on nearby Rock Creek. Later he opened a store in his house, hauling goods by team and pack horse from Fort Smith, Arkansas. The name means "sweet potato" in the Creek language.

The Frisco railway arrived in 1886, and for a time Sapulpa was a terminus and an important cattle-shipping center. Development of the Glenpool oil strike in 1905-06 provided the impetus for Sapulpa's growth. It is now a manufacturing center, best known for glass factories and pottery.

The 1946 Route 66 guidebook noted that two unidentified Sapulpa investors started with $700 during the Glenn Pool oil boom and ran their fortune up $35 million in eleven years.

EXCURSION

—Sand Springs - US 64—OK 97————

Sand Springs is one of the Oklahoma communities that could put up a sign saying "Washington Irving slept here." In his *A Tour on the Prairies*, Irving told of seeing the Cimarron River—the "Red Fork of the Arkansas River," he called it. Irving was on Beattie's Knob, a hill north of town. That was in 1832.

The next year there was a Creek Indian settlement named Adams Springs, but the town didn't get its start unitl 1907, when an oilman named Charles Page bought a plot of land to establish a home for widows and orphans. He built an interurban line from Tulsa. The community was platted as Sand Springs in 1911 and quickly drew industries. Charles Page died in 1926; his wife built the $100,000 Page Memorial Library in his honor.

—Mule Barn - US 64————

This town is not on the official state highway map, and there is no marker by the road, but it is on the ground. About twenty miles west of Tulsa on US 64, a sign on a gate announces Mule Barn, Oklahoma— a legally incorporated municipality with a population of three. It has been that way since February 14, 1977.

Back in 1977, by virtue of the state constitution, it took only three people to form a town. Robert L. and Eleanor Brown and their son turned their 15.99-acre plot into a municipality. On the peninsula between Keystone Lake and the Arkansas River, Mule Barn has maintained its independence ever since.

That year seventeen such towns were born in one day. Mule Barn may be the only one remaining. It is Oklahoma's smallest town.

—Walnut Creek State Park - US 64—OK 51————

Walnut Creek State Park and Keystone State Park, recreation areas west of Sand Springs, were established in 1964 by a dam on the Arkansas River that formed the sprawling Keystone Reservoir. Towns were inundated—Keystone, Prue, and Mannford—including the Berryhill Farm, which had been a hide-out for the Dalton gang. It was believed locally that the expanding lake covered large sums of money taken from banks by the Daltons.

Keystone disappeared from the map; the old towns of Mannford (OK 51) and Prue (now New Prue) moved and took on new life as they geared up to serve visitors to the newly formed recreation areas.

—Kellyville - OK 66————

This town was established in 1893. For many years annual dance celebrations of the Creek and Euchee Indians took place just southwest of town during June and July. In 1971 promoters came up with the idea for a ski area north of town; the project died before artificial snow machines could be turned on. The 1946 Route 66 guide noted for the benefit of westbound motorists:

> By this time you will have noticed the famous red soil of Oklahoma, which will become a deeper, richer red as you proceed farther west in the state. The road is good, but detours are quite difficult in wet weather if you are routed over a dirt road of this red earth.

—Bristow - OK 66————

This town began in 1897 as a trading post catering to the Creek Indians. The post office was established the following year, but the town did not exist until the Frisco railroad arrived in 1901. From 1916 until 1922 petroleum development in the area created an oil boom. During the 1940s travelers found it well supplied with accommodations. Between Bristow and Stroud, unseen by motorists, there is an underground "tank farm," a depleted gas field into which the El Paso Natural Gas Company injects surplus gas for storage during periods of low consumption.

—Stroud - OK 66-99————

Founded in 1892 only two miles from the border of Indian Territory, Stroud became not only a shipping point for cattle from the Creek lands but a whiskey supply point for the Indians as well. The whiskey was commonly hidden in wagonloads of groceries destined for Indian Territory. In 1907, the coming of statehood closed down nine saloons slaking the thirst of cowhands who brought cattle to Stroud. Stroud's population began to dwindle, but discovery of the Stroud oil field in 1923 brought an upsurge.

Route 66 went down Stroud's main street, a brick road. The 1946 Route 66 guide noted that it was a "busy farm trading center" but "short on tourist accommodations." In 1953 Turner Turnpike opened and Stroud was established as the "midway service center." Since that time Stroud has organized numerous events to lure visitors, including the International Brick and Rolling Pin Throwing Championship.

EXCURSION

—The Sac and Fox National Capitol——
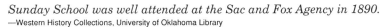

The old Sac and Fox Agency and the national capitol grounds are on OK 99 five miles south of Stroud.

The Sac and Fox story begins in the upper peninsula of the Great Lakes region of the United States. The Sac or Sauk (People of the Yellow Earth) and the Fox (People of the Red Earth) were separate but neighboring tribes. In 1804 they banded together for protection and survival. During the "Indian removal," the tribes were victims of a succession of moves from Wisconsin through Illinois, Iowa, Missouri, and Kansas.

In 1869 they settled in Indian Territory on 750,000 square miles of land they purchased in what became Lincoln, Payne, and

Sunday School was well attended at the Sac and Fox Agency in 1890.
—Western History Collections, University of Oklahoma Library

Pottawatomie counties. In 1885 they wrote and adopted a constitution, established a court system, a police department, a mission school, and a large farming operation.

The Sac and Fox Agency became a center of activity. Located at the halfway point on a trail between Pawnee and Shawnee, the agency was a stagecoach stop, a military post, and a meeting place for cowboys, Indian traders, hunters, homeseekers, gamblers, and outlaws long before the opening of Indian Territory to settlers.

From 1869 until 1910 the Sac and Fox Agency was a flourishing town with more than twenty-five businesses and dwellings. A council house stood on the ceremonial grounds where feasts, powwows, ball games, and horseracing took place. The agency and the mission school were moved to Shawnee in 1917 and 1919, and soon the old town was abandoned.

Today the site is once more occupied by the Sac and Fox. Visitors to the capitol grounds can see the tribal courthouse, an art gallery in the Sac and Fox Tribal Office, and buildings on the capitol grounds.

—Davenport - OK 66————

Founded in 1892 as a rural trade center, Davenport soon rivaled Stroud. The town moved to its present location in 1898 to be on the Frisco railroad. In 1903, Southern Methodists from Kentucky arrived to establish a community. Oil brought boom times in the 1920s, but when the Seminole Oil Field came in some thirty-five miles to the south, many Davenport residents moved on to the new field.

—Chandler - OK 18-66————

The Chandler townsite was platted in 1891. Located at the intersection of the east-west Frisco railroad and the north-south Rock Island line, Chandler showed promise of becoming an industrial center. There was a flour and feed mill, a cotton gin, and a brick plant that turned out bricks imprinted "Chandler, O.T." The Southland Cotton Oil Company employed nearly fifty people at peak season, the cattle pens were busy, and fruit-packing sheds bustled during the picking season.

On March 30, 1897, six years of effort was wiped out. A tornado struck virtually without warning. A few people had time to take shelter in the Presbyterian Church. It took less than a minute for the storm to roar past. When people came out of the church they found it was the only complete building left standing. Fourteen people died and many were injured.

William Tilghman, premier lawman who had been marshal of Dodge City during its wildest days, came to Oklahoma in 1889. He was elected

William Matthew Tilghman, Jr., "went West" in 1870 and worked as a buffalo hunter. Before becoming a lawman he rode with a "bad crowd" and was twice arrested on suspicion of train robbery and horse-stealing. This 1873 photograph shows buffalo hunters Jim Elder and Bill Tilghman (on the right). —Western History Collections, University of Oklahoma Library

sheriff of Lincoln County. During his first thirty days he was handed nine warrants for the arrest of horse thieves. He arrested eight and recovered the stolen animal in the ninth case.

Today there are enough pecan growers, buyers, and processors in the area that Chandler proclaims itself the "Pecan Capital of the World."

—*Wellston* - OK 66B————

This community began in 1880 as a trading post operated by Christian T. Wells on the Kickapoo Indian reservation, thus qualifying as the county's first permanent white settlement. Like a number of other Oklahoma communities, Wellston has a middle school facility underground. With an earthen roof three feet thick, the building quadruples in brass as a school and storm, bomb, and fallout shelter.

335

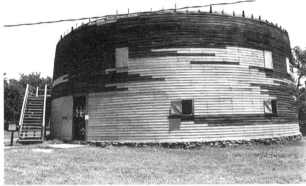

The century-old round red barn was long a fixture in Arcadia on Route 66, the scene of lively barn dances. It deteriorated, and the roof fell in. By community effort, it is being restored in accordance with a faded photograph from the past to serve as a museum and theater-in-the-round.

—Fallis————

This rural hamlet on a county road west of Wellston was settled as Mission in 1892. The name was changed to Fallis in 1894. Once at the crossing of the Katy and Fort Smith and Western railroads, Fallis had a brief day in the sun as a bustling railroad center during the early 1900s. It had two newspapers. The *Fallis Blade* was a "Negro newspaper," and the *Fallis Star* adhered to "the principles and policies of the Republican party."

—Arcadia - OK 66————

The eastern boundary of the unassigned lands opened for white settlement by the run of '89 is about four and a half miles east of Arcadia. The town of Arcadia, now just outside of the city limits of Oklahoma City, was founded in 1890, the year following the run. The author of the 1946 guide to Route 66 was not impressed. He noted, "Once this was a fair-sized little town, but its growth has stopped."

The eastern edge of Arcadia is designated as the spot where the Washington Irving party and a troop of U.S. Rangers camped in October

1832. Southwest of Arcadia, on the north bank of the North Canadian River, is the site of Camp Alice, a Boomer encampment established by David L. Payne and a party of settlers who attempted to occupy the area before the opening. They were driven back to Kansas by United States troops.

—Oklahoma City - OK 66————

During their trek to California via Route 66, as portrayed by John Steinbeck in *The Grapes of Wrath,* the Joad family drove through Oklahoma City without stopping:

> ... and then Oklahoma City—the big city. Tom drove straight on. Ma waked up and looked at the streets as they went through the city. And the family, on top of the truck, stared about at the stores, at the big houses, at the office buildings. And then the buildings grew smaller and the stores smaller. The wrecking yards and hot-dog stands, the out-city dance halls.
>
> Ruthie and Winfield saw it all, and it embarrassed them with its bigness and its strangeness, and it frightened them with the fine-clothed people they saw. They did not speak of it to each other. Later—they would, but not now. They saw the oil derricks in the town, on the edge of the town; oil derricks black, and the smell of oil and gas in the air. But they did not exclaim. It was so big and so strange it frightened them.

For historical information on Oklahoma City, see Chapter IV.

I-40—OK 40
Bridgeport—Texola

—Bridgeport (Exit 108)I-40—US 281————

This community began in the 1890s at a point where travelers waited for low water before fording the treacherous South Canadian River. There was a series of rickety wooden bridges until 1898 when the Rock Island railroad built the bridge that started the town. Four people lost their lives when the Rock Island bridge was taken out by a flood in 1914.

In 1921 a 900-foot suspension bridge was opened on the trans-Oklahoma highway, which preceded Route 66. It was a toll bridge—$1 for automobiles, $1.50 for trucks. In response to public pressure, when US 66 was opened in 1930 it was made a free bridge. When US 66 was rerouted, a longer bridge was opened downstream and Bridgeport began

Crossing the treacherous South Canadian River was risky business until the 900-foot suspension bridge was opened at Bridgeport. —Oklahoma Department of Transportation, David Lopez

to fade. In 1946 a guidebook noted that Bridgeport was "a small town about a mile off US 66." The opening of I-40 completed isolation of the town.

—*Hydro* (Exit 88) - OK 58————

Grain elevators and feed mills followed arrival of the Rock Island railroad in 1898. Peanuts were an important part of Hydro's agricultural base. The superior quality of well water in the area was the source of the town's name, a fact trumpeted by the *Hydro Journal* and the *Caddo County Review*. In 1946, although the town was a mile off Route 66, there were "several gas stations and three tourist courts."

—*Weatherford* (Exits 84, 82, 80A-B) - I-40—OK 54

On the morning of April 19, 1892, William John Weatherford and his daughter Carra dashed into the newly opened Cheyenne-Arapaho country to stake a 160-acre claim about two miles northeast of the present site of Weatherford. A wagon road developed between El Reno, the nearest supply point to the east, and Arapaho, the new county seat of Custer County. It passed the Weatherford's farm. Mrs. Weatherford had previous experience as a postmistress in Arkansas, and a post office opened on the Weatherford homestead. Receipts were about $4 a month. Mrs. Weatherford hid the money under her mattress.

Weatherford remained a tiny community until the railroad came past about two miles to the southwest. Beeks Erick promoted the new townsite. A bank opened for business the first day and within two

Street scene in Weatherford, about 1920. —Western History Collections, University of Oklahoma Library

months there were 15 wagon yards, 8 lumberyards, 14 saloons, and 5 dance halls; Weatherford was on its way with a reputation for being the "wildest and wooliest" town in the area.

In 1901 the territorial legislature authorized a normal school to educate public school teachers somewhere in southwestern Oklahoma. The community was required to provide a 40-acre site within a mile of town, an 80-foot-wide road around the campus, and $5,000 for fencing, trees, and landscaping of the campus. Weatherford won out over Mangum and Granite, and became a "college town." Today the institution is known as Southwestern Oklahoma State University, a strong buttress to Weatherford's economy.

—*Clinton* (Exit 66) - I-40—US 183————

In 1901, if the citizens of Arapaho had raised money to help the Frisco railroad "pay for the necessary right of way" for a new line, the area occupied by Clinton might still be a cow pasture. However, they did not, and Frisco changed the route to cross the north-south Rock Island line south of Arapaho. In spite of threats from people in Arapaho, Thomas J. Nance, an Arapaho banker, proceeded to establish a town at the junction.

Nance negotiated with four Indians—Nowahy, Shoe Boy, Darwin Hays, and Night Killer—to buy 80 acres from each at $2,000. A railroad lawyer helped him get congressional approval for the purchase. As soon as he got approval, Nance left Arapaho in his horse and buggy with a satchel containing $8,000 to consummate purchase of the 320-acre townsite before someone else did.

Nance and his associates planned to call the new town Washita Junction. The townsite was advertised and the railroads ran excursion trains for the sale of lots on June 3-5, 1903. Buyers flocked in, and the promoters took in $50,000 during the three days. The town became a tent city overnight. The Post Office Department refused to accept "Washita Junction" as a name, and the town was called Clinton for Clinton F. Irwin, a federal judge.

Clinton prospered as a railroad junction, and Arapaho's growth began to deteriorate. Located at the intersection of US 66 and US 183, Clinton dubbed itself "Hub City of Western Oklahoma." The community survived the demise of Route 66 and bought one of the old highway signs at auction for display in the Western Trails Museum.

—*Arapaho* (Exit 66) - US 183————

On March 23, 1892, in far-away Washington, D.C., "Arapaho" appeared in various documents to christen a post office that did not yet exist. Shortly thereafter, the newly appointed postmaster, John D. Nicholas, arrived at a designated site in the middle of a prairie west of El Reno to find a survey crew laying out a town as the county seat of "G" County.

Nicholas pitched a tent and hung up a sign: "U.S. Post Office, Arapaho." At first his only duties were to send weekly mail back and forth between his post office and El Reno, the nearest railroad station to the government land office. The mail was carried by soldiers stationed at Fort Reno. A stamp cost 2 cents, and a postcard could be mailed for a penny.

On April 19, 1892, the day of the territory's opening to white settlement, Postmaster Nicholson's business picked up. His post office tent was surrounded by other tents housing more than 400 settlers.

By 1899 Arapaho had grown to 2,500, and the Rock Island railroad was building west from Weatherford. Officials demanded $10,000 to come through Arapaho. Arapaho's city fathers refused to pay. Arapaho was the largest town west of El Reno; they thought the railroad couldn't afford to pass it by. Besides, there was a transportation law that forbid railroads to build within three miles of a town without coming to that town.

Railroad officials circumvented both Arapaho and the law. They built the line four miles away and put Arapaho passengers and mail off at a stop called Washita Junction, later renamed Clinton. Arapaho continued as county seat of County G, renamed Custer.

—*Foss* (Exit 53) - OK 44————

Exit 53 off I-40 leads to Foss, now almost a ghost town. The community started in the late 1890s, when settlers found they could get water for home use by digging wells only twenty-five feet deep. A man named

Graham wanted the town named after him, but there was already a post office named Graham in the territory. The Post Office Department turned Graham's name backwards to spell "Maharg."

Residents disliked the name, and J. M. Foss, the postmaster at Cordell, said he would help get it changed if they would name the town after him. That was in 1901. The first train also came to Foss that year, and the town was off to a promising start. Financial problems of the late 1920s and the Dust Bowl era of the 1930s caused an exodus. Today Foss has few residents.

HISTORICAL HIGHLIGHT
Great Western Cattle Trail

About three miles east of Canute, I-40 crosses the route of the Great Western Trail to Dodge City. In 1872 the Santa Fe Railway forged westward and established Dodge City, Kansas. Settlers along the Texas Road and the Chisholm Trail to the east despised the herds of longhorn stock carrying ticks that infected their cattle with fever.

In 1874 a herd was driven over what later became the Western Trail, but the warlike Kiowas and Comanches became a deterrent to drives through their territory. In 1875, Quanah Parker and his Comanche band became the last hostile group to surrender and accept reservation life, finally opening the route for safe passage.

Doan's Store at the Red River crossing of the cattle trail was a trading post for drovers and Indians. This photograph was made in 1880. —Western History Collections, University of Oklahoma Library

341

In 1876 John H. Slaughter assembled a herd to drive over the western trail. He had so many longhorns that he divided the cattle into three different herds. Lewis Warren Neatherlin was in charge of the drive. A key factor in selecting the western route was Neatherlin's experience the previous year. He had "bossed" a herd up the Chisholm Trail, and his drovers had been arrested for trailing their cattle over private property.

The drive started in San Antonio, Texas, March 12, 1876. The trail entered Oklahoma at what later became known as Doan's Crossing on the Red River. The route went a few miles east of present-day Altus, Warren, Granite, Canute, and Fargo. In the northern part of the state, the trail veered west of Woodward, May, and Buffalo.

For a number of years thereafter, the Western Cattle Trail received regular use. The peak year was probably 1881. Herds averaged 3,000. It took ten men to handle such a herd and each cowboy required about seven horses. In 1881 some 300,000 head of cattle, 7,000 horses, and 1,000 men crossed the prairies of Oklahoma from the Texas ranges to the railhead at Dodge City.

In the nineteen or twenty years of the trail's existence, more than seven million cattle waded and swam the Red River at Doan's Crossing. Land openings and range fencing in Oklahoma, along with the construction of railroads into Texas, caused use of the Great Western Cattle Trail to cease about 1888. In the extensive literature about the trail it is variously called Texas Cattle Trail, Western Cattle Trail, Abilene & Fort Dodge Trail, Fort Griffin-Fort Dodge Trail, and Dodge City Trail.

—*Canute* (Exit 47) - I-40————

The first settlers to the country around Canute came in April 1892, when four pistol shots sounded the opening of the Cheyenne-Arapaho reservation to settlement. More than 5,000 homesteaders raced into County H, later named Washita. Canute was started in 1902 by the Southwest Townsite Company, which surveyed the land and marked it off into lots. Prospective residents paid $10 for a chance to put slips of paper bearing their names into a box. Lot numbers were placed in another box and slips were drawn from the two boxes simultaneously.

The citizens of Canute secured railroad facilities after a heated battle with residents in the Cordell area, and the community began to grow. Canute won out over Cordell to get Route 66 through town. Road construction provided welcome jobs and a promise for the future. After construction was completed jubilant citizens held a street dance under the overpass on the night before the highway opened to traffic.

Today nostalgic travelers bent on following old Route 66 leave I-40 to search for the remains of Mahl Brothers Garage and to visit the Catholic cemetery noted in the 1946 guide for its unusual bronze statuary.

—*Elk City* (Exits 38, 40, 41) - I-40————

The land occupied by present-day downtown Elk City was homesteaded by J. M. Allee in 1897. In 1899 a post office was established three miles to the south in a dugout occupied by Cisero Sitton. The post office was supposed to have been named Crone to honor a settler of that name; however, a government official misread the application, and the name came out Crowe.

In 1900 land promoters learned that the Choctaw, Oklahoma and Gulf Railroad was coming to the area, and Allee's land on Elk Creek appeared to be an ideal spot for a town. The promoters bought the homestead for $2,500. They acquired three adjacent tracts for similar prices and laid out a town. The land company began selling lots on March 20, 1901. On that day they sold $32,000 worth of property. Allee did not retain property for his homesite and years later he paid much more for one lot than he received for the entire tract.

Initially, the town was named Busch after Adolphus Busch of the Anheuser-Busch Brewing Company in the hope that he would feel sufficiently flattered to make a contribution to the growing town or to establish a brewery. Many early settlers, particularly women, objected to their town taking its name from a beer label. As the railroad

The Western Oklahoma Historical Society occupies a fine old Victorian house in Elk City.

approached, the proprietress of a boardinghouse refused to serve railroad men. When a painter showed up to letter the despised name on the new railroad station, irate citizens threatened to kick the ladder out from under him. Locally, the community was called Elk City from 1901 on, but the name change did not become official until July 20, 1907.

—*Sayre* (Exits 20, 23, 25) - US 40B————

In 1901 the Choctaw Townsite and Improvement Company bought land from five western Oklahoma pioneer ranchers to build a town that would be reached by an extension of the Choctaw, Oklahoma and Gulf Railroad from Weatherford. The community was named for Robert H. Sayre, a stockholder in the railroad. Subsequently, the line was leased by the Chicago, Rock Island and Pacific Railway Co. The line was completed to Amarillo, Texas, and Sayre became a division point on the Rock Island.

During its days as a rest stop on old Route 66, Sayre gained some fame from the fact that Jess Willard, former world's heavyweight boxing champion, drove a freight wagon in the town and ran a rooming house.

—*Erick* (Exits 11, 7) - US 40B————

Erick's post office dates from November 16, 1901. The town was named for Beeks Erick, president of the Choctaw Townsite and Improvement Company, which developed the town. The original plot of 80 acres was inhabited by "267 souls."

In the midst of rich farming land and cattle ranches, the town grew rapidly; however, the 1930s brought hard times and empty brick houses rented for $10 a month. So many houses were being moved from Erick to outlying farms that the city council passed an ordinance making it unlawful to move a house over an alley or a street to prevent decimation of the town.

Erick began to bounce back when it was bisected by Route 66. One writer in a 1946 guidebook to the highway cited Erick as the first town the westbound motorist encountered "which has any of the true 'western' look, with its wide, sun-baked streets, frequent horsemen, occasional sidewalk awnings, and similar touches."

Then progress came. The old highway that had carried so many dispirited farmers westward toward the promised land in California fell victim to "improving the flow of high-volume traffic." Old Route 66 was widened, repaved, straightened, and carefully routed around towns. Erick was bypassed; however, a state welcome center continues to lure eastbound travelers off the interstate highway.

—*Texola* (Exit 1) - US 40B————

This pioneer farming community was the last town in Oklahoma on old Route 66. It was founded in 1901. Two townsite plats had been surveyed and given the names Texoma and Texokla. Texola was suggested as a compromise and an election was held to determine whether the town should be incorporated. The vote was 26 to 25 in favor of incorporation.

Texola became an agricultural trade center and merchants profited from traffic on Route 66. Bypassed by the freeway, the town is now about a mile off I-40. However, many motorists who are dedicated to following the old route to California find their way there.

X. Indian Nations in Transition

The triangular slice of east-central Oklahoma tapering southward from I-44 on the north to Lake Texhoma on the Texas border is a microcosm of Oklahoma's history. As part of Indian Territory, the area was made up of Indian nations: Sac and Fox, Seminole, Creek, and Chickasaw. County names reflect its Indian heritage: Creek, Okfuskee, Pottawatomie, Seminole, Pontotoc.

Beginning with the arrival of the Five Civilized Tribes during the late 1830s, the area has experienced virtually every facet of Oklahoma's historical development. Early missionaries seeking to establish schools in the area often faced prejudice from Indian chiefs who feared the Christian religion would destroy their influence. In September 1845, a Methodist missionary reported to Col. James Logan, the Creek agent, that some of the Indians were "driven from home! tied up and whipt, like slaves!! for no other reason than that they worship God."

Nevertheless, the missionaries developed some of the most influential educational institutions in Indian Territory, only to have them relegated to oblivion by opening the area to white settlement and abolishing the Indians' tribal governments.

The land was criss-crossed by gold-seekers en route to California and by drovers taking cattle to railheads in Kansas. The development of mineral and petroleum resources created raucous boom towns, which peaked and faded into rusty remains. Farmers tilled the fertile lands, only to be scourged by the drought and the Great Depression of the 1930s.

This triangle of Oklahoma contains a variety of communities: cities that have survived economic disaster by developing local industry, historic towns that are now mere scatterings of houses by the roadside or along abandoned railroad sidings, and once-thriving villages that have become peaceful rural havens for people who work in nearby cities.

—Coweta - OK 51-72————

The forced resettlement march known as the Trail of Tears led a group of Creek Indians away from the town of Koweta, Georgia, and settled them southeast of present-day Coweta in 1839.

Actual settlement began in 1843 when Presbyterians established a mission school. When the Reverend Robert M. Loughridge discussed the school with the Creek Indians, the tribal council said, "We want a school, but we don't want any preaching; for we find that preaching breaks up all our old customs—our feasts, ball plays and dances—which we want to keep up."

In 1891 a Creek census counted 583 people in Coweta. With the coming of white settlers and the railroad, the town moved northwest. The first post office had a black postmaster, a former slave. Peacekeeping was carried out by Creek "light horsemen" under "Tacky" Grayson, also a freed slave.

—Red Bird - OK 51B————

A few years prior to 1900, families began to settle in the fertile valley between the Arkansas and Verdigris rivers. When the railroad came through in 1902 from Muskogee to Tulsa, a town was laid out on the allotment of Fus Chata ("red bird" in the Creek language) and a post office opened.

The Red Bird Investment Company organized in Muskogee to recruit black families to move to this newly established all-black town. More than six hundred people attended the "grand opening" on August 10, 1907. In 1919, Professor J. F. Cathey saw the need for a high school for blacks in Wagoner County. The school flourished until 1959.

—Porter - OK 51B————

Established in 1903, this town was named for Pleasant Porter, principal chief of the Cherokee Nation. In the early 1890s, Benjamin Marshall started the business that became an economic mainstay of the community. He planted peaches about five miles southeast of the townsite. In 1904 Marshall's peaches won acclaim at the St. Louis World's Fair, and Porter established itself as the "Peach Capital of Oklahoma," a title now contested by Stratford.

In addition to peaches, the early-day economy was based primarily upon cotton and corn. Other cash crops were wheat, spinach, soybeans, and hay. More recently, Porter has become a bedroom community for people employed in Broken Arrow, Muskogee, and Tulsa.

—*Tullahassee* - OK 51B————

This town was established in 1899, and took its name from the nearby Tullahassee Mission, which had been opened in 1850 by Rev. Robert M. Loughridge. The community was largely black. The population was principally descendants of former slaves of the Creek Indians.

The Tullahassee Manual Labor School became an important institution. The school continued until the Civil War. In 1880 the buildings were destroyed by fire. The Creeks rebuilt the school and used it to educate their former slaves. Today only a few foundation stones remain on the outskirts of Tullahassee.

US 62—OK 67
Leonard—Council Hill

—*Leonard* - OK 67————

This farm community was established in 1908 as a result of the construction of the Midland Valley Railroad (later Missouri Pacific) between Muskogee and Tulsa. The site of the Wealaka Mission is northwest of town. This mission was established by the Creek National Council in 1881. Rev. Robert M. Loughridge was superintendent of the mission under the auspices of the Presbyterian Board of Missions. The mission was built on land once belonging to Chief Pleasant Porter. His grave is not far from the site.

—*Haskell—Choska* - US 62—OK 67-104————

Prior to the platting of Haskell, there had been a country post office called Sawokla a mile and a half south. The post office was established in 1902. The town consisted of a store and a cotton gin. Haskell was platted in 1904, shortly after completion of the railroad. The store and cotton gin moved, and Sawokla disappeared from the map. Haskell was nurtured by the surrounding agricultural area. It continues to prosper.

Choska appears on many maps east of Haskell across the Arkansas River, but the town is only a memory. The name means "post oak"; the townsite owner was Polly Postoak. Established in 1890, the town grew to 500. There was a drugstore, cotton gin, hotel, blacksmith shop, and pool hall. The approach of the Midland Valley Railroad offered a promising future, but there was a problem.

People west of Choska also wanted a railroad. They played politics. They named their town Haskell to honor the chief surveyor for the Midland Valley Railroad, and he returned the favor by routing the line through their town. Charles N. Haskell went on to become the first governor after Oklahoma achieved statehood. Choska gradually faded. All that remain are a few graves in private cemeteries.

—Boynton - US 62————

The appearance of this small agricultural community does not reflect its past. In 1902, when the Shawnee, Oklahoma and Missouri Coal and Railway Company surveyed a line, Muskogee bankers decided that halfway between Muskogee and Okmulgee would be a good spot for a trading center. The resulting town was named for E. W. Boynton, chief engineer on the railroad.

In addition to a dozen stores, five churches, and a three-story hotel, there was a grain mill and elevator, two cotton gins, and the Francis Vitrified Brick Company. After oil was discovered in the vicinity, a refinery capable of processing of 10,000 barrels a day was built. When the railroad line was abandoned, Boynton passed its peak.

—Wainwright ————

This railroad siding to the east of US 62 was established in 1905 and named for W. H. Wainwright. Two newspapers tried successively to lure the trade of farmers in the surrounding area, but apparently their voices were not loud enough. Both the *Wainwright American* and the *Wainwright Tribune* were short-lived.

—Council Hill - OK 72————

This small agricultural community was established in 1905 as a result of the railroad. It took its name from a mound to the west long used by the Creek Indians for ceremonial purposes. On March 4, 1906, Indian tribal government ceased. In October, the *Council Hill Eagle* published Chief Green McCurtain's message to the last session of the Choctaw Senate and House of Representatives.

HISTORICAL HIGHLIGHT

The Creek Nation

After the Indian removal from the East, some 13,000 Creeks settled in Indian Territory. Prior to the move, a population of 21,792 enrolled under the Treaty of 1832. No count was made after the removal until 1859, when a census of the Creek Nation showed 13,537. The difference is indicative of the toll taken by the forced march over the Trail of Tears.

Until 1868, when the Council House was built at Okmulgee, tribal meetings were held at High Springs, near Council Hill, some twenty miles southeast of Okmulgee. On October 12, 1867, a constitution was adopted by a vote of the Creek people. The National Council, composed of the House of Kings and the House of Warriors, was given the power to pass laws. Each town elected one member to the House of Kings; members of the lower house were apportioned roughly on the basis of population.

The Creek Nation was divided into six districts. The National Council elected a judge for each district, and the principal chief appointed six district attorneys. Voters of each district elected a captain and four privates to serve as a lighthorse police force. The principal chief was responsible for law enforcement. Trial by jury was provided for civil and criminal cases. All suits at law in which the disputed amount was more than $100 were tried before the tribal supreme court.

When the Intertribal Council, composed of delegates from various tribes residing in Indian Territory, met at the Creek National Capitol to devise a system of government, the United States government made it known that it would exercise supreme authority in Indian Territory and brought pressure upon the Five Civilized Tribes to accept individual land allotments and dissolve their tribal governments.

In 1894, after the question of allotting Creek lands had been hotly debated between Indian leaders and representatives of the federal government, Chief Legus C. Perryman called for a vote. He asked all who opposed allotment to go to the west side of the Council House grounds and all who favored it to the east. All but one went west. Only Moty Tiger stepped east and turned to face three thousand who opposed allotment. Called upon to explain his stand, he said that no matter what the Indians did, the whites would overwhelm them. It would be best to accede and obtain what they could from the white man's government. Five years later, allotment was accepted and Moty Tiger's stand was vindicated.

In 1906, over protests of the Creeks, the sovereignty of the tribal government was ignored by the United States. Statehood for Oklahoma abolished tribal government, and the old Creek Council House became the Okmulgee County Courthouse.

In 1923, the Creek Indian Memorial Association was organized to protect and collect materials relating to Creek history and culture. In 1961, the Creek National Capitol was designated by the National Park Service as a National Historic Landmark. In 1979, the Muscogee Creek Nation ratified its constitution and reaffirmed its sovereignty as a tribal government.

US 62-75
Okmulgee—Lehigh

—*Okmulgee* - US 62-75————

As a modern city, Okmulgee's history began after the Creek tribal lands ceased to be held in communal ownership and the Creek Nation was opened to settlement. Okmulgee began to grow from an Indian trading village with a population of perhaps 200 to an incorporated municipality. By the end of 1905, thanks to oil discoveries nearby, the city's population rose to 4,000.

Okmulgee citizens called 1907 their "year of years." It brought statehood and the first of several gusher oil fields to be opened in the area. In April a well was brought in that produced 500 barrels a day. In June a 1,000-barrel well blew in, and the rush of drillers, lease hounds, speculators, and oil camp followers soon boosted the population to 6,000. By 1910 a refinery was operating. Okmulgee adopted the slogan "Where oil flows, gas blows, and glass flows," the latter a reference to local glassmaking plants.

Okmulgee's Indian heritage is kept green by Indian powwows and a museum. Although a past mayor attempted to have it removed as an eyesore, the historic Creek Council House still stands, sedate and serene, a two-story structure of brown stone, topped by a cupola. It serves as a museum of Creek history.

—*Henryetta* - I-40—US 62-75————

As railroad surveyors forded Deep Fork Creek near Okmulgee, they lost their grub box. In looking about for food, they ended up at the ranch of a Creek Indian named Hugh Henry. The rancher shared his food supply. During the course of conversation, the surveyors asked him if he knew of any place nearby where there was coal. Again, Henry obliged. He showed them an open vein mined by blacksmiths for several years. The surveyors drilled test holes; every sample showed signs of coal. They forthwith changed the route of the railroad to run through the area.

Townsite agents made a deal with Henry to divide up his allotment and sell town lots, but Henry's ownership was restricted; he could not transfer title to a townsite firm. Again he obliged. He abandoned his allotment and took up 160 acres adjoining it. Settlers flocked in, and Henryetta began to grow.

J. W. Scott from Holdenville began mining coal before the town had a name. After dirt was scraped off the top, coal could be taken out with picks and shovels. Henryetta offset the boom-and-bust aspect of mining by attracting other industrial enterprises. Jim Shoulders, a favorite son,

United Mine Workers of America a parade in Henryetta. —Western History
Collections, University of Oklahoma Library

gave the town a publicity boost when he began winning World Championship Rodeo titles.

—*Weleetka* - US 75————————

This trade center was established in 1902 at the junction of the Frisco and Fort Smith and Western railroads. Principal crops in the area are pecans and watermelons. The Old Hickory Stomp Ground is located on Coal Creek fifteen miles east of Weleetka. This was the headquarters of the Crazy Snake Rebellion under Chitto Harjo.

Harjo gathered some 500 malcontents who opposed allotment of Indian lands and the abolishment of tribal government. Chitto Harjo said, "Away back in Alabama the Government said, 'Go to this country and we will give it to you forever,' and now we are only asking them to live up to that treaty they made before we came here." Despite the logic of this approach, Harjo and some of his followers were arrested in 1902 and sent to prison at Leavenworth, Kansas, for two years. There was trouble again after their release in 1907, and still again in 1909.

—**Wetumka** - US 75—OK 9-27————————

This community was formed as a trading post in 1858 when a group of Creek Indians came over the Trail of Tears from Alabama. They brought the name of their former home with them, a Creek word meaning "noisy water." The Creeks also brought living fire from their communal hearth in Alabama. Two braves were charged with keeping the fire, blowing it to life every night for cooking, and carrying the new coals onward the next day. Upon arrival, at the dedication of a new communal hearth, the leader of the band said, "Here is our town, we shall go no farther west."

As the result of a scam, Wetumka has one of the most unusual community celebrations in the nation, Sucker Day. In 1950 F. Bam Morrison came through town acting as advance man for a non-existent circus. He convinced merchants to lay in supplies: hot dogs, buns, soda pop, and even hay for elephants. While taking orders and promoting the mythical circus he collected hundreds of dollars for tickets before leaving town.

With all the fixin's on hand, the bilked merchants decided they might as well stage a celebration. Since that time, Sucker Day has been an annual affair with parades, dances, and other festivities attracting crowds that number into the thousands. A number of years after the inauguration of Sucker Day, Bam Morrison, the perpetrator of the scam, was invited to attend.

—*Calvin* - US 75-270————

This crossroads settlement on the south bank of the Canadian River has seen better days. Prior to statehood, three weekly newspapers vied for the readership of farmers and ranchers in the area, and in 1907 the *Calvin Enterprise* advertised that it had 434 subscribers.

Just east of Calvin a historical marker commemorates an 1853 survey for a transcontinental railroad route conducted by Lt. Amiel W. Whipple under orders from Secretary of War Jefferson Davis. Whipple's reports and observations gave an invaluable picture of Oklahoma in the mid-nineteenth century.

—*Coalgate* - US 75—OK 31————

In 1889 this emerging town was called Liddle for William Liddle, a coal-mining superintendent. Within a few months, the name of the post office was changed to Coalgate. The first coal mine opened in 1882 within a hundred feet of what is now Main Street. The vein was so close to the surface that the overburden was removed with plows and scrapers; coal was taken out with sledges, steel coal pins, and shovels.

By 1956, in all of Coal County, only one coal mine was still operating. Coalgate made plans to manufacture overalls, and a factory opened in 1957, saving the community from possible ghost-town status.

Hudson's Big Country Store is a local attraction. It claims to be "the state's largest country department store." During the early 1920s, Hudson's attracted crowds each year by throwing $500 in dimes from the top of the store. The practice was stopped because men, in their scramble for dimes, injured too many women and children.

—Lehigh - US 75————

Coal was first mined here in 1880, and the settlement was named for Pennsylvania's coal-mining city. It was little more than a coal company commissary and a few shacks until 1887, when a mine disaster at Savanna closed the mines. Mining equipment and housing were moved to Lehigh. In its turn, Lehigh suffered a similar disaster, and the community began to decline. In 1956 a destructive fire almost finished off the town.

US 75 ALT
Mounds—Beggs

—Mounds - US 75 ALT————

Established on the Frisco railroad in 1898, this farming community took its name from nearby geographical features. It experienced a boom during the development of the Glenn Pool oil field and then settled back into its quiet rural ways.

After he made it as a movie and singing star, Gene Autry was welcomed in Oklahoma as a favorite son. While he occupied a barber's chair, his horse Champion was treated to a "hooficure."
—Western History Collections, University of Oklahoma Library

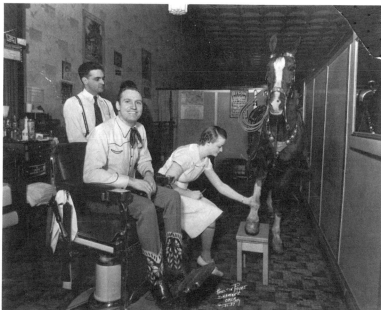

—Beggs - US 75 ALT—OK 16————

Established in 1900 with the coming of the Frisco railroad, Beggs experienced boom times between 1910 and 1915 because of the spread of the Glenn Pool oil field. Nearly 5,000 people made their way into the fledgling town. Ten buses ran through town daily and two northbound and two southbound passenger trains stopped every day.

At one time fifteen oil companies were represented. There were five theaters including the Liberty. Gene Autry worked at the Frisco depot and sometimes in the oil fields. During intermissions at the Liberty Theater he entertained spectators with songs. He was once turned down by a group of local Western singers practicing in the city square because "he couldn't carry a note in a tin bucket."

OK 16-162
Taft—Bald Hill

—*Taft* - OK 162————

Located a mile north of OK 16 on OK 162, this town was established in 1902 as an all-black town on a sixteen-acre townsite purchased from a freedman. It was first named for W. H. Twine, a prominent citizen. The United States required the Creek Indians to adopt their former slaves, and many allotments in this area near the confluence of the Arkansas and Verdigris rivers were awarded to blacks who were listed on the tribal rolls of the Creek Nation. In 1904 the name of the town was changed to Taft, honoring President William H. Taft.

Taft remained predominately black, and in 1974 Lelia Foley became the first black woman in the United States to be elected mayor. She was honored by President Gerald Ford as one of the year's Ten Outstanding Young Women of America.

—*Bald Hill* - OK 16————

The post office of this tiny rural community was established in 1896; it closed in 1908. Although the name is retained on the state highway map, little of the town remains on the ground. Enos Wilson once maintained an elaborate home in the community. Wilson, who died in 1937, was one of the world's richest Indians because of oil and gas royalties on the 160-acre allotment he received in 1899 from the Creek Nation.

—Okemah - OK 56————

This town occupies ground declared surplus after the allotment of land in the Creek Nation. It was opened to white settlement in 1902, and lots were sold at an auction attended by an estimated 3,000 people. Tents were the only buildings for months; drinking water was hauled in and sold at 25 cents a barrel.

When the Fort Smith and Western Railroad survey was completed in 1901, developers platted the townsite of Okemah to be at the intersection of that railroad and the Ozark and Cherokee Central, but the latter line never got that far. While the town was developing, a fight broke out between Okemah and an older settlement to the southeast called McDermott. As building progressed, promoters for Okemah moved twenty-four stores from McDermott, and McDermott faded with the growth of Okemah.

During the early days, a barbed-wire fence was built around Okemah to keep the thousands of longhorns grazed on the surrounding prairie out of town. Eventually, the prairies produced pecans, corn, sweet potatoes, and cotton to make the town a thriving agricultural trading center. Petroleum development and a clothing factory have also contributed to the local economy.

Broadway, the main street of Okemah, in 1909. —Western History Collections, University of Oklahoma Library

Passing motorists on I-40 may become curious about a pair of water towers on a hill by the highway. They are painted black and gold; the larger one is labeled COLD and the smaller HOT. This bit of whimsy came from the city officials; black and gold are the local school colors.

It took some soul searching before a third water tower was labeled HOME OF WOODY GUTHRIE. The folksinger was born in Okemah in 1912. He lived there until he left home at the age of fifteen to become a balladeer of Oklahoma's Dust Bowl-Depression days. Most of Okemah's citizens resented what they viewed as the singer's communistic leanings. It was only after his death in 1967 that they agreed to advertise Okemah as Woody Guthrie's birthplace.

—*Cromwell* - OK 56————

In 1924 this town resulted from development of the Greater Seminole oil field. It was named for Joe I. Cromwell, an oil producer. The population swelled to nearly 10,000. Gambling dens, bootleggers, dope peddlers, and prostitutes soon caused it to earn a reputation as "Cromwell, the Wicked, the Wildest town in the United States."

One night a messenger came to tell District Judge George C. Crump that a prostitute was dying a few doors down the street. He found a 16-year-old girl overdosed on morphine. Before she died the judge learned that she had been brought to the house against her will.

Judge Crump launched what became known as the "chain gang drive." He bought padlocks and chains for the doors of illegal establishments. Then he conducted raids and made arrests until Cromwell was cleaned up. One of the illicit houses turned out to belong to a lifelong friend of the judge.

Cromwell is now a faded remnant of an oil-boom town.

—*Grayson—Kusa* - US 266—OK 52————

This area of Oklahoma was underlaid by rich beds of coal, close to the surface, easily available. When J. J. McAlester began mining coal in 1872 in the Choctaw Nation, he found a ready market in the expanding railroads of the region. After 1903 there was a temporary slump until 1910. In the decade from 1910 until 1920, coal production in Oklahoma rose steadily until a peak of almost 5 million tons was produced in 1920.

It was during this period that the small communities in this area came to life—Grayson, Dewar, Hitchita, Hoffman, Kusa. The availability of cheap fuel made it profitable to establish smelters. Raw ore from Colorado and Montana was brought in to be processed. After 1920, coal production declined in the face of increasing competition from cheap oil. This may have been a boon to Oklahoma's petroleum industry, but it was the beginning of the end for the coal industry. By 1933 Oklahoma's annual coal production had dropped to less than a million tons and the small towns between Okmulgee and Henryetta were sliding toward obsolescence.

—Kusa - OK 52————

Some of the towns had explosive growth. Kusa started with a tent in 1915 and grew to a stretch of smelters occupying twelve city blocks; LaHarp Smelter, Kusa Smelter, United Smelter, Standard Smelter, U.S. Zinc Smeltering Company, Berkley Mining Company, Whitehead Mine, Lantz Mining, Kelley Mining, and Central Mining were some of the names.

Built between Kusa and Dewar, a general freight and passenger depot was used by both the St. Louis and San Francisco Railway and the Missouri, Oklahoma and Gulf. Dewar had a population of 2,700. Between 700 and 1,000 men were employed in nearby mines. While most of the smelters and mining companies operated company stores, there was plenty of business to go around and an interurban ran between Dewar and Kusa.

Many of the smelting companies and mining operations sold real estate. Kusa was formed by the Kusa Townsite Development Company. There is debate among historians regarding origin of the name. Some say it came from a Creek town in Alabama called Coosa; others say it was the name of a Creek Indian girl. However, more likely, it was coined from the initials of the Kansas United Smelter's Association when the Kusa Townsite Development Company was formed.

When ore played out in an area, most of those employed in mining and smelting moved on to other boom towns, leaving the small Oklahoma communities to fade to near oblivion. Most of their present residents now engage in agricultural pursuits or commute to work in Okmulgee and Henryetta.

—*Dustin* - OK 9-84————

This town seemed to have a perennial identity problem. In 1898 it began as Watsonville. In 1902 the name was changed to Spokogee for reasons unknown. Located at the crossing of the Kansas, Oklahoma and Western and the Fort Smith and Western railroads, the town again changed its name to Dustin, in honor of Henry C. Dustin, a Fort Smith and Western official. Mr. Dustin did not come to his namesake's rescue. The Fort Smith and Western line abandoned Dustin in 1939.

—*Stuart* - US 270—OK 1————

A log house with a white stone chimney, said to have been constructed in 1828, served as a landmark for travelers on an early road through this area. An Indian named Hoyuby (sometimes spelled "Honubby," Choctaw for "woman killer") occupied the house. In 1892 the nearby town, present-day Stuart, was named for him. After he moved, the house became a rendezvous for outlaws. There were many stories of criminal activities, and one tenant supposedly found human bones while digging the cellar. In 1896, the town's name was changed from Hoyuby to Stuart.

—*Calvin* - US 270—OK 1————

This settlement was initially called Riverview because of its location on the Canadian River; however, in 1895, after only three months, the name of the post office was changed to honor Calvin Perry, a railroad official. This area had a mixture of small farmhouses and pretentious ranch houses interspersed with the homes of full-blooded Choctaws who were described as "conservatives" by whites and mixed bloods because they adhered to "the old way of life."

—*Steedman* - OK 1————

As the railroad was building the line, the siding here was known as Ford Switch. However, in 1901 the Post Office Department officially dubbed the community Black Rock. In 1910 the name was changed to Steedman to honor E. L. Steed, an Ada businessman. The post office closed in 1932 as both the community and the nation suffered under the effects of the Depression.

OK 48
Tupelo—Kenefic

—*Tupelo* - OK 3-48————

This rural town was formed in 1900 when the town of Jeffs, which had been established six years earlier, moved to this site. It was then a junction of the Kansas, Oklahoma and Gulf and the Oklahoma City, Ada and Atoka railroads. The new name was imported from Mississippi, homeland of the Choctaw Indians, original settlers in this area. Prior to the coming of the railroads, this site was on the West Shawnee Trail, a cattle trail between Texas and railheads in Kansas.

—Wapanucka - OK 7-48————

This community began in 1852 when the Wapanucka Female Manual Labor School opened, one of the first schools in the Chickasaw Nation. The name is a Delaware Indian word meaning "eastern people." Except for the Civil War years, the girls' school operated until the limestone building was condemned in 1901. After the building was repaired, it reopened in 1903 as a boys' school and served until 1907. The building was demolished in 1948.

A post office was opened at the school in 1883. In 1888 the post office was moved four miles east to the present location of Wapanucka. The *Wapanucka Press* began publication in 1901. The March 29, 1906, issue contained an illustrated history of Wapanucka.

One story told of pioneer ingenuity. Contemplating construction of a branch line, a railroad official wanted to know the distance to Boggy Depot. A local resident made a "horse-and-buggy survey." He tied a red rag to a wheel of his buggy and drove to Boggy Depot, counting revolutions of the wheel en route. When railroad surveyors got around to checking the distance with their instruments, it tallied exactly with what the driver of the buggy had said.

—Bromide - OK 7D————

This virtual ghost town northwest of Wapanucka on OK 7D started life as Zenobia in 1906. The name was changed to Bromide the following year, taking the new name from the nearby mineral springs. From 1913 until the early 1920s, Bromide was a flourishing health spa. According to press agents, the bubbling springs spewed "35 million gallons of healing waters daily." Excursion trains came from Texas. At its height, Bromide boasted four hotels, a bathhouse, a swimming pool, a bank, a theater, and other businesses. Little remains from that heyday. Today, residents in a scattering of homes enjoy the beauty of the area's natural setting.

—Kenefic - OK 48————

Originally called Nail, this community took its name from Nail's Crossing where the Butterfield stage line crossed the Blue River. It is just east of the junction of OK 48 with OK 22. In 1850 a Choctaw citizen named Joel H. Nail built a six-room log house on the east side of the creek. From 1858 until 1861, it was known as Nail's Station on the Butterfield Overland Mail route. Here passengers rested while horses were being changed. The house was about two miles southwest of present-day Kenefic. It was destroyed by fire in 1930.

On the first trip of the Butterfield Mail, September 20, 1858, Waterman L. Ormsby, a correspondent for the *New York Herald*, was pleased to find

The bridge at Nail's Crossing on the Blue River west of Caddo near Kenefic.
Stages on the Butterfield Overland Mail route used this bridge. The photo-
graph was taken in 1900. —Western History Collections, University of Oklahoma Library

that Joel Nail subscribed to his newspaper. "Here I saw a copy of the
Weekly *Herald*—a distance of over six hundred miles from St. Louis and
nearly seventeen hundred miles from New York, overland, and twenty-
five miles from any postoffice."

A post office was established at Nail in 1888. The name was changed
to Kenefic in 1910 in deference to William Kenefic, president of the
Kansas, Oklahoma and Gulf Railroad.

OK 3
Centrahoma—Stonewall

—*Centrahoma* - OK 3————

This community started in 1892 as Byrd, named for William L. Byrd,
governor of the Chickasaw Nation. At that time it was a few miles
northeast of its present site. In 1894 the post office name was changed
to Owl. Newspapers began publishing—the *Tribune* in 1905 and the *Owl*
in 1906.

In 1907, the town moved to its present location to be on the Oklahoma
City, Ada and Atoka Railroad, and its name was changed to Centrahoma.
The railroad has been abandoned and the town is a shadow of its past.

—Stonewall - OK 3————

This historic Chickasaw town dates back to the Civil War. It was named for Confederate General T. J. "Stonewall" Jackson. Pontotoc County was organized in 1856 under the Chickasaw Constitution. Stonewall was the county seat from the early 1870s until 1907, when statehood ended the Indian nations. The Collins Institute and the Chickasaw National Academy, both important educational institutions, were nearby. The original site was some three miles west of the town's present location.

—Wardville - OK 131————

The first settlement at the present site of Wardville consisted of tents housing a surveying crew for the Rock Island railroad. That was 1902, and the post office was called Herbert. The railroad built a depot. The railroad station became the focal point for two cotton gins, several general stores, a barber shop, bank, drugstore, school, and two churches. The name of the post office was changed to Wardville in 1907.

Two passenger trains and two freight trains came through Wardville every day running between Ardmore and Haileyville. The town thrived on the sale of cotton and cattle until the drought and the Great Depression of the 1930s. In writing about the recent fate of the community, Maria Reinking Overstreet noted:

> Ranches, operated mostly by retirees and "sundown cowboys" who work nearby, make the greatest contribution to the gross national product. The living is easy and traffic is light in this little village still viable after these eighty-odd years.

—Milburn - OK 87————

The name of this small trading center was a bone of contention during its early days. The first post office was called Ellen, for the daughter of an early-day resident. W. J. Milburn, a merchant, proposed renaming the place Condon, but the Post Office Department would have no part of it. Meantime, the railroad was calling its station Morris and then McLish. A miniature war ensued until the railroad and the townsite came to agreement on Milburn in 1901.

Things did not go well during the early days in Milburn, at least for its newspapers. Two publishers had a go at it and failed, and in December 1903, the editor of the *Earlsboro Echo* sarcastically remarked that Milburn was a "newspaper cemetery." Nevertheless, in 1905 R. T. Bland started the *Milburn News*, and two years later reported that he had 500 sub-scribers.

Today's residents occupy a scattering of neat homes, but they shop elsewhere, leaving vacant, boarded-up buildings in the center of the community. The post office is in the old bank building.

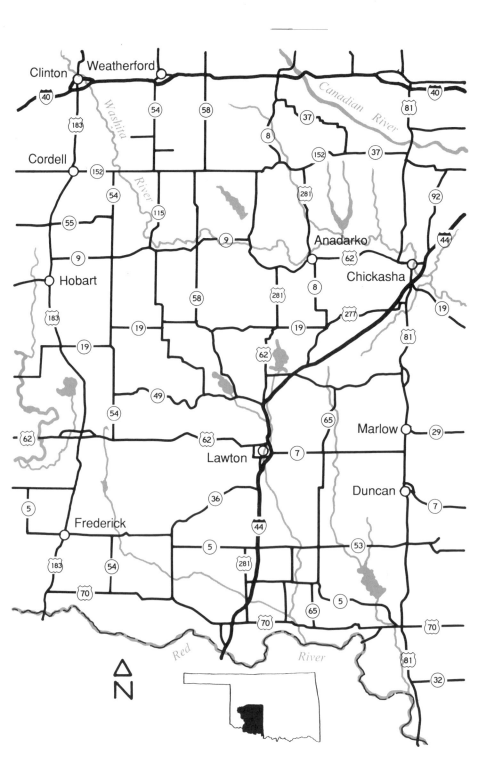

XI. Domain of the Plains Indians

The first human occupants of Oklahoma were big-game hunters, wandering in family groups, searching out mammoths and giant bison to kill for food and hides. The debris of their camps have been found along streams and around springs, in caves and under rock ledges. Archaeologists named these primitive hunters the Clovis man and the Folsom man. Tests upon the fragments they left behind reveal that they roamed the country some 10,000 to 15,000 years ago.

By the time the white man came, the land was in the midst of a vast area occupied by the Plains Indians, primarily the Comanches, a Shoshonean offshoot. About the beginning of the eighteenth century the Comanches had left their country between the Yellowstone and Platte rivers. They came to the South Plains where buffalo drifted across the land by the thousands. For 150 years the Commanches mounted forays against both red and white people along the borders of their territory and resisted the approach of intruders.

Early defensive efforts on the part of the United States were directed toward protecting travelers and traders on trails leading to the west—to Oregon, Salt Lake, New Mexico, and California. Hunting was the principal business pursuit of the Plains Indian; he never engaged in it for fun. Warfare was the driving force behind Plains Indian society. To have property, authority, or prestige—even to take a mate—a Plains Indian first had to distinguish himself on the warpath. Personal vengeance was a religious duty and a social obligation.

Warfare was also the Plains Indian's principal sport. Warriors "counted coups" on their enemies in a variety of ways including killing, scalping, stealing horses, and touching a foe in battle with a coup stick. Each coup increased a warrior's status in his tribe.

As the Plains Indians were herded onto reservations, the invisible boundaries so important to the white man meant little to the Indian. The

United States built forts to protect those boundaries, and troops rode out to enforce the white man's law.

The Indians were supposed to be able to pursue their tribal ways within the reservations. However, ultimately the white man killed off the buffalo and other game that traditionally provided them with food and clothing. One Indian agent reported that within his jurisdiction whites were killing 400,000 buffalo a year and his Indians were starving.

While white administrators in faraway Washington nursed a vain hope that these "wild people" would settle down and learn to make a living from the soil, the Indians grew increasingly dependent upon largesse distributed by Indian agents who were frequently more interested in lining their pockets than in attending to the needs of their charges. In the meantime, Congress fell under increasing political pressure to distribute lands the Indians were not "using" to white settlers.

The Cheyenne-Arapaho reservation consisted of 4,297,771 acres. In 1890 the Indians were persuaded, after more than forty days of negotiation, that each tribal member should receive 160 acres. The remainder would be ceded to the United States, in consideration for which the Indians would be paid $1.5 million.

The Indians refused to participate until they saw the money. During the summer of 1891, four shipments of silver dollars in canvas bags containing $1,000 each were brought to the Darlington Agency near Fort Reno. Each Indian got six pounds of silver dollars, $75. A total of 3,329 allotments were made—529,682.06 acres. Schools were allotted 230,000 acres; military and agency use, 32,000. That left 3,500,000 acres for settlers. The land was opened by a run on April 19, 1892.

By 1901 similar agreements had been struck for the Wichita-Caddo reservation and the Comanche-Kiowa-Apache lands. There had been no land openings in Oklahoma for four years, and land-hungry people all over the United States and even in foreign countries were clamoring for information about the projected settlement. Arrangements were made to conduct a lottery instead of a run.

Those desiring allotments went to registration offices to fill out applications. Offices were opened at El Reno and Lawton, the new town at Fort Sill. There were only 13,000 allotments available for 150,253 registrants.

Filing for the land began on August 6. The lucky 13,000 filed at the rate of 125 per day in each of the two districts. Filing consisted of the applicant indicating by legal description the land he had selected. If it had not already been assigned to another, it became his. He paid $1.75 per acre. When the paper work was completed, the majority of the lands that had once nurtured the bodies and the spirits of Plains Indians belonged to white settlers.

Cheyenne-Arapaho Ghost Dance camp on the North Canadian River near Fort Reno, about 1891. An Indian messiah was attempting to incite an uprising with the promise of disappearance of the whites and return of the buffalo. —
Western History Collections, University of Oklahoma Library

US 70-281—OK 8
Hinton—Devol

—*Hinton* - US 281—OK 8-37————

Settlement in this prosperous farming community began in 1902, a year after opening of the Kiowa-Apache-Comanche lands to settlement. The Rock Island railroad was the catalyst. Initially, on April 18, 1902, the post office was named Crosby, honoring the county attorney of "I" County. However, the name was changed three months later. Hinton was the maiden name of the wife of Ivan G. Conkin, the townsite developer.

Underground reservoirs provide irrigation for wheat, cotton, peanuts, and pasturage. The area prospered. In 1931 Hinton staged a rodeo under sponsorship of the Kiwanis Club. It became an annual event, now claiming to be Oklahoma's oldest continuously operating rodeo.

The area southeast of Hinton is slashed by canyons from fifty to a hundred feet wide and several miles long. Springs gush from crevices in the rocks. Red Rock Canyon State Park, formerly a haven for horse and cattle thieves, now provides recreational opportunities for visitors.

About 7,000 land-hungry people camped near Fort Sill in July 1901 to register for the drawing for allotments in the Indian lands. —Fort Sill Museum

—*Binger* - US 281—OK 152————

Settled in 1901, Binger was named for Binger Hermann. He was commissioner of the General Land Office, which staged the land lottery at the opening of the Kiowa-Comanche-Apache lands. The townsite was platted in 1902 at the arrival of the Rock Island railroad. As with other agricultural communities in the area, Binger's economy centers around cotton, peanuts, and cattle raising. It is the boyhood home of Johnny Bench, who became a star catcher for the Cincinnati Reds.

—*Riverside* - US 281————

The Riverside Indian School is to the west of US 281-OK 8 just outside the northern city limit of Anadarko. The school began in 1871 when Quaker Indian Agent Jonathan Richards erected a one-room building on Sugar Creek to house supplies. The school opened that year with eight non-English-speaking Wichita and Caddo children. Slowly the student body grew as it encompassed other tribes, including Najavos from the Southwest. In 1971 Riverside Indian School celebrated its centennial. It is the oldest U.S. Indian Service boarding school in operation.

—*Anadarko* - US 62-281————

This city was founded on August 6, 1901, when the surrounding Indian reservations were opened to white settlement. Before the opening, Anadarko had been surveyed as a county seat for the newly created Caddo County. Auction of lots began on August 6. Not more than one business and one residential lot could be sold to an individual. The sale of lots brought $132,593 to be used for building bridges, improving roads, and constructing a courthouse not to exceed $10,000 in cost.

Three weeks before the land opening, a bank set up business in a tent. Liquor had been brought in via the Rock Island. Saloons and gambling houses catered to the 20,000 people on hand awaiting the outcome of their chances for obtaining land. About half that number remained in Anadarko for several months; then the population shrank to about 3,000.

A substantial business district soon developed. By December 1901, there were 30 saloons, 11 lumberyards, 10 barbershops, 6 bakeries, 8 meat markets, 15 hardware stores, 25 lawyers, 9 lodging accommodations, and 8 wagon and feed yards. Anadarko soon became a trading center for farmers. Alfalfa, cotton, wheat, corn, peanuts, and watermelons were the principal crops.

An Indian agency north of the townsite was established during the 1870s to tend the welfare of the Indians in western Oklahoma. Today it continues as the Bureau of Indian Affairs Area Office.

The first business establishments in the area were Indian trading posts. Far from being a recent phenomenon, a credit-card system was established for the Indians in this area just after the turn of the twentieth century. The head of an Indian family was given an orange card about the size of a postcard. It showed the Indian's name, his family number, and his credit limit that is, the amount he could charge within a given period, usually three months.

One store in each community was under bond to sell only merchandise listed in a booklet issued in 1904 at a stipulated profit. The government guaranteed the Indians' credit. Indians had no word for "orange," so the process became known as the "red card" system. The credit-card program was short-lived. The procedure made a serious dent in the profits of nonparticipating stores. Merchants brought pressure upon the government to stop the plan.

For more than a century, Anadarko has been steeped in Indian culture. Today a wealth of museums display artifacts and memorabilia from the past, and tourism has become an economic mainstay.

One of the nation's outstanding Indian events is the American Indian Exposition during the second week of August at the Caddo County Fairgrounds on the east edge of Anadarko. Indians come from all over the nation. Hundreds of brush arbors and teepees nestle side by side with modern campers and tents as the tribes of Cheyenne, Caddo, Washita, Delaware, Kiowa, Apache, and Comanche gather.

For the Indians, the exposition is a time for social gathering, a reunion with seldom-seen relatives and an opportunity to relive traditions of the old days. For visitors, it is a chance to witness a colorful and unusual spectacle as the years roll back and the days of the great chiefs, war parties, and buffalo hunts are revived.

The highlight of the exposition is the National War Dance contest. A panel of tribal elders, including former dance champions, serve as judges. The field is narrowed until finally only one—the champion—receives the cheers of the crowd and the silent but proud approval of the elders.

EXCURSION

—*Verden* - US 62—OK 9————

This small farming community in the Washita Valley east of Anadarko was established in 1899 and named for A. N. Verden, the townsite developer. In 1865 Camp Napoleon was nearby. Camp Napoleon was briefly used, but during the Civil War the campground hosted one of the largest gatherings of Indians in Oklahoma. At that time, the site of present-day Verden was called Cottonwood Grove. Today business establishments have moved to the highway, leaving the grain elevators around which the town grew along the railroad track.

—*Washita*————

About eight miles west of Anadarko on US 62, where a small road leads north to Washita, a historical marker commemorates the first U.S. Indian Agency in western Oklahoma. The site is about five and a half miles north of US 62.

The agency opened in 1859 for the Wichitas and exiled tribes from Texas including Caddo, Anadarko, Tawakoni, Waco, and Ionie. Confederate treaties with eleven tribes were negotiated at this agency in 1861 by Commissioner Albert Pike. On the night of October 23, 1862, Union Indian forces of Delaware, Caddo, Cherokee, Osage, and others attacked the agency.

Several agency employees were killed and the agency was burned during the attack. The following morning, the Northern Indians attacked the Confederate Tonkawas who lived nearby and all but exterminated the tribe. The attackers were maddened by a report that the Tonkawas were about to engage in the cannibalistic practice of killing a Caddo captive and holding a feast.

The Wichita Agency was reopened at Anadarko several years after the Civil War. Today only a grove of chinaberry trees marks the site of the old Wichita Agency.

The small farming community of Washita is farther to the north in a bend of the Washita River. Established in 1910 on a branch of the Rock Island railroad, it took its name from the river.

—*Fort Cobb* - OK 9————

This farming community was established in 1899 and named Cobb. In 1902 the name was changed to Fort Cobb in memory of the old military post that had stood about a mile to the east. Peanuts are the principal crop in the area, and the annual Caddo County Peanut Festival is held in September.

Fort Cobb is the southern gateway to Fort Cobb State Park and Fort Cobb Reservoir. The surrounding area provides some of the best hunting in the state. Deer, quail, rabbit, and turkey are plentiful. The area is scourged by crows. They begin to arrive in late October and reach a peak of about 20 million in January; farmers in the vicinity welcome crow hunters. They must, however, do their crow hunting outside of a nearby game refuge that attracts as many as 60,000 ducks during the winter.

—*Apache* - US 281—OK19————

This community began in 1901 when Indian lands were opened to white settlement. The following year the Rock Island railroad arrived, and the settlement grew as farmers raised wheat, corn, alfalfa, and cotton in the rich land nurtured by Cache Creek. However, during the early days, life was not easy. After living on a rented farm in Nebraska, Frank X. and Lizzie Pape came to Oklahoma Territory with hopes of owning their own land. L. Sue Hoy remembered her grandmother's accounts:

> Living in the tent was a dreadful experience for Grandmother. She stood petrified a number of times when several Indians silently and suddenly appeared inside the tent flap. They asked for "brot," the German word for bread. Upon receiving it, they silently disappeared.
>
> On one such occasion Grandmother had no bread. She tried to tell them the dough was rising in the pans but not yet baked. . . . Not understanding, one Indian walked over to the cradle and held his knife poised over the sleeping infant. Horrified, Grandmother reached for the pearl-handled revolver and, brandishing it, walked toward the cradle. The intruders left without a sound. Her heart still pounding, she shakily put the unloaded revolver away.
>
> Needless to say, Grandmother was less than elated with the Oklahoma Territory.

—*Cement* - US 277—OK 19————

Settled in 1902, Cement is primarily an agricultural community that took its name from a nearby gypsum quarry. In addition to gypsum mining, the town profited economically from development of the Cement oil field during the early 1920s.

—*Cyril* - US 277—OK 19————

Four miles southwest of Cement, Cyril also began as an agricultural community in 1906 and was named for Cyril Lookingglass, owner of the townsite. During the early 1920s, with development of the Cement oil field, it became an oil-boom town; production supported an oil refinery at Cyril.

—*Fletcher* - US 277————

Fletcher Dodge had a 180-acre homestead on a ridge above the headwaters of a branch of Beaver Creek. The Frisco railroad clipped a corner off his claim, and Dodge donated eighty acres for a townsite. In 1902 the community consisted of five one-room shacks along the railroad, but it grew quickly. Fletcher immediately entered into competition with Elgin, just four miles down the track. When the railroad built a depot in Elgin but not in Fletcher, the people of Fletcher put on a drive for funds to construct a depot and sent the money to the railroad. The depot was built in 1904.

Frank James, the retired outlaw brother of Jesse James, lived in Fletcher for a time during the 1920s. Locals were certain the old bank robber and his brother had hidden some of their loot nearby. When Frank James went for a ride in the mountains, he usually had a following. The community suffered during the Dust Bowl days and the decline of the cotton market, but more recently it prospered from expansion of the Fort Sill military reservation after World War II and from development of the Fletcher Trend gas field in the 1970s.

—*Elgin* - US 277————

When this community was founded in 1902 with the coming of the Frisco railroad, application was submitted for a post office to be named Cee Gee (or Ceegee), the initials of C. G. Jones, the townsite promoter. The Post Office Department turned down the name. A local resident had just returned from a trip to Elgin, Illinois; he liked that name, and the Post Office Department concurred. Like other agricultural communities in the area, Elgin suffered during the 1930s, but it too has profited from its proximity to Fort Sill.

*Medicine Bluff above
Medicine Creek on the
Fort Sill reservation. The
Indians believed the
water in the stream had
medicinal powers.* —Fort Sill
Museum

—*Medicine Park* - US 281—OK 49——————

This summer playground on OK 49, four miles west of US 281 along
Medicine Creek, was the brainchild of Senator J. Elmer Thomas. Its
opening "on a limited basis" took place on July 4, 1908, with soda pop and
fireworks stands the principal concessions. Picnickers spread blankets
under blackjack and post oak trees. A band played the "Star Spangled
Banner."

The following year a dam 60 feet high and 375 feet long was constructed
in a narrow granite gorge on Medicine Creek above the growing community
to impound Lake Lawtonka, Lawton's water supply. Local Indians
believed the pure water of the stream had medicinal powers.

Medicine Park was boomed as a health spa and labeled the "Queen of
the Southwest" and "Gateway of the Wichitas." During the 1920s and

A 1912 view of Medicine Park, the health spa which developed on Medicine Creek. —Fort Still Museum

1930s it became a highly fashionable resort. The old hotel has been restored and is now called the Old Plantation Restaurant. The restaurant occupies the former hotel's ballroom.

The stylish aura is diminished, but many of the recreational facilities remain, and the folklore that grew up about the place is still bruited about: There was the wealthy traveling salesman, reputed to have been killed by a fancy lady and buried in the basement; a snoopy federal agent looking for a whiskey still is supposed to have met the same fate; and there was the tale about George "Machine Gun" Kelly kidnapping a wealthy oil baron and holding him for ransom in one of Medicine Park's cottages.

—*Fort Sill* - I-44—US 281————

Fort Sill was established as the result of a suggestion by Capt. Randolph B. Marcy to the secretary of war on July 19, 1852.

However, it was not until January 1869, that Gen. Philip H. Sheridan selected the site along Medicine Bluff Creek. At first it was called Camp Wichita for an abandoned Indian village, but on July 2 Sheridan changed the name to honor Brig. Gen. Joshua W. Sill, his classmate at West Point and fellow officer who was killed during the Civil War.

Soldiers built the fort. Stone was found in Quarry Hill, southeast of the post; lime for mortar was prepared in crude ovens along the banks of Cache Creek. Lumber, bricks, tools, and a sawmill were hauled from Fort Arbuckle. Twenty-five wagons from Kansas brought tools, hardware, and civilian workmen.

Troops E, F, H, and K of the 5th Cavalry on the old parade ground at Fort Sill in 1890. —Fort Sill Museum

Gen. U. S. Grant became president on March 4, 1869. A few days after his inauguration a delegation of Quakers visited him and proposed that the Society of Friends take over management of the Plains Indian tribes and substitute brotherly love for the sword. Lawrie Tatum, a Quaker farmer from Iowa who had no previous experience handling Indians, arrived at Fort Sill to serve as Indian agent.

The Kiowas and Comanches harassed the Fort Sill garrison by stealing horses and mules almost at will. Young braves could raid their

Indian Agent Lawrie Tatum with Mexican captives taken from Comanches and Kiowas at the Fort Sill agency in the 1870s. —Fort Sill Museum

traditional enemies in Texas and count coup to attain status as warriors or chiefs, then scurry back to the Fort Sill vicinity where the Quaker agent's "peace policy" would not let the army chastise them. By Indian logic, if the Indians lost as many as they killed during a raid, they were "even" and could see no reason why they should be punished.

On one occasion, Lawrie Tatum caught a wizened old chief named Satank (Sitting Bear) with a mule that had belonged to a Texan. Satank had an explanation: One of his sons had gone to Texas to steal a few animals with no intent of hurting anybody but the Texans killed him. Satank went to the same area and stole the mule, which he had grown to love as his son. Therefore, he reasoned, he should be allowed to keep it. He made Lawrie Tatum a proposition. The two of them should go out on the prairie alone and fight; whoever killed the other would keep the mule. Tatum declined the proposal.

Finally, Tatum's patience wore thin. He violated his religious precepts and tarnished his reputation as a Quaker by having the post commander arrest three ringleaders of an attack upon a wagon train. Satanta, Satank, and Big Tree were loaded into a wagon to be taken to Texas for

Satank ("Sitting Bear"), a Kiowa chief who challenged the Indian agent to a duel. Satank later sang his death song and committed suicide by trying to escape from U.S. troops at Fort Sill.
—Fort Sill Museum

A Ghost Dance was staged in front of the trader's store at Fort Sill for the benefit of people who had missed seeing the real thing. —Fort Sill Museum

trial. Satank, Tatum's old adversary, sang his death song and committed suicide by attempting to escape before the wagon was off the Fort Sill reservation. He was the first Indian buried in the Fort Sill cemetery. Satanta and Big Tree were tried and convicted.

Continued forays led to discontinuance of the Quaker Peace Policy in 1874. The last important resistance was that of Quanah Parker and the Quohada Comanches. They surrendered in June 1875, the last of the Plains Indian tribes to yield to the inevitable.

The last threat of Indian disturbance occurred in 1890 when the Ghost Dance or "Messiah Craze" spread across the Great Plains. Leaders of the movement believed the whites would disappear forever and both Indian dead and the great buffalo herds would return. The ceremony involved men, women, and children dancing in a circle.

Quartermaster Lt. Hugh L. Scott and a Kiowa assistant, I-see-o, managed to keep the Fort Sill Indians from going on the warpath. When the self-appointed prophets did not produce the messiah and the almost-extinct buffalo, the threat of rebellion collapsed of its own weight.

At Fort Sill there was a footnote to the affair. Lieutenant Scott learned that many officers and their families had not seen a ghost dance and were curious to do so. He recruited a number of Cheyennes and Arapahoes and gave them several beeves to stage a mock ghost dance in front of the trader's store. Dancing continued two or three nights—until the beef ran

Geronimo and his family in a melon patch near Fort Sill, 1895. —Fort Sill Museum

out. A few participants got caught up in the dance and went into trances, but the most enthusiastic participants were Indian children dancing in imitation of their elders.

In 1905, with the frontier vanished, Fort Sill was extensively rebuilt and expanded as an artillery center. Today its emphasis is upon guided missiles. Fort Sill is an "open post," allowing virtually unrestricted access to visitors. Most of the stone buildings of the original post are still standing and are still in use. Maps and descriptive material can be obtained at any of the several gates to the post and at the visitor's center.

The Geronimo Guardhouse, once called "Geronimo Hotel," is now a museum. The Apache chief Geronimo and his men were captured in 1886 and sent to Florida and Alabama. In 1894 they were brought to Fort Sill.

Geronimo at the wheel of an early model Cadillac.
—Fort Sill Museum

Geronimo was subject to military control but was free to roam the reservation. Addicted to spirits, he was frequently confined in the guardhouse to sober up, and Fort Sill inhabitants got used to seeing the notoriously bloodthirsty Indian recovering from a hangover while splitting wood at the rear of the jail.

Geronimo was in demand for traveling fairs and shows, and he obtained leave for this purpose as often as possible. He made appearances during world expositions at Omaha in 1898, Buffalo in 1901, and St. Louis in 1904. He traveled for a time with Pawnee Bill's Wild West Circus. He had a prominent place in President Roosevelt's inaugural parade. Geronimo learned to write his name and sold signed photographs for two dollars each.

Geronimo died of pneumonia February 17, 1909, and was buried in the Apache Cemetery near Cache Creek on the post grounds. The War Department declared February 18 a holiday for the Apaches to observe mourning and funeral rites. It took considerable effort to keep Geronimo's wife from killing his favorite horse so that it could accompany him to the spirit land.

Geronimo's grave in the Apache cemetery on the Fort Sill reservation.

Lawton began on August 6, 1901, just six days after the opening by lottery of the 3 million-acre Kiowa-Comanche-Apache reservation. The site had been designated by the land office as one of three county seats to be established. Almost overnight Lawton gained a population of 10,000.

The people came in the hope of bidding successfully at the sale of lots. By August 3, three days before the sale, there were three streets, four business establishments, and a newspaper. F. M. English's bank—a one-room frame shack—was poised on rollers, ready to be wheeled to the lot he intended to buy.

On August 6 a government auctioneer stood on a packing box beside a tent and cried the lots, beginning at the northern limit of the platted townsite. When he shouted "Sold!" a soldier escorted the successful bidder into the tent where, if he paid the total price in cash, he received a title to his lot. If the buyer did not have the full amount with him, he could pay $25 down to hold the property for half an hour. The first lot sold for $420. The top price was $4,555 for a lot opposite the land office.

James R. Woods had first choice. Instead of selecting the usual square homestead, Woods took a strip a mile long and a quarter of a mile wide alongside the Lawton townsite plat. This cut off the person with the second choice from access to the townsite. It turned out to be a young lady named Mattie Beal.

The owner of this frame and canvas saloon in Lawton did not want a visit by Carrie Nation, the saloon-busting temperance activist of the day. —Western History Collections, University of Oklahoma Library

As a result of nationwide publicity over her plight, Miss Beal received five hundred proposals for marriage from all parts of the United States and James R. Woods earned the nickname "Hog." Both homesteads were eventually taken into the city. Mattie Beal's home became a social center of early-day Lawton, and she realized a tidy fortune from the sale of lots in what would become one of the city's better neighborhoods.

Lawton's "ragtown" section of tents and shacks grew along a street called Goo-Goo Avenue, from the popular song containing the line, "When you make dem goo-goo eyes at me!" By November 1901, there were eighty-six saloons, one for every hundred inhabitants. One displayed a sign: ALL NATIONS WELCOME BUT "CARRIE." There is no record of the temperance crusader visiting Lawton.

Although Lawton has developed some industrial base, Fort Sill has been its principal source of economic sustenance. The Museum of the Great Plains provides an outstanding display of the history, archaeology, and anthropology of the Great Plains from prehistoric times through the early 1900s.

EXCURSION

—*Cache* - US 62—OK 115—————

Settlers began moving into the area during the 1890s. Some were lured by tales of Spanish gold mines and invested in unproductive mining operations in the Wichita Mountains. The first townsite plat for Cache was surveyed in 1901, but it did not conform to government requirements by setting aside land for parks and playgrounds, and approval was delayed until 1909.

The town was first named Quanah in honor of the Comanche chief who lived in the area, but both the railroad and the Post Office Department protested because Texas had a town of that name some hundred miles to the southwest. The community was finally called Cache after the creek that runs through town.

During the early years, fire was a persistent problem. After fires wiped out downtown Cache in 1903 and 1911, merchants replaced their frame buildings with brick and moved the business district farther from the railroad. Cinders from the snorting, coal-burning locomotives periodically started grass fires. The first person to see a fire would shoot a gun several times to alert the town; men grabbed buckets and gunny sacks and ran to fight the blaze.

Of particular interest is the former home of Comanche chief Quanah Parker, which was moved from its original location to the north side of Cache. During his declining years, Quanah was a local celebrity. His 22-room "Comanche Whitehouse" became a showplace for visiting dignitaries. It was also known as the "Star House."

Quanah had some fourteeb white stars painted on the roof to signify to the generals at Fort Sill that he, as "Eagle of the Comanches," was a chief, just as they were chiefs.

Quanah's house accommodated five wives and twenty-three children. Each wife had a bedroom, but they were not identical, as popular folklore has maintained. There was a hierarchy among the helpmates, and each was responsible for a particular area of household activity.

HISTORICAL HIGHLIGHT

Quanah Parker

Born about 1845, Quanah Parker was the son of white captive Cynthia Ann Parker and Comanche chief Peta Nocona. His mother had been captured at the age of nine. Years later she was identified and urged to return to her people. By this time, her marriage and the birth of three half-Comanche children had made her a Comanche at heart. She died soon after she was forcibly returned to live with whites.

Quanah followed his father in raids, proved himself as a warrior, and became a subchief of the Quohada band of Comanches. He refused to have anything to do with the Medicine Lodge treaty council in 1867. He continued to lead his band in raids and became the scourge of the Staked Plains in Texas.

Not until 1875 did he realize the futility of further resistance. By June 2, 1875, he had convinced the majority of his warriors that they should surrender. On that day he walked into Fort Sill and gave himself up.

Quanah added "Parker" to his name in honor of his mother. He rose quickly in the Indian reservation's political structure. He became a favorite of both Indian agents and Texas cattlemen who grazed herds on reservation ranges. By 1890 he became the principal Comanche chief. He also acquired considerable property.

He made several trips to Washington and became a friend and hunting companion of President Theodore Roosevelt. On one of his trips to Washington, a federal official suggested that he should give up all but one of his several wives and live like a white man. Quanah replied:

"*You* tell 'em which one I keep."

In 1886 Quanah was appointed a tribal judge to hear cases involving Indians, one of three Indians so designated by the government. He was not only a keen observer of the white man's culture, but he had an adroit sense of humor. On one occasion a writer for *Sturm's Oklahoma Magazine* asked him what his duties were. His response appeared in the May 1911, issue:

Quanah Parker and two of his wives, Pi uuh (left) and So hnee (right), on the porch of Parker's house. —Western History Collections, University of Oklahoma Library

"You see," he said, illustrating with appropriate gestures as he went along, "me open desk and sit down in chair so—and lean back, and put feet up on desk and lighting seegar, and hold newspaper in front of me, all same white-man sabe? Then by-m-by white man come in and knock at door, and he say: 'Quanah, me want talk t'you a minute.' And me swing round in chair—so—and puff lots of smoke in his face and me say, 'What can I do for you today?'"

Between entertaining visitors and conducting tribal business at his home in the foothills of the Wichita Mountains, he managed his ranch and invested in securities. Even though his Quohada band had taken to the warpath against the incursion of railroads into Indian lands, he eventually owned $40,000 worth of stock in a railroad. Quanah proved to be an astute bargainer in negotiating leases for grazing rights on Comanche lands.

He went to Washington to participate in President Theodore Roosevelt's inauguration parade. He accepted invitations to appear in parades and to make speeches. After a trip to Mexico to visit his mother's relatives, he was asked why he did not go live with them. He replied, "Down there, I just plain Indian, here I am great chief."

Quanah opted to follow the religion of his people, particularly when the wife of the Indian agent told him that to embrace Christianity he would have to dispense with all but one wife. He was not moved by the Ghost Dance furor and its promise of an Indian messiah: "Mebbe-so Messiah he come? Mebbe-so No. Anyway me going to keep one hand on government—then me safe." He used peyote, and modern peyotists credit him with being responsible for the Native American Church of Oklahoma receiving a charter in 1910, placing peyote worship on a level with other religions.

Quanah Parker died on February 23, 1911.

—*Indiahoma* - US 62————

In 1894, the Mennonite missionary Rev. Henry Kohfeld approached Comanche chief Quanah Parker, obtained a grant of land, and established the Post Oak Mission. The Comanche and Kiowa families in the area had names such as Chebahtah, Kowena, Codopony, Saupitty, Tahmahker, and Asenap; following the 1901 land lottery, they were joined by Dillons, Potters, Brentons, and others. The names of early settlers and merchants are commemorated by Indiahoma's north-south streets.

In 1902 when the Frisco railroad built between Lawton and Snyder, the Indiahoma post office was established with its name coined from "Indian" and "Oklahoma." Cotton formed Indiahoma's economic base until the Dust Bowl days. The community has survived adversity.

The site of the old Post Oak Mission and the mission cemetery was abandoned in 1957 because of the expansion of the Fort Sill firing range. The graves of Quanah Parker and Cynthia Ann Parker, Quanah's mother, were moved to the post cemetery at Fort Sill.

—*Geronimo* - US 277-281————

On January 13, 1902, thirteen miles south of Lawton, people gathered to buy lots in a town to be named Junction City. The Rock Island railroad had not reached there yet, but it was coming. Some of the lots sold for as little as $2 each. A year later, two miles farther down the railroad track, a rival community developed: Geronimo. Geronimo got a depot; Junction City did not. Geronimo boomed and Junction City faded.

In 1910 Geronimo had a population of 186. It declined to 103 by 1950; however, thanks to a preference for rural living by many people who work in Lawton, Geronimo experienced a suburban boom during the next two decades.

—*Randlett* - US 277-281————

One of five townsites platted at the opening of the grazing area known as the "Big Pasture," Randlett was established in 1907 and named for an Indian agent at Anadarko. The *Randlett Enterprise* helped the campaign to raise $50,000 to build a railroad, but the railroad missed Randlett by a mile and went to Devol instead. Randlett suffered as a result of the Depression, and the H. E. Bailey Turnpike, three miles to the west, siphoned much traffic from the highways that formerly went through town; however, it has profited from its location between Sheppard Air Force Base and Fort Sill, and many residents commute to jobs in Wichita Falls, Texas, and Lawton.

—*Devol* - US 70—OK 70D————

West of Randlett just off US 70, Devol was established in 1908 as a railroad-siding community. From 1918 until 1922, Devol experienced its greatest period of prosperity during the Burkburnett oil boom across the Red River in Texas. People were certain that since there was so much oil on the south side of the river there should be some on the north side. Land was leased and hundreds of dry holes were drilled. Finally, the land was used for refining and storing the wealth from Texas. At one time seven refineries and hundreds of storage tanks dotted the landscape around Devol.

A toll bridge was built across the Red River and people came to live and work. As activity in Burkburnett slowed, drillers and roughnecks left to work in new fields, and Devol's population dwindled. Today it is primarily a residential community.

OK 65
Sterling—Temple

—*Sterling* - OK 17-65————

Sterling was preceded by a village called Hamlin, Indian Territory. Prior to its opening to settlement in 1901, this part of the Kiowa-Comanche-Apache reservation was under lease as grazing land to Texas cattlemen. One of these was Capt. Charles Sterling, a Texas Ranger for whom the town was renamed in 1901. Principal crops in the area were corn, broomcorn, and cotton.

—Pumpkin Center - OK 7-65————

Most residents of this crossroads scattering of neat houses work and shop in nearby Lawton and pronounce the name of their village "Punkin Center." Birdwatchers who want to add an exotic specimen to their sightings can visit the 4-C Ostrich Farm on OK 65 a short distance north of its intersection with OK 7. During recent years in the Southwest there has been considerable development in the "ratite industry"—raising ostriches, emus, and rheas on a commercial basis.

————— EXCURSION

—Walters - OK 5-53—————

This prosperous agricultural community to the west of OK 65 at the junction of OK 5 and OK 53 was established in 1901 with the opening of the territory to the north along Cache Creek. Initially it was called McKnight for a Major McKnight, but there was already a McKnight in another county; so people then called it Walter for Walter McKnight, the major's son. In 1902 Cache Creek flooded, and the residents moved south and established another community called "Townsite Addition Walters"; this one was named for Bill Walters, a city official. The name controversy was not officially settled until 1917.

In the meantime, on November 18, 1912, Walters won out over other communities to become the county seat of Cotton County. Walters has profited by the development of oil and gas fields in the area. It is the home of the Cotton Electric Cooperative, the largest rural electrification cooperative in Oklahoma, serving customers in nine counties. Grain elevators testify to the town's agricultural base.

—Temple - OK 5-65—————

Drawing for lots in a town called Botsford began on November 11, 1901. By 1902 it was a substantial community with three grocery stores and an equal number of saloons. The *Botsford Tribune* boasted about the town's location with Lawton to the north, Addington on the east, and Wichita Falls, Texas, to the south. It said "all roads lead to Botsford," and predicted the railroad would be coming shortly.

Alas! The railroad bypassed Botsford by a mile to the north, and everybody moved. The new town on the railroad was called Temple, for Temple Houston, an Oklahoma lawyer and the son of Sam Houston.

—*Eakly* - OK 58————

This rural community started in 1902. Its name was supposed to be Ackly, for Ackly Montague, the daughter of a resident. The Post Office Department added the initial letter. Cotton and peanut crops form the economic base of the town. Most towns have service clubs. Eakly is the national headquarters of the Eakly Gobblers Lodge. Dedicated to the entertainment of its members, this organization was started in 1928 by a retired medicine show operator. Since then, affiliates have sprung up in various surrounding communities.

—*Carnegie* - OK 9-58————

Peanuts form the principal basis of the economy of this strong agricultural community. The town dates from the opening of the Kiowa-Apache-Comanche lands to white settlement in 1901. The Kiowa Tribal Museum is in Carnegie, and the annual Kiowa Gourd Clan Ceremonials are held on July 4, drawing participants and visitors from a wide area. Since 1945, the annual World Championship Domino Tournament has been held at the fairgrounds on the last Friday in February.

—*Boone* - OK 19————

Only a few scattered stones from a fireplace are left here of what was once "The Half Way House" on the old wagon road between Fort Cobb and Fort Sill. Jim Myers leased grazing land and operated a ranch in the area from 1872 until white settlement in 1901. A post office was established in 1895. This area was the scene of large-scale slaughter of buffalo.

HISTORICAL HIGHLIGHT
The Buffalo Hunters

The period of 1870-83 was doomsday for the vast herds of buffalo that roamed the plains. Cheap transportation by new railroads into Kansas increased the market for buffalo hides, and thousands of hunters swarmed the plains to supply the demand. After the last large kill of 1883, all but a few herds had vanished. Poverty-stricken farmers gathered and sold the weathered bones as fertilizer and for use in making bone china.

The stupidity of the buffalo was remarkable. When one was killed the smell of blood excited the rest of the herd, but instead of stampeding they would gather around the dead buffalo, pawing, bellowing, and hooking it viciously. Taking advantage of this well-known habit, a hunter could kill one animal and then wipe out virtually the entire herd one at a time.

Killing buffalo became a cold-blooded business, not a sport. Typically, there were one or two hunters in a party with two or three skinners for each shooter. It took two or three wagons to bring supplies to the camp and freight hides back. The most popular rifle was the "Big Fifty," the .50-90 Sharps Special with a 473-grain bullet and 90 grains of powder, a powerful weapon.

The hunter tried to shoot buffalo through the lungs the "lights," as he said. An animal shot through the lungs would go a step or two and drop, whereas a heart-shot buffalo might run several hundred yards. On a successful kill, the hunter could expect to slaughter 100-500 animals. After the hunter shot out his stand, skinners took over.

A good skinner could handle forty to fifty buffalo a day. First he ripped the hide down the belly from throat to tail, then he slashed down each leg, and again around the head up to the ears. The rest of the head was not skinned out. The hide was rolled back for a starter and a rope was drawn tight around the neck flap. A team was hitched to the other end, and the skin shucked off by brute force. The carcasses were left to rot.

Buffalo hunters skinning a buffalo. —Fort Sill Museum

Buffalo hunters' camp with hides pegged out on the ground to dry.
—Western History Collections, University of Oklahoma Library

Green hides, each weighing from 60 to more than 100 pounds, were hauled back to camp and pegged out on the ground to dry, flesh side up. They were turned after three to five days and, finally, the "flint hides," as they were called, were freighted to town to await buyers. The long curly hair on big heads was sometimes taken for mattress or cushion stuffing.

At first, hides brought only $1 to $2, since buffalo skin is too spongy for shoe-sole leather. As other uses developed—lap robes for open vehicles, coats, buff leather for belts, saddle coverings, and especially belts to drive industrial machinery—prices rose to $2 and up for cow hides, and $4 for bull hides. The panic of 1873 brought thousands of jobless men out to the prairies to share in this bloody bonanza, and that spelled the end of the buffalo herds.

In 1898 a Mennonite Brethern Convention at Corn was well attended. —Western Hstory Collection, University of Oklahoma Library

OK 54-115
Corn—Meers

—*Corn* - OK 54A————

The name of this rural German Mennonite community, west of OK 54 on OK 54A, was Korn from 1896 until 1918, when it was anglicized to Corn to avoid any implication of sympathy with Germany. A sturdy Mennonite Brethern Church building testifies that the town retains its religious heritage, and the menus in cafes are sprinkled with German dishes.

—*Colony* - OK 54B————

In 1872 John H. Seger, a Union veteran, came to the Darlington Indian Agency to serve the Cheyennes and Arapahos. In 1885 he was sent to the present site of Colony, east of OK 54 on OK 54B, with about 500 Indians to establish an experimental agricultural community. The post office, established in 1890, took its name from the "Seger Colony." He established the Seger Indian School in 1893 and served as superintendent until 1905. The school and a mission founded by the Dutch Reformed Church did not close until 1941.

—*Mountain View* - OK 9—OK 115————

This farming and ranching community began as Oakdale in 1893. In 1900, with the coming of the Rock Island railroad, it moved to its present site. The name was changed to Mountain View, in recognition of the panorama of the Wichita Mountains to the south. During the 1880s, Bill Wilbourn, a cattleman in the area, adopted "a brand you could read in the moonlight," as stockmen put it. He discouraged brand-changing and rustling by emblazoning the flanks of his stock with HELL in large letters.

—*Saddle Mountain* - OK 115————

This community took its name from the Saddle Mountain Indian Mission. In 1893, Isabel Crawford came to Kiowa country at the age of twenty-eight to begin missionary work. She held her first meeting on Easter Sunday, April 12, 1896. The Indians called her "the little Jesus woman" and admired her courage. "We like this. You, one woman all alone among Indians and no skeered."

The Saddle Mountain Church was built in 1903. Miss Crawford retired and returned to her home in Canada in 1906. The Saddle Mountain Indian Cemetery, a quarter mile east of the church, is of particular interest. Some of the graves are marked by body-sized tombs decorated with seashells.

—*Meers* - OK 115————

This fragment of a town is a reminder of the gold fever that swept the Wichita Mountains during the 1890s and continued into the twentieth century. It started with tales of old Spanish mines and was fueled by such stories as the report of a housewife near Meers who found a gold nugget "as large as No. 8 birdshot" in the craw of a chicken she was preparing for Christmas dinner.

On May 23, 1901, about forty miners met at the foot of Mt. Sheridan and organized a mining district. It mattered not to them that it was an Indian reservation, thus not open to prospectors or miners. The land was opened to settlers on August 6, and a mining camp was named for Col. Andrew Jackson Meers, who had found an outcropping of quartzite, "peacock ore," in 1900. At the peak of activity, Meers had a population of about 500, three grocery stores, two drugstores, a cafe, a confectionery, three doctors, a smelter, a post office, and *The Mt. Sheridan Miner.*

A University of Oklahoma geologist investigated on behalf of the United States Geological Survey and reported that minerals in the Wichita Mountains were hardly worth the effort to extract them. The geologist was lambasted by financiers and prospectors, but his report put a damper on the mining activities, and Meers began to shrink.

The old store from the ghost town of Meers has become an "in" place to eat "Meersburgers"—dinnerplate-size hamburgers made with longhorn beef.

The last remnant of Meers is a building that has been moved a half mile north of the original site. Constructed in 1901 and now on the National Register of Historic Places, the former store, doctor's office, and newspaper office is a flourishing restaurant.

OK 54
Cloud Chief—Cooperton

—*Cloud Chief* - OK 54——————

This community began in 1882 when the Cheyenne and Arapaho reservation was opened. It was named Tacola for an Arapaho subchief; the name was changed to the English equivalent when the post office was established. For ten years following the opening, Cloud Chief was the county seat. When the Frisco railroad built through the territory, nearby Cordell moved to the railroad and a bitter county seat fight broke out. A county attorney who was in favor of Cordell as the county seat was tarred and feathered by Cloud Chief citizens. Cordell finally won the honor, and Cloud Chief began to fade.

—*Gotebo* - OK 9-54——————

This town started in 1901, and was named Harrison to pay tribute to President Benjamin Harrison. In 1904 President Harrison lost out when the town's name was changed to Gotebo for a Kiowa subchief. The fact that mail destined for Harrison, Oklahoma Territory, ended up in Harrison, Arkansas, may have had something to do with the change. In 1902, a settler drilling for water struck oil at 102 feet. However, oil production in the area was spotty; not too far away a hole reached 31,441 feet without showing a trace of oil. It was touted as the "world's deepest hole."

—*Cooperton* - OK 54————

This community was established in 1902 by a townsite company. The settlers' problems illustrate the confusion that prevailed during land openings. The three hundred members of the company drew for business lots, 25 by 50 feet, and residential lots, 50 by 150 feet, only to discover the area was a government townsite. After a government surveyor laid out the town, members of the company had to pay $10 per lot to register. Before the town could be granted a charter, there had to be a home on every forty acres of land.

OK 36-54
Chattanooga—Grandfield

—*Chattanooga* - OK 36————

On December 18, 1902, a patent was issued to N. C. Sisson and two associates to form the Chattanooga Town Company. Capital stock of $16,000 funded the enterprise, and the town of Chattanooga was laid out and so named because Chattanooga, Tennessee, was Sisson's hometown. The *Chattanooga Weekly News* featured a two-column headline in each issue: "Chattanooga the Big Pasture Town."

The Big Pasture was the last section of Indian Territory to be opened to settlement. The treaty by which the Indians ceded their surplus lands provided that each individual would retain an allotment of 160 acres while the tribes as a whole retained 480,000 acres in two or three large tracts as pasture lands for their surplus livestock. The largest of these tracts in southwestern Indian Territory became known as the Big Pasture.

As a matter of fact, the Indians had no surplus livestock. They had been encouraged by ranchmen pasturing herds on their reservations to insist upon the clause. These pasture lands were immediately leased to cattlemen and herds were pastured there until 1906 when the Indians were induced to surrender their title. The land was then sold to settlers by sealed bids.

—Loveland————

This railroad-siding community to the west of OK 36 was platted in July 1908 and named for G. V. Harris, the townsite owner. In October, the name was changed to Loveland at the suggestion of a local merchant named E. T. Duncan. For many years the post office experienced a rush of business just prior to February 14 by people who wanted the LOVELAND postmark on their Valentine's Day greetings.

—Grandfield - US 70—OK 36————

This community began in 1907 as Eschiti and was named for a Comanche medicine man. The name was changed to Grandfield in 1909. During its days as Eschiti, there was a strong rivalry between this town and Kell City, two miles away. The *Kell City Enterprise* started the fight with an editorial on October 17, 1907:

> Kell City is only a small town, yet we jar the earth and strike fire from the cobblestones as we walk. . . . Eschiti essays to be the business rival of Kell City, but she is not making any more noise than the passing of a regiment of pussy-footed catterpillars.

The *Eschiti Banner* replied with a full-page editorial, and the battle of words was on.

Rev. A. J. Fant bought and homesteaded the present site of Grandfield. He called his community Kell and offered free lots to Eschiti and Kell City residents who would quit feuding and move.

Residents of Kell would not go to Eschiti for mail. They took outgoing mail to Wichita Falls, Texas, where they picked up incoming mail from a rented box. One night in 1908 the Eschiti post office building was loaded on wagons and moved to the center of what is now Main Street in Grandfield.

Two U.S. deputy marshals arrived to question citizens, and the next night the post office building was moved back to Eschiti. Reverend Fant finally got Kell City, Kell, and Eschiti welded into a single community called Grandfield.

Grandfield is in the heart of the Big Pasture, a fact commemorated by a granite marker in a downtown park. The marker displays a map of the area and tells the story of the Big Pasture. This is still ranching country, and grain elevators along the railroad testify to bounteous wheat crops.

—*Bessie* - OK 183A————

It took this town a while to settle on a name. Located near Boggy Creek, in 1895 it started out as Boggy. In 1899 the name was changed to Stout, for Benjamin W. Stout, the first postmaster. In 1903 the Blackwell, Enid and Southwestern Railroad arrived—popularly called "The Bess Line" because of its initials—and residents finally found a name they could live with. During its formative years, Bessie attracted German-Russian farmers.

—*Cordell* - US 183—OK 152————

Established west of its present site in 1892 at the opening of the Cheyenne-Arapaho reservation, Cordell moved to the railroad and launched a campaign to become the county seat of Washita County. After a bitter fight, in 1900 a special election gave Cordell the right to move the courthouse from Cloud Chief to Cordell. In 1909 the old courthouse was destroyed by a mysterious fire and a new one had to be built.

The Oklahoma-based chain of variety stores—T.G.&Y.—originated in Cordell, founded by E. L. "Les" Gosselin, the "G" of T.G.&Y. The firm consolidated Gosselin's store with the "T" store, then located in Frederick, and a "Y" store located in Kingfisher.

After the demise of Navajoe, this hotel was moved to Cordell where it became the City Hotel. Meals cost 25 cents. —Western History Collections, University of Oklahoma Library

Beginning in 1889, there was a post office called Hardin. The name was changed to Speed on February 20, 1901, but there was not yet an accumulation of people large enough to warrant being called a town. With opening of the Kiowa-Comanche reservation in August, a crowd estimated at 13,000 arrived and pitched a sea of tents to await the lottery for the sale of lots on August 6. As was the case with many other towns on the Oklahoma frontier, they called it Rag Town.

Gamblers, preachers, outlaws, businessmen, and cowboys rubbed elbows. One enterprising young man sold admissions to the first "rest home"—an outdoor privy. Others made money by selling water at five cents a glass. After the lots sold, 2,530 people stayed to become the nucleus of Hobart.

It was the following spring before most of them could replace their tents with more substantial dwellings. The lucky ones had pot-bellied stoves to heat their tents. During winter they held sheets around the stoves to warm them before going to bed; they heated bricks and wrapped them in blankets to put at their children's feet.

Hobart drew its sustenance from agriculture. The valley lands produced heavy crops of alfalfa, cotton, and forage crops, supplemented by dairying and poultry. The uplands grew wheat, small grains, kaffir, and sorghum crops. The pastures supported cattle and sheep. At the southeastern corner of the city, where the Rock Island and Frisco railroads crossed, cotton gins, compresses, a cottonseed oil mill, and

The Kiowa County Courthouse Square in Hobart, circa 1923. —Western History Collections, University of Oklahoma Library

stock pens grew. In 1939 an oil field opened to the northeast, and shallow wells, from 1,000 to 1,100 feet, gave the economy a boost to help Hobart recover from the effects of the Depression.

—*Babbs* - US 183————

Most maps designate this town as Babbs, but its official name was Babbs Switch, named for Edith "Babbs" Babcock who delivered the first load of wheat to the grain elevator on the railroad siding. A historical marker commemorates the loss of thirty-six lives—men, women, and children—in a schoolhouse fire on December 24, 1924. During a Christmas Eve celebration, a candle ignited the Christmas tree. The doors of the one-room frame building became blocked during the ensuing panic. This fire resulted in design changes to make schools safer throughout the nation.

—*Roosevelt* - US 183—OK 19————

This community began as a land promotion prior to the opening of the territory to settlement. A plan fostered by the Parkersburg Development Company called for a town to be laid out in the new county on a railroad not yet built. The plan went awry when a farmer refused to donate land to the townsite. This resulted in the development of a rival adjacent townsite.

Charley Hunter, the developer of the new town, had been a Rough Rider during the Spanish-American War. He named the town after his old commanding officer and succeeded in getting President Roosevelt to come to Oklahoma in 1905. Later, L. C. Cheuvront described President Roosevelt as "just one of the fellows. He didn't need guards, he could have whipped a half dozen men by himself."

—*Cold Springs*————

The first town in the area was called Mondamin, an Indian word meaning "corn," apparently adopted from Longfellow's *Hiawatha*. Litigation over land title developed, and Mondamin's plat was never filed. The town was absorbed by South Cold Springs in 1908.

In the meantime, J. H. D. Terral had started North Cold Springs. Terral was a promoter who appreciated the natural beauty of the area. His town consisted of a two-story hotel, seven or eight houses, a grocery store, and a depot. He succeeded in luring tourists on weekend excursions from as far away as Clinton. According to the story, every Friday evening, Terral imported two 300-pound cakes of ice from the ice plant at Hobart via the Frisco railroad and slipped them into his spring-fed well. One summer evening, a tourist remarked that it was the "coldest damn' spring water she had ever tasted." That was the day he named the town Cold Springs.

—*Mountain Park* - US 183————————

Mountain Park was first known as Burford, a trading post for Indians and cowboys. The name was changed to Mountain Park in 1902. The government had set aside a half-section of land for the present site of Mountain Park. The proposed railroad had not been built, but 2,000-3,000 early settlers came in covered wagons and on horseback for the opening.

The town followed the usual pattern. A tent-town sprang up. Saloons, gambling houses, and other forms of vice were prevalent. Frame buildings replaced the tents. Hopes were high as the Oklahoma City and Southwestern Railroad, later the Frisco, approached. The railroad wanted a cash bonus along with a quarter-section of land adjoining the townsite upon which to build a depot and other buildings.

Arrangements were made to purchase the necessary 160 acres from Sol Bracken for $6,000. However, as Bracken assayed the situation, he became convinced the railroad would have to pass through his place, and they would be compelled to buy his land at any price he asked. He doubled the price. Angry railroad officials obtained land in Snyder and changed the route to run two miles south of Mountain Park. All but seven of the forty-eight business establishments in Mountain Park moved to Snyder. Sol Bracken was left with land at a greatly deflated value and the ill will of the few residents who remained in Mountain Park.

In 1915 Anton Soukup, a Bohemian-born citizen, arrived and bought 160 acres of land on the rugged slopes of nearby Mount Radziminski. The land appeared to be suitable only for raising goats, and that was what Soukup did. He bought a herd of goats; he also bought other portions of the mountain, for additional pasture, as he explained it. Locally, Soukup became known as "that crazy Bohemian."

But when the crazy Bohemian finally had title to the entire mountain, he sent for a fellow Bohemian, Frank Svoboda, a granite-finisher from Omaha, Nebraska, who had been financing Soukup's purchase of land. Svoboda promptly began exploitating the massive granite pile that is Mount Radziminski. At one time as many as 500 granite cutters and finishers were employed in the area. Today most of the granite industry is concentrated in Snyder, and Mountain Park's economy is primarily dependent upon farming and ranching.

Wichita Mountains Wildlife Refuge

When the Kiowa-Comanche lands were opened to white settlement in 1901, a portion was set aside as a forest preserve. In 1905, President Theodore Roosevelt established the 59,200-acre Wichita Mountains Wildlife Refuge.

By 1889 only a few hundred buffalo stood between survival and extinction of the species. In 1907 the New York Zoological Society donated fifteen choice specimens for the beginning of a buffalo herd in the Wichita Mountains.

The train from New York was met at Cache by Quanah Parker and a band of his warriors dressed in their finest regalia. They followed closely behind the wagons containing the crates that held the shaggy beasts. They watched as each was sprayed with crude oil as protection from the dreaded Texas fever tick. Many of the older Indians were nearly overcome by emotion as they watched the "Great Spirit's Cattle" being turned into a twelve-square-mile fenced pasture. Today the herd is maintained at about 525. Surplus buffalo are rounded up each fall and sold at auction.

In 1927, thirty head of Texas longhorns were brought to the refuge to begin a herd now maintained at about 300. Visitors can also see deer and elk. A prairie dog town provides hours of entertainment as the residents go about their endless daily chores of feeding and grooming.

The Holy City of the Wichitas

This picturesque natural amphitheater at the base of Mount Roosevelt is the setting for an annual Easter pageant. The pageant was started by the Reverend Anthony Mark Wallock. He noticed a similarity between the granite outcrops of the Wichita Mountains and the terrain of the Holy Land. The first pageant was staged in 1926 at Medicine Park by Reverend Wallock's Sunday school class.

In 1933, the U.S. government set aside 160 acres of land in the Wichita National Forest Preserve for the pageant. The event gained national fame in 1948 with filming of *The Prince of Peace* on location in the Holy City with local people cast in the leading roles.

—*Snyder* - US 62-183————

Established in 1902 with the coming of the railroad, Snyder was named for Bryan Snyder, a railroad official. In 1905 a devastating tornado virtually destroyed the town and claimed 105 lives. Today there are few homes in Snyder without storm caves or cellars.

In 1911 Snyder suffered economic misfortune when Swanson County was dissolved. It survived as a trading center for the surrounding farming area and to become the center of the granite industry that began to thrive a few years later. Today a number of companies process the distinctive pink Snyder granite, which comes from several quarries in the area.

—*Manitou* - US 183————

This railroad-siding community was established in 1902, after the arrival of the Frisco railroad. Its name is the Algonquin word for "god" or "Great Spirit."

The city fathers planned a celebration for August 6, 1906. They asked Quanah Parker to attend. He agreed and, on August 5, showed up with three wives and about 150 members of his tribe. They pitched camp on the north side of town. Officials prepared a barbecue to feed the Indians and the spectators. They had figured eight beeves would be adequate. The following day, after parading down Main Street, the Indian guests took all of the beef and retired to their camp, leaving the city fathers to figure out how to feed the rest of their guests.

—*Tipton* - OK 5————

Located on OK 5 to the west of US 183, Tipton is a prosperous farming and ranching community which was established on the Wichita Falls and Northwestern (now Katy) Railway in 1909. The townsite was initially called Stinson, but the name did not last long enough to become a post office. Cotton is the principal crop in the area. The community is perhaps best known for the Tipton Children's Home located on the north edge of town.

—*Frederick* - US 183—OK 5————

Originally known as Gosnell for the townsite owner, Robert L. Gosnell, this town was founded in 1901 with the opening of the Indian lands to settlement. Shortly after, the name was changed to Frederick. The town prospered along with the surrounding farming and ranching area and as the county seat of Tillman County. Frederick was the first town in the territory to vote out saloons and pool halls, but that did not dampen its Western flavor. The discovery of oil in the area sweetened the

After the wolf hunt, the party posed for a picture. The group includes Theodore Roosevelt, Jack Abernathy, Quanah Parker, and, of course, the dead wolf. —
Western History Collections, University of Oklahoma Liibrary

economic kitty for Frederick, and the city now has a comfortable base of industrial development.

In 1905 President Theodore Roosevelt visited Frederick to participate in a six-day wolf hunt with U.S. Marshal John R. (Jack) Abernathy. The story goes that one day Abernathy found one of his dogs slashed and dying with a big wolf standing by. He took after the wolf. The wolf leaped for Abernathy's throat. Somehow Abernathy got his hand into the wolf's mouth and closed his fingers on the lower jaw behind the sharp canine teeth. Both went down in a rough-and-tumble fight, but Jack found he could hold the wolf without being bitten. From that day he hunted wolves and coyotes bare-handed. He carried baling wire to wire the jaws of his captives shut and carried them home alive across his saddle.

President Roosevelt wrote about the hunt, during which Abernathy caught sixteen coyotes, commonly called prairie wolves, with his bare hands. Abernathy and President Roosevelt were photographed with Abernathy holding one of the animals.

—*Davidson* - US 70-183————

This was the first town in southwestern Oklahoma to boast a railroad after the Blackwell and Southern Railway came north from Vernon, Texas. It was called Texawa ("Texas" plus "Kiowa") and later Olds before the name was changed to Davidson to honor a railroad official. Davidson had a population of 200 in 1907.

Originally, the Red River was crossed by ferry. Texas and Oklahoma got together in 1924 to build the longest wooden bridge in the world. It was washed out by a flood in 1934 and finally replaced by another spanning 5,460 feet. It is Oklahoma's longest bridge, located three miles south of Davidson.

OK 44
Burns Flat—Lugert

—*Burns Flat* - OK 44—————

In 1894, this community was named Burns for Sarah Burns, the first postmistress. The town didn't last long, but its name was revived with development of the Clinton-Sherman Air Force Base during World War II. In 1950, the U.S. Census Bureau counted 2,280 people in Burns Flat. In 1971 the Strategic Air Command closed the base, and the town shrank to a sprinkling of residents. Development of an industrial park rejuvenated the area.

—*Sentinel* - OK 44-55—————

This farming community was established in 1899 by a post office designated as Barton, and the townsite plat was filed in 1901. However, the name was not popular, and it was changed to Sentinel for the *Herald Sentinel*, a newspaper published in Cloud Chief, at that time the county seat of Washita County.

Sentinel is in the center of the Elk Creek Watershed Development Project, which provides fishing, recreational facilities, and flood protection for surrounding farm land. Cotton, wheat, and alfalfa are augmented by natural gas in support of the economy.

—*Lone Wolf* - OK 9-44—————

This quiet agricultural community on former Kiowa Indian land commemorates the name of a Kiowa chief. Chief Lone Wolf died of malaria in 1879. He was succeeded as principal chief by Mamay-day-te, who took the name Lone Wolf. The town was established when the Kiowa lands were opened to white settlement in 1901. The community now profits from its proximity to Quartz Mountain State Park and Altus Lake.

Although the name remains on the map, there is little left of Frank Lugert's General Store. Frank Lugert was a Russian immigrant who came to the United States at the age of twelve. He taught himself English, worked as a logger in Wisconsin, and participated in the run into the Cherokee Outlet. In 1901, he filed on a claim at the foot of the Wichita Mountains and was appointed to sell lots in the town that would bear his name.

The town thrived, and there were several general stores besides Lugert's. There was also a problem—a shortage of money. Frank Lugert issued small metal tokens in denominations from one cent to one dollar, redeemable only at his store.

Lugert's store prospered. It contained the post office and carried prospectors' supplies, groceries, dry goods, boots, shoes, books, school supplies, patent medicines, guns, ammunition, blasting supplies, pictures, hardware, stoves, pots and pans, dishes, tubs, washboards, well buckets, pumps, harness, axes, hoes, picks, meat, cheese, cracker barrels, cold drinks, cookies, candy, coal, and later installed gasoline pumps.

Things were going well in Lugert until April 27, 1912. The morning dawned hot and sultry. Clouds gathered, warning of an impending storm. Vivid flashes of lightning were followed by thunder as residents headed for storm cellars. The noon train was just entering the north part of the Lugert railyard when the wind increased to a roar. Within a few minutes there was silence—deathly silence—followed by torrential rain.

When people emerged from their cellars they found homes, businesses, and personal possessions destroyed. The train was scattered; only one or two railroad cars and the caboose remained on the track. The town never rebuilt. People left and Lugert dwindled. The final indignity came in the 1940s when water from Altus Reservoir backed up to cover most of what was left.

Frank Lugert's General Store. —Western History Collections, University of Oklahoma Library

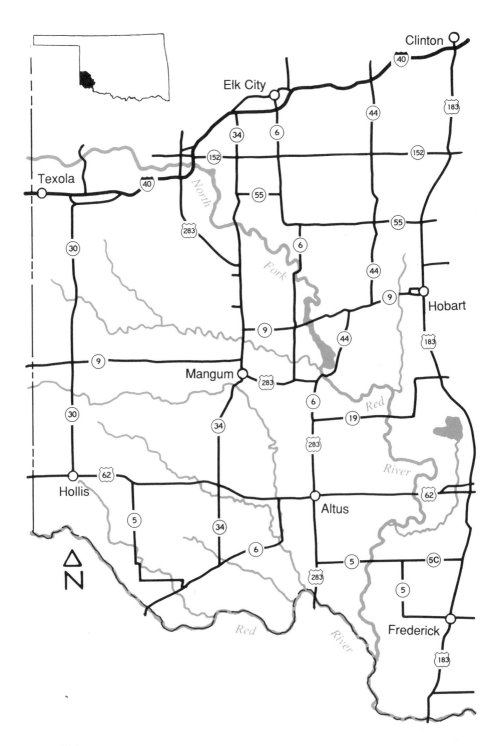

XII. Old Greer County

The southwest corner of Oklahoma between the Red River and the North Fork of the Red River was disputed territory from 1860 to 1896. Since 1629, when the land was granted to Sir Robert Heath of the North Carolina Colony, the area—some 2,300 square miles—has been claimed by fourteen different governments. The United States Supreme Court finally settled the controversy over "Old Greer County."

In 1819, the Adams-Onís Treaty between Spain and the United States set the boundary between the two nations as the Red River up to the 100th meridian (the western border of Oklahoma). In 1852, Capt. R. B. Marcy commanded an expedition to explore the headwaters of the Canadian and Red rivers. He discovered that not one but two main branches of the Red River intersected the 100th meridian.

After winning independence from Spain and becoming a state, Texas took steps to claim territory up to the North Fork of the Red River. On February 8, 1860, the Texas legislature passed an act providing for the formation of Greer County. The Civil War interrupted the efforts to organize a county government.

In 1883, the Day Land and Cattle Company of Austin, Texas, bought up land certificates that had been issued to veterans of the Texas war for independence. The cattle company used these certificates to patent 144,000 acres in Greer County. The company leased an additional 203,000 acres in the area.

In June 1884, a detachment was sent out from Fort Sill, Indian Territory, to eject settlers from the county. The officer in charge of the detachment returned to report that the county had been parcelled out among cattle owners. There were ten families and 60,000 head of cattle belonging to different firms. The Francklyn Land and Cattle Company owned 40,000 head.

President Chester A. Arthur issued a proclamation on July 1, 1884, warning people not to enter Greer County. Settlers in Greer County responded by meeting at Mobeetie in Wheeler County, Texas, and organizing a county government with Mangum as the county seat. They built a jail and strengthened their claim by getting the Post Office Department to establish post offices at Mangum and Frazier in Greer County, *Texas*.

The following year the designations of the post offices were changed from Texas to Indian Territory, and on December 30, 1887, President Grover Cleveland issued a proclamation declaring the disputed lands to be part of Indian Territory and warning against selling or purchasing any of the land. On May 2, 1890, Congress created Oklahoma Territory; however, Greer County was excluded until title to the land could be determined.

On October 27, 1890, the Attorney General of the United States filed suit against Texas to determine title to Greer County: United States *vs.* Texas, 162 U.S. *Reports* (1895). The point at issue could be stated simply: Was the north or the south branch of the Red River the main stream? If the North Fork was the main stream, the land between the two branches had belonged to Spain and subsequently to Texas.

Residents of Old Greer County remained in limbo while the Supreme Court debated the issue. The United States maintained that the South Fork (then known as the Prairie Dog Town Fork) was the natural east-west continuation of the Red River indicated in the treaty with Spain. Texas claimed the land by right of possession and occupation extending back thirty-five years, resulting in a well-ordered and prosperous land.

After six years and the accumulation of fifty thick volumes of testimony, on March 16, 1896, the United States Supreme Court decreed the South Fork of the Red River the main stream and hence the boundary between Texas and Oklahoma Territory. District Judge G. A. Brown was presiding at a trial in Mangum when he heard the news. He immediately stopped the trial, announced that his jurisdiction had been terminated, and departed for his home in Burnham, Texas.

The decision created pandemonium as people worried about titles to land on which they had settled while it was claimed by Texas. Congress enacted legislation declaring former Greer County, Texas, to be Greer County, Oklahoma, and extending Oklahoma laws to encompass former Texan legal proceedings affecting the area. Some 8,500 settlers and residents found themselves Oklahomans instead of Texans; their land titles were secure.

On January 18, 1897, the new county was made a separate land district with provision for opening the unoccupied lands to settlement. The district contained 1,372,666 acres. Of this, 640,000 acres were subject to preference by some 2,000 resident settlers as of March 16, 1896, leaving 732,666 acres open to settlement, room for more than 4,000 new homesteads.

Old Greer County was subsequently subdivided into Greer, Harmon, and Jackson counties and a portion of Beckham County. The North Fork of the Red River marks the northern and eastern boundaries Old Greer County. A historical marker on the western boundary of Oklahoma in Texola designates the area as the "Empire of Greer."

A tour of Old Greer County leads through areas where the grass and streams have scarcely changed since Indians ruled as "Lords of the High Plains" and through other areas where civilization has molded the land beyond recognition. There are pastures that once teemed with fattening longhorns, mountain haunts of Kiowas and Comanches, the old Western Cattle Trail that led cattle to northern markets, the remains of towns where homesteaders fought and lost battles with depression and drought, rich farming areas where irrigation and conservation have brought the land back, and pumps that suck oil from the earth. Old Greer County presents the traveler with a constantly changing scene. Its museums preserve the historical past.

US 283
Willow—Elmer

—*Willow* - OK 34A————

The Beeson family came to the site of present-day Willow in December 1888. They plowed a furrow around four sections of land and then used three yokes of oxen and a Cassidy plow to break out 200 acres of sod. Coyotes followed the furrows, sometimes coming within a few feet of the plow. Bunk Beeson kept a monkey wrench handy to throw at them.

The Beesons farmed during the spring and summer and supplemented their income by hunting during the winter. Using shotguns and rifles, they killed deer, turkeys, prairie chickens, and quail. These were loaded in a hack and taken to Quanah, Texas, for shipment to Kansas City and Chicago. They sometimes killed as many as a hundred quail in a day.

This small farming community just west of OK 34 was built on the Beesons' claim. The town was named for Will O'Connell, the town's first postmaster. The post office was established October 17, 1899. The principal crop in the area is now cotton, as evidenced by cotton gins in town and the crops and equipment on surrounding farms.

—*Brinkman* - OK 34B————

This farming community just west of US 283 was established in 1910 on the Wichita Falls and Northwestern Railway (now the Katy). It was initially named Kell for an official of the railroad, but the name was changed to honor John Brinkman, an early resident who helped finance the townsite.

During early days, more wheat was shipped from Brinkman than all other markets combined in Greer County. The railroad line has been abandoned and the community now gives the appearance of a ghost town, with only one brick building and widely scattered grain elevators still standing.

EXCURSION

—*Granite* - OK 6-9

This community was founded in 1889, taking its name from gigantic granite formations in the nearby Wichita Mountains. By 1910 a monument works had been established. The quarry is still operating, and street signs point the way to the "world's largest granite portrait": A likeness of Will Rogers is carved on massive slabs

Oklahoma's mountains furnished building materials. —Western History Collections, University of Oklahoma Library

When aggregations of Indians visited Washington, they attired themselves after the fashion of white men. This party consisted of (standing left to right): Col. E. B. Hunt, Indian agent; E. L. Cook, interpreter. (seated) Ko-di-a-ko (Wichita), White Man (Apache), Stumbling Bear (Kiowa), Wild Horse (Comanche). —Western History Collections, University of Oklahoma Library

of granite forming a 32-foot-square mosaic. Today, the largest local industry is the Oklahoma State Reformatory for the rehabilitation of youthful offenders.

HISTORICAL HIGHLIGHT

The Death of Yellow Bear

George W. Briggs came to the area of Granite in 1880 as a "trail cutter," preceding the herds of cattle being driven north. In 1881 he settled in a dugout near Comanche Springs, five miles northeast of present-day Granite. Later he served as county commissioner and was elected Greer County's representative to the first legislature of the state of Oklahoma.

Briggs was an unwitting participant in a bizarre tragedy that resulted in the death of Yellow Bear, a famous Comanche chief. Briggs was serving as escort for Yellow Bear and Quanah Parker on a trip. They were staying in the Pickwick Hotel in Fort Worth, Texas. The two Indians retired to their room, and Briggs went to his.

409

When they were ready to go to sleep, the Indians blew out the gas jet providing light in their room. The following morning Briggs found Yellow Bear asphyxiated and Quanah Parker near death. Quanah recovered.

—*Mangum* - US 283—OK 34————

Soon after becoming a state, Texas awarded land script to veterans of its war to gain independence from Mexico. Capt. A. S. Mangum received a grant for 320 acres wherever he could find unappropriated lands. Mangum entered into contract with Henry C. Sweet, a Dallas civil engineer, to claim his land in Greer County near the Western Cattle Trail. Sweet was to survey the land, lay out a townsite, and receive part of the lots as payment.

Sweet surveyed the land in 1883, naming the townsite Mangum after the owner. Captain Mangum, quite elderly when the land script was issued, did not live to see the town named for him. Sweet became sole owner of the tract in 1884, moved to the area with his family, and platted the town. He opened a store in a 9- by 12-foot frame shack built of rough-cut planks and was named postmaster.

The store was a boon to cowboys in the area who previously had to ride to Doan's Store on the Red River for supplies. Sweet stocked canned fruits, lunch goods, and a large stock of tobacco. Cowboy appetites ran to canned goods, and Sweet unfolded the tin cans and used them to patch knotholes and cracks in his store. The community became known as "Tin Town" or "Tin City."

In Mangum, settled primarily by Texans, there were lots of participants when Confederate veterans turned out for a parade, even as late as 1910. —Western History Collections, University of Oklahoma Library

The cattlemen of Greer County eventually objected to inroads by the settlers and secured a proclamation from the president of the United States warning settlers to move on. Soldiers from Fort Sill presented the ultimatum and added an injunction of their own making, threatening to raze the town if the citizens were still there when they returned. But Mangum persevered and nothing came of the order. In 1896, by a Supreme Court decision, Greer County became part of Oklahoma Territory instead of Texas.

Years ago, ranchers in the area organized an annual rattlesnake hunt to rid the ranges of the pests. The Mangum Rattlesnake Derby has become an annual three-day carnival attracting hundreds of hunters and thousands of spectators who come to sample rattlesnake meat and witness the weighing and measuring to determine winners in various categories.

HISTORICAL HIGHLIGHT

Devil's Canyon

Devil's Canyon is a rugged pass in the Wichita Mountains. Its mouth is a few miles northeast of the confluence of Elk Creek and the North Fork of the Red River. In 1834 it was the site of the first formal contact between United States emissaries and the Plains Indians in an attempt to promote peace.

Vague stories of earlier happenings in the canyon are more intriguing than recorded history. Known to early hunters as "Spanish Town" more than a century ago, the area has been visited by a succession of treasure hunters in search of Spanish gold and hidden mines. Because of its historical significance, Devil's Canyon has been placed on the National Register of Historic Places; however, it is on privately owned land.

In July 1834, Brig. Gen. Henry Leavenworth left Fort Gibson with the First Regiment of the United States Dragoons to contact the wild Indians and bring them back to Fort Gibson for conference and treaty. The army wanted to secure safe passage along the Santa Fe Trail for hunters, trappers, and traders, and for the Five Civilized Tribes being settled in the eastern part of the territory.

The force left Fort Gibson some five hundred strong, dressed in resplendent uniforms and bearing fluttering guidons. The troops were guaranteed to produce a lasting effect upon the Kiowas and Comanches. Experienced frontiersmen accompanied the dragoons, including Capt. Nathan Boone, son of Daniel Boone. First Lt. Jefferson Davis was a member of the group. Montfort Stokes, ex-governor of North Carolina, served as a commissioner. A talented Philadelphia artist named George Catlin joined the force as a guest of General Leavenworth. The wagon train contained commissary supplies, ammunition, gifts for the Indians, and two Wichita prisoners to trade for any white captives they might discover.

Disaster plagued the expedition from the start. The proud dragoons suffered from heat stroke and exhaustion in their heavy uniforms. A gastrointestinal malady struck the unit. A hospital called Camp Leavenworth had to be established on the prairie. Here General Leavenworth fell from his horse while chasing a buffalo calf and went to his deathbed. Before he died he ordered Col. Henry Dodge to select 250 healthy men and continue the expedition.

Colonel Dodge sent word ahead that they were coming to shake hands, to make peace not war. Dodge found some 2,000 Wichitas living in a village composed of bottle-shaped grass huts at the mouth of Devil's Canyon. Kiowas, Comanches, and Wichitas came to parley.

The Indians were impressed by the mounted regiment. They had nothing but scorn for "walk-a-heaps" (infantrymen) who moved on foot like squaws. Maybe now they realized that in the future they would have to deal with a different species of enemy. Two prisoners were exchanged. The Indians told Dodge that Spanish traders had recently visited from the west, and Dodge told the Indians that American traders would give them better goods at lower prices. Future conferences were agreed upon.

When Colonel Dodge and his party arrived at Devil's Canyon, they found a settlement of about 2,000 Wichitas living in bottle-shaped grass houses at the mouth of the canyon. —Fort Sill Museum

The negotiations yielded treaties with the Comanches and Wichitas in 1835 and with the Kiowas in 1837.

The treaties may have had passing value, but the artist George Catlin produced a lasting effect. After completion of the talks, the dragoons spent two days visiting the Indian village and bartering cheap trade knives for good horses. George Catlin had an umbrella coveted by the Indians. Since Catlin was ill and needed the umbrella as a sunshade he would not part with it. The Indians apparently remembered. Years later, when traders were established at Fort Sill, virtually every Indian equipped himself with an umbrella.

During the next century, rumors of Spanish gold and buried treasure in Devil's Canyon proliferated. Some historians maintained that Fray Juan de Salas, a Spanish priest, established a mission there in 1629 and was followed by gold-seekers. Adobe ruins and primitive mine shafts have been found; some say the Mexicans operated smelters. Indians turned up fragments of armament and horse gear said to have belonged to Spanish conquistadors. Cryptic petroglyphs have been found, reputed to point the way to buried loot if they could be translated. Devil's Canyon remained a part of the Kiowa-Comanche-Apache reservation, but Indian police and soldiers from Fort Sill regularly had to remove interlopers bent on uncovering riches.

To date, no one has come forward to admit locating a treasure trove, but an occasional hunter still appears to roam the area with the bright light of gold fever shining from his eyes.

—*Blair* - US 283—OK 19—————

Blair began in 1890-91 as a subscription school. A one-room building was used for a school during winter when weather conditions made it impossible for children to work in the fields. B. B. Zinn moved to the area, opened a store, and chartered a post office named Dot for one of his daughters.

One day a buggy pulled into Zinn's yard and the occupants identified themselves as officials of the Kansas City, Mexico and Orient Railway. The railroad was interested in building a line from Kansas City to Mexico. They would come through Dot if the town would provide title to a quarter-section of land across from the Dot store. Zinn and a neighbor bought the land for $1,500. The town's name was changed to honor John A. Blair, a railroad official.

Blair turned into a survivor. It survived a tornado in 1928 and eleven subsequent years of agricultural depression. Today it survives as a typical rural crossroads community because of irrigation water from Altus Lake.

—*Warren* - OK 19————————

This small farming community is located on the Western Cattle Trail just south of the North Fork of the Red River. Herds were driven across the river at this point, then known simply as Trail Crossing. The cattlemen's association had an inspection station to make certain that trail herds did not contain cattle belonging to local ranchers. A scattered town grew, "two miles long and a hundred feet wide," according to one resident. It obtained a post office in 1888, named after an early resident.

Nathaniel Jacob McElroy, who came to Warren in 1886, played an important role in the community. He served as a translator with Indians on the Kiowa-Comanche reservation just across the river. On his way home from school when he was eleven years old, Uncle Jake, as he was called, had been captured by Comanches. His father ransomed him for $950, but during the year and a half he was a prisoner he had learned the Comanche language. Throughout his life, he continued to wear his hair long, as the Indians had taught him.

—*Martha*————————

In 1888, this faded farming community to the west of US 283 had its beginning as a school organized by Martha Medlin, daughter of a pioneer Baptist minister. The school was a dugout, so common on the prairie, about a mile north of the present town. There were twelve pupils the first year. One settler, fearful that his children might lose their way in bad weather, plowed a furrow from their home to the school to serve as a guide. The post office was opened in 1889 and named for the first teacher.

In September 1891, Martha underwent an Indian scare, sparked by the killing of a man named Bob Polant near Warren. Both Indians and settlers armed themselves. The citizens of Martha took every type of weapon they could find to the blacksmith shop and turned the building into a fortress. Guards were sent out to give warning if Indians crossed the North Fork of the Red River. The alarm spread to Mangum, where men turned out for target practice; organizations in other parts of the county prepared to take defensive measures. Fortunately, the military arrived from Fort Sill and civic leaders were able to settle the dispute. Life returned to normal.

Martha began to shrink with abandonment of the railroad.

Navajoe

This community was established in 1887 when Joseph S. Works, a land promoter known as Buckskin Joe, settled on the site. He and his family lived in a half-dugout while he built a two-story hotel. Works published a small paper, *The Emigrant Guide*, and traveled about the country encouraging settlers to come and live in the area. In the August 1888 issue of *The Emigrant Guide* he billed himself as "Founder and Manager of the Texas-Oklahoma Colony, Numbering over 400 Families." He painted a glowing picture:

> Navajoe is situated one and one-half miles south of North Fork of [the] Red river and twenty-five miles north of South Fork, and is situated at the foot of the Navajoe mountains (a spur of the Wichita range of mountains), and we can say, without fear of successful contradiction, that from the summit of the Navajoe mountains, for twenty miles around the base, lies as grand and magnificent a country, take it as a whole, as can be seen on God's green earth. The north and east of Navajoe is Indian Territory proper, and is used for ranching purposes by Texas cattlemen. This land can not be intruded

In spite of Buckskin Joe's newspaper, The Emigrant Guide, *Navajoe relapsed to become a ghost town.*

—Western History Collections, University of Oklahoma Library

by settlers. The south and west, stretching away into a beautiful prairie, is Greer county, disputed territory. Greer is about ninety miles long and fifty miles wide, and contains over five thousand people. There is timber in Greer for fuel and posts. . . .

People coming into Greer do not pay anything whatever for land, but settle down on 160 acres and go to work. . . . Navajoe is the gate to the new territory to be opened up, and has vacant homesteads for thousands of people in its vicinity.

Buckskin Joe described the typical homesteader as living in a new house with his land under cultivation, his stock feeding on green grass in February, and nearby mountains "yielding up their hoarded wealth of precious metals." He described Navajoe: four grocery stores, one drugstore, a wagon yard, a hotel, a schoolhouse, and a Masonic hall. He had an excursion leaving for Navajoe on September 3, 1888, in a "special chartered car." His town company would donate alternate lots to colonists who built before December 1, 1888, as long as odd-numbered lots lasted.

Settlers came, and Navajoe became a trading center. Indians visited town regularly every quarter when they were paid. After a few days of gambling, drinking, and wild spending, they would fold their tents and teepees and leave. Cowboys came to spend their idle hours in the saloons. Settlers came to buy staples.

The settlers soon got tired of the wild life in the saloons. They invited Carrie Nation, the fiery prohibitionist, to visit Navajoe on behalf of temperance. There is no record of Carrie Nation wielding her hatchet, but the temperance league was successful in closing the saloons. Action

A gold mine in the Wichita Mountains.

immediately shifted to the drugstores where bitters, heady potions of nearly 100 percent alcohol, could be bought.

There was a brief boom during the 1890s when prospectors came to the Wichita Mountains in unsuccessful pursuit of gold. When the railroad bypassed Navajoe in 1902, residents began to move away. Now, only the cemetery remains.

—*Altus* - US 283-62———

Motorists are welcomed with the slogan "Altus is a city with a future to share." Early in its career, the community did not appear to have much future. It began with a buffalo hunter named Frazier, who came to the area in the 1870s and built a half-dugout. Frazier found his services less and less in demand. In 1890, when the last wild buffalo in the area was killed near Cold Springs, he turned to other means of making a living.

A settlement grew up around the dugout on Bitter Creek and was given the old buffalo hunter's name. It was the first post office in Old Greer County, then claimed by Texas. In 1891 floods drove the settlers to higher ground two miles east. Someone with a penchant for Latin called the new location Altus because it was on higher ground.

The first railroad entered Greer County in 1901, giving access to markets and consequent stimulation of growth. However, the pioneers had to pay a price for this progress. Railroads sought to increase their profits by developing towns or by obtaining inducements from towns that already existed. Large tracts of land were set aside, percentages of business profits were pledged, bonds were secured, and cash was raised to induce a railroad to pass through a particular town.

The citizens of Altus raised $50,000 and briefly changed its name to Leger to honor a railroad official. It was considered a worthwhile investment. In 1897 two hundred bales of cotton were ginned in a sixty-saw gin run by a threshing machine engine. Within a few years the annual total rose to 124,000 bales.

The Depression severely affected this region because of its dependence upon agriculture, particularly cotton. After the boom period of the late 1920s, cotton prices fell to record lows and stayed at those levels for the better part of a decade. The problem was compounded by drought conditions of record duration during the Dust Bowl era.

Relief came with the construction of Altus Reservoir to the north, making irrigation possible. With crop diversification, wheat and alfalfa were soon sharing honors with cotton.

World War II brought a boon to the economy of Altus. Altus Army Air Field was established on the east edge of the city in 1943. The facility was closed down after the war but reactivated in 1953 as Altus Air Force

In 1909, the Cole Transfer & Storage Company, of Altus, had a fleet of four stake-wagons. —Western History Collections, University of Oklahoma Library

Base. In 1968 the base became part of the Military Airlift Command, home of the C-5 Galaxy, at that time the world's largest airplane.

EXCURSION

—*Ozark* - US 62———

The community took its name from location on a branch of the Ozark Trail, Oklahoma's early effort to generate tourist travel. Today there are no businesses along the highway. The few remaining residents in this rural area obviously shop in nearby Altus.

—*Friendship* - OK 62———

This barely perceptible rural community north of Ozark is located on the Western Cattle Trail. During trail driving days it was known as the Friendship Store.

—*Headrick* - OK 62——— ——

In 1902, the residents of Navajoe, located about four miles northwest of present-day Headrick, firmly believed that the Frisco railroad line planned between Oklahoma City and Quanah, Texas, would come through their town. However, as was so often the case, railroad officials changed their minds, dealing a death blow to Navajoe.

Developers platted Headrick on the railroad, and most of the inhabitants of Navajoe moved to the new town, bringing buildings with them. On April 21, 1902, the post office was established, named for T. B. Headrick, owner of the townsite. The red granite hills just north of town mark the beginning of the Wichita Mountains.

—*Humphreys*————

As early as 1897, there were settlers in the vicinity of this faded community to the east of US 283 on the Katy railroad. Mrs. Hugh Minor started a Sunday school in a half-dugout in 1897. With the coming of the railroad, the townsite plat was filed in September 1909. Naming the town was hotly discussed and finally put to a vote. Jim Humphrey, a local rancher, won.

The land was flat and fertile; crops were abundant except during drought years and the grasshopper plague. Two cotton gins and two grain elevators served the needs of farmers in the area.

—*Hess*————

This scattering of houses off US 283 southeast of Elmer is the remains of a farming community established in 1889 just after the flow of cattle ceased over the Western Cattle Trail. The famous Doan's Crossing of the Red River, then called Prairie Dog Town Fork, was about eight miles southeast of Hess.

The crossing was at a relatively shallow point about three miles upstream from where the North Fork enters the main stream of the Red River. The peak year on the trail was 1881, when an estimated 301,000 cattle swam or waded the river and were driven through Indian Territory to northern railheads. Drovers obtained supplies at Doan's Store, on the Texas side of the river.

—*Elmer* - US 283————

This small agricultural community was founded in 1901 by W. T. Thaggard and J. H. Barr, owners of a general store. It was named for Elmer W. Slocum, an official of the Kansas City, Mexico and Orient Railway (now the Santa Fe). An earlier community named Yeldell had been established nearby in 1892. When Elmer was founded, most of Yeldell's residents moved to Elmer.

Elmer got a post office in 1902, but it was not incorporated until 1926. The railroad was completed through town in 1908. During its heyday, Elmer had four grocery stores, three lumberyards, two cotton gins, a bank, a hardware and furniture store, a coal yard, a dry goods store, and a theater. B. C. Bennett edited the *Elmer Record.*

—*Reed* - OK 9————————

This tiny community was founded in 1892 near the north bank of the Salt Fork of the Red River, taking its name from John Reed Graham, the first postmaster. Cave Creek is between two and three miles south of Reed. A series of tunnels and grottos along the creek have long been known as Bat Caves because of thousands of bats that fly out after sunset on their nightly hunting expeditions. One cavern is reputed to be six feet high and reach a half mile underground.

Jaybuckle Springs is four miles north of Reed on the Elm Creek Fork of the Red River. This old landmark was the headquarters of the Haney-Handy-Powers-Murphy Cattle Company, dating from 1880, when Old Greer County was part of Texas.

—*Vinson* - OK 9————————

This community started during the early 1890s when cattlemen from Texas moved into Old Greer County. Initially, the post office was named for William P. Francis. The name was changed to Trotter in 1902, and the following year the post office took on the last name of Henry B. Vinson, owner of the townsite.

Rock Bridge is three miles from Vinson. It is a 100-foot rock formation overlooking an area studded with caves and springs. The Salt Fork of the Red River took its name from the salt produced from these springs.

US 62 —OK 34
Duke —Hollis

—*Duke* - US 62—OK 34————————

Duke's history began in 1890 when Mr. and Mrs. A. L. Perry left Texas to make their home in Old Greer County. They left the train at Quanah, Texas, and proceeded by wagon. They were told they would have to cross the Red River by a "straw bridge." They found it consisted of bales of hay strewn across the river to keep wagons from sinking in the sand.

The community was named Duke after F. B. Duke, a territorial judge, and a post office was established September 11, 1890. Mrs. Perry predicted this new town would become the "duke" of the prairie. By 1910 there were twenty-six business establishments when word was received that the railroad was coming, causing controversy that would divide the town for years.

In those days, when a railroad was coming, promoters would buy land in places they thought the railroad would pass and sell lots for businesses and residences. A. L. Perry bought land and promoted a site about a quarter mile east of the old location. The community chose up sides between supporters of Old Town and New Town.

On March 31, 1910, an advertisement in the *Altus Weekly News* extolled the benefits of Old Town: Trade was booming and only five of the twenty-six businesses were moving to New Town. The town offered two free residential lots to anyone who wished to build. When the railroad built its depot in New Town, the advantage shifted, but Old Town forces refused to give up. The dispute became so heated that the railroad moved the depot to an area between the two contesting communities. It was called "no man's land."

In 1910 a fire destroyed many businesses in the new town, but it did not stop the controversy. Finally—in 1915—the two factions settled the dispute with a strange ceremony. A horse-drawn hearse drove from Old Town to New Town. The hearse carried a bloody hatchet as a symbol of the division of the community. A grave was dug and the hatchet was deposited; the ceremony was accompanied by appropriate speeches, and representatives of the two factions shook hands over the grave.

Dubbing their community East Duke, leaders of New Town agreed to provide a lot to anyone who wanted to leave West Duke. Within a short time West Duke was deserted and East Duke reverted to its original name.

Duke's economy was based primarily upon cotton until 1964, when the Republic Gypsum Company constructed a plant at the west edge of town.

—*Gould* - US 62—OK 5———————

In 1908, Samuel L. Gibson filed a townsite plat and called the community Gibson. The following year John A. Gould became postmaster and renamed the town.

The bench marks used by the United States Geological Survey in determining the location of the 100th meridian, the southern part of Oklahoma's western border, are west of Gould. The initial survey for location of the meridian was made in 1818, with an error of about eighty miles. Capt. George B. McClellan made another survey in 1853 and moved the boundary forty miles farther west. Additional surveys were made in 1859, 1892, 1902, and—finally—in 1927. A concrete slab surrounds the marker, as if to make certain that it will not move.

Texas ranchers came to this far-southwestern corner of Old Greer County as early as 1880. In 1898, the Clemons brothers—James M., Alonzo T., and Eugene M.—rented the land they farmed in Texas. They heard about land in Greer County obtainable simply by filing on it. They arrived in a covered wagon. Each man had a saddle horse and two work horses. They filed on three adjoining quarter-sections just east of present-day Hollis. To fulfill the requirement of sleeping on their land, the brothers built a single dugout over the corners where their homesteads joined. Each put a bed in his own corner.

The present-day county seat of Harmon County did not come to life until the opening of the Kiowa-Comanche-Apache lands. George W. Hollis, the townsite owner, platted the community. The railroad arrived in 1910, but the line has since been abandoned.

The town still serves the surrounding agricultural area. A cotton oil mill manufactures animal feed for the export market. The Harmon County Historical Museum displays exhibits highlighting the county's history from the days of its earliest settlers to the present.

OK 6
Olustee—Eldorado

—*Olustee*————————

This farming and ranching community was established in 1895. The name is a Seminole word meaning "pond"; it had also been the name of a battle during the Seminole War in Florida. There is no record of how the name was chosen.

In 1903 the Frisco railway came on its way between Altus and Quanah, Texas. Olustee became a center of trade and real estate development. The Bentley Hotel was constructed to house potential settlers who came looking for land. Beginning in the fall of 1903 excursion trains arrived every two weeks.

A carnival atmosphere prevailed. A dance was staged to welcome the visitors. Mrs. Bentley insisted on placing two guests to a bed, whether they knew each other or not. The hotel overflowed and many nights found fifteen or twenty people sleeping on the floor in the lobby. As much as fifty pounds of flour would be used in the preparation of biscuits for breakfast. Guests often killed quail while they were out looking at land, and Mrs. Bentley spent much of her time cleaning the birds to serve the following morning for breakfast.

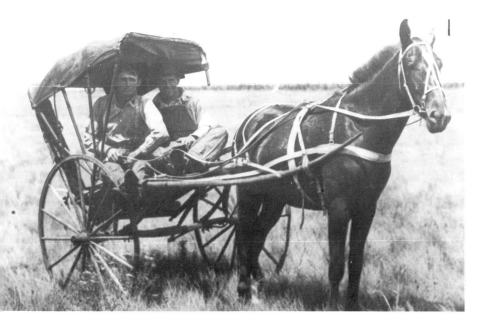

Prospective settlers would ride out across the prairies in a horse and buggy to inspect the land. As automobiles supplanted horse-and-buggy transportation and Rural Free Delivery expanded, many small towns which had served as ranching and farming trading centers faded from the face of the land. —Western History Collections, University of Oklahoma Library

Today the real estate business is somewhat less lively. However, in 1965 a strip copper mine was opened a few miles southwest of Olustee— Oklahoma's only copper production. Operation of the mine is dependent upon the price of copper.

HISTORICAL HIGHLIGHT
Cross S Ranch

The limestone headquarters building of the old Cross S Ranch stands forlorn and lonely just south of Olustee. It was once the social center of the area, rocking to music almost every evening as cowboys with guitars, fiddles, and banjos played "After the Ball," "Over the Waves," and "Black Hawk Waltz."

During its best days, the ranch reached from the Red River on the south almost to present-day Altus on the north. L. Z. Eddleman and his cousin, Everett Walcott, crossed the Red River from Round Timbers, Texas, in 1881. They found a well of exceptionally soft water that had been dug by a previous settler. They built a picket house, and set up operations.

At first they raised longhorn cattle, driving them across the territory to the nearest market in Kiowa, Kansas. Later they changed to shorthorn cattle. After being flooded out in 1891, Eddleman engaged two passing Swedes to build a rock house. His cowboys gathered limestone from nearby hills. It was a good house; its sturdy walls are still standing.

Soft water was a scarce commodity on the prairie, and nearby settlers would go to the Cross S to get water to use in their homes. They kept the water in barrels in front of their houses. Some of the Cross S cowboys took to riding by the settlers' houses at night and shooting holes in the barrels. Eddleman put a stop to this form of amusement after a shot not only punctured a water barrel but killed a settler's dog sleeping behind the barrel.

—Creta———

Originally Era, the name of this village on Boggy Creek was changed to Creta (Latin for "chalk") on February 20, 1904. Creta was the site of a rock quarry that furnished building material for many homes in the county. The post office was short-lived; it closed on October 31, 1904, and the residents had to wait for their mail to be delivered from Olustee.

—Eldorado - OK 5-6———

During the late 1880s, Eldorado got a headstart on other towns in the area. Prospective settlers rode the train to Quanah, Texas, and continued to Greer County by wagon or buggy. The wagon yard on the Quanah-Mangum road was close to the border, and the surrounding tall prairie grass was an invitation to stop. As the town began to grow, business-oriented leaders of the community made every effort to get travelers to stop and settle in the area.

As with many other towns, the community made a couple of moves, first to be closer to the post office, and finally to be close to the railroad. On Saturday, February 7, 1903, the tracks of the long-awaited St. Louis and San Francisco Railway were laid through town. With the introduction of cotton, Eldorado became the shipping point for a large section of Jackson and Harmon counties.

In 1906 the *Eldorado Light* advertised a circulation of 800, and in 1910 it listed the population of Eldorado at 1,500. Today it has about half that number.

424

Sources for Additional Reading

Alfalfa County Historical Society. *Our Alfalfa County Heritage, 1893-1976.* Cherokee: 1977.

Alley, John. *City Beginnings in Oklahoma Territory.* Norman: University of Oklahoma Press, 1939.

Anon. *Bella Starr, The Bandit Queen or the Female Jesse James.* New York: Richard K. Fox, 1889.

Ashley, Velma Dolphin. *A History of Boley, Oklahoma.* Master's thesis: Kansas State Teachers College, Pittsburg, Kansas, 1940.

Atoka County Historical Society. *Tales of Atoka County Heritage.* Atoka: 1983.

Bailey, Mary Hewett. *A History of Grady County, Oklahoma.* Master's thesis: University of Oklahoma, 1937.

Bass, Althea. *Cherokee Messenger.* Norman: University of Oklahoma Press, 1936.

Beaver County Historical Society, Inc., Pauline Bond & Gladys Eagen, eds. *A History of Beaver County.* 2 vols. Oklahoma City: Taylor Publishing Co., 1970, 1971.

Beck, Warren A. & Ynez D. Haase. *Historical Atlas of the American West.* Norman: University of Oklahoma Press, 1989.

Benedict, John D. *Muskogee and Northeastern Oklahoma...* Chicago: S. J. Clark Pub. Co., 1922.

Briehan, Carl W. *Badmen of the Frontier Days.* New York: Robert M. McBride Co., 1957.

Brown, Opal Hartsell. *Murray County, Oklahoma: In the Heart of Eden.* Wichita Falls: Nortex Press, 1977.

Bryan County Heritage Association, Inc. *The History of Bryan County, Oklahoma.* Dallas: National ShareGraphics, Inc., 1983.

Burns, Hoyt, ed. *Early History of the Town Washington, Oklahoma.* Del City: Del City Publishing Co., 1990.

Carter, L. Edward. *The Story of Oklahoma Newspapers, 1844-1984.* Muskogee: pub. for Oklahoma Heritage Association by Western Heritage Books, c1984.

Carter, W. A. *McCurtain County and Southeast Oklahoma: History, Biography, Statistics.* Idabel: Tribune Pub. Co., 1923.

Chambers, Homer S. *The Enduring Rock: History and Reminiscences of Blackwell, Okla., and the Cherokee Strip.* Blackwell: Blackwell Publications, Inc., 1954.

Chapman, Berlin Basil. *The Founding of Stillwater: A Case Study in Oklahoma History.* Oklahoma City: Times Journal Publishing Co., 1948.

Cherokee Strip Volunteer League. *Pioneer Footprints Across Woods County.* San Angelo: Newsfoto Yearbooks, 1976.

Chesser, Dean Cecil. *Across the Lonely Years: The Story of Jackson County.* Altus: Altus Printing Co., 1971.

Claremore College Foundation. *The History of Rogers County, Oklahoma.* Tulsa: Heritage Publishing Co., 1979.

Conkling, Roscoe P. & Margaret B. Conkling. *The Butterfield Overland Mail, 1857-1869.* 3 vols. Glendale, California: Arthur H. Clark Co., 1947.

Cotterill, R. S. *The Southern Indians: The Story of the Civilized Tribes Before Removal.* Norman: University of Oklahoma Press, 1954.

Cotton County Historical Society, Inc. *History of Cotton County: Family and Area Stories.* Walters: Herald Publishing Co., 1979.

Craig County Heritage Association. *The Story of Craig County: Its People and Places.* Vinita: Curtis Media Corp., 1984.

Crawford, Isabel. *Kiowa: The History of a Blanket Indian Mission.* New York: Fleming H. Revell Co., 1915.

Cunningham, Robert E. *Perry: Pride of the Prairie.* Stillwater: Frontier Printers, Inc., n.d.

Dale, Edward Everett. *The Range Cattle Industry: Ranching on the Great Plains from 1865 to 1925.* Norman: University of Oklahoma Press, 1960.

——————— & Gaston Litton. *Cherokee Cavaliers: Forty Years of Cherokee History as Told in the Correspondence of the Ridge-Watie-Boudinot Family.* Norman: University of Oklahoma Press, 1939.

——————— & Jesse Lee Rader. *Readings in Oklahoma History.* Evanston, Illinois: Row, Peterson and Co., 1930.

Dalton, Emmett. *When the Dalton's Rode.* Garden City, New York: Sun Dial Press, Inc., 1937.

Dawson, E. Lomax. *The Cheyenne-Arapahoe Country.* New York: Carlton Press, Inc., 1968.

Debo, Angie. *Oklahoma: Foot-loose and Fancy-free.* Norman: University of Oklahoma Press, 1949.

———————. *The Road to Disappearance.* Norman: University of Oklahoma Press, 1941.

———————. *Tulsa: From Creek Town to Oil Capital.* Norman: University of Oklahoma Press, 1943.

Deloria, Vine, Jr. *Behind the Trail of Broken Treaties: An Indian Declaration of Independence.* Austin, Texas: University of Texas Press, 1985.

Dewey County Historical Society. *Spanning the River.* Camargo: Dewey County Historical Society, 1973-78.

Dickson, Jerry, ed. *Prairie Fire: A Pioneer History of Western Oklahoma.* Western Oklahoma Historical Society, 1987.

——————, ed. *Prairie Wedding: A Pioneer History of Western Oklahoma.* Western Oklahoma Historical Society, 1987.

Dott, Robert H. et al. *Rock Mary and the California Road.* Oklahoma City: Oklahoma Historical Society, 1960.

Ellenbrook, Edward Charles. *Outdoor and Trail Guide to the Wichita Mountains of Southwest Oklahoma.* Lawton: In-the-Valley-of-the-Wichitas House, 1988.

Ellis County Historical Society. *Our Ellis County Heritage.* 2 vols. Oklahoma City: Ellis County Historical Society, 1974, 1979.

Ellsworth, Henry Leavitt. *Washington Irving on the Prairie, or a Narrative of a Tour of the Southwest in the Year 1832.* New York: American Book Company, 1937.

Farley, Gloria. "The Heavener Runestone," *Oklahoma Today,* Autumn, 1968.

Faulk, Odie B. & Billie M. Jones. *Tahlequah, NSU, and the Cherokees.* Tahlequah: Northeastern State University Educational Association, 1984.

Ferber, Edna. *Cimarron.* Garden City, N.Y.: Doubleday, Doran and Co., Inc., 1930.

Flint, Timothy. *Recollections of the Last Ten Years, in the Valley of the Mississippi.* Boston: Cummings, Hilliard, and Co., 1826.

Foreman, Carolyn Thomas. *Oklahoma Imprints, 1835-1907: A History of Printing in Oklahoma Before Statehood.* Norman: University of Oklahoma Press, 1936.

Foreman, Grant. *Advancing the Frontier, 1830-1860.* Norman: University of Oklahoma Press, 1933.

——————, ed. *Adventure On Red River: Report on the Exploration of the Headwaters of the Red River by Captain Randolph B. Marcy and Captain G. B. McClellan.* Norman: University of Oklahoma Press, 1937.

——————. *Down the Texas Road: Historic Places Along Highway 69 Through Oklahoma.* Norman: University of Oklahoma Press, 1936.

——————. *The Five Civilized Tribes.* Norman: University of Oklahoma Press, 1934.

——————. *A History of Oklahoma.* Norman: University of Oklahoma Press, 1942.

——————. *Indians & Pioneers: The Story of the American Southwest Before 1830.* Rev. Ed. Norman: University of Oklahoma Press, 1936.

————. *Marcy & the Gold Seekers: The Journal of Captain R. B. Marcy, with an Account of the Gold Rush Over the Southern Route.* Norman: University of Oklahoma Press, 1939.

————. *Muskogee: The Biography of an Oklahoma Town.* Norman: University of Oklahoma Press, 1943.

————. *Sequoyah.* Norman: University of Oklahoma Press, 1938.

Fortson, John Lake. *Pott County and What Came of It: A History of Pottawatomie County.* [Shawnee: Pottawatomie County Historical Society, 1936.]

Frame, Paul Nelson. *A History of Ardmore, Oklahoma, from the Earliest Beginnings to 1907.* Master's thesis: University of Oklahoma, 1949.

Frazer, Robert W. *Forts of the West.* Norman: University of Oklahoma Press, 1965.

Gabriel, Ralph Henry. *Elias Boudinot, Cherokee, & His America.* Norman: University of Oklahoma Press, 1941.

Garfield County Historical Society. Stella Campbell Rockwell, ed. *Garfield County, Oklahoma, 1893-1982.* 2 vols. Topeka: Josten's Publications, 1982.

George, Preston & Sylvan R. Wood. *The Railroads of Oklahoma, Bulletin No. 60.* Boston: Railway & Locomotive Historical Society, Inc., January, 1943.

Gibson, A[rrell] M[organ]. "Early Mining Camps in Northeastern Oklahoma," *Chronicles of Oklahoma,* Vol. 34, Summer, 1956.

————. *Oklahoma: A History of Five Centuries.* 2d ed. Norman: University of Oklahoma Press, 1981.

Gittinger, Roy. *The Formation of the State of Oklahoma, 1803-1906.* Norman: University of Oklahoma Press, 1939.

Goode, William Henry. *Outposts of Zion, with Limnings of Mission Life . . .* Cincinnati: Poe & Hitchcock, 1836.

Gould, Charles N. *Oklahoma Place Names.* Norman: University of Oklahoma Press, 1933.

Harmon County Historical Association. *Planning The Route: A History of Harmon County.* Hollis: 1980.

Harper County Historical Society. *Sage and Sod: Harper County, Oklahoma, 1885-1973.* Virginia Boldes, Rose Douglas, Sarah Moore, eds. 2 vols. N.p.: 1974-1975.

Harris, Phil. *This Is Three Forks Country.* Muskogee: Hoffman Printing Co., Inc., 1965, 1966, 1976.

Hart, Herbert M. *Old Forts of the Southwest.* Seattle, Wash.: Superior Publishing Co., 1964.

Haskell County Historical Society. *Haskell County History: Indian Territory— 1988.* Dallas: Curtis Media Corporation, 1989.

Hill, Mozell. "The All-Negro Communities of Oklahoma," *Journal of Negro History,* July, 1946.

Hofsommer, Donovan L., ed. *Railroads in Oklahoma.* Oklahoma City: Oklahoma Historical Society, 1977.

Holmes, Helen Freudenberger. *The Logan County History: The County and Its Communities.* Topeka, Kans.: Josten/American Yearbook Co., 1980.

The Hooker Advance. *A History of Hooker: A Diamond in the Rough.* 2 vols. Hooker: The Hooker Advance, 1983-1986.

Hughes, William Hankins. *Old Fort Supply.* Master's thesis: Oklahoma Agricultural & Mechanical College, Stillwater, 1931.

Hurst, Irwin. *The 46th Star.* Oklahoma City: Semco Color Press, 1957.

Imon, Frances. *Smoke Signals from Indian Territory.* 2 vols. Wolfe City, Texas: Henington Publishing Co., 1976, 1977.

Interested Citizens of Shattuck, Okla. *A Pioneer History of Shattuck.* N.p.: 1970.

Irving, Washington. *A Tour on the Prairies.* John Francis McDermott, ed. Norman: University of Oklahoma Press, 1956.

Jackson, Berenice, Jewel Carlisle, Iris Colwell. *Man and the Oklahoma Panhandle.* North Newton, Kan.: Mennonite Press, Inc., c1892.

James, Louise Boyd. "Woodward: First Century on the Sand-Sage Prairie, 1887-1987," *Chronicles of Oklahoma,* Fall, 1986.

Jones, W. F. *The Experiences of a Deputy U. S. Marshal of the Indian Territory.* Muskogee: Stan-Hill Associates, 1976.

Kaho, Noel. *The Will Rogers Country.* Norman: University of Oklahoma Press, 1941.

Kansas Pacific Railway Co. *Guide Map of the Great Texas Cattle Trail from Red River Crossing to the Old Reliable Kansas Pacific Railway.* Kansas City: Ramsey, Millett & Hudson, 1874.

Kiowa County Historical Society. *Pioneering in Kiowa County.* 6 vols. Hobart: Kiowa County Historical Society, 1976-1982.

Knight, Oliver. *Life and Manners in the Frontier Army.* Norman: University of Oklahoma Press, 1978.

Lackey, Vinson. *The Forts of Oklahoma.* Tulsa: Tulsa Printing Co., 1963.

Landsverk, O. G. "Norsemen in Oklahoma," *Oklahoma Today,* Summer, 1970.

Laune, Seigniora Russell. *Sand in My Eyes.* Philadelphia: J. B. Lippincott Co., 1956.

Leonhardy, Frank C., ed. *Domebo: A Paleo-Indian Mammoth Kill in the Prairie-Plains.* Lawton: Great Plains Historical Association, 1966.

Lester, Herschel. *LeFlore County's History Is Colorful.* Poteau: n.p., 1988.

Library of Congress. *Oklahoma: The Semicentennial of Statehood, 1907-1957: An Exhibition in the Library of Congress.* Washington: Library of Congress, 1957.

A Look at Wagoner County: Wagoner County History. Wagoner: Wagoner County Extension Homemakers Council, 1980.

McCoy, Joseph G. Ralph P. Bieber, ed. *Historic Sketches of the Cattle Trade of the West and Southwest*. Glendale, Calif.: Arthur H. Clark Co., 1940.

MacCreary, Henry. *A Story of Durant: "Queen of Three Valleys."* Durant: n.p., n.d.

McDermott, John Francis, ed. *The Western Journals of Washington Irving*. Norman: University of Oklahoma Press, 1944.

McKennon, C. H. *Iron Men: A Saga of the Deputy United States Marshals Who Rode the Indian Territory*. Garden City: Doubleday & Company, Inc., 1967.

McRill, Leslie A. "Ferdinandina: First White Settlement in Oklahoma," *Chronicles of Oklahoma,* Summer, 1963.

Madill City Library, Calvin Harkins et al. *Memories of Marshall County, Oklahoma, Then and Now*. Dallas: Media Corp., 1988.

[Marlow, Charles & George]. *Life of the Marlows: A True Story of Frontier of Early Days, as Related by Themselves*. Revised by William Rathmell. Ouray, Colorado: Ouray Herald, print, W. S. Olexa, publisher, n.d.

Marriott, Alice & Carol R. Rachlin. *Oklahoma: The Forty-Sixth Star*. Garden City: Doubleday & Company, Inc., 1973.

Mathews, John Joseph. *Wah'Kon-Tah: The Osage and the White Man's Road*. Norman: University of Oklahoma Press, 1932.

Mayes County Historical Society. *Historical Highlights of Mayes County*. Pryor: 1977.

Milsten, David Randolph. *Will Rogers—The Cherokee Kid*. West Chicago: Glenheath Publishers, 1987.

Mooney, Charles W. *Localized History of Pottawatomie County, Oklahoma, to 1907*. Midwest City: 1971.

Morris, John W. *Ghost Towns of Oklahoma*. Norman: University of Oklahoma Press, 1977.

————— & Edwin C. McReynolds. *Historical Atlas of Oklahoma*. Norman: University of Oklahoma Press, 1965.

Morrison, William Brown. *Military Posts and Camps in Oklahoma*. Oklahoma City: Harlow Publishing Corp., 1936.

Munn, Irvin. *Chickasha—A Journey Back In Time*. Chickasha: University of Science and Arts of Oklahoma, 1982.

Musick, Velma, ed. *Pioneers of Kingfisher County, 1889-1976*. San Angelo: Newsfoto Yearbooks, 1976.

Neatherlin, Lewis Warren. "Up the Trail in '76," *Chronicles of Oklahoma,* Spring, 1988.

Nieberding, Velma. *The History of Ottawa County, Oklahoma*. Marceline, Missouri: Walsworth Publishing Co., 1983.

Norton, Patty Virginia & Layton R. Sutton. *Indian Territory and Carter County, Oklahoma, Pioneers Including Pickens County, Chickasaw Nation.* Vol. I, 1840-1926. Dallas: Taylor Publishing Co., 1983.

Nye, Col. W. S. *Carbine & Lance: The Story of Old Fort Sill.* Norman: University of Oklahoma Press, 1943.

Officers and Members of the 1913 Study Club. *A Place Called Poteau . . . the people and their neighbors.* Poteau: 1976.

Okmulgee Historical Society and the Heritage Society of America. *History of Okmulgee County, Oklahoma.* Tulsa: Historical Enterprises, Inc., 1985.

Old Greer County Museum & Hall of Fame, Inc. *A History of Old Greer County And Its Pioneers.* Mangum: 1980.

Osage County Historical Society. *Osage County Profiles.* Pawhuska: 1978.

Peck, Henry L. *The Proud History of Le Flore County: a History of an Oklahoma County.* [Van Buren, Ark.: Press Argus, 1963.]

Peery, Dan W. "The First Two Years," *Chronicles of Oklahoma,* Vols. VII, 278-322, 419-457; VIII, 94-127.

Pierce, David Washington. *A History of Alfalfa County.* Master's thesis: University of Oklahoma, 1926.

Ponca City Chapter, D.A.R. *The Last Run: Kay County, Oklahoma, 1893.* Ponca City: Courier Printing Co., 1939.

Pottawatomie County History Book Committee. *Pottawatomie County, Oklahoma, History.* Claremore: Country Lane Press, 1987.

Preece, Harold. *The Dalton Gang: End of an Outlaw Era.* New York: Hastings House, 1963.

Rascoe, Burton. *Belle Starr: "The Bandit Queen."* New York: Random House, 1941.

Reubin, Carl E., ed. *Johnston County History, 1855-1979.* Oklahoma City: Johnston County Historical Society, 1979.

Rex, Joyce, ed. *McClain County, Oklahoma: History and Heritage.* Book I. Pauls Valley: Lanham Campbell, 1986.

Richardson, Albert D. *Beyond the Mississippi: From the Great River to the Great Ocean.* New York: 1867.

Rister, Carl Coke. *No Man's Land.* Norman: University of Oklahoma Press, 1948.

—————. "Satanta: Orator of the Plains," *Southwest Review,* Autumn, 1931.

Rittenhouse, Jack D. *A Guide Book to Highway 66.* Facsimile, 1946 ed. Albuquerque: University of New Mexico Press, 1989.

Roe, Frances M. *Army Letters from an Officer's Wife, 1871-1888.* New York: Appleton, 1909.

Rose, F. P. "Early History of Catesby and Vicinity," *Chronicles of Oklahoma,* Summer, 1951.

Royce, Charles C. "The Cherokee Nation of Indians," *Bureau of American Ethnology, Fifth Annual Report 1883-84.* Washington: Government Printing Office, 1887.

Ruth, Kent. *Oklahoma Travel Handbook.* Norman: University of Oklahoma Press, 1977.

──────. *Window on the Past: Historical Sites in Oklahoma.* Oklahoma City: Oklahoma Publishing Co., 1973.

────── et al. *Oklahoma: A Guide to the Sooner State.* Norman: University of Oklahoma Press, 1957.

Scott, A. C. "The Story of Oklahoma City," *The Daily Oklahoman,* April 22, 1929.

Scott, Quinta & Susan Croce Kelly. *Route 66: The Highway and Its People.* Norman: University of Oklahoma Press, 1988.

Seekers of Oklahoma Heritage Association. *Alva, Oklahoma: The First 100 Years, 1886-1986.* Dallas: Curtis Media Corporation, 1987.

Sequoyah County Historical Society. *The History of Sequoyah County, 1828-1975.* N.p., n.d.

Shirk, George N. *Oklahoma Place Names.* Norman: University of Oklahoma Press, 1974.

Shirley, Glenn. *Belle Starr and Her Times: The Literature, the Facts, and the Legends.* Norman: University of Oklahoma Press, 1982.

──────. *West of Hell's Fringe: Crime, Criminals, and the Federal Peace Officer in Oklahoma Territory, 1889-1907.* Norman: University of Oklahoma Press, 1978.

Spaulding, George F. *On the Western Tour with Washington Irving: The Journal and Letters of Count de Pourtales.* Norman: University of Oklahoma Press, 1968.

Speer, Bonnie. *Cleveland County, Pride of the Promised Land: An Illustrated History.* Norman: Traditional Publishers, 1988.

Starr, Emmet. *History of the Cherokee Indians and Their Legends and Folklore.* Muskogee: Hoffman Printing Co., Inc., 1984.

Steinbeck, John. *The Grapes of Wrath.* New York: Viking Press, 1939.

Stephens County Historical Society. *History of Stephens County.* Duncan: 1982.

Strickland, Rennard. *The Indians in Oklahoma.* Norman: University of Oklahoma Press, 1980.

Sutton, Fred E. & A. B. MacDonald. *Hands Up! Stories of the Six-Gun Fighters of the Old West.* New York: Bobbs-Merril Company, 1927.

Tallack, William. *The California Overland Express.* London: 1865.

Teall, Kaye M. *Black History in Oklahoma: A Resource Book.* Oklahoma City: Oklahoma City Public Schools, 1971.

Thoburn, Joseph B. & Muriel H. Wright. *Oklahoma: A History of the State and Its People.* 2 vols. New York: Lewis Historical Publishing Company, 1929.

Tillman County Historical Society. *A Diamond Jubilee History of Tillman County, 1901-1976.* 2 vols. Frederick: 1976, 1978.

Troup, Bob. "You Get Your Kicks On Route 66." Londontown Music, Inc., 1946.

Vestal, Stanley. *Short Grass Country.* New York: Duell, Sloan & Pearce, 1941.

Vogel, Virgil J. *American Indian Medicine.* Norman: University of Oklahoma Press, 1970.

Wade, Henry F. *Ship of State on a Sea of Oil.* Oklahoma City: Oklahoma State Capitol, 1975.

Wallis, Michael. *Route 66: The Mother Road.* New York: St. Martin's Press, 1990.

Wardell, Morris L. *A Political History of the Cherokee Nation, 1838-1907.* Norman: University of Oklahoma Press, 1938.

Washita County History Committee, Inc. *Wagon Tracks: Washita County Heritage, 1892-1976.* [Cornell:] Washita County Historical Commission, 1976.

Webb, Guy P. *History of Grant County, Oklahoma, 1811-1970.* North Newton, Kansas: Mennonite Press, 1971.

Wellman, Paul I. *A Dynasty of Western Outlaws.* New York: Bonanza Books, 1959.

Wells, Laura Lou. *Young Cushing in Oklahoma Territory.* Perkins: 1985.

West, C. W. "Dub." *Muscogee, I.T.: The Queen City of the Southwest, 1872-1972.* Muskogee: Muscogee Publishing Company, 1972.

Williams, Joe. Bartlesville: *Remembrance of Times Past, Reflections of Today.* Bartlesville: TRW Reda Pump Division, 1978.

Wilson, Steve. *Oklahoma Treasures and Treasure Tales.* Norman: University of Oklahoma Press, 1976.

Wise, Donald A., ed. *Myriads of the Past.* Broken Arrow: ReTvkv'cke Press, c1987.

Womack, John. *Cleveland County, Oklahoma, Highlights.* Norman: 1982.

——————. *Cleveland County, Oklahoma, Place Names.* Norman, 1977.

——————. *Norman—An Early History, 1820-1900.* Norman: 1976.

Wooldridge, Clyde E. *Wilburton: I.T. and OK, 1890-1970.* N.p., n.d.

Work Projects Administration. *Oklahoma: A Guide to the Sooner State.* Norman: University of Oklahoma Press, 1941.

Wright, Muriel H. *A Guide to the Indian Tribes of Oklahoma.* Norman: University of Oklahoma Press, 1951.

——————, George H. Shirk & Kenny A. Franks. *Mark of Heritage.* Oklahoma City: Oklahoma Historical Society, 1976.

Wyatt III, Robert Lee. *Grandfield: The Hub of the Big Pasture,* 2 vols. Marceline, Missouri: Walsworth Publishers, 1974, 1975.

Index

Wister: 80
Wister State Park: 80
Witteville: 76
Wood, L. L.: 202
Woods, James R.: 380-81
Woods, S. H.: 113-14
Woodville: 202
Woodward: 253-54, 342
Woolaroc Museum: 225-26; *illus.* 226
Worcester, Rev. Samuel Austin: 29, 32-33
Worcester Mission Cemetery: 33
Works, Joseph S.: 415-17; *illus.* 415

World Museum-Art Centre: 329
World War I: 5, 10, 50, 60, 93, 96, 160
World War II: 5, 10, 19, 93-94, 152, 185, 417-18
Woten, Joe: 281
Wright, Rev. Alfred: 100-101
Wright, Frank Lloyd: illus, 224
Wright, William W.: 96
Wright City: 96
Wyandotte, 13-14
Wybark: 175
Wynnewood: 160, 163
Wynona: 230

Yahola, Chief Achee: 327
Yale: 187, 189
Yanush: 87
Yeldell: 419
Yellow Bear, Chief: 409-10
Yewed: 275
Younger, Cole: 52
Younger's Bend: 51, 53
Yuba: 107
Yuhnke, August F.: 129
Yukon: 123

Zenobia: 361
Zinn, B. B.: 413
Zinn, Dot: 413